O'REILLY®
Strata
Making Data Work

Learn how to turn data into decisions.

From startups to the Fortune 500, smart companies are betting on data-driven insight, seizing the opportunities that are emerging from the convergence of four powerful trends:

- New methods of collecting, managing, and analyzing data

- Cloud computing that offers inexpensive storage and flexible, on-demand computing power for massive data sets

- Visualization techniques that turn complex data into images that tell a compelling story

- Tools that make the power of data available to anyone

Get control over big data and turn it into insight with O'Reilly's Strata offerings. Find the inspiration and information to create new products or revive existing ones, understand customer behavior, and get the data edge.

O'REILLY®

Visit oreilly.com/data to learn more.

SECOND EDITION

Mining the Social Web

Matthew A. Russell

O'REILLY®

Beijing · Cambridge · Farnham · Köln · Sebastopol · Tokyo

Mining the Social Web, Second Edition

by Matthew A. Russell

Printed in the United States of America.

Published by O'Reilly Media, Inc., 1005 Gravenstein Highway North, Sebastopol, CA 95472.

O'Reilly books may be purchased for educational, business, or sales promotional use. Online editions are also available for most titles (*http://my.safaribooksonline.com*). For more information, contact our corporate/institutional sales department: 800-998-9938 or *corporate@oreilly.com*.

Editor: Mary Treseler	**Indexer:** Lucie Haskins
Production Editor: Kristen Brown	**Cover Designer:** Karen Montgomery
Copyeditor: Rachel Monaghan	**Interior Designer:** David Futato
Proofreader: Rachel Head	**Illustrator:** Rebecca Demarest

October 2013:   Second Edition

Revision History for the Second Edition:

2013-09-25:   First release

See *http://oreilly.com/catalog/errata.csp?isbn=9781449367619* for release details.

ISBN: 978-1-449-36761-9

[LSI]

If the ax is dull and its edge unsharpened, more strength is needed,
but skill will bring success.

—Ecclesiastes 10:10

Table of Contents

Part II.   Twitter Cookbook

Part III. Appendixes

Preface

*The Web is more a social creation
than a technical one.
I designed it for a social effect—to
help people work together—and not as a
technical toy. The ultimate goal of the Web
is to support and improve our weblike existence
in the world. We clump into families, associations,
and companies. We develop trust across the miles
and distrust around the corner.*

—Tim Berners-Lee, *Weaving the Web* (Harper)

README.1st

This book has been carefully designed to provide an incredible learning experience for a particular target audience, and in order to avoid any unnecessary confusion about its scope or purpose by way of disgruntled emails, bad book reviews, or other misunderstandings that can come up, the remainder of this preface tries to help you determine whether you are part of that target audience. As a very busy professional, I consider my time my most valuable asset, and I want you to know right from the beginning that I believe that the same is true of you. Although I often fail, I really do try to honor my neighbor above myself as I walk out this life, and this preface is my attempt to honor you, the reader, by making it clear whether or not this book can meet your expectations.

Managing Your Expectations

Some of the most basic assumptions this book makes about you as a reader is that you want to learn how to mine data from popular social web properties, avoid technology hassles when running sample code, and have *lots* of fun along the way. Although you could read this book solely for the purpose of learning what is possible, you should know up front that it has been written in such a way that you really could follow along with the many exercises and become a data miner once you've completed the few simple steps to set up a development environment. If you've done some programming before, you should find that it's relatively painless to get up and running with the code examples. Even if you've never programmed before but consider yourself the least bit tech-savvy, I daresay that you could use this book as a starting point to a remarkable journey that will stretch your mind in ways that you probably haven't even imagined yet.

To fully enjoy this book and all that it has to offer, you need to be interested in the vast possibilities for mining the rich data tucked away in popular social websites such as Twitter, Facebook, LinkedIn, and Google+, and you need to be motivated enough to download a virtual machine and follow along with the book's example code in IPython Notebook, a fantastic web-based tool that features all of the examples for every chapter. Executing the examples is usually as easy as pressing a few keys, since all of the code is presented to you in a friendly user interface. This book will teach you a few things that you'll be thankful to learn and will add a few indispensable tools to your toolbox, but perhaps even more importantly, it will tell you a story and entertain you along the way. It's a story about data science involving social websites, the data that's tucked away inside of them, and some of the intriguing possibilities of what you (or anyone else) could do with this data.

If you were to read this book from cover to cover, you'd notice that this story unfolds on a chapter-by-chapter basis. While each chapter roughly follows a predictable template that introduces a social website, teaches you how to use its API to fetch data, and introduces some techniques for data analysis, the broader story the book tells crescendos in complexity. Earlier chapters in the book take a little more time to introduce fundamental concepts, while later chapters systematically build upon the foundation from earlier chapters and gradually introduce a broad array of tools and techniques for mining the social web that you can take with you into other aspects of your life as a data scientist, analyst, visionary thinker, or curious reader.

Some of the most popular social websites have transitioned from fad to mainstream to household names over recent years, changing the way we live our lives on and off the Web and enabling technology to bring out the best (and sometimes the worst) in us. Generally speaking, each chapter of this book interlaces slivers of the social web along with data mining, analysis, and visualization techniques to explore data and answer the following representative questions:

- Who knows whom, and which people are common to their social networks?
- How frequently are particular people communicating with one another?
- Which social network connections generate the most value for a particular niche?
- How does geography affect your social connections in an online world?

- Who are the most influential/popular people in a social network?

- What are people chatting about (and is it valuable)?

- What are people interested in based upon the human language that they use in a digital world?

The answers to these basic kinds of questions often yield valuable insight and present lucrative opportunities for entrepreneurs, social scientists, and other curious practitioners who are trying to understand a problem space and find solutions. Activities such as building a turnkey killer app from scratch to answer these questions, venturing far beyond the typical usage of visualization libraries, and constructing just about anything state-of-the-art are not within the scope of this book. You'll be really disappointed if you purchase this book because you want to do one of those things. However, this book does provide the fundamental building blocks to answer these questions and provide a springboard that might be exactly what you need to build that killer app or conduct that research study. Skim a few chapters and see for yourself. This book covers a lot of ground.

Python-Centric Technology

This book intentionally takes advantage of the Python programming language for all of its example code. Python's intuitive syntax, amazing ecosystem of packages that trivialize API access and data manipulation, and core data structures that are practically JSON (*http://bit.ly/1a1kFaF*) make it an excellent teaching tool that's powerful yet also very easy to get up and running. As if that weren't enough to make Python both a great pedagogical choice and a very pragmatic choice for mining the social web, there's IPython Notebook (*http://bit.ly/1a1kFr4*), a powerful, interactive Python interpreter that provides a notebook-like user experience from within your web browser and combines code execution, code output, text, mathematical typesetting, plots, and more. It's difficult to imagine a better user experience for a learning environment, because it trivializes the problem of delivering sample code that you as the reader can follow along with and execute with no hassles. Figure P-1 provides an illustration of the IPython Notebook experience, demonstrating the dashboard of notebooks for each chapter of the book. Figure P-2 shows a view of one notebook.

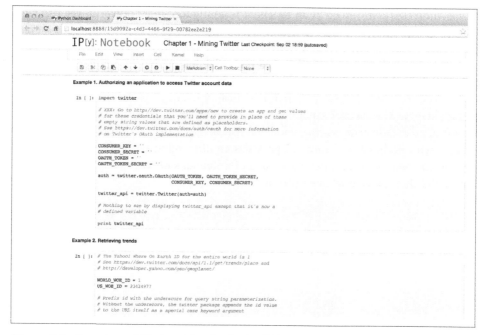

Figure P-1. Overview of IPython Notebook; a dashboard of notebooks

Figure P-2. Overview of IPython Notebook; the "Chapter 1-Mining Twitter" notebook

Every chapter in this book has a corresponding IPython Notebook with example code that makes it a pleasure to study the code, tinker around with it, and customize it for your own purposes. If you've done some programming but have never seen Python syntax, skimming ahead a few pages should hopefully be all the confirmation that you need. Excellent documentation is available online, and the official Python tutorial (*http://bit.ly/1a1kDj8*) is a good place to start if you're looking for a solid introduction to Python as a programming language. This book's Python source code is written in Python 2.7, the latest release of the 2.x line. (Although perhaps not entirely trivial, it's not too difficult to imagine using some of the automated tools to up-convert it to Python 3 for anyone who is interested in helping to make that happen.)

IPython Notebook is great, but if you're new to the Python programming world, advising you to just follow the instructions online to configure your development environment would be a bit counterproductive (and possibly even rude). To make your experience with this book as enjoyable as possible, a turnkey virtual machine is available that has IPython Notebook and all of the other dependencies that you'll need to follow along with the examples from this book preinstalled and ready to go. All that you have to do is follow a few simple steps, and in about 15 minutes, you'll be off to the races. If you have a programming background, you'll be able to configure your own development environment, but my hope is that I'll convince you that the virtual machine experience is a better starting point.

 See Appendix A for more detailed information on the virtual machine experience for this book. Appendix C is also worth your attention: it presents some IPython Notebook tips and common Python programming idioms that are used throughout this book's source code.

Whether you're a Python novice or a guru, the book's latest bug-fixed source code and accompanying scripts for building the virtual machine are available on GitHub (*http://bit.ly/1a1kFHM*), a social Git (*http://bit.ly/16mhOep*) repository that will always reflect the most up-to-date example code available. The hope is that social coding will enhance collaboration between like-minded folks who want to work together to extend the examples and hack away at fascinating problems. Hopefully, you'll fork, extend, and improve the source—and maybe even make some new friends or acquaintances along the way.

 The official GitHub repository containing the latest and greatest bug-fixed source code for this book is available at *http://bit.ly/MiningThe SocialWeb2E*.

Improvements Specific to the Second Edition

When I began working on this second edition of *Mining the Social Web*, I don't think I quite realized what I was getting myself into. What started out as a "substantial update" is now what I'd consider almost a rewrite of the first edition. I've extensively updated each chapter, I've strategically added new content, and I really do believe that this second edition is superior to the first in almost every way. My earnest hope is that it's going to be able to reach a much wider audience than the first edition and invigorate a broad community of interest with tools, techniques, and practical advice to implement ideas that depend on munging and analyzing data from social websites. If I am successful in this endeavor, we'll see a broader awareness of what it is possible to do with data from social websites and more budding entrepreneurs and enthusiastic hobbyists putting social web data to work.

A book is a product, and first editions of any product can be vastly improved upon, aren't always what customers ideally would have wanted, and can have great potential if appropriate feedback is humbly accepted and adjustments are made. This book is no exception, and the feedback and learning experience from interacting with readers and consumers of this book's sample code over the past few years have been incredibly important in shaping this book to be far beyond anything I could have designed if left to my own devices. I've incorporated as much of that feedback as possible, and it mostly boils down to the theme of *simplifying the learning experience for readers*.

Simplification presents itself in this second edition in a variety of ways. Perhaps most notably, one of the biggest differences between this book and the previous edition is that the technology toolchain is vastly simplified, and I've employed configuration management by way of an amazing virtualization technology called Vagrant (*http://bit.ly/1a1kGeH*). The previous edition involved a variety of databases for storage, various visualization toolkits, and assumed that readers could just figure out most of the installation and configuration by reading the online instructions.

This edition, on the other hand, goes to great lengths to introduce as few disparate technology dependencies as possible and presents them all with a virtual machine experience that abstracts away the complexities of software installation and configuration, which are sometimes considerably more challenging than they might initially seem. From a certain vantage point, the core toolbox is just IPython Notebook and some third-party package dependencies (all of which are versioned so that updates to open source software don't cause code breakage) that come preinstalled on a virtual machine. Inline visualizations are even baked into the IPython Notebooks, rendering from within IPython Notebook itself, and are consolidated down to a single JavaScript toolkit (D3.js (*http://d3js.org*)) that maintains visually consistent aesthetics across the chapters.

Continuing with the theme of simplification, spending less time introducing disparate technology in the book affords the opportunity to spend more time engaging in fundamental exercises in analysis. One of the recurring critiques from readers of the first edition's content was that more time should have been spent analyzing and discussing the implications of the exercises (a fair criticism indeed). My hope is that this second edition delivers on that wonderful suggestion by augmenting existing content with additional explanations in some of the void that was left behind. In a sense, this second edition does "more with less," and it delivers significantly more value to you as the reader because of it.

In terms of structural reorganization, you may notice that a chapter on GitHub has been added to this second edition. GitHub is interesting for a variety of reasons, and as you'll observe from reviewing the chapter, it's not all just about "social coding" (although that's a big part of it). GitHub is a very social website that spans international boundaries, is rapidly becoming a general purpose collaboration hub that extends beyond coding, and can fairly be interpreted as an interest graph—a graph that connects people and the things that interest them. Interest graphs, whether derived from GitHub or elsewhere, are a very important concept in the unfolding saga that is the Web, and as someone interested in the social web, you won't want to overlook them.

In addition to a new chapter on GitHub, the two "advanced" chapters on Twitter from the first edition have been refactored and expanded into a collection of more easily adaptable Twitter recipes that are organized into Chapter 9. Whereas the opening chapter of the book starts off slowly and warms you up to the notion of social web APIs and data mining, the final chapter of the book comes back full circle with a battery of diverse building blocks that you can adapt and assemble in various ways to achieve a truly enormous set of possibilities. Finally, the chapter that was previously dedicated to microformats has been folded into what is now Chapter 8, which is designed to be more of a forward-looking kind of cocktail discussion about the "semantically marked-up web" than an extensive collection of programming exercises, like the chapters before it.

 Constructive feedback is always welcome, and I'd enjoy hearing from you by way of a book review, tweet to @SocialWebMining (*http://bit.ly/ 1a1kHzq*), or comment on *Mining the Social Web*'s Facebook wall (*http://on.fb.me/1a1kHPQ*). The book's official website and blog that extends the book with longer-form content is at *http://MiningTheSo cialWeb.com*.

Conventions Used in This Book

This book is *extensively* hyperlinked, which makes it ideal to read in an electronic format such as a DRM-free PDF that can be purchased directly from O'Reilly as an ebook. Purchasing it as an ebook through O'Reilly also guarantees that you will get automatic updates for the book as they become available. The links have been shortened using the *bit.ly* service for the benefit of customers with the printed version of the book. All hyperlinks have been vetted.

The following typographical conventions are used in this book:

Italic

> Indicates new terms, URLs, email addresses, filenames, and file extensions.

`Constant width`

> Indicates program listings, and is used within paragraphs to refer to program elements such as variable or function names, databases, data types, environment variables, statements, and keywords.

`Constant width bold`

> Shows commands or other text that should be typed literally by the user. Also occasionally used for emphasis in code listings.

`Constant width italic`

> Shows text that should be replaced with user-supplied values or values determined by context.

 This icon signifies a tip, suggestion, or general note.

 This icon indicates a warning or caution.

Using Code Examples

The latest sample code for this book is maintained on GitHub at *http://bit.ly/Mining TheSocialWeb2E*, the official code repository for the book. You are encouraged to monitor this repository for the latest bug-fixed code as well as extended examples by the author and the rest of the social coding community. If you are reading a paper copy of this book, there is a possibility that the code examples in print may not be up to date, but so long as you are working from the book's GitHub repository, you will always have the latest bug-fixed example code. If you are taking advantage of this book's virtual machine experience, you'll already have the latest source code, but if you are opting to work on your own development environment, be sure to take advantage of the ability to download a source code archive directly from the GitHub repository.

Please log issues involving example code to the GitHub repository's issue tracker as opposed to the O'Reilly catalog's errata tracker. As issues are resolved in the source code at GitHub, updates are published back to the book's manuscript, which is then periodically provided to readers as an ebook update.

In general, you may use the code in this book in your programs and documentation. You do not need to contact us for permission unless you're reproducing a significant portion of the code. For example, writing a program that uses several chunks of code from this book does not require permission. Selling or distributing a CD-ROM of examples from O'Reilly books does require permission. Answering a question by citing this book and quoting example code does not require permission. Incorporating a significant amount of example code from this book into your product's documentation does require permission.

We require attribution according to the OSS license under which the code is released. An attribution usually includes the title, author, publisher, and ISBN. For example: "*Mining the Social Web, 2nd Edition*, by Matthew A. Russell. Copyright 2014 Matthew A. Russell, 978-1-449-36761-9."

If you feel your use of code examples falls outside fair use or the permission given above, feel free to contact us at *permissions@oreilly.com*.

Safari® Books Online

 Safari Books Online (*www.safaribooksonline.com*) is an on-demand digital library that delivers expert content in both book and video form from the world's leading authors in technology and business.

Technology professionals, software developers, web designers, and business and creative professionals use Safari Books Online as their primary resource for research, problem solving, learning, and certification training.

Safari Books Online offers a range of product mixes and pricing programs for organizations, government agencies, and individuals. Subscribers have access to thousands of books, training videos, and prepublication manuscripts in one fully searchable database from publishers like O'Reilly Media, Prentice Hall Professional, Addison-Wesley Professional, Microsoft Press, Sams, Que, Peachpit Press, Focal Press, Cisco Press, John Wiley & Sons, Syngress, Morgan Kaufmann, IBM Redbooks, Packt, Adobe Press, FT Press, Apress, Manning, New Riders, McGraw-Hill, Jones & Bartlett, Course Technology, and dozens more. For more information about Safari Books Online, please visit us online.

How to Contact Us

Please address comments and questions concerning this book to the publisher:

O'Reilly Media, Inc.
1005 Gravenstein Highway North
Sebastopol, CA 95472
800-998-9938 (in the United States or Canada)
707-829-0515 (international or local)
707-829-0104 (fax)

We have a web page for this book, where we list *non-code-related errata* and additional information. You can access this page at:

http://bit.ly/mining_social_web_2e

Any errata related to the sample code should be submitted as a ticket through GitHub's issue tracker at:

http://github.com/ptwobrussell/Mining-the-Social-Web/issues

Readers can request general help from the author and publisher through GetSatisfaction at:

http://getsatisfaction.com/oreilly

To comment or ask technical questions about this book, send email to:

bookquestions@oreilly.com

For more information about our books, conferences, Resource Centers, and the O'Reilly Network, see our website at:

http://www.oreilly.com

Acknowledgments for the Second Edition

I'll reiterate from my acknowledgments for the first edition that writing a book is a tremendous sacrifice. The time that you spend away from friends and family (which happens mostly during an extended period on nights and weekends) is quite costly and can't be recovered, and you really do need a certain amount of moral support to make it through to the other side with relationships intact. Thanks again to my very patient friends and family, who really shouldn't have tolerated me writing another book and probably think that I have some kind of chronic disorder that involves a strange addiction to working nights and weekends. If you can find a rehab clinic for people who are addicted to writing books, I promise I'll go and check myself in.

Every project needs a great project manager, and my incredible editor Mary Treseler and her amazing production staff were a pleasure to work with on this book (as always). Writing a technical book is a long and stressful endeavor, to say the least, and it's a remarkable experience to work with professionals who are able to help you make it through that exhausting journey and deliver a beautifully polished product that you can be proud to share with the world. Kristen Brown, Rachel Monaghan, and Rachel Head truly made all the difference in taking my best efforts to an entirely new level of professionalism.

The detailed feedback that I received from my very capable editorial staff and technical reviewers was also nothing short of amazing. Ranging from very technically oriented recommendations to software-engineering-oriented best practices with Python to perspectives on how to best reach the target audience as a mock reader, the feedback was beyond anything I could have ever expected. The book you are about to read would not be anywhere near the quality that it is without the thoughtful peer review feedback that I received. Thanks especially to Abe Music, Nicholas Mayne, Robert P.J. Day, Ram Narasimhan, Jason Yee, and Kevin Makice for your *very* detailed reviews of the manuscript. It made a tremendous difference in the quality of this book, and my only regret is that we did not have the opportunity to work together more closely during this process. Thanks also to Tate Eskew for introducing me to Vagrant, a tool that has made all the difference in establishing an easy-to-use and easy-to-maintain virtual machine experience for this book.

I also would like to thank my many wonderful colleagues at Digital Reasoning for the enlightening conversations that we've had over the years about data mining and topics in computer science, and other constructive dialogues that have helped shape my professional thinking. It's a blessing to be part of a team that's so talented and capable. Thanks especially to Tim Estes and Rob Metcalf, who have been supportive of my work on time-consuming projects (outside of my professional responsibilities to Digital Reasoning) like writing books.

Finally, thanks to every single reader or adopter of this book's source code who provided constructive feedback over the lifetime of the first edition. Although there are far too many of you to name, your feedback has shaped this second edition in immeasurable ways. I hope that this second edition meets your expectations and finds itself among your list of useful books that you'd recommend to a friend or colleague.

Acknowledgments from the First Edition

To say the least, writing a technical book takes a *ridiculous* amount of sacrifice. On the home front, I gave up more time with my wife, Baseeret, and daughter, Lindsay Belle, than I'm proud to admit. Thanks most of all to both of you for loving me in spite of my ambitions to somehow take over the world one day. (It's just a phase, and I'm really trying to grow out of it—honest.)

I sincerely believe that the sum of your decisions gets you to where you are in life (especially professional life), but nobody could ever complete the journey alone, and it's an honor to give credit where credit is due. I am truly blessed to have been in the company of some of the brightest people in the world while working on this book, including a technical editor as smart as Mike Loukides, a production staff as talented as the folks at O'Reilly, and an overwhelming battery of eager reviewers as amazing as everyone who helped me to complete this book. I especially want to thank Abe Music, Pete Warden, Tantek Celik, J. Chris Anderson, Salvatore Sanfilippo, Robert Newson, DJ Patil, Chimezie Ogbuji, Tim Golden, Brian Curtin, Raffi Krikorian, Jeff Hammerbacher, Nick Ducoff, and Cameron Marlowe for reviewing material or making particularly helpful comments that absolutely shaped its outcome for the best. I'd also like to thank Tim O'Reilly for graciously allowing me to put some of his Twitter and Google+ data under the microscope; it definitely made those chapters much more interesting to read than they otherwise would have been. It would be impossible to recount all of the other folks who have directly or indirectly shaped my life or the outcome of this book.

Finally, thanks to you for giving this book a chance. If you're reading this, you're at least thinking about picking up a copy. If you do, you're probably going to find something wrong with it despite my best efforts; however, I really do believe that, in spite of the few inevitable glitches, you'll find it an enjoyable way to spend a few evenings/weekends and you'll manage to learn a few things somewhere along the line.

A Guided Tour of the Social Web

Part I of this book is called "a guided tour of the social web" because it presents some practical skills for getting immediate value from some of the most popular social websites. You'll learn how to access APIs and analyze social data from Twitter, Facebook, LinkedIn, Google+, web pages, blogs and feeds, emails, and GitHub accounts. In general, each chapter stands alone and tells its own story, but the flow of chapters throughout Part I is designed to also tell a broader story. It gradually crescendos in terms of the complexity of the subject matter before resolving with a light-hearted discussion about some aspects of the semantic web that are relevant to the current social web landscape.

Because of this gradual increase in complexity, you are encouraged to read each chapter in turn, but you also should be able to cherry-pick chapters and follow along with the examples should you choose to do so. Each chapter's sample code is consolidated into a single IPython Notebook that is named according to the number of the chapter in this book.

The source code for this book is available at GitHub (*http://bit.ly/ 1a1kNqy*). You are highly encouraged to take advantage of the virtual machine experience so that you can work through the sample code in a pre-configured development environment that "just works."

Prelude

Although it's been mentioned in the preface and will continue to be casually reiterated in every chapter at some point, this isn't your typical tech book in which there's an archive of sample code that accompanies the text. It's a book that attempts to rock the status quo and define a new standard for tech books in which the code is managed as a first-class, open source software project, with the book being a form of "premium" support for that code base.

To address that objective, serious thought has been put into synthesizing the discussion in the book with the code examples into as seamless a learning experience as possible. After much discussion with readers of the first edition and reflection on lessons learned, it became apparent that an interactive user interface backed by a server running on a virtual machine and rooted in solid configuration management was the best path forward. There is not a simpler and better way to give you total control of the code while also ensuring that the code will "just work"—regardless of whether you use Mac OS, Windows, or Linux; whether you have a 32-bit or 64-bit machine; and whether third-party software dependencies change APIs and break.

Take advantage of this powerful environment for interactive learning.

 Read "Reflections on Authoring a Minimum Viable Book" (*http:// bit.ly/1a1kPyJ*) for more reflections on the process of developing a virtual machine for this second edition.

Although Chapter 1 is the most logical place to turn next, you should take a moment to familiarize yourself with Appendixes A and C when you are ready to start running the code examples. Appendix A points to an online document and accompanying screencasts that walk you through a quick and easy setup process for the virtual machine. Appendix C points to an online document that provides some background information you may find helpful in getting the most value out of the interactive virtual machine experience.

Even if you are a seasoned developer who is capable of doing all of this work yourself, give the virtual machine a try the first time through the book so that you don't get derailed with the inevitable software installation hiccup.

## CHAPTER 1

Mining Twitter: Exploring Trending Topics, Discovering What People Are Talking About, and More

This chapter kicks off our journey of mining the social web with Twitter, a rich source of social data that is a great starting point for social web mining because of its inherent openness for public consumption, clean and well-documented API, rich developer tooling, and broad appeal to users from every walk of life. Twitter data is particularly interesting because tweets happen at the "speed of thought" and are available for consumption as they happen in near real time, represent the broadest cross-section of society at an international level, and are so inherently multifaceted. Tweets and Twitter's "following" mechanism link people in a variety of ways, ranging from short (but often meaningful) conversational dialogues to interest graphs that connect people and the things that they care about.

Since this is the first chapter, we'll take our time acclimating to our journey in social web mining. However, given that Twitter data is so accessible and open to public scrutiny, Chapter 9 further elaborates on the broad number of data mining possibilities by providing a terse collection of recipes in a convenient problem/solution format that can be easily manipulated and readily applied to a wide range of problems. You'll also be able to apply concepts from future chapters to Twitter data.

 Always get the latest bug-fixed source code for this chapter (and every other chapter) online at *http://bit.ly/MiningTheSocialWeb2E*. Be sure to also take advantage of this book's virtual machine experience, as described in Appendix A, to maximize your enjoyment of the sample code.

1.1. Overview

In this chapter, we'll ease into the process of getting situated with a minimal (but effective) development environment with Python, survey Twitter's API, and distill some analytical insights from tweets using frequency analysis. Topics that you'll learn about in this chapter include:

- Twitter's developer platform and how to make API requests
- Tweet metadata and how to use it
- Extracting entities such as user mentions, hashtags, and URLs from tweets
- Techniques for performing frequency analysis with Python
- Plotting histograms of Twitter data with IPython Notebook

1.2. Why Is Twitter All the Rage?

Most chapters won't open with a reflective discussion, but since this is the first chapter of the book and introduces a social website that is often misunderstood, it seems appropriate to take a moment to examine Twitter at a fundamental level.

How would you define Twitter?

There are many ways to answer this question, but let's consider it from an overarching angle that addresses some fundamental aspects of our shared humanity that any technology needs to account for in order to be useful and successful. After all, the purpose of technology is to enhance our human experience.

As humans, what are some things that we want that technology might help us to get?

- We want to be heard.
- We want to satisfy our curiosity.
- We want it easy.
- We want it now.

In the context of the current discussion, these are just a few observations that are generally true of humanity. We have a deeply rooted need to share our ideas and experiences, which gives us the ability to connect with other people, to be heard, and to feel a sense of worth and importance. We are curious about the world around us and how to organize and manipulate it, and we use communication to share our observations, ask questions, and engage with other people in meaningful dialogues about our quandaries.

The last two bullet points highlight our inherent intolerance to friction. Ideally, we don't want to have to work any harder than is absolutely necessary to satisfy our curiosity or get any particular job done; we'd rather be doing "something else" or moving on to the next thing because our time on this planet is so precious and short. Along similar lines, we want things *now* and tend to be impatient when actual progress doesn't happen at the speed of our own thought.

One way to describe Twitter is as a microblogging service that allows people to communicate with short, 140-character messages that roughly correspond to thoughts or ideas. In that regard, you could think of Twitter as being akin to a free, high-speed, global text-messaging service. In other words, it's a glorified piece of valuable infrastructure that enables rapid and easy communication. However, that's not all of the story. It doesn't adequately address our inherent curiosity and the value proposition that emerges when you have over 500 million curious people registered, with over 100 million of them actively engaging (*http://bit.ly/1a1kNXR*) their curiosity on a regular monthly basis.

Besides the macro-level possibilities for marketing and advertising—which are always lucrative with a user base of that size—it's the underlying network dynamics that created the gravity for such a user base to emerge that are truly interesting, and that's why Twitter is all the rage. While the communication bus that enables users to share short quips at the speed of thought may be a *necessary* condition for viral adoption and sustained engagement on the Twitter platform, it's not a *sufficient* condition. The extra ingredient that makes it sufficient is that Twitter's asymmetric following model satisfies our curiosity. It is the asymmetric following model that casts Twitter as more of an interest graph than a social network, and the APIs that provide just enough of a framework for structure and self-organizing behavior to emerge from the chaos.

In other words, whereas some social websites like Facebook and LinkedIn require the mutual acceptance of a connection between users (which usually implies a real-world connection of some kind), Twitter's relationship model allows you to keep up with the latest happenings of *any* other user, even though that other user may not choose to follow you back or even know that you exist. Twitter's *following* model is simple but exploits a fundamental aspect of what makes us human: our curiosity. Whether it be an infatuation with celebrity gossip, an urge to keep up with a favorite sports team, a keen interest in a particular political topic, or a desire to connect with someone new, Twitter provides you with boundless opportunities to satisfy your curiosity.

Although I've been careful in the preceding paragraph to introduce Twitter in terms of "following" relationships, the act of *following* someone is sometimes described as "friending" (albeit it's a strange kind of one-way friendship). While you'll even run across the "friend" nomenclature in the official Twitter API documentation (*http://bit.ly/1a1kOuI*), it's probably best to think of Twitter in terms of the following relationships I've described.

Think of an *interest graph* as a way of modeling connections between people and their arbitrary interests. Interest graphs provide a profound number of possibilities in the data mining realm that primarily involve measuring correlations between things for the objective of making intelligent recommendations and other applications in machine learning. For example, you could use an interest graph to measure correlations and make recommendations ranging from whom to follow on Twitter to what to purchase online to whom you should date. To illustrate the notion of Twitter as an interest graph, consider that a Twitter user need not be a real person; it very well could be a person, but it could also be an inanimate object, a company, a musical group, an imaginary persona, an impersonation of someone (living or dead), or just about anything else.

For example, the @HomerJSimpson (*http://bit.ly/1a1kQD1*) account is the official account for Homer Simpson, a popular character from *The Simpsons* television show. Although Homer Simpson isn't a real person, he's a well-known personality throughout the world, and the @HomerJSimpson Twitter persona acts as an conduit for him (or his creators, actually) to engage his fans. Likewise, although this book will probably never reach the popularity of Homer Simpson, @SocialWebMining (*http://bit.ly/1a1kHzq*) is its official Twitter account and provides a means for a community that's interested in its content to connect and engage on various levels. When you realize that Twitter enables you to create, connect, and explore a community of interest for an arbitrary topic of interest, the power of Twitter and the insights you can gain from mining its data become much more obvious.

There is very little governance of what a Twitter account can be aside from the badges on some accounts that identify celebrities and public figures as "verified accounts" and basic restrictions in Twitter's Terms of Service agreement (*http://bit.ly/1a1kRXl*), which is required for using the service. It may seem very subtle, but it's an important distinction from some social websites in which accounts must correspond to real, living people, businesses, or entities of a similar nature that fit into a particular taxonomy. Twitter places no particular restrictions on the persona of an account and relies on self-organizing behavior such as following relationships and folksonomies that emerge from the use of hashtags to create a certain kind of order within the system.

Taxonomies and Folksonomies

A fundamental aspect of human intelligence is the desire to classify things and derive a hierarchy in which each element "belongs to" or is a "child" of a parent element one level higher in the hierarchy. Leaving aside some of the finer distinctions between a taxonomy and an ontology (*http://bit.ly/1a1kRXy*), think of a *taxonomy* as a hierarchical structure like a tree that classifies elements into particular parent/child relationships, whereas a *folksonomy* (*http://bit.ly/1a1kU5C*) (a term coined around 2004) describes the universe of collaborative tagging and social indexing efforts that emerge in various ecosystems of the Web. It's a play on words in the sense that it blends *folk* and *taxonomy*. So, in essence, a folksonomy is just a fancy way of describing the decentralized universe of tags that emerges as a mechanism of *collective intelligence* when you allow people to classify content with labels. One of the things that's so compelling about the use of hashtags on Twitter is that the folksonomies that organically emerge act as points of aggregation for common interests and provide a focused way to explore while still leaving open the possibility for nearly unbounded serendipity.

1.3. Exploring Twitter's API

Now having a proper frame of reference for Twitter, let us now transition our attention to the problem of acquiring and analyzing Twitter data.

1.3.1. Fundamental Twitter Terminology

Twitter might be described as a real-time, highly social microblogging service that allows users to post short status updates, called *tweets*, that appear on timelines. Tweets may include one or more entities in their 140 characters of content and reference one or more places that map to locations in the real world. An understanding of users, tweets, and timelines is particularly essential to effective use of Twitter's API (*http://bit.ly/1a1kSKQ*), so a brief introduction to these fundamental Twitter Platform objects (*http://bit.ly/1a1kSL8*) is in order before we interact with the API to fetch some data. We've largely discussed Twitter users and Twitter's asymmetric following model for relationships thus far, so this section briefly introduces tweets and timelines in order to round out a general understanding of the Twitter platform.

Tweets are the essence of Twitter, and while they are notionally thought of as the 140 characters of text content associated with a user's status update, there's really quite a bit more metadata there than meets the eye. In addition to the textual content of a tweet itself, tweets come bundled with two additional pieces of metadata that are of particular note: *entities* and *places*. Tweet entities are essentially the user mentions, hashtags, URLs, and media that may be associated with a tweet, and places are locations in the real world that may be attached to a tweet. Note that a place may be the actual location in which a tweet was authored, but it might also be a reference to the place described in a tweet.

To make it all a bit more concrete, let's consider a sample tweet with the following text:

> @ptwobrussell is writing @SocialWebMining, 2nd Ed. from his home office in Franklin, TN. Be #social: http://on.fb.me/16WJAf9

The tweet is 124 characters long and contains four tweet entities: the user mentions @ptwobrussell and @SocialWebMining, the hashtag #social, and the URL *http://on.fb.me/16WJAf9*. Although there is a place called Franklin, Tennessee that's explicitly mentioned in the tweet, the *places* metadata associated with the tweet might include the location in which the tweet was authored, which may or may not be Franklin, Tennessee. That's a lot of metadata that's packed into fewer than 140 characters and illustrates just how potent a short quip can be: it can unambiguously refer to multiple other Twitter users, link to web pages, and cross-reference topics with hashtags that act as points of aggregation and horizontally slice through the entire Twitterverse in an easily searchable fashion.

Finally, *timelines* are the chronologically sorted collections of tweets. Abstractly, you might say that a timeline is any particular collection of tweets displayed in chronological order; however, you'll commonly see a couple of timelines that are particularly noteworthy. From the perspective of an arbitrary Twitter user, the *home timeline* is the view that you see when you log into your account and look at all of the tweets from users that you are following, whereas a particular *user timeline* is a collection of tweets only from a certain user.

For example, when you log into your Twitter account, your home timeline is located at *https://twitter.com*. The URL for any particular user timeline, however, must be suffixed with a context that identifies the user, such as *https://twitter.com/SocialWebMining*. If you're interested in seeing what a particular user's home timeline looks like from that user's perspective, you can access it with the additional *following* suffix appended to the URL. For example, what Tim O'Reilly sees on his home timeline when he logs into Twitter is accessible at *https://twitter.com/timoreilly/following*.

An application like TweetDeck provides several customizable views into the tumultuous landscape of tweets, as shown in Figure 1-1, and is worth trying out if you haven't journeyed far beyond the Twitter.com user interface.

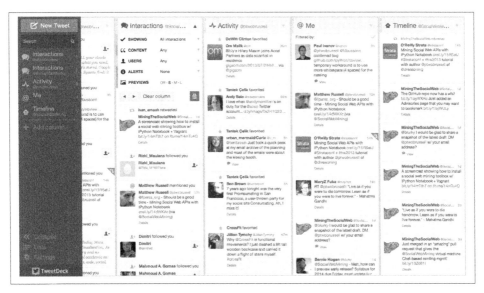

Figure 1-1. TweetDeck provides a highly customizable user interface that can be helpful for analyzing what is happening on Twitter and demonstrates the kind of data that you have access to through the Twitter API

Whereas timelines are collections of tweets with relatively low velocity, *streams* are samples of public tweets flowing through Twitter in realtime. The *public firehose* of all tweets has been known to peak at hundreds of thousands of tweets per minute (*http://bit.ly/1a1kV9N*) during events with particularly wide interest, such as presidential debates. Twitter's public firehose emits far too much data to consider for the scope of this book and presents interesting engineering challenges, which is at least one of the reasons that various third-party commercial vendors have partnered with Twitter to bring the firehose to the masses in a more consumable fashion. That said, a small random sample of the public timeline (*http://bit.ly/1a1kVq7*) is available that provides filterable access to enough public data for API developers to develop powerful applications.

The remainder of this chapter and Part II of this book assume that you have a Twitter account, which is required for API access. If you don't have an account already, take a moment to create onem and then review Twitter's liberal terms of service (*http://bit.ly/1a1kWKB*), API documentation (*http://bit.ly/1a1kSKQ*), and Developer Rules of the Road (*http://bit.ly/1a1kX1a*). The sample code for this chapter and Part II of the book generally don't require you to have any friends or followers of your own, but some of the examples in Part II will be a lot more interesting and fun if you have an active account with a handful of friends and followers that you can use as a basis for social web mining. If you don't have an active account, now would be a good time to get plugged in and start priming your account for the data mining fun to come.

1.3.2. Creating a Twitter API Connection

Twitter has taken great care to craft an elegantly simple RESTful (*http://bit.ly/ 1a1kVX5*) API that is intuitive and easy to use. Even so, there are great libraries available to further mitigate the work involved in making API requests. A particularly beautiful Python package that wraps the Twitter API and mimics the public API semantics almost one-to-one is `twitter`. Like most other Python packages, you can install it with `pip` by typing **pip install twitter** in a terminal.

 See Appendix C for instructions on how to install `pip`.

Python Tip: Harnessing pydoc for Effective Help During Development

We'll work though some examples that illustrate the use of the `twitter` package, but just in case you're ever in a situation where you need some help (and you will be), it's worth remembering that you can always skim the documentation for a package (its `pydoc` (*http://bit.ly/1a1kVXg*)) in a few different ways. Outside of a Python shell, running `pydoc` in your terminal on a package in your PYTHONPATH is a nice option. For example, on a Linux or Mac system, you can simply type **pydoc twitter** in a terminal to get the package-level documentation, whereas **pydoc twitter.Twitter** provides documentation on the `Twitter` class included with that package. On Windows systems, you can get the same information, albeit in a slightly different way, by executing `pydoc` as a package. Typing **python -mpydoc twitter.Twitter**, for example, would provide information on the `twitter.Twitter` class. If you find yourself reviewing the documentation for certain modules often, you can elect to pass the `-w` option to `pydoc` and write out an HTML page that you can save and bookmark in your browser.

However, more than likely, you'll be in the middle of a working session when you need some help. The built-in `help` function accepts a package or class name and is useful for an ordinary Python shell, whereas IPython (*http://bit.ly/1a1kXyf*) users can suffix a package or class name with a question mark to view inline help. For example, you could type **help(twitter)** or **help(twitter.Twitter)** in a regular Python interpreter, while you could use the shortcut **twitter?** or **twitter.Twitter?** in IPython or IPython Notebook.

It is highly recommended that you adopt IPython as your standard Python shell when working outside of IPython Notebook because of the various convenience functions, such as tab completion, session history, and "magic functions," (*http://bit.ly/1a1kXyf*) that it offers. Recall that Appendix A provides minimal details on getting oriented with recommended developer tools such as IPython.

We'll opt to make programmatic API requests with Python, because the `twitter` package so elegantly mimics the RESTful API. If you're interested in seeing the raw requests that you could make with HTTP or exploring the API in a more interactive manner, however, check out the developer console (*http://bit.ly/1a1kWui*) or the command-line tool Twurl (*http://bit.ly/1a1kZq1*).

Before you can make any API requests to Twitter, you'll need to create an application at *https://dev.twitter.com/apps*. Creating an application is the standard way for developers to gain API access and for Twitter to monitor and interact with third-party platform developers as needed. The process for creating an application is pretty standard, and all that's needed is read-only access to the API.

In the present context, *you* are creating an app that you are going to authorize to access *your* account data, so this might seem a bit roundabout; why not just plug in your username and password to access the API? While that approach might work fine for *you*, a third party such as a friend or colleague probably wouldn't feel comfortable forking over a username/password combination in order to enjoy the same insights from *your* app. Giving up credentials is never a sound practice. Fortunately, some smart people recognized this problem years ago, and now there's a standardized protocol called OAuth (*http://bit.ly/1a1kZWN*) (short for Open Authorization) that works for these kinds of situations in a generalized way for the broader social web. The protocol is a social web standard at this point.

If you remember nothing else from this tangent, just remember that OAuth is a means of allowing users to authorize third-party applications to access their account data without needing to share sensitive information like a password. Appendix B provides a slightly broader overview of how OAuth works if you're interested, and Twitter's OAuth documentation (*http://bit.ly/1a1kZWW*) offers specific details about its particular implementation.[1]

For simplicity of development, the key pieces of information that you'll need to take away from your newly created application's settings are its consumer key, consumer secret, access token, and access token secret. In tandem, these four credentials provide everything that an application would ultimately be getting to authorize itself through a series of redirects involving the user granting authorization, so treat them with the same sensitivity that you would a password.

---

1. Although it's an implementation detail, it may be worth noting that Twitter's v1.1 API still implements OAuth 1.0a, whereas many other social web properties have since upgraded to OAuth 2.0.

See Appendix B for details on implementing an OAuth 2.0 flow that you would need to build an application that requires an arbitrary user to authorize it to access account data.

Figure 1-2 shows the context of retrieving these credentials.

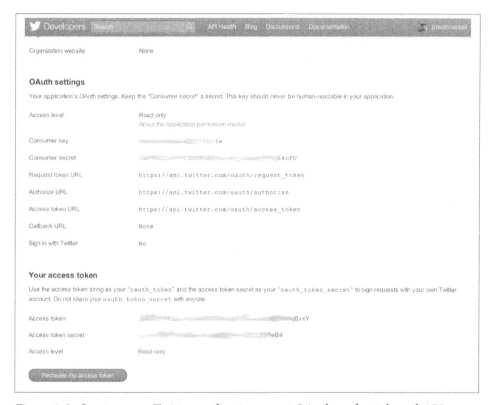

Figure 1-2. Create a new Twitter application to get OAuth credentials and API access at https://dev.twitter.com/apps; the four (blurred) OAuth fields are what you'll use to make API calls to Twitter's API

Without further ado, let's create an authenticated connection to Twitter's API and find out what people are talking about by inspecting the trends available to us through the GET trends/place resource (*http://bit.ly/1a1kYSQ*). While you're at it, go ahead and bookmark the official API documentation (*http://bit.ly/1a1kSKQ*) as well as the REST API v1.1 resources (*http://bit.ly/1a1kZ9i*), because you'll be referencing them regularly as you learn the ropes of the developer-facing side of the Twitterverse.

As of March 2013, Twitter's API operates at version 1.1 and is significantly different in a few areas from the previous v1 API that you may have encountered. Version 1 of the API passed through a deprecation cycle of approximately six months and is no longer operational. All sample code in this book presumes version 1.1 of the API.

Let's fire up IPython Notebook and initiate a search. Follow along with Example 1-1 by substituting your own account credentials into the variables at the beginning of the code example and execute the call to create an instance of the Twitter API. The code works by using your OAuth credentials to create an object called auth that represents your OAuth authorization, which can then be passed to a class called Twitter that is capable of issuing queries to Twitter's API.

Example 1-1. Authorizing an application to access Twitter account data

```
import twitter

# XXX: Go to http://dev.twitter.com/apps/new to create an app and get values
# for these credentials, which you'll need to provide in place of these
# empty string values that are defined as placeholders.
# See https://dev.twitter.com/docs/auth/oauth for more information
# on Twitter's OAuth implementation.

CONSUMER_KEY = ''
CONSUMER_SECRET = ''
OAUTH_TOKEN = ''
OAUTH_TOKEN_SECRET = ''

auth = twitter.oauth.OAuth(OAUTH_TOKEN, OAUTH_TOKEN_SECRET,
                           CONSUMER_KEY, CONSUMER_SECRET)

twitter_api = twitter.Twitter(auth=auth)

# Nothing to see by displaying twitter_api except that it's now a
# defined variable

print twitter_api
```

The results of this example should simply display an unambiguous representation of the twitter_api object that we've constructed, such as:

```
<twitter.api.Twitter object at 0x39d9b50>
```

This indicates that we've successfully used OAuth credentials to gain authorization to query Twitter's API.

1.3.3. Exploring Trending Topics

With an authorized API connection in place, you can now issue a request. Example 1-2 demonstrates how to ask Twitter for the topics that are currently trending worldwide, but keep in mind that the API can easily be parameterized to constrain the topics to more specific locales if you feel inclined to try out some of the possibilities. The device for constraining queries is via Yahoo! GeoPlanet's (*http://yhoo.it/1a1kZ9u*) Where On Earth (WOE) ID system, which is an API unto itself that aims to provide a way to map a unique identifier to any named place on Earth (or theoretically, even in a virtual world). If you haven't already, go ahead and try out the example that collects a set of trends for both the entire world and just the United States.

Example 1-2. Retrieving trends

```
# The Yahoo! Where On Earth ID for the entire world is 1.
# See https://dev.twitter.com/docs/api/1.1/get/trends/place and
# http://developer.yahoo.com/geo/geoplanet/

WORLD_WOE_ID = 1
US_WOE_ID = 23424977

# Prefix ID with the underscore for query string parameterization.
# Without the underscore, the twitter package appends the ID value
# to the URL itself as a special case keyword argument.

world_trends = twitter_api.trends.place(_id=WORLD_WOE_ID)
us_trends = twitter_api.trends.place(_id=US_WOE_ID)

print world_trends
print
print us_trends
```

You should see a semireadable response that is a list of Python dictionaries from the API (as opposed to any kind of error message), such as the following truncated results, before proceeding further. (In just a moment, we'll reformat the response to be more easily readable.)

```
[{u'created_at': u'2013-03-27T11:50:40Z', u'trends': [{u'url':
    u'http://twitter.com/search?q=%23MentionSomeoneImportantForYou'...
```

Notice that the sample result contains a URL for a trend represented as a search query that corresponds to the hashtag #MentionSomeoneImportantForYou, where %23 is the URL encoding for the hashtag symbol. We'll use this rather benign hashtag throughout the remainder of the chapter as a unifying theme for examples that follow. Although a sample data file containing tweets for this hashtag is available with the book's source code, you'll have much more fun exploring a topic that's trending at the time you read this as opposed to following along with a canned topic that is no longer trending.

The pattern for using the `twitter` module is simple and predictable: instantiate the `Twitter` class with an object chain corresponding to a base URL and then invoke methods on the object that correspond to URL contexts. For example, `twitter_api._trends.place(WORLD_WOE_ID)` initiates an HTTP call to GET *https://api.twitter.com/1.1/trends/place.json?id=1*. Note the URL mapping to the object chain that's constructed with the `twitter` package to make the request and how query string parameters are passed in as keyword arguments. To use the `twitter` package for arbitrary API requests, you generally construct the request in that kind of straightforward manner, with just a couple of minor caveats that we'll encounter soon enough.

Twitter imposes *rate limits* on how many requests an application can make to any given API resource within a given time window. Twitter's rate limits (*http://bit.ly/1a1l257*) are well documented, and each individual API resource also states its particular limits for your convenience. For example, the API request that we just issued for trends limits applications to 15 requests per 15-minute window (see Figure 1-3). For more nuanced information on how Twitter's rate limits work, see REST API Rate Limiting in v1.1 (*http://bit.ly/1a1l2ly*). For the purposes of following along in this chapter, it's highly unlikely that you'll get rate limited. Section 9.16 on page 378 (Example 9-16) will introduce some techniques demonstrating best practices while working with rate limits.

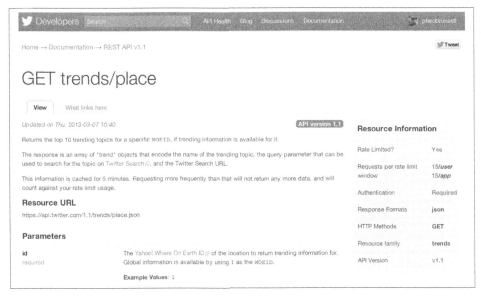

Figure 1-3. Rate limits for Twitter API resources are identified in the online documentation for each API call; the particular API resource shown here allows 15 requests per "rate limit window," which is currently defined as 15 minutes

The developer documentation states that the results of a Trends API query are updated only once every five minutes, so it's not a judicious use of your efforts or API requests to ask for results more often than that.

Although it hasn't explicitly been stated yet, the semireadable output from Example 1-2 is printed out as native Python data structures. While an IPython interpreter will "pretty print" the output for you automatically, IPython Notebook and a standard Python interpreter will not. If you find yourself in these circumstances, you may find it handy to use the built-in json package to force a nicer display, as illustrated in Example 1-3.

JSON (*http://bit.ly/1a1l2lJ*) is a data exchange format that you will encounter on a regular basis. In a nutshell, JSON provides a way to arbitrarily store maps, lists, primitives such as numbers and strings, and combinations thereof. In other words, you can theoretically model just about anything with JSON should you desire to do so.

Example 1-3. Displaying API responses as pretty-printed JSON

```
import json

print json.dumps(world_trends, indent=1)
print
print json.dumps(us_trends, indent=1)
```

An abbreviated sample response from the Trends API produced with json.dumps would look like the following:

```
[
 {
  "created_at": "2013-03-27T11:50:40Z",
  "trends": [
   {
    "url": "http://twitter.com/search?q=%23MentionSomeoneImportantForYou",
    "query": "%23MentionSomeoneImportantForYou",
    "name": "#MentionSomeoneImportantForYou",
    "promoted_content": null,
    "events": null
   },
   ...
  ]
 }
]
```

Although it's easy enough to skim the two sets of trends and look for commonality, let's use Python's set (*http://bit.ly/1a1l2Sw*) data structure to automatically compute this for us, because that's exactly the kind of thing that sets lend themselves to doing. In this instance, a *set* refers to the mathematical notion of a data structure that stores an unordered collection of unique items and can be computed upon with other sets of items and setwise operations. For example, a setwise intersection computes common items between sets, a setwise union combines all of the items from sets, and the setwise difference among sets acts sort of like a subtraction operation in which items from one set are removed from another.

Example 1-4 demonstrates how to use a Python list comprehension (*http://bit.ly/ 1a1l1hy*) to parse out the names of the trending topics from the results that were previously queried, cast those lists to sets, and compute the setwise intersection to reveal the common items between them. Keep in mind that there may or may not be significant overlap between any given sets of trends, all depending on what's actually happening when you query for the trends. In other words, the results of your analysis will be entirely dependent upon your query and the data that is returned from it.

 Recall that Appendix C provides a reference for some common Python idioms like list comprehensions that you may find useful to review.

Example 1-4. Computing the intersection of two sets of trends

```
world_trends_set = set([trend['name']
                       for trend in world_trends[0]['trends']])

us_trends_set = set([trend['name']
                    for trend in us_trends[0]['trends']])

common_trends = world_trends_set.intersection(us_trends_set)

print common_trends
```

 You should complete Example 1-4 before moving on in this chapter to ensure that you are able to access and analyze Twitter data. Can you explain what, if any, correlation exists between trends in your country and the rest of the world?

Set Theory, Intuition, and Countable Infinity

Computing setwise operations may seem a rather primitive form of analysis, but the ramifications of set theory for general mathematics are considerably more profound since it provides the foundation for many mathematical principles.

Georg Cantor is generally credited with formalizing the mathematics behind set theory, and his paper "On a Characteristic Property of All Real Algebraic Numbers" (1874) formalized set theory as part of his work on answering questions related to the concept of infinity. To understand how it worked, consider the following question: is the set of positive integers larger in cardinality than the set of both positive and negative integers?

Although common intuition may be that there are twice as many positive and negative integers than positive integers alone, Cantor's work showed that the cardinalities of the sets are actually equal! Mathematically, he showed that you can map both sets of numbers such that they form a sequence with a definite starting point that extends forever in *one* direction like this: *{1, –1, 2, –2, 3, –3, ...}*.

Because the numbers can be clearly enumerated but there is never an ending point, the cardinalities of the sets are said to be *countably infinite*. In other words, there is a definite sequence that could be followed deterministically if you simply had enough time to count them.

1.3.4. Searching for Tweets

One of the common items between the sets of trending topics turns out to be the hashtag #MentionSomeoneImportantForYou, so let's use it as the basis of a search query to fetch some tweets for further analysis. Example 1-5 illustrates how to exercise the GET search/tweets resource (*http://bit.ly/1a1l398*) for a particular query of interest, including the ability to use a special field that's included in the metadata for the search results to easily make additional requests for more search results. Coverage of Twitter's Streaming API (*http://bit.ly/1a1l1ya*) resources is out of scope for this chapter but is introduced in Section 9.8 on page 365 (Example 9-8) and may be more appropriate for many situations in which you want to maintain a constantly updated view of tweets.

 The use of *args and **kwargs as illustrated in Example 1-5 as parameters to a function is a Python idiom for expressing arbitrary arguments and keyword arguments, respectively. See Appendix C for a brief overview of this idiom.

Example 1-5. Collecting search results

```
# XXX: Set this variable to a trending topic,
# or anything else for that matter. The example query below
# was a trending topic when this content was being developed
# and is used throughout the remainder of this chapter.

q = '#MentionSomeoneImportantForYou'

count = 100
```

```
# See https://dev.twitter.com/docs/api/1.1/get/search/tweets

search_results = twitter_api.search.tweets(q=q, count=count)

statuses = search_results['statuses']


# Iterate through 5 more batches of results by following the cursor

for _ in range(5):
    print "Length of statuses", len(statuses)
    try:
        next_results = search_results['search_metadata']['next_results']
    except KeyError, e: # No more results when next_results doesn't exist
        break

    # Create a dictionary from next_results, which has the following form:
    # ?max_id=313519052523986943&q=NCAA&include_entities=1
    kwargs = dict([ kv.split('=') for kv in next_results[1:].split("&") ])

    search_results = twitter_api.search.tweets(**kwargs)
    statuses += search_results['statuses']

# Show one sample search result by slicing the list...
print json.dumps(statuses[0], indent=1)
```

 Although we're just passing in a hashtag to the Search API at this point, it's well worth noting that it contains a number of powerful operators (*http://bit.ly/1a1l3pN*) that allow you to filter queries according to the existence or nonexistence of various keywords, originator of the tweet, location associated with the tweet, etc.

In essence, all the code does is repeatedly make requests to the Search API. One thing that might initially catch you off guard if you've worked with other web APIs (including version 1 of Twitter's API) is that there's no explicit concept of *pagination* in the Search API itself. Reviewing the API documentation reveals that this is a intentional decision, and there are some good reasons (*http://bit.ly/1a1l4K6*) for taking a *cursoring* approach instead, given the highly dynamic state of Twitter resources. The best practices for cursoring vary a bit throughout the Twitter developer platform, with the Search API providing a slightly simpler way of navigating search results than other resources such as timelines.

Search results contain a special `search_metadata` node that embeds a `next_results` field with a query string that provides the basis of a subsequent query. If we weren't using a library like `twitter` to make the HTTP requests for us, this preconstructed query string would just be appended to the Search API URL, and we'd update it with additional parameters for handling OAuth. However, since we are not making our

HTTP requests directly, we must parse the query string into its constituent key/value pairs and provide them as keyword arguments.

In Python parlance, we are *unpacking* the values in a dictionary into keyword arguments that the function receives. In other words, the function call inside of the for loop in Example 1-5 ultimately invokes a function such as twitter_api.search.tweets (q='%23MentionSomeoneImportantForYou', include_entities=1, max_id=313519 052523986943) even though it appears in the source code as twitter_api .search.tweets(**kwargs), with kwargs being a dictionary of key/value pairs.

 The search_metadata field also contains a refresh_url value that can be used if you'd like to maintain and periodically update your collection of results with new information that's become available since the previous query.

The next sample tweet shows the search results for a query for #MentionSomeoneImportantForYou. Take a moment to peruse (all of) it. As I mentioned earlier, there's a lot more to a tweet than meets the eye. The particular tweet that follows is fairly representative and contains in excess of 5 KB of total content when represented in uncompressed JSON. That's more than 40 times the amount of data that makes up the 140 characters of text that's normally thought of as a tweet!

```
[
 {
  "contributors": null,
  "truncated": false,
  "text": "RT @hassanmusician: #MentionSomeoneImportantForYou God.",
  "in_reply_to_status_id": null,
  "id": 316948241264549888,
  "favorite_count": 0,
  "source": "<a href=\"http://twitter.com/download/android\"...",
  "retweeted": false,
  "coordinates": null,
  "entities": {
   "user_mentions": [
    {
     "id": 56259379,
     "indices": [
      3,
      18
     ],
     "id_str": "56259379",
     "screen_name": "hassanmusician",
     "name": "Download the NEW LP!"
    }
   ],
   "hashtags": [
```

```
  {
   "indices": [
    20,
    50
    ],
    "text": "MentionSomeoneImportantForYou"
   }
  ],
  "urls": []
 },
 "in_reply_to_screen_name": null,
 "in_reply_to_user_id": null,
 "retweet_count": 23,
 "id_str": "316948241264549888",
 "favorited": false,
 "retweeted_status": {
  "contributors": null,
  "truncated": false,
  "text": "#MentionSomeoneImportantForYou God.",
  "in_reply_to_status_id": null,
  "id": 316944833233186816,
  "favorite_count": 0,
  "source": "web",
  "retweeted": false,
  "coordinates": null,
  "entities": {
   "user_mentions": [],
   "hashtags": [
    {
     "indices": [
      0,
      30
      ],
      "text": "MentionSomeoneImportantForYou"
     }
    ],
    "urls": []
  },
  "in_reply_to_screen_name": null,
  "in_reply_to_user_id": null,
  "retweet_count": 23,
  "id_str": "316944833233186816",
  "favorited": false,
  "user": {
   "follow_request_sent": null,
   "profile_use_background_image": true,
   "default_profile_image": false,
   "id": 56259379,
   "verified": false,
   "profile_text_color": "3C3940",
   "profile_image_url_https": "https://si0.t...",
   "profile_sidebar_fill_color": "95E8EC",
```

```
"entities": {
 "url": {
  "urls": [
   {
    "url": "http://t.co/yRX89YM4J0",
    "indices": [
     0,
     22
    ],
    "expanded_url": "http://www.datpiff...",
    "display_url": "datpiff.com/mixtapes-detai\u2026"
   }
  ]
 },
 "description": {
  "urls": []
 }
},
"followers_count": 105041,
"profile_sidebar_border_color": "000000",
"id_str": "56259379",
"profile_background_color": "000000",
"listed_count": 64,
"profile_background_image_url_https": "https://si0.t...",
"utc_offset": -18000,
"statuses_count": 16691,
"description": "#TheseAreTheWordsISaid LP",
"friends_count": 59615,
"location": "",
"profile_link_color": "91785A",
"profile_image_url": "http://a0.twimg.com/...",
"following": null,
"geo_enabled": true,
"profile_banner_url": "https://si0.twimg.com/pr...",
"profile_background_image_url": "http://a0.twi...",
"screen_name": "hassanmusician",
"lang": "en",
"profile_background_tile": false,
"favourites_count": 6142,
"name": "Download the NEW LP!",
"notifications": null,
"url": "http://t.co/yRX89YM4J0",
"created_at": "Mon Jul 13 02:18:25 +0000 2009",
"contributors_enabled": false,
"time_zone": "Eastern Time (US & Canada)",
"protected": false,
"default_profile": false,
"is_translator": false
},
"geo": null,
"in_reply_to_user_id_str": null,
"lang": "en",
```

```
  "created_at": "Wed Mar 27 16:08:31 +0000 2013",
  "in_reply_to_status_id_str": null,
  "place": null,
  "metadata": {
   "iso_language_code": "en",
   "result_type": "recent"
  }
 },
 "user": {
  "follow_request_sent": null,
  "profile_use_background_image": true,
  "default_profile_image": false,
  "id": 549413966,
  "verified": false,
  "profile_text_color": "3D1957",
  "profile_image_url_https": "https://si0.twimg...",
  "profile_sidebar_fill_color": "7AC3EE",
  "entities": {
   "description": {
    "urls": []
   }
  },
  "followers_count": 110,
  "profile_sidebar_border_color": "FFFFFF",
  "id_str": "549413966",
  "profile_background_color": "642D8B",
  "listed_count": 1,
  "profile_background_image_url_https": "https:...",
  "utc_offset": 0,
  "statuses_count": 1294,
  "description": "i BELIEVE do you? I admire n adore @justinbieber ",
  "friends_count": 346,
  "location": "All Around The World ",
  "profile_link_color": "FF0000",
  "profile_image_url": "http://a0.twimg.com/pr...",
  "following": null,
  "geo_enabled": true,
  "profile_banner_url": "https://si0.twimg.com/...",
  "profile_background_image_url": "http://a0.tw...",
  "screen_name": "LilSalima",
  "lang": "en",
  "profile_background_tile": true,
  "favourites_count": 229,
  "name": "KoKo :D",
  "notifications": null,
  "url": null,
  "created_at": "Mon Apr 09 17:51:36 +0000 2012",
  "contributors_enabled": false,
  "time_zone": "London",
  "protected": false,
  "default_profile": false,
  "is_translator": false
```

```
  },
  "geo": null,
  "in_reply_to_user_id_str": null,
  "lang": "en",
  "created_at": "Wed Mar 27 16:22:03 +0000 2013",
  "in_reply_to_status_id_str": null,
  "place": null,
  "metadata": {
   "iso_language_code": "en",
   "result_type": "recent"
  }
 },
 ...
]
```

Tweets are imbued with some of the richest metadata that you'll find on the social web, and Chapter 9 elaborates on some of the many possibilities.

1.4. Analyzing the 140 Characters

The online documentation is always the definitive source for Twitter platform objects, and it's worthwhile to bookmark the Tweets (*http://bit.ly/1a1I3WL*) page, because it's one that you'll refer to quite frequently as you get familiarized with the basic anatomy of a tweet. No attempt is made here or elsewhere in the book to regurgitate online documentation, but a few notes are of interest given that you might still be a bit overwhelmed by the 5 KB of information that a tweet comprises. For simplicity of nomenclature, let's assume that we've extracted a single tweet from the search results and stored it in a variable named t. For example, t.keys() returns the top-level fields for the tweet and t['id'] accesses the identifier of the tweet.

 If you're following along with the IPython Notebook for this chapter, the exact tweet that's under scrutiny is stored in a variable named t so that you can interactively access its fields and explore more easily. The current discussion assumes the same nomenclature, so values should correspond one-for-one.

- The human-readable text of a tweet is available through t['text']:

      RT @hassanmusician: #MentionSomeoneImportantForYou God.

- The entities in the text of a tweet are conveniently processed for you and available through t['entities']:

      {
       "user_mentions": [
        {
         "indices": [
```
```

```
    3,
    18
   ],
   "screen_name": "hassanmusician",
   "id": 56259379,
   "name": "Download the NEW LP!",
   "id_str": "56259379"
  }
 ],
 "hashtags": [
  {
   "indices": [
    20,
    50
   ],
   "text": "MentionSomeoneImportantForYou"
  }
 ],
 "urls": []
}
```

- Clues as to the "interestingness" of a tweet are available through t['favor ite_count'] and t['retweet_count'], which return the number of times it's been bookmarked or retweeted, respectively.

- If a tweet has been retweeted, the t['retweeted_status'] field provides significant detail about the original tweet itself and its author. Keep in mind that sometimes the text of a tweet changes as it is retweeted, as users add reactions or otherwise manipulate the text.

- The t['retweeted'] field denotes whether or not the authenticated user (via an authorized application) has retweeted this particular tweet. Fields that vary depending upon the point of view of the particular user are denoted in Twitter's developer documentation as *perspectival*, which means that their values will vary depending upon the perspective of the user.

- Additionally, note that only original tweets are retweeted from the standpoint of the API and information management. Thus, the retweet_count reflects the total number of times that the original tweet has been retweeted and should reflect the same value in both the original tweet and all subsequent retweets. In other words, retweets aren't retweeted. It may be a bit counterintuitive at first, but if you think you're retweeting a retweet, you're actually just retweeting the original tweet that you were exposed to through a proxy. See Section 1.4.4 on page 34 later in this chapter for a more nuanced discussion about the difference between retweeting vs quoting a tweet.

A common mistake is to check the value of the `retweeted` field to determine whether or not a tweet has ever been retweeted by anyone. To check whether a tweet has ever been retweeted, you should instead see whether a `retweeted_status` node wrapper exists in the tweet.

You should tinker around with the sample tweet and consult the documentation to clarify any lingering questions you might have before moving forward. A good working knowledge of a tweet's anatomy is critical to effectively mining Twitter data.

1.4.1. Extracting Tweet Entities

Next, let's distill the entities and the text of the tweets into a convenient data structure for further examination. Example 1-6 extracts the text, screen names, and hashtags from the tweets that are collected and introduces a Python idiom called a *double* (or *nested*) *list comprehension*. If you understand a (single) list comprehension, the code formatting should illustrate the double list comprehension as simply a collection of values that are derived from a nested loop as opposed to the results of a single loop. List comprehensions are particularly powerful because they usually yield substantial performance gains over nested lists and provide an intuitive (once you're familiar with them) yet terse syntax.

List comprehensions are used frequently throughout this book, and it's worth consulting Appendix C or the official Python tutorial (*http://bit.ly/1a1l1hy*) for more details if you'd like additional context.

Example 1-6. Extracting text, screen names, and hashtags from tweets

```
status_texts = [ status['text']
                 for status in statuses ]

screen_names = [ user_mention['screen_name']
                 for status in statuses
                     for user_mention in status['entities']['user_mentions'] ]

hashtags = [ hashtag['text']
             for status in statuses
                 for hashtag in status['entities']['hashtags'] ]

# Compute a collection of all words from all tweets
words = [ w
          for t in status_texts
              for w in t.split() ]

# Explore the first 5 items for each...
```

```
print json.dumps(status_texts[0:5], indent=1)
print json.dumps(screen_names[0:5], indent=1)
print json.dumps(hashtags[0:5], indent=1)
print json.dumps(words[0:5], indent=1)
```

Sample output follows; it displays five status texts, screen names, and hashtags to provide a feel for what's in the data.

 In Python, syntax in which square brackets appear after a list or string value, such as status_texts[0:5], is indicative of *slicing*, whereby you can easily extract items from lists or substrings from strings. In this particular case, [0:5] indicates that you'd like the first five items in the list status_texts (corresponding to items at indices 0 through 4). See Appendix C for a more extended description of slicing in Python.

```
[
 "\u201c@KathleenMariee_: #MentionSomeOneImportantForYou @AhhlicksCruise...,
 "#MentionSomeoneImportantForYou My bf @Linkin_Sunrise.",
 "RT @hassanmusician: #MentionSomeoneImportantForYou God.",
 "#MentionSomeoneImportantForYou @Louis_Tomlinson",
 "#MentionSomeoneImportantForYou @Delta_Universe"
]
[
 "KathleenMariee_",
 "AhhlicksCruise",
 "itsravennn_cx",
 "kandykisses_13",
 "BMOLOGY"
]
[
 "MentionSomeOneImportantForYou",
 "MentionSomeoneImportantForYou",
 "MentionSomeoneImportantForYou",
 "MentionSomeoneImportantForYou",
 "MentionSomeoneImportantForYou"
]
[
 "\u201c@KathleenMariee_:",
 "#MentionSomeOneImportantForYou",
 "@AhhlicksCruise",
 ",",
 "@itsravennn_cx"
]
```

As expected, #MentionSomeoneImportantForYou dominates the hashtag output. The output also provides a few commonly occurring screen names that are worth investigating.

1.4.2. Analyzing Tweets and Tweet Entities with Frequency Analysis

Virtually all analysis boils down to the simple exercise of counting things on some level, and much of what we'll be doing in this book is manipulating data so that it can be counted and further manipulated in meaningful ways.

From an empirical standpoint, counting observable things is the starting point for just about everything, and thus the starting point for any kind of statistical filtering or manipulation that strives to find what may be a faint signal in noisy data. Whereas we just extracted the first 5 items of each unranked list to get a feel for the data, let's now take a closer look at what's in the data by computing a frequency distribution and looking at the top 10 items in each list.

As of Python 2.7, a `collections` (*http://bit.ly/1a1l4tC*) module is available that provides a counter that makes computing a frequency distribution rather trivial. Example 1-7 demonstrates how to use a `Counter` to compute frequency distributions as ranked lists of terms. Among the more compelling reasons for mining Twitter data is to try to answer the question of what people are talking about *right now*. One of the simplest techniques you could apply to answer this question is basic frequency analysis, just as we are performing here.

Example 1-7. Creating a basic frequency distribution from the words in tweets

```
from collections import Counter

for item in [words, screen_names, hashtags]:
    c = Counter(item)
    print c.most_common()[:10] # top 10
    print
```

Here are some sample results from frequency analysis of tweets:

```
[(u'#MentionSomeoneImportantForYou', 92), (u'RT', 34), (u'my', 10),
 (u',', 6), (u'@justinbieber', 6), (u'<3', 6), (u'My', 5), (u'and', 4),
 (u'I', 4), (u'te', 3)]

[(u'justinbieber', 6), (u'Kid_Charliej', 2), (u'Cavillafuerte', 2),
 (u'touchmestyles_', 1), (u'aliceorr96', 1), (u'gymleeam', 1), (u'fienas', 1),
 (u'nayely_1D', 1), (u'angelchute', 1)]

[(u'MentionSomeoneImportantForYou', 94), (u'mentionsomeoneimportantforyou', 3),
 (u'NoHomo', 1), (u'Love', 1), (u'MentionSomeOneImportantForYou', 1),
 (u'MyHeart', 1), (u'bebesito', 1)]
```

The result of the frequency distribution is a map of key/value pairs corresponding to terms and their frequencies, so let's make reviewing the results a little easier on the eyes by emitting a tabular format. You can install a package called `prettytable` by typing **pip install prettytable** in a terminal; this package provides a convenient way to emit a fixed-width tabular format that can be easily copied-and-pasted.

Example 1-8 shows how to use it to display the same results.

Example 1-8. Using prettytable to display tuples in a nice tabular format

```
from prettytable import PrettyTable

for label, data in (('Word', words),
                    ('Screen Name', screen_names),
                    ('Hashtag', hashtags)):
    pt = PrettyTable(field_names=[label, 'Count'])
    c = Counter(data)
    [ pt.add_row(kv) for kv in c.most_common()[:10] ]
    pt.align[label], pt.align['Count'] = 'l', 'r' # Set column alignment
    print pt
```

The results from Example 1-8 are displayed as a series of nicely formatted text-based tables that are easy to skim, as the following output demonstrates.

```
+------------------------------+-------+
| Word                         | Count |
+------------------------------+-------+
| #MentionSomeoneImportantForYou |    92 |
| RT                           |    34 |
| my                           |    10 |
| ,                            |     6 |
| @justinbieber                |     6 |
| &lt;3                        |     6 |
| My                           |     5 |
| and                          |     4 |
| I                            |     4 |
| te                           |     3 |
+------------------------------+-------+
+-----------------+-------+
| Screen Name     | Count |
+-----------------+-------+
| justinbieber    |     6 |
| Kid_Charliej    |     2 |
| Cavillafuerte   |     2 |
| touchmestyles_  |     1 |
| aliceorr96      |     1 |
| gymleeam        |     1 |
| fienas          |     1 |
| nayely_1D       |     1 |
| angelchute      |     1 |
+-----------------+-------+
+------------------------------+-------+
| Hashtag                      | Count |
+------------------------------+-------+
| MentionSomeoneImportantForYou |    94 |
| mentionsomeoneimportantforyou |     3 |
| NoHomo                       |     1 |
| Love                         |     1 |
| MentionSomeOneImportantForYou |     1 |
```

```
| MyHeart                        |     1 |
| bebesito                       |     1 |
+--------------------------------+-------+
```

A quick skim of the results reveals at least one marginally surprising thing: Justin Bieber is high on the list of entities for this small sample of data, and given his popularity with tweens on Twitter he may very well have been the "most important someone" for this trending topic, though the results here are inconclusive. The appearance of <3 is also interesting because it is an escaped form of <3, which represents a heart shape (that's rotated 90 degrees, like other emoticons and smileys) and is a common abbreviation for "loves." Given the nature of the query, it's not surprising to see a value like <3, although it may initially seem like junk or noise.

Although the entities with a frequency greater than two are interesting, the broader results are also revealing in other ways. For example, "RT" was a very common token, implying that there were a significant number of retweets (we'll investigate this observation further in Section 1.4.4 on page 34). Finally, as might be expected, the #MentionSomeoneImportantForYou hashtag and a couple of case-sensitive variations dominated the hashtags; a data-processing takeaway is that it would be worthwhile to normalize each word, screen name, and hashtag to lowercase when tabulating frequencies since there will inevitably be variation in tweets.

1.4.3. Computing the Lexical Diversity of Tweets

A slightly more advanced measurement that involves calculating simple frequencies and can be applied to unstructured text is a metric called *lexical diversity*. Mathematically, this is an expression of the number of *unique* tokens in the text divided by the *total* number of tokens in the text, which are both elementary yet important metrics in and of themselves. Lexical diversity is an interesting concept in the area of interpersonal communications because it provides a quantitative measure for the diversity of an individual's or group's vocabulary. For example, suppose you are listening to someone who repeatedly says "and stuff" to broadly generalize information as opposed to providing specific examples to reinforce points with more detail or clarity. Now, contrast that speaker to someone else who seldom uses the word "stuff" to generalize and instead reinforces points with concrete examples. The speaker who repeatedly says "and stuff" would have a lower lexical diversity than the speaker who uses a more diverse vocabulary, and chances are reasonably good that you'd walk away from the conversation feeling as though the speaker with the higher lexical diversity understands the subject matter better.

As applied to tweets or similar online communications, lexical diversity can be worth considering as a primitive statistic for answering a number of questions, such as how broad or narrow the subject matter is that an individual or group discusses. Although an overall assessment could be interesting, breaking down the analysis to specific time periods could yield additional insight, as could comparing different groups or individuals. For example, it would be interesting to measure whether or not there is a significant difference between the lexical diversity of two soft drink companies such as Coca-Cola (*http://bit.ly/1a1l5xR*) and Pepsi (*http://bit.ly/1a1l7pt*) as an entry point for exploration if you were comparing the effectiveness of their social media marketing campaigns on Twitter.

With a basic understanding of how to use a statistic like lexical diversity to analyze textual content such as tweets, let's now compute the lexical diversity for statuses, screen names, and hashtags for our working data set, as shown in Example 1-9.

Example 1-9. Calculating lexical diversity for tweets

```
# A function for computing lexical diversity
def lexical_diversity(tokens):
    return 1.0*len(set(tokens))/len(tokens)

# A function for computing the average number of words per tweet
def average_words(statuses):
    total_words = sum([ len(s.split()) for s in statuses ])
    return 1.0*total_words/len(statuses)

print lexical_diversity(words)
print lexical_diversity(screen_names)
print lexical_diversity(hashtags)
print average_words(status_texts)
```

 Prior to Python 3.0, the division operator (/) applies the floor function and returns an integer value (unless one of the operands is a floating-point value). Multiply either the numerator or the denominator by 1.0 to avoid truncation errors.

The results of Example 1-9 follow:

```
0.67610619469
0.955414012739
0.0686274509804
5.76530612245
```

There are a few observations worth considering in the results:

- The lexical diversity of the words in the text of the tweets is around 0.67. One way to interpret that figure would be to say that about two out of every three words is unique, or you might say that each status update carries around 67% unique information. Given that the average number of words in each tweet is around six, that translates to about four unique words per tweet. Intuition aligns with the data in that the nature of a #MentionSomeoneImportantForYou trending hashtag is to solicit a response that will probably be a few words long. In any event, a value of 0.67

is on the high side for lexical diversity of ordinary human communication, but given the nature of the data, it seems very reasonable.

- The lexical diversity of the screen names, however, is even higher, with a value of 0.95, which means that about 19 out of 20 screen names mentioned are unique. This observation also makes sense given that many answers to the question will be a screen name, and that most people won't be providing the same responses for the solicitous hashtag.

- The lexical diversity of the hashtags is extremely low at a value of around 0.068, implying that very few values other than the #MentionSomeoneImportantForYou hashtag appear multiple times in the results. Again, this makes good sense given that most responses are short and that hashtags really wouldn't make much sense to introduce as a response to the prompt of mentioning someone important for you.

- The average number of words per tweet is very low at a value of just under 6, which makes sense given the nature of the hashtag, which is designed to solicit short responses consisting of just a few words.

What would be interesting at this point would be to zoom in on some of the data and see if there were any common responses or other insights that could come from a more qualitative analysis. Given an average number of words per tweet as low as 6, it's unlikely that users applied any abbreviations to stay within the 140 characters, so the amount of noise for the data should be remarkably low, and additional frequency analysis may reveal some fascinating things.

1.4.4. Examining Patterns in Retweets

Even though the user interface and many Twitter clients have long since adopted the native Retweet API used to populate status values such as `retweet_count` and `retwee ted_status`, some Twitter users may prefer to quote a tweet (*http://bit.ly/1a1l7FZ*), which entails a workflow involving copying and pasting the text and prepending "RT @*username*" or suffixing "/via @*username*" to provide attribution.

When mining Twitter data, you'll probably want to both account for the tweet metadata and use heuristics to analyze the 140 characters for conventions such as "RT @*username*" or "/via @*username*" when considering retweets, in order to maximize the efficacy of your analysis. See Section 9.14 on page 374 for a more detailed discussion on retweeting with Twitter's native Retweet API versus "quoting" tweets and using conventions to apply attribution.

A good exercise at this point would be to further analyze the data to determine if there was a particular tweet that was highly retweeted or if there were just lots of "one-off" retweets. The approach we'll take to find the most popular retweets is to simply iterate over each status update and store out the retweet count, originator of the retweet, and text of the retweet if the status update is a retweet. Example 1-10 demonstrates how to capture these values with a list comprehension and sort by the retweet count to display the top few results.

Example 1-10. Finding the most popular retweets

```
retweets = [
            # Store out a tuple of these three values ...
            (status['retweet_count'],
             status['retweeted_status']['user']['screen_name'],
             status['text'])

            # ... for each status ...
            for status in statuses

            # ... so long as the status meets this condition.
                if status.has_key('retweeted_status')
           ]

# Slice off the first 5 from the sorted results and display each item in the tuple

pt = PrettyTable(field_names=['Count', 'Screen Name', 'Text'])
[ pt.add_row(row) for row in sorted(retweets, reverse=True)[:5] ]
pt.max_width['Text'] = 50
pt.align= 'l'
print pt
```

Results from Example 1-10 are interesting:

```
+-------+----------------+----------------------------------------------------+
| Count | Screen Name    | Text                                               |
+-------+----------------+----------------------------------------------------+
| 23    | hassanmusician | RT @hassanmusician: #MentionSomeoneImportantForYou |
|       |                | God.                                               |
| 21    | HSweethearts   | RT @HSweethearts: #MentionSomeoneImportantForYou   |
|       |                | my high school sweetheart ❤                        |
| 15    | LosAlejandro_  | RT @LosAlejandro_: ¿Nadie te menciono en           |
|       |                | "#MentionSomeoneImportantForYou"? JAJAJAJAJAJAJA    |
|       |                | JAJAJAJAJAJAJAJAJAJAJAJAJAJAJAJAJAJAJAJA Ven, ...   |
| 9     | SCOTTSUMME     | RT @SCOTTSUMME: #MentionSomeoneImportantForYou My   |
|       |                | Mum. Shes loving, caring, strong, all in one. I    |
|       |                | love her so much ❤❤❤❤                              |
| 7     | degrassihaha   | RT @degrassihaha: #MentionSomeoneImportantForYou I  |
|       |                | can't put every Degrassi cast member, crew member, |
|       |                | and writer in just one tweet....                   |
+-------+----------------+----------------------------------------------------+
```

"God" tops the list, followed closely by "my high school sweetheart," and coming in at number four on the list is "My Mum." None of the top five items in the list correspond to Twitter user accounts, although we might have suspected this (with the exception of @justinbieber) from the previous analysis. Inspection of results further down the list does reveal particular user mentions, but the sample we have drawn from for this query is so small that no trends emerge. Searching for a larger sample of results would likely yield some user mentions with a frequency greater than one, which would be interesting to further analyze. The possibilities for further analysis are pretty open-ended, and by now, hopefully, you're itching to try out some custom queries of your own.

 Suggested exercises are at the end of this chapter. Be sure to also check out Chapter 9 as a source of inspiration: it includes more than two dozen recipes presented in a cookbook-style format.

Before we move on, a subtlety worth noting is that it's quite possible (and probable, given the relatively low frequencies of the retweets observed in this section) that the original tweets that were retweeted may not exist in our sample search results set. For example, the most popular retweet in the sample results originated from a user with a screen name of @hassanmusician and was retweeted 23 times. However, closer inspection of the data reveals that we collected only 1 of the 23 retweets in our search results. Neither the original tweet nor any of the other 22 retweets appears in the data set. This doesn't pose any particular problems, although it might beg the question of who the other 22 retweeters for this status were.

The answer to this kind of question is a valuable one because it allows us to take content that represents a concept, such as "God" in this case, and discover a group of other users who apparently share the same sentiment or common interest. As previously mentioned, a handy way to model data involving people and the things that they're interested in is called an *interest graph*; this is the primary data structure that supports analysis in Chapter 7. Interpretative speculation about these users could suggest that they are spiritual or religious individuals, and further analysis of their particular tweets might corroborate that inference. Example 1-11 shows how to find these individuals with the GET statuses/retweets/:id API (*http://bit.ly/1a1l64H*).

Example 1-11. Looking up users who have retweeted a status

```
# Get the original tweet id for a tweet from its retweeted_status node
# and insert it here in place of the sample value that is provided
# from the text of the book

_retweets = twitter_api.statuses.retweets(id=317127304981667841)
print [r['user']['screen_name'] for r in _retweets]
```

Further analysis of the users who retweeted this particular status for any particular religious or spiritual affiliation is left as an independent exercise.

1.4.5. Visualizing Frequency Data with Histograms

A nice feature of IPython Notebook is its ability to generate and insert high-quality and customizable plots of data as part of an interactive workflow. In particular, the `matplotlib` (*http://bit.ly/1a1l7Wv*) package and other scientific computing tools that are available for IPython Notebook are quite powerful and capable of generating complex figures with very little effort once you understand the basic workflows.

To illustrate the use of `matplotlib`'s plotting capabilities, let's plot some data for display. To get warmed up, we'll consider a plot that displays the results from the `words` variable as defined in Example 1-9. With the help of a `Counter`, it's easy to generate a sorted list of tuples where each tuple is a `(word, frequency)` pair; the x-axis value will correspond to the index of the tuple, and the y-axis will correspond to the frequency for the word in that tuple. It would generally be impractical to try to plot each word as a value on the x-axis, although that's what the x-axis is representing. Figure 1-4 displays a plot for the same words data that we previously rendered as a table in Example 1-8. The y-axis values on the plot correspond to the number of times a word appeared. Although labels for each word are not provided, x-axis values have been sorted so that the relationship between word frequencies is more apparent. Each axis has been adjusted to a logarithmic scale to "squash" the curve being displayed. The plot can be generated directly in IPython Notebook with the code shown in Example 1-12.

Figure 1-4. A plot displaying the sorted frequencies for the words computed by Example 1-8

 If you are using the virtual machine, your IPython Notebooks should be configured to use plotting capabilities out of the box. If you are running on your own local environment, be sure to have started IPython Notebook with PyLab (*http://bit.ly/1a1l6BN*) enabled as follows:

```
ipython notebook --pylab=inline
```

Example 1-12. Plotting frequencies of words

```
word_counts = sorted(Counter(words).values(), reverse=True)

plt.loglog(word_counts)
plt.ylabel("Freq")
plt.xlabel("Word Rank")
```

A plot of frequency values is intuitive and convenient, but it can also be useful to group together data values into bins that correspond to a range of frequencies. For example, how many words have a frequency between 1 and 5, between 5 and 10, between 10 and 15, and so forth? A *histogram* (*http://bit.ly/1a1l6Sk*) is designed for precisely this purpose and provides a convenient visualization for displaying tabulated frequencies as adjacent rectangles, where the area of each rectangle is a measure of the data values that fall within that particular range of values. Figures 1-5 and 1-6 show histograms of the tabular data generated from Examples 1-8 and 1-10, respectively. Although the histograms don't have x-axis labels that show us which words have which frequencies, that's not really their purpose. A histogram gives us insight into the underlying frequency distribution, with the x-axis corresponding to a range for words that each have a frequency within that range and the y-axis corresponding to the total frequency of all words that appear within that range.

When interpreting Figure 1-5, look back to the corresponding tabular data and consider that there are a large number of words, screen names, or hashtags that have low frequencies and appear few times in the text; however, when we combine all of these low-frequency terms and bin them together into a range of "all words with frequency between 1 and 10," we see that the total number of these low-frequency words accounts for most of the text. More concretely, we see that there are approximately 10 words that account for almost all of the frequencies as rendered by the area of the large blue rectangle, while there are just a couple of words with much higher frequencies: "#MentionSomeoneImportantForYou" and "RT," with respective frequencies of 34 and 92 as given by our tabulated data.

Likewise, when interpreting Figure 1-6, we see that there are a select few tweets that are retweeted with a much higher frequencies than the bulk of the tweets, which are retweeted only once and account for the majority of the volume given by the largest blue rectangle on the left side of the histogram.

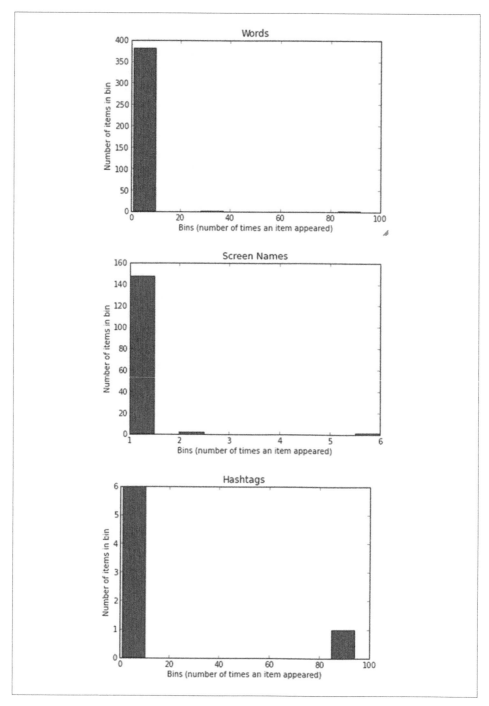

Figure 1-5. Histograms of tabulated frequency data for words, screen names, and hash-tags, each displaying a particular kind of data that is grouped by frequency

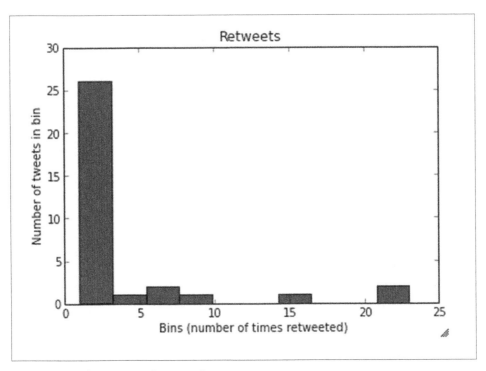

Figure 1-6. A histogram of retweet frequencies

The code for generating these histograms directly in IPython Notebook is given in Examples 1-13 and 1-14. Taking some time to explore the capabilities of matplotlib and other scientific computing tools is a worthwhile investment.

 Installation of scientific computing tools such as matplotlib can potentially be a frustrating experience because of certain dynamically loaded libraries in their dependency chain, and the pain involved can vary from version to version and operating system to operating system. It is highly recommended that you take advantage of the virtual machine experience for this book, as outlined in Appendix A, if you don't already have these tools installed.

Example 1-13. Generating histograms of words, screen names, and hashtags

```
for label, data in (('Words', words),
                    ('Screen Names', screen_names),
                    ('Hashtags', hashtags)):

    # Build a frequency map for each set of data
    # and plot the values
```

```
c = Counter(data)
plt.hist(c.values())

# Add a title and y-label ...
plt.title(label)
plt.ylabel("Number of items in bin")
plt.xlabel("Bins (number of times an item appeared)")

# ... and display as a new figure
plt.figure()
```

Example 1-14. Generating a histogram of retweet counts

```
# Using underscores while unpacking values in
# a tuple is idiomatic for discarding them

counts = [count for count, _, _ in retweets]

plt.hist(counts)
plt.title("Retweets")
plt.xlabel('Bins (number of times retweeted)')
plt.ylabel('Number of tweets in bin')

print counts
```

1.5. Closing Remarks

This chapter introduced Twitter as a successful technology platform that has grown virally and become "all the rage," given its ability to satisfy some fundamental human desires relating to communication, curiosity, and the self-organizing behavior that has emerged from its chaotic network dynamics. The example code in this chapter got you up and running with Twitter's API, illustrated how easy (and fun) it is to use Python to interactively explore and analyze Twitter data, and provided some starting templates that you can use for mining tweets. We started out the chapter by learning how to create an authenticated connection and then progressed through a series of examples that illustrated how to discover trending topics for particular locales, how to search for tweets that might be interesting, and how to analyze those tweets using some elementary but effective techniques based on frequency analysis and simple statistics. Even what seemed like a somewhat arbitrary trending topic turned out to lead us down worthwhile paths with lots of possibilities for additional analysis.

 Chapter 9 contains a number of Twitter recipes covering a broad array of topics that range from tweet harvesting and analysis to the effective use of storage for archiving tweets to techniques for analyzing followers for insights.

One of the primary takeaways from this chapter from an analytical standpoint is that counting is generally the first step to any kind of meaningful quantitative analysis. Although basic frequency analysis is simple, it is a powerful tool for your repertoire that shouldn't be overlooked just because it's so obvious; besides, many other advanced statistics depend on it. On the contrary, frequency analysis and measures such as lexical diversity should be employed early and often, for precisely the reason that doing so is so obvious and simple. Oftentimes, but not always, the results from the simplest techniques can rival the quality of those from more sophisticated analytics. With respect to data in the Twitterverse, these modest techniques can usually get you quite a long way toward answering the question, "What are people talking about right now?" Now that's something we'd all like to know, isn't it?

 The source code outlined for this chapter and all other chapters is available at GitHub (*http://bit.ly/1a1kNqy*) in a convenient IPython Notebook format that you're highly encouraged to try out from the comfort of your own web browser.

1.6. Recommended Exercises

- Bookmark and spend some time reviewing Twitter's API documentation (*http://bit.ly/1a1kSKQ*). In particular, spend some time browsing the information on the REST API (*http://bit.ly/1a1kZ9i*) and platform objects (*http://bit.ly/1a1kSL8*).

- If you haven't already, get comfortable working in IPython (*http://bit.ly/1a1laRY*) and IPython Notebook (*http://bit.ly/1a1laSf*) as a more productive alternative to the traditional Python interpreter. Over the course of your social web mining career, the saved time and increased productivity will really start to add up.

- If you have a Twitter account with a nontrivial number of tweets, request your historical tweet archive from your account settings (*http://bit.ly/1a1lb8D*) and analyze it. The export of your account data includes files organized by time period in a convenient JSON format. See the *README.txt* file included in the downloaded archive for more details. What are the most common terms that appear in your tweets? Who do you retweet the most often? How many of your tweets are retweeted (and why do you think this is the case)?

- Take some time to explore Twitter's REST API with its developer console (*http://bit.ly/1a1kWui*). Although we opted to dive in with the `twitter` Python package in a programmatic fashion in this chapter, the console can be useful for exploring the API, the effects of parameters, and more. The command-line tool Twurl (*http://bit.ly/1a1kZq1*) is another option to consider if you prefer working in a terminal.

- Complete the exercise of determining whether there seems to be a spiritual or religious affiliation for the users who retweeted the status citing "God" as someone important to them, or follow the workflow in this chapter for a trending topic or arbitrary search query of your own choosing. Explore some of the advanced search features (*http://bit.ly/1a1l3pN*) that are available for more precise querying.

- Explore Yahoo! GeoPlanet's Where On Earth ID API (*http://yhoo.it/1a1kZ9u*) so that you can compare and contrast trends from different locales.

- Take a closer look at `matplotlib` (*http://bit.ly/1a1l7Wv*) and learn how to create beautiful plots of 2D and 3D data with IPython Notebook (*http://bit.ly/1a1lccP*).

- Explore and apply some of the exercises from Chapter 9.

1.7. Online Resources

The following list of links from this chapter may be useful for review:

- Beautiful plots of 2D and 3D data with IPython Notebook (*http://bit.ly/1a1lccP*)
- IPython "magic functions" (*http://bit.ly/1a1kXyf*)
- json.org (*http://bit.ly/1a1l2lJ*)
- PyLab (*http://bit.ly/1a1l6BN*)
- Python list comprehensions (*http://bit.ly/1a1l1hy*)
- The official Python tutorial (*http://bit.ly/1a1l1hy*)
- OAuth (*http://bit.ly/1a1kZWN*)
- Twitter API documentation (*http://bit.ly/1a1kSKQ*)
- Twitter API Rate Limiting in v1.1 (*http://bit.ly/1a1l2ly*)
- Twitter developer console (*http://bit.ly/1a1kWui*)
- Twitter Developer Rules of the Road (*http://bit.ly/1a1kX1a*)
- Twitter's OAuth documentation (*http://bit.ly/1a1kZWW*)
- Twitter Search API operators (*http://bit.ly/1a1l3pN*)
- Twitter Streaming API (*http://bit.ly/1a1l1ya*)
- Twitter terms of service (*http://bit.ly/1a1kWKB*)
- Twurl (*http://bit.ly/1a1kZq1*)
- Yahoo! GeoPlanet's Where On Earth ID API (*http://yhoo.it/1a1kZ9u*)

## CHAPTER 2

Mining Facebook: Analyzing Fan Pages, Examining Friendships, and More

In this chapter, we'll tap into the Facebook platform through its (Social) Graph API and explore some of the vast possibilities. Facebook is arguably the heart of the social web and is somewhat of an all-in-one wonder, given that more than half of its 1 billion users[1] are active each day updating statuses, posting photos, exchanging messages, chatting in real time, checking in to physical locales, playing games, shopping, and just about anything else you can imagine. From a social web mining standpoint, the wealth of data that Facebook stores about individuals, groups, and products is quite exciting, because Facebook's clean API presents incredible opportunities to synthesize it into information (the world's most precious commodity), and glean valuable insights. On the other hand, this great power commands great responsibility, and Facebook has instrumented the most sophisticated set of online privacy controls (*http://on.fb.me/ 1a1llg9*) that the world has ever seen in order to help protect its users from exploit.

It's worth noting that although Facebook is self-proclaimed as a social graph, it's been steadily transforming into a valuable interest graph as well, because it maintains relationships between people and the things that they're interested in through its Facebook pages and "Likes" feature. In this regard, you may increasingly hear it framed as a "social interest graph." For the most part, you can make a case that interest graphs implicitly exist and can be bootstrapped from most sources of social data. As an example, Chapter 1 made the case that Twitter is actually an interest graph because of its asymmetric "following" (or, to say it another way, "interested in") relationships between people and other people, places, or things. The notion of Facebook as an interest graph will come

---

1. Internet usage statistics (*http://bit.ly/1a1ljF8*) show that the world's population is estimated to be approximately 7 billion, with the estimated number of Internet users being almost 2.5 billion.

up throughout this chapter, and we'll return to the idea of explicitly bootstrapping an interest graph from social data in Chapter 7.

The remainder of this chapter assumes that you have an active Facebook account (*http://on.fb.me/1a1lkcd*), which is required to gain access to the Facebook APIs. Although there are plenty of fun things that you can do to analyze public information, you may find that it's a little bit more fun if you are analyzing data from your own social network, so it's worth adding a few friends if you are new to Facebook.

 Always get the latest bug-fixed source code for this chapter (and every other chapter) online at *http://bit.ly/MiningTheSocialWeb2E*. Be sure to also take advantage of this book's virtual machine experience, as described in Appendix A, to maximize your enjoyment of the sample code.

2.1. Overview

As this is the second chapter in the book, the concepts we'll cover are a bit more complex than those in Chapter 1, but should still be highly accessible for a very broad audience. In this chapter you'll learn about:

- Facebook's Social Graph API and how to make API requests
- The Open Graph protocol and its relationship to Facebook's Social Graph
- Analyzing likes from Facebook pages and from Facebook friends
- Techniques such as clique analysis for analyzing social graphs
- Visualizing social graphs with the D3 JavaScript library

2.2. Exploring Facebook's Social Graph API

The Facebook platform is a mature, robust, and well-documented gateway into what may be the most comprehensive and well-organized information store ever amassed, both in terms of breadth and depth. It's broad in that its user base represents about one-seventh of the entire living population, and it's deep with respect to the amount of information that's known about any one of its particular users. Whereas Twitter features an asymmetric friendship model that is open and predicated on following other users without any particular consent, Facebook's friendship model is symmetric and requires a mutual agreement between users to gain visibility into one another's interactions and activities.

Furthermore, whereas virtually all interactions except for private messages between users on Twitter are public statuses, Facebook allows for much more finely grained privacy controls in which friendships can be organized and maintained as lists with varying levels of visibility available to a friend on any particular activity. For example, you might choose to share a link or photo only with a particular list of friends as opposed to your entire social network.

As a social web miner, the only way that you can access a Facebook user's account data is by registering an application and using that application as the entry point into the Facebook developer platform. Moreover, the only data that's available to an application is whatever the user has explicitly authorized it to access. For example, as a developer writing a Facebook application, you'll be the user who's logging into the application, and the application will be able to access any data that you explicitly authorize it to access. In that regard, as a Facebook user you might think of an application a bit like any of your Facebook friends, in that you're ultimately in control of what the application can access and you can revoke access at any time. The Facebook Platform Policies document (*http://bit.ly/1a1lm3C*) is a must-read for any Facebook developer, as it provides the comprehensive set of rights and responsibilities for all Facebook users as well as the spirit and letter of the law for Facebook developers. If you haven't already, it's worth taking a moment to review Facebook's developer policies and to bookmark the Facebook Developers home page (*http://bit.ly/1a1lm3Q*), since it is the definitive entry point into the Facebook platform and its documentation.

Keep in mind that as a developer mining your own account, you may not have a problem allowing your own application to access *all* of your account data. Beware, however, of aspiring to develop a successful *hosted* application that requests access to more than the minimum amount of data necessary to complete, because it's quite likely that a user will not recognize or trust your application to command that level of privilege (and rightly so).

Although we'll programmatically access the Facebook platform later in this chapter, Facebook provides a number of useful developer tools (*http://bit.ly/1a1lnVf*), including a Graph API Explorer app (*http://bit.ly/1a1lnVv*) that we'll be using for initial familiarization with the Social Graph. The app provides an intuitive and turnkey way of querying the Social Graph, and once you're comfortable with how the Social Graph works, translating queries into Python code for automation and further processing comes quite naturally. Although we'll work through the Graph API as part of the discussion, you may benefit from an initial review of the well-written "Getting Started: The Graph API" document (*http://bit.ly/1a1lobU*) as a comprehensive preamble.

In addition to the Graph API, you may also encounter the Facebook Query Language (FQL (*http://bit.ly/1a1lmRd*)) and what is now referred to as the Legacy REST API (*http://bit.ly/1a1lmRo*). Be advised that although FQL is still very much alive and will be briefly introduced in this chapter, the Legacy REST API is in deprecation and will be phased out soon. Do not use it for any development that you do with Facebook.

2.2.1. Understanding the Social Graph API

As its name implies, Facebook's Social Graph is a massive graph (*http://bit.ly/1a1loIX*) data structure representing social interactions and consisting of nodes and connections between the nodes. The Graph API provides the primary means of interacting with the Social Graph, and the best way to get acquainted with the Graph API is to spend a few minutes tinkering around with the Graph API Explorer (*http://bit.ly/1a1lnVv*).

It is important to note that the Graph API Explorer is not a particularly special tool of any kind. Aside from being able to prepopulate and debug your access token, it is an ordinary Facebook app that uses the same developer APIs that any other developer application would use. In fact, the Graph API Explorer is handy when you have a particular OAuth token that's associated with a specific set of authorizations for an application that you are developing and you want to run some queries as part of an exploratory development effort or debug cycle. We'll revisit this general idea shortly as we programmatically access the Graph API. Figures 2-1 through 2-4 illustrate a progressive series of Graph API queries that result from clicking on the plus (+) symbol and adding connections and fields. There are a few items to note about this particular query:

Access token

> The access token that appears in the application is an OAuth (*http://bit.ly/1a1kZWN*) token that is provided as a courtesy for the logged-in user; it is the same OAuth token that your application would need to access the data in question. We'll opt to use this access token throughout this chapter, but you can consult Appendix B for a brief overview of OAuth, including details on implementing an OAuth flow for Facebook in order to retrieve an access token. As mentioned in Chapter 1, if this is your first encounter with OAuth, it's probably sufficient at this point to know that the protocol is a social web standard that stands for Open Authorization. In short, OAuth is a means of allowing users to authorize third-party applications to access their account data without needing to share sensitive information like a password.

 See Appendix B for details on implementing an OAuth 2.0 flow that you would need to build an application that requires an arbitrary user to authorize it to access account data.

Node IDs

The basis of the query is a node with an ID (identifier) of "644382747," corresponding to a person named "Matthew A. Russell," who is preloaded as the currently logged-in user for the Graph Explorer. The "id" and "name" values for the node are called *fields*. The basis of the query could just as easily have been any other node, and as we'll soon see, it's very natural to "walk" or traverse the graph and query other nodes (which may be people or things as books or TV shows).

Connection constraints

You can modify the original query with a "friends" connection, as shown in Figure 2-2, by clicking on the + and then scrolling to "friends" in the "connections" pop-up menu. The "friends" connections that appear in the console represent nodes that are connected to the original query node. At this point, you could click on any of the blue ID fields in these nodes and initiate a query with that particular node as the basis. In network science terminology, we now have what is called an *ego graph*, because it has an actor (or *ego*) as its focal point or logical center, which is connected to other nodes around it. An ego graph would resemble a hub and spokes if you were to draw it.

Likes constraints

A further modification to the original query is to add "likes" connections for each of your friends, as shown in Figure 2-3. Before you can retrieve likes connections for your friends, however, you must authorize the Graph API Explorer application to explicitly access your friends' likes by updating the access token that it uses and then approve this access, as shown in Figure 2-4. The Graph API Explorer allows you to easily authorize it by clicking on the Get Access Token button and checking the "friends_likes" box on the Friends Data Permissions tab. In network science terminology, we still have an ego graph, but it's potentially much more complex at this point because of the many additional nodes and connections that could exist among them.

Debugging

The Debug button can be useful for troubleshooting queries that you think should be returning data but aren't doing so based on the authorizations associated with the access token.

JSON response format

The results of a Graph API query are returned in a convenient JSON format that can be easily manipulated and processed.

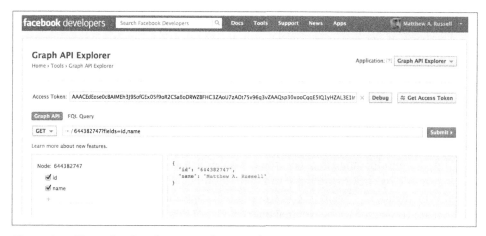

Figure 2-1. Using the Graph API Explorer application to progressively build up a query for friends' interests: a query for a node in the Social Graph

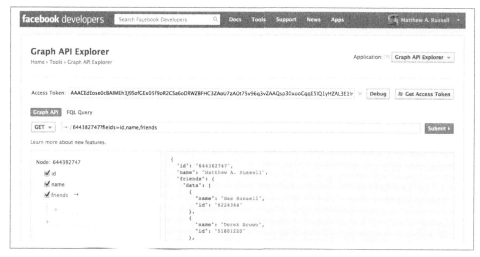

Figure 2-2. Using the Graph API Explorer application to progressively build up a query for friends' interests: a query for a node and connections to friends

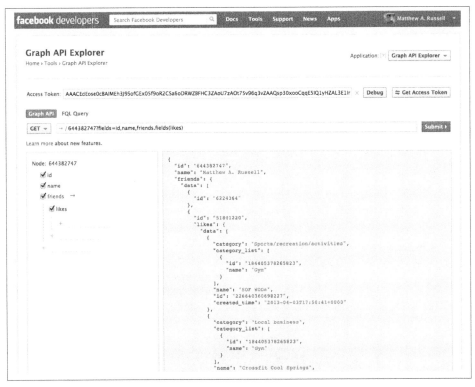

Figure 2-3. Using the Graph API Explorer application to progressively build up a query for friends' interests: a query for a node, connections to friends, and likes for those friends

Figure 2-4. Facebook applications must explicitly request authorization to access a user's account data. Top: The Graph API Explorer permissions panel. Bottom: A Facebook dialog requesting authorization for the Graph API Explorer application to access friends' likes data.

Facebook Query Language

In addition to the Graph API, FQL provides a fine alternative fpr querying Facebook's Social Graph and has a SQL-inspired syntax that most developers find intuitive. It seems to be the case that any data you could query with the Graph API, you could also query via FQL, and although it may be true that some advanced queries that are possible with FQL may not be possible with the Graph API, it appears that Facebook's longer-term plan is to ensure that the Graph API is at full parity with FQL. For example, some recent investments in the Graph API resulted in a number of powerful new features, such as field expansion and nesting (*http://bit.ly/1a1lsIE*). If you're interested in learning more about FQL, consult the FQL Reference (*http://bit.ly/1a1lmRd*), and try out a query with the FQL Query console that's available as an alternate option from the Graph API Explorer. For example, you could query the first and last names of your friends in the FQL Query tab of the Graph API Explorer with the following FQL query:

```
select first_name, last_name
from user
where uid in (
  select uid2
  from friend
  where uid1 = me()
)
```

Although we'll programmatically explore the Graph API with a Python package later in this chapter, you could opt to make Graph API queries more directly over HTTP yourself by mimicking the request that you see in the Graph API Explorer. For example, Example 2-1 uses the `requests` (*http://bit.ly/1a1lrEt*) package to simplify the process of making an HTTP request (as opposed to using a much more cumbersome package from Python's standard library, such as `urllib2`) for fetching your friends and their likes. You can install this package in a terminal with the predictable **pip install re quests** command. The query is driven by the values in the `fields` parameter and is the same as what would be built up interactively in the Graph API Explorer. Of particular interest is that the `friends.limit(10).fields(likes.limit(10))` syntax uses a relatively new feature of the Graph API called field expansion (*http://bit.ly/1a1lsIE*) that is designed to make and parameterize multiple queries in a single API call.

Example 2-1. Making Graph API requests over HTTP

```
import requests # pip install requests
import json

base_url = 'https://graph.facebook.com/me'

# Get 10 likes for 10 friends
fields = 'id,name,friends.limit(10).fields(likes.limit(10))'
```

```
url = '%s?fields=%s&access_token=%s' % \
    (base_url, fields, ACCESS_TOKEN,)

# This API is HTTP-based and could be requested in the browser,
# with a command line utlity like curl, or using just about
# any programming language by making a request to the URL.
# Click the hyperlink that appears in your notebook output
# when you execute this code cell to see for yourself...
print url

# Interpret the response as JSON and convert back
# to Python data structures
content = requests.get(url).json()

# Pretty-print the JSON and display it
print json.dumps(content, indent=1)
```

If you attempt to run a query for all of your friends' likes by setting `fields = 'id,name,friends.fields(likes)`, and the script appears to hang, it is probably because you have a lot of friends who have a lot of likes. If this happens, you may need to add limits and offsets to the fields in the query, as described in Facebook's field expansion (*http://bit.ly/1a1lsIE*) documentation. However, the `facebook` package that you'll learn about later in this chapter handles some of these issues, so it's recommended that you hold off and try it out first. This initial example is just to illustrate that Facebook's API is built on top of HTTP. A couple of field limit/offset examples that illustrate the possibilities with field selectors follow:

```
# Get all likes for 10 friends
fields = 'id,name,friends.limit(10).fields(likes)'

# Get all likes for 10 more friends
fields = 'id,name,friends.offset(10).limit(10).fields(likes)'

# Get 10 likes for all friends
fields = 'id,name,friends.fields(likes.limit(10))'
```

It appears as though the default limit for queries at the time of this writing is to return up to 5,000 items. It's possible but somewhat unlikely that you'll be making Graph API queries that could return more than 5,000 items; if you do, consult the pagination documentation (*http://bit.ly/1a1ltMP*) for information on how to navigate through the "pages" of results.

2.2.2. Understanding the Open Graph Protocol

In addition to sporting a powerful Graph API that allows you to traverse the Social Graph and query familiar Facebook objects, you should also know that Facebook unveiled something called the Open Graph protocol (*http://bit.ly/1a1lu3m*) (OGP) back in April 2010, at the same F8 conference at which it introduced the Social Graph. In short, OGP is a mechanism that enables developers to make any web page an object in Facebook's Social Graph by injecting some RDFa metadata (*http://bit.ly/1a1lujR*) into the page. Thus, in addition to being able to access from within Facebook's "walled garden" the dozens of objects that are described in the Graph API Reference (*http://bit.ly/1a1lvEr*) (users, pictures, videos, checkins, links, status messages, etc.), you might also encounter pages from the Web that represent meaningful concepts that have been grafted into the Social Graph. In other words, OGP is a means of "opening up" the Social Graph, and you'll see these concepts described in Facebook's developer documentation as its "Open Graph."[2]

There are practically limitless options for leveraging OGP to graft web pages into the Social Graph in valuable ways, and the chances are good that you've already encountered many of them and not even realized it. For example, consider Figure 2-5, which illustrates a page for the movie *The Rock* from IMDb.com. In the sidebar to the right, you see a rather familiar-looking Like button with the message "19,319 people like this. Be the first of your friends." IMDb enables this functionality by implementing OGP for each of its URLs that correspond to objects that would be relevant for inclusion in the Social Graph. With the right RDFa metadata in the page, Facebook is then able to unambiguously enable *connections* to these objects and incorporate them into activity streams and other key elements of the Facebook user experience.

Figure 2-5. An IMDb page featuring an implementation of OGP for The Rock

Implementation of OGP manifesting as Like buttons on web pages may seem a bit obvious if you've gotten used to seeing them over the past few years, but the fact that

---

2. Throughout this section describing the implementation of OGP, the term *Social Graph* is generically used to refer to both the Social Graph and Open Graph, unless explicitly emphasized otherwise.

Facebook has been fairly successful at opening up its development platform in a way that allows for arbitrary inclusion of objects on the Web is rather profound and has some potentially significant consequences.

For example, at the time of this writing in early 2013, Facebook has just started the process of launching its new Graph Search product (*http://on.fb.me/1a1lv7b*) to a limited audience. Whereas companies like Google crawl and index the entire Web in order to enable search, the basic idea behind Facebook's Graph Search is that you type something into a search box, just like in the typical Google user experience, but you get back results that are personalized to you based upon the vast amount of your information that Facebook has. The rub, now that OGP is fairly well established, is that Facebook's Graph Search results won't be limited to things within the Facebook user experience, since connections from the Web are inherently incorporated into the Social Graph. It's out of scope to ponder the wider ramifications of how disruptive Graph Search *could* be to the Web given Facebook's user base, but it's a thought exercise well worth your time.

Let's briefly take a look at the gist of implementing OGP before moving on to Graph API queries. The canonical example from the OGP documentation that demonstrates how to turn IMDb's page on *The Rock* into an object in the Open Graph protocol as part of an XHTML document that uses namespaces looks something like this:

```
<html xmlns:og="http://ogp.me/ns#">
<head>
<title>The Rock (1996)</title>
<meta property="og:title" content="The Rock" />
<meta property="og:type" content="movie" />
<meta property="og:url" content="http://www.imdb.com/title/tt0117500/" />
<meta property="og:image" content="http://ia.media-imdb.com/images/rock.jpg" />
...
</head>
...
</html>
```

These bits of metadata have great potential once realized at a massive scale, because they enable a URI like *http://www.imdb.com/title/tt0117500* to unambiguously represent any web page—whether it's for a person, company, product, etc.—in a machine-readable way and further the vision for a semantic web. In addition to being able to "like" *The Rock*, users could potentially interact with this object in other ways through custom actions. For example, users might be able to indicate that they have watched *The Rock* (*http://bit.ly/1a1lwrU*), since it is a movie. OGP allows for a wide and flexible set of actions between users and objects as part of the Social Graph.

 If you haven't already, go ahead and view the source HTML for *http://www.imdb.com/title/tt0117500* and see for yourself what the RDFa looks like out in the wild.

At its core, querying the Graph API for *Open Graph* objects is incredibly simple: append a web page URL or an object's ID to *http(s)://graph.facebook.com/* to fetch details about the object. For example, fetching the URL *http://graph.facebook.com/http://www.imdb.com/title/tt0117500* in your web browser would return this response:

```
{
    "id": "114324145263104",
    "name": "The Rock (1996)",
    "picture": "http://profile.ak.fbcdn.net/hprofile-ak-snc4/hs344.snc4/...jpg",
    "link": "http://www.imdb.com/title/tt0117500/",
    "category": "Movie",
    "description": "Directed by Michael Bay.  With Sean Connery, ...",
    "likes" : 3
}
```

If you inspect the source for the URL *http://www.imdb.com/title/tt0117500*, you'll find that fields in the response correspond to the data in the meta tags of the page, and this is no coincidence. The delivery of rich metadata in response to a simple query is the whole idea behind the way OGP is designed to work. Where it gets more interesting is when you explicitly request additional metadata for an object in the page by appending the query string parameter metadata=1 to the request. Here is a sample response for the query *https://graph.facebook.com/114324145263104?metadata=1* in which we use its ID instead of the IMDB web page URL:

```
{
    "id": "114324145263104",
    "name": "The Rock (1996)",
    "picture": "http://profile.ak.fbcdn.net/hprofile-ak-snc4/..._s.jpg",
    "link": "http://www.imdb.com/title/tt0117500",
    "category": "Movie",
    "website": "http://www.imdb.com/title/tt0117500",
    "description": "Directed by Michael Bay.  With Sean Connery,  ...",
    "about": "Directed by Michael Bay.  With Sean Connery, Nicolas Cage, ...",
    "likes": 8606,
    "were_here_count": 0,
    "talking_about_count": 0,
    "is_published": true,
    "app_id": 115109575169727,
    "metadata": {
        "connections": {
            "feed": "http://graph.facebook.com/http://www.imdb.com/title/...",
            "posts": "http://graph.facebook.com/http://www.imdb.com/title/...",
            "tagged": "http://graph.facebook.com/http://www.imdb.com/title/...",
            "statuses": "http://graph.facebook.com/http://www.imdb.com/title/...",
            "links": "http://graph.facebook.com/http://www.imdb.com/title/...",
            "notes": "http://graph.facebook.com/http://www.imdb.com/title/...",
            "photos": "http://graph.facebook.com/http://www.imdb.com/title/...",
            "albums": "http://graph.facebook.com/http://www.imdb.com/title/...",
            "events": "http://graph.facebook.com/http://www.imdb.com/title/...",
            "videos": "http://graph.facebook.com/http://www.imdb.com/title/...",
        },
```

```
      "fields": [
        {
          "name": "id",
          "description": "The Page's ID. Publicly available. A JSON string."
        },
        {
          "name": "name",
          "description": "The Page's name. Publicly available. A JSON string."
        },
        {
          "name": "category",
          "description": "The Page's category. Publicly available. ..."
        },
        {
          "name": "likes",
          "description": "\\* The number of users who like the Page..."
        },

        ...

      ]
    },
    "type": "page"
}
```

The items in `metadata.connections` are pointers to other nodes in the graph that you can crawl to get to other intriguing bits of data. For example, you could follow the "photos" link to pull down photos associated with the movie, and potentially walk links associated with the photos to discover who posted them or see comments that might have been made about them. In case it hasn't already occurred to you, you are also an object in the graph. Try visiting the same URL prefix, but substitute in your own Facebook ID or username as the URL context and see for yourself (e.g., visit *https:// graph.facebook.com/<YOUR_FB_ID>* in your web browser).

> Try using the Facebook ID "MiningTheSocialWeb" to retrieve details about the official Facebook fan page for this book (*http://on.fb.me/ 1a1lAI8*) with the Graph API Explorer. You could also modify Example 2-1 to programmatically query for *https://graph.face-book.com/MiningTheSocialWeb* to retrieve basic page information, including content posted to the page. For example, appending a query string with a qualifier such as `"?fields=posts"` to that URL would return a listing of its posted content.

As a final note of advice before moving on to programmatically accessing the Graph API, when considering the possibilities with OGP be forward-thinking and creative, but bear in mind that it's still evolving. As it relates to the semantic web and web standards in general, the use of "open" (*http://tcrn.ch/1a1lAYF*) has understandably generated some consternation. Various kinks in the spec have been worked out along the way

---

(*http://bit.ly/1a1lAbd*), and some are still probably being worked out. You could also make the case that OGP is essentially a single-vendor effort, and it's little more than on par with the capabilities of meta elements (*http://bit.ly/1a1lBMa*) from the much earlier days of the Web, although the social effects appear to be driving a very different outcome.

Whether OGP and Graph Search will one day dominate the Web is a highly contentious topic, the potential is certainly there; the indicators for its success are trending in a positive direction, and many exciting things may happen as the future unfolds and innovation continues to take place. Let's now turn back and hone in on how to access the Graph API to work now that you have an appreciation for the fuller context of the Social Graph.

2.3. Analyzing Social Graph Connections

An official Python SDK for the Graph API is a community fork of that repository previously maintained by Facebook and can be installed per the standard protocol with pip via pip install facebook-sdk. This package contains a few useful convenience methods that allow you to interact with Facebook in a number of ways, including the ability to make FQL queries and post statuses or photos. However, there are really just a few key methods from the GraphAPI class (defined in the *facebook.py* source file) that you need to know about in order to use the Graph API to fetch data as shown next, so you could just as easily opt to query over HTTP directly with requests (as was illustrated in Example 2-1) if you prefer. The methods are:

get_object(self, id, **args)
    Example usage: get_object("me", metadata=1)

get_objects(self, id, **args)
    Example usage: get_objects(["me", "some_other_id"], metadata=1)

get_connections(self, id, connection_name, **args)
    Example usage: get_connections("me", "friends", metadata=1)

request(self, path, args=None, post_args=None)
    Example usage: request("search", {"q" : "social web", "type" : "page"})

 Unlike with other social networks, there don't appear to be clearly published guidelines about Facebook API rate limits (*http://on.fb.me/1a1lDDU*). Although the availability of the APIs seems to be quite generous, you should still carefully design your application to use the APIs as little as possible and handle any and all error conditions as a recommended best practice.

The most common (and often, the only) keyword argument you'll probably use is `metadata=1`, in order to get back the connections associated with an object in addition to just the object details themselves. Take a look at Example 2-2, which introduces the `GraphAPI` class and uses its `get_objects` method to query for information about you, information about your friends, and the term *social web*. This example also introduces a helper function called `pp` that is used throughout the remainder of this chapter for pretty-printing results as nicely formatted JSON to save some typing.

Example 2-2. Querying the Graph API with Python

```python
import facebook # pip install facebook-sdk
import json

# A helper function to pretty-print Python objects as JSON

def pp(o):
    print json.dumps(o, indent=1)

# Create a connection to the Graph API with your access token

g = facebook.GraphAPI(ACCESS_TOKEN)

# Execute a few sample queries

print '---------------'
print 'Me'
print '---------------'
pp(g.get_object('me'))
print
print '---------------'
print 'My Friends'
print '---------------'
pp(g.get_connections('me', 'friends'))
print
print '---------------'
print 'Social Web'
print '---------------'
pp(g.request("search", {'q' : 'social web', 'type' : 'page'}))
```

Sample results for the queries from Example 2-2 are shown below and are predictable enough. If you were using the Graph API Explorer, the results would be identical. During development, it can often be very handy to use the Graph API Explorer and an IPython or IPython Notebook in tandem, depending on your specific objective. The advantage of the Graph API Explorer is the ease with which you can click on ID values and spawn new queries during exploratory efforts. Sample results from Example 2-2 follow:

```
---------------
Me
---------------
{
```

```
"last_name": "Russell",
"relationship_status": "Married",
"locale": "en_US",
"hometown": {
 "id": "104012476300889",
 "name": "Princeton, West Virginia"
},
"quotes": "The only easy day was yesterday.",
"favorite_athletes": [
 {
  "id": "112063562167357",
  "name": "Rich Froning Jr. Fan Site"
 }
],
"timezone": -5,
"education": [
 {
  "school": {
   "id": "112409175441352",
   "name": "United States Air Force Academy"
  },
  "type": "College",
  "year": {
   "id": "194603703904595",
   "name": "2003"
  }
 }
],
"id": "644382747",
"first_name": "Matthew",
"middle_name": "A.",
"languages": [
 {
  "id": "106059522759137",
  "name": "English"
 },
 {
  "id": "312525296370",
  "name": "Spanish"
 }
],
"location": {
 "id": "103078413065161",
 "name": "Franklin, Tennessee"
},
"email": "ptwobrussell@gmail.com",
"username": "ptwobrussell",
"bio": "How I Really Feel About Using Facebook (Or: A Disclaimer)...",
"birthday": "06/17/1981",
"link": "http://www.facebook.com/ptwobrussell",
"verified": true,
"name": "Matthew A. Russell",
```

```
  "gender": "male",
  "work": [
   {
    "position": {
     "id": "135722016448189",
     "name": "Chief Technology Officer (CTO)"
    },
    "start_date": "0000-00",
    "employer": {
     "id": "372007624109",
     "name": "Digital Reasoning"
    }
   }
  ],
  "updated_time": "2013-04-04T14:09:22+0000",
  "significant_other": {
   "name": "Bas Russell",
   "id": "6224364"
  }
 }
```

```
---------------
My Friends
---------------
```

```
{
 "paging": {
  "next": "https://graph.facebook.com/644382747/friends?...",
 },
 "data": [
  {
   "name": "Bas Russell",
   "id": "6224364"
  },
  ...
  {
   "name": "Jamie Lesnett",
   "id": "100002388496252"
  }
 ]
}
```

```
---------------
Social Web
---------------
```

```
{
 "paging": {
  "next": "https://graph.facebook.com/search?q=social+web&type=page...",
 },
 "data": [
  {
   "category": "Book",
   "name": "Mining the Social Web",
```

```
    "id": "146803958708175"
  },
  {
   "category": "Internet/software",
   "name": "Social & Web Marketing",
   "id": "172427156148334"
  },
  {
   "category": "Internet/software",
   "name": "Social Web Alliance",
   "id": "160477007390933"
  },
  ...
  {
   "category": "Local business",
   "name": "Social Web",
   "category_list": [
    {
     "id": "2500",
     "name": "Local Business"
    }
   ],
   "id": "145218172174013"
  }
 ]
}
```

At this point, you have the power of both the Graph API Explorer and the Python console —and all that they have to offer—at your fingertips. Now that we've scaled the walled garden, let's turn our attention to analyzing some of its data.

2.3.1. Analyzing Facebook Pages

Although Facebook started out as more of a pure social networking site without a Social Graph or a good way for businesses and other entities to have a presence, it quickly adapted to take advantage of the market needs. Fast-forward a few years, and now businesses, clubs, books, and many other kinds of nonperson entities have Facebook pages (*http://on.fb.me/1a1lCzQ*) with a fan base. Facebook pages are a powerful tool for businesses to engage their customers, and Facebook has gone to some lengths to provide tools that allow Facebook page administrators to understand their fans with a small toolbox that is appropriately called "Insights."

If you're already a Facebook user, the chances are pretty good that you've already liked one or more Facebook pages that represent something that you approve of or think is interesting, and in this regard, Facebook pages significantly broaden the possibilities for the Social Graph as a platform. The explicit accommodation of nonperson user entities through Facebook pages, the Like button, and the Social Graph fabric collectively provide a powerful arsenal for an interest graph platform, which carries with it a profundity of possibilities. (Refer back to Section 1.2 on page 6 for a discussion of why interest graphs are so abundant with useful possibilities.)

2.3.1.1. Analyzing this book's Facebook page

Given that this book has a corresponding Facebook page that happened to turn up as the top result in a search for "social web," it seems natural enough that we could use it as an illustrative starting point for some instructive analysis here in this chapter.[3] Here are just a few questions that might be worth considering with regard to this book's Facebook page, or just about any other Facebook page:

- How popular is the page?
- How engaged are the page's fans?
- Are any of the fans for the page particularly outspoken and participatory?
- What are the most common topics being talked about on the page?

Your imagination is the only limitation to what you can ask of the Graph API for a Facebook page when you are mining its content for insights, and these questions should get you headed in the right direction. Along the way, we'll also use these questions as the basis of some comparisons among other pages.

Recall that the starting point for our journey might have been a search for "social web" that revealed a book entitled *Mining the Social Web* per the following search result item:

```
{
    "category": "Book",
    "name": "Mining the Social Web",
    "id": "146803958708175"
}
```

For any of the items in the search results, we could use the ID as the basis of a graph query through get_object with an instance of facebook.GraphAPI. If you don't have a numeric string ID handy, just use the page name (such as "MiningTheSocialWeb") that appears in the URL bar of your browser when you visit the page. The code is a quick one-liner that produces the results shown in Example 2-3.

---

3. Throughout this section, keep in mind that the responses to these queries reflect data for the first edition of the book, since that's what's available at the time of this writing. Your exact query results may vary somewhat.

Example 2-3. Results for a Graph API query for Mining the Social Web

```
# Get an instance of Mining the Social Web
# Using the page name also works if you know it.
# e.g. 'MiningTheSocialWeb' or 'CrossFit'
mtsw_id = '146803958708175'
pp(g.get_object(mtsw_id))
```

Sample output for the query reveals the data that backs the object's Facebook page, as shown here:

```
{
  "category": "Book",
  "username": "MiningTheSocialWeb",
  "about": "Analyzing Data from Facebook, Twitter, LinkedIn, and Other Social...",
  "talking_about_count": 22,
  "description": "Facebook, Twitter, and LinkedIn generate a tremendous ...",
  "company_overview": "Like It here on Facebook!\n\nFollow @SocialWebMining...",
  "release_date": "January 2011",
  "can_post": true,
  "cover": {
   "source": "https://sphotos-b.xx.fbcdn.net/...",
   "cover_id": 474206292634605,
   "offset_x": -41,
   "offset_y": 0
  },
  "mission": "Teaches you how to...\n\n* Get a straightforward synopsis of ...",
  "name": "Mining the Social Web",
  "founded": "January 2011",
  "website": "http://amzn.to/d1Ci8A",
  "link": "http://www.facebook.com/MiningTheSocialWeb",
  "likes": 911,
  "were_here_count": 0,
  "general_info": "Analyzing Data from Facebook, Twitter, LinkedIn, ...",
  "id": "146803958708175",
  "is_published": true
}
```

The interesting analytical results from the query response are the book's `talking_about_count` and `like_count`. The `like_count` is a good indicator of the page's overall popularity, so a reasonable response to the query "How popular is the page?" is that there are 911 Facebook fans for the page, and 22 of them have recently been engaging in discussion. Given that *Mining the Social Web* is a fairly niche technical book, this seems like a reasonable fan base.[4]

For any kind of popularity analysis, however, comparables are essential for understanding the broader context. There are a lot of ways to draw comparisons, but a couple of striking data points are that the book's publisher, O'Reilly Media (*http://on.fb.me/*

---

4. This summary was generated circa March 2013.

1a1lD6F), has around 34,000 likes, and the Python programming language (*http://on.fb.me/1a1lD6V*) has around 80,000 likes. Thus, the popularity of *Mining the Social Web* is approaching 3% of the publisher's entire fan base and just over 1% of the programming language's fan base. Clearly, there is a lot of room for this book's popularity to grow, even though it's a niche topic.

Although another good comparison would have been to a niche book similar to *Mining the Social Web*, it isn't easy to find any good apples-to-apples comparisons by reviewing Facebook page data, because at the time of this writing it isn't possible to search for pages and limit by constraints such as "book" as a category. For example, you can't search for pages and limit the result set to books in order to find a good comparable; instead, you'd have to search for pages and then filter the result set by category to retrieve only the books. Still, there are a couple of options to consider.

One option is to search for another O'Reilly title that you know is a similar kind of niche book, such as *Programming Collective Intelligence*, and see what turns up. The Graph API search results for a query of "Programming Collective Intelligence" do turn up a community page (*http://on.fb.me/1a1lEYn*) with almost 400 likes; all things being equal, it's interesting that a six-year-old book has almost half the number of likes as *Mining the Social Web* without an active author maintaining a page for it.

Another option to consider is taking advantage of concepts from Facebook's Open Graph Protocol in order to draw a comparison. For example, the O'Reilly online catalog contains entries and implements OGP for all of O'Reilly's titles, and there are pages (and thus Like buttons) for both *Mining the Social Web*, 2nd Edition and *Programming Collective Intelligence*. We can easily make requests to the Graph API to see what data is available and keep tabs on it by simply querying for these URLs in the browser as follows:

Graph API query for Mining the Social Web
    https://graph.facebook.com/http://shop.oreilly.com/product/0636920030195.do

Graph API query for Programming Collective Intelligence
    https://graph.facebook.com/http://shop.oreilly.com/product/9780596529321.do

In terms of a programmatic query with Python, the URLs are the objects that we are querying (just like the URL for the IMDb entry for *The Rock* was what we were querying earlier), so in code, we can query these objects as shown in Example 2-4. As a subtle but very important distinction, keep in mind that even though both the O'Reilly catalog page and the Facebook fan page for *Mining the Social Web* logically represent the same book, the nodes (and accompanying metadata, such as the number of likes) that correspond to the Facebook page versus the O'Reilly catalog page are completely independent. It just so happens that each represents the same real-world concept. Figure 2-6 demonstrates an exploration of the Graph API with IPython Notebook.

An entirely separate kind of analysis known as *entity resolution* (or *entity disambiguation*, depending on how you frame the problem) is the process of aggregating mentions of things into a single platonic concept. For example, in this case, an entity resolution process could observe that there are multiple nodes in the Open Graph that actually refer to the same platonic idea of *Mining the Social Web* and create connections between them indicating that they are in fact equivalent as an entity in the real world. Entity resolution is an exciting field of research that will continue to have profound effects on how we use data as the future unfolds.

Example 2-4. Querying the Graph API for Open Graph objects by their URLs

```
# MTSW catalog link
pp(g.get_object('http://shop.oreilly.com/product/0636920030195.do'))


# PCI catalog link
pp(g.get_object('http://shop.oreilly.com/product/9780596529321.do'))
```

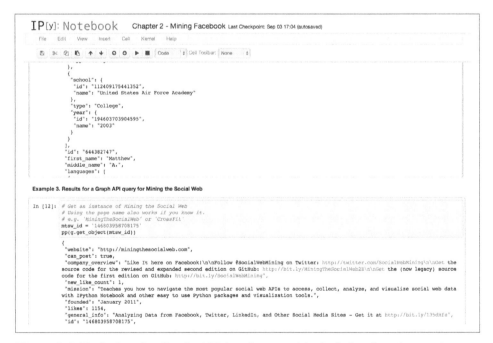

Figure 2-6. Exploring the Graph API is a breeze with the help of an interactive programming environment like IPython Notebook

Although it's often not the case that you'll be able to make an apples-to-apples comparison that provides an authoritative result when data mining, there's still a lot to be learned. Exploring a data set long enough to accumulate strong intuitions about the data often provides all the insight that you'll initially need when encountering a problem space for the first time. Hopefully, enhancements to the Graph API as part of the new Graph Search product will facilitate more sophisticated queries and lower the barriers to entry for data miners in the future.

2.3.1.2. Analyzing Coke vs Pepsi Facebook pages

As an alternative to analyzing tech books, let's take just a moment to broaden the scope of the discussion to something *much* more mainstream and see what turns up. The never-ending soft drink war between Coke and Pepsi seems like an innocuous but potentially interesting topic to consider, so let's set out to determine which one is the most popular according to Facebook. As you now know, the answer is just a couple of graph queries away, as illustrated in Example 2-5.

Example 2-5. Comparing likes between Coke and Pepsi fan pages

```
# Find Pepsi and Coke in search results

pp(g.request('search', {'q' : 'pepsi', 'type' : 'page', 'limit' : 5}))
pp(g.request('search', {'q' : 'coke', 'type' : 'page', 'limit' : 5}))

# Use the ids to query for likes

pepsi_id = '56381779049' # Could also use 'PepsiUS'
coke_id = '40796308305'  # Could also use 'CocaCola'

# A quick way to format integers with commas every 3 digits
def int_format(n): return "{:,}".format(n)

print "Pepsi likes:", int_format(g.get_object(pepsi_id)['likes'])
print "Coke likes:", int_format(g.get_object(coke_id)['likes'])
```

The results are somewhat striking:

```
Pepsi likes: 9,677,881
Coke likes: 62,735,664
```

Would you have expected that Coke has almost *seven times* the popularity of Pepsi on Facebook? As one possible source of investigation, you might consult stock market information and see if the number of likes correlates at all with the overall market capitalization, which could be an indicator of the overall size of the companies. If you were to look up this information, however, the results might surprise you: at the time of this writing (circa March 2013), the market capitalization of Coke (NYSE:KO) is around 178B, whereas Pepsi (NYSE:PEP) is 121B. Although analysis of companies at a financial level is a very complex exercise in and of itself, the overall market capitalization of the companies differs by only around 30%, which is a far cry from a 700% difference in Facebook popularity. It seems reasonable to think that each company probably has similar means available to it and probably sells similar amounts of product.

A worthwhile exercise would be to drill down further and try to determine what might be the cause of this disparity. In approaching a question like this one, bear in mind that although there are likely to be indicators in the Facebook data itself, the overall scope is very broad, and there may be a number of dependent variables outside of what you might find in Facebook data. For example, are there particular indicators you can find in the data that suggest that Coke launches massive advertising campaigns or does anything special to engage users in a way that Pepsi does not?

Digging further into what now seems like a bit of a phenomenon is left as an exercise. However, here's a hint to get you on your way: a shallow search of the Web reveals articles on reputable sites such as Forbes entitled "Coca-Cola and Procter and Gamble Lead the Way into the New Advertising Era of SocialTV... A Money Machine" (*http://onforb.es/ 1a1lIY9*) and "Coca-Cola Leveraging Social to Drive Leadership in Social Media Marketing," (*http://onforb.es/1a1lHDt*) indicating that Coca-Cola has intentionally developed marketing campaigns that make extensive use of social media.

There are practically limitless possibilities for analyzing a Facebook page, and a great transition point after you've performed frequency analysis is to examine the human language data in the page's *feed*, although more specific kinds of filters (such as the page's shared links) can be queries for analysis as well. We can't solve every problem in each short chapter, but once you've read up on some techniques for processing human language data in Chapters 4 and 5, you'll be able to return to this problem and apply those techniques to better understand how Coca-Cola's social media team engages its Facebook fans to gain insight into the communication that takes place between them. Meanwhile, you could frame your intuition by spending a few minutes skimming Coca-Cola's and Pepsi's Facebook pages. After all, glossing over the data at a high level whenever possible is an essential prerequisite to programmatic analysis.

Example 2-6 provides a starting point for data collection if you'd like to examine the human language data from a page by treating its content as a bag of words (*http://bit.ly/ 1a1lHDF*) with basic frequency analysis techniques as explained in Chapter 4. In other words, you could just split the text into words by approximating word boundaries with whitespace and feed the words into a Counter to compute the more frequent terms as a starting point.

Example 2-6. Querying a page for its "feed" and "links" connections

```
pp(g.get_connections(pepsi_id, 'feed'))
pp(g.get_connections(pepsi_id, 'links'))

pp(g.get_connections(coke_id, 'feed'))
pp(g.get_connections(coke_id, 'links'))
```

If you choose to examine the human language data in the pages, here are a few questions for your consideration:

- Can you determine which posts in the feed are the most popular, as indicated by either the number of comments posted or the number of likes?

- Are any particular kinds of posts more popular than others? For example, are posts with links more popular than posts with photos?

- What characteristics can you identify that make a post go viral as opposed to just getting a couple of likes?

 Example 2-6 demonstrates how to query for the page's feed and links to get you started. The differences between feeds, posts, and statuses can initially be a bit confusing. In short, feeds include anything that users might see on their own wall, posts include most any content users have created and posted to their own or a friend's wall, and statuses include only status updates posted on a user's own wall. See the Graph API documentation for a user (*http://bit.ly/1a1lHU1*) for more details.

2.3.2. Examining Friendships

Let's now use our knowledge of the Graph API to examine the friendships from your own social network. Here are some questions to get the creative juices flowing:

- Are there any topics or special interests that are especially pronounced within your social network?

- Does your social network contain many mutual friendships or even larger cliques (*http://bit.ly/1a1lJLJ*)?

- How well connected are the people in your social network?

- Are any of your friends particularly outspoken or passionate about anything you might also be interested in learning more about?

The remainder of this section walks through exercises that involve analyzing likes as well as analyzing and visualizing mutual friendships. Although we are framing this section in terms of *your* social network, bear in mind that the conversation generalizes to any other user's account and could be realized through a Facebook application you could create and make available.

2.3.2.1. Analyzing things your friends "like"

Let's set out to examine the question about whether or not any topics or special interests exist within your social network and explore from there. A logical starting point for answering this query is to aggregate the likes for each of your friends and try to determine if there are any particularly high-frequency items that appear. Example 2-7 demonstrates how to build a frequency distribution of the likes in your social network as the basis for further analysis. Keep in mind that if any of your friends may have privacy settings set to not share certain types of personal information such as their likes with apps, you'll often see empty results as opposed to any kind of explicit error message.

Example 2-7. Querying for all of your friends' likes

```
# First, let's query for all of the likes in your social
# network and store them in a slightly more convenient
# data structure as a dictionary keyed on each friend's
# name. We'll use a dictionary comprehension to iterate
# over the friends and build up the likes in an intuitive
# way, although the new "field expansion" feature could
# technically do the job in one fell swoop as follows:
#
# g.get_object('me', fields='id,name,friends.fields(id,name,likes)')
#
# See Appendix C for more information on Python tips such as
# dictionary comprehensions

friends = g.get_connections("me", "friends")['data']

likes = { friend['name'] : g.get_connections(friend['id'], "likes")['data']
          for friend in friends }

print likes
```

 Reducing the scope of the expected data tends to speed up the response. If you have a lot of Facebook friends, the previous query may take some time to execute. Consider trying out the option to use field expansion and make a single query, or try limiting results with a list slice such as `friends[:100]` to limit the scope of analysis to 100 of your friends while you are initially exploring the data.

There's nothing particularly tricky about collecting your friends' likes and building up a nice data structure, although this might be one of your first encounters with a dictionary comprehension. Just like a list comprehension, a dictionary comprehension iterates over a list of items and collects values (key/value pairs in this case) that are to be returned. You may also want to try out the Graph API's new field expansion feature and issue a single query for all of your friends' likes in a a single request. With the facebook package, you could do it like this: `g.get_object('me', fields='id,name,friends.fields(id,name,likes)')`.

See Appendix C for more information on dictionary comprehensions and other Python tips and tricks.

With a useful data structure called likes in hand that contains your friends and their likes, let's start off our analysis by calculating the most popular likes across all of your friends. The Counter class provides an easy way to build a frequency distribution that will do just the trick, as illustrated in Example 2-8, and we can use the prettytable package (**pip install prettytable** if you don't have it already) to neatly format the results so that they're more readable.

Example 2-8. Calculating the most popular likes among your friends

```
# Analyze all likes from friendships for frequency

# pip install prettytable
from prettytable import PrettyTable
from collections import Counter
friends_likes = Counter([like['name']
                         for friend in likes
                             for like in likes[friend]
                                 if like.get('name')])

pt = PrettyTable(field_names=['Name', 'Freq'])
pt.align['Name'], pt.align['Freq'] = 'l', 'r'
[ pt.add_row(fl) for fl in friends_likes.most_common(10) ]

print 'Top 10 likes amongst friends'
print pt
```

Sample results follow:

```
Top 10 likes amongst friends
+-------------------------+------+
| Name                    | Freq |
+-------------------------+------+
| Crossfit Cool Springs   |   14 |
| CrossFit                |   13 |
| The Pittsburgh Steelers |   13 |
| Working Out             |   13 |
| The Bible               |   13 |
| Skiing                  |   12 |
| Star Trek               |   12 |
| Seinfeld                |   12 |
| Jesus                   |   12 |
+-------------------------+------+
```

It appears that exercise/sports is a common theme within this social network, with religion/Christianity possibly being a common theme as well. Let's dig a little bit further and analyze the categories of likes that exist within the social network to see if the same themes exist. Example 2-9 illustrates a variation of the previous example that shows how.

Example 2-9. Calculating the most popular categories for likes among your friends

```
# Analyze all like categories by frequency

friends_likes_categories = Counter([like['category']
                                    for friend in likes
                                        for like in likes[friend]])

pt = PrettyTable(field_names=['Category', 'Freq'])
pt.align['Category'], pt.align['Freq'] = 'l', 'r'
[ pt.add_row(flc) for flc in friends_likes_categories.most_common(10) ]

print "Top 10 like categories for friends"
print pt
```

Sample results from the query are a tuple with a similar structure as before:

```
Top 10 like categories for friends
+-------------------------+------+
| Category                | Freq |
+-------------------------+------+
| Musician/band           |   62 |
| Book                    |   46 |
| Movie                   |   43 |
| Interest                |   40 |
| Tv show                 |   31 |
| Public figure           |   31 |
| Local business          |   25 |
| Community               |   24 |
| Non-profit organization |   21 |
| Product/service         |   17 |
+-------------------------+------+
```

There are no explicit mentions of sports or religion, but it is interesting how much higher the frequencies are on some of the "unexpected" categories such as "Musician/band" or "Book." It may be that there are simply a lot of highly eclectic, nonoverlapping interests within the social network.

Something that may shed further light on the situation and be compelling in and of itself is to calculate how many likes exist for each friend. For example, do most friends have a similar number of likes, or is the number of likes highly skewed? Having additional insight into the underlying distribution helps to inform some of the things that may be happening when the data is aggregated. In Example 2-10, we'll calculate a frequency distribution that shows the number of likes for each friend to get an idea of how the categories from the previous example may be skewed.

Example 2-10 introduces the operator.itemgetter function, which is commonly used in combination with the sorted function to sort a list of tuples (as returned from calling items() on an instance of a dictionary) based upon a particular slot in the tuple. For example, passing key=itemgetter(1) to the sorted function returns a sorted list that uses the second item in the tuple as the basis of sorting. See Appendix C for more details.

Example 2-10. Calculating the number of likes for each friend and sorting by frequency

```
# Build a frequency distribution of number of likes by
# friend with a dictionary comprehension and sort it in
# descending order

from operator import itemgetter

num_likes_by_friend = { friend : len(likes[friend])
                        for friend in likes }


pt = PrettyTable(field_names=['Friend', 'Num Likes'])
pt.align['Friend'], pt.align['Num Likes'] = 'l', 'r'
[ pt.add_row(nlbf)
  for nlbf in sorted(num_likes_by_friend.items(),
                key=itemgetter(1),
                reverse=True) ]

print "Number of likes per friend"
print pt
```

Sample results have the familiar form of a tuple with a friend and frequency value. Some results (sanitized of last names) follow:

```
Number of likes per friend
+--------------------+-----------+
| Friend             | Num Likes |
+--------------------+-----------+
| Joshua             |       187 |
| Derek              |       146 |
| Heather            |        84 |
| Rick               |        69 |
| Patrick            |        42 |
| Bryan              |        38 |
| Ray                |        17 |
| Jamie              |        14 |
| ...                |       ... |
| Bas                |         0 |
+--------------------+-----------+
```

The more time you spend really trying to understand the data, the more insights you'll glean, and by now I hope you are starting to get a more holistic picture of what's happening. We now know that the distribution of likes across the data is enormously skewed across a small number of friends and that any one friend's results could be highly contributing to the results that break down the frequencies of category for each like. There are a number of directions that we could go in at this point. One possibility would be to start to compare smaller samples of friends for some kind of similarity or to further analyze likes. For example, does Joshua account for 90% of the liked TV shows? Does Derek account for the most significant majority of liked music? The answers to these questions are well within your grasp at this point.

Instead, however, let's ask another question : which friends are most similar to the ego[5] in the social network? To make any kind of useful similarity comparison between two things, we'll need a similarity function. The simplest possibility is likely to be one of the best starting points, so let's start out with "number of shared likes" to compute similarity between the ego and friendships. To compute the similarity between the ego of the network and the friendships, all we need is the ego's likes and some help from the set object's intersection operator, which makes it possible to compare two lists of items and compute the overlapping items from each of them. Example 2-11 illustrates how to compute the overlapping likes between the ego and friendships in the network as the first step in finding the most similar friends in the network.

Example 2-11. Finding common likes between an ego and its friendships in a social network

```
# Which of your likes are in common with which friends?
my_likes = [ like['name']
             for like in g.get_connections("me", "likes")['data'] ]

pt = PrettyTable(field_names=["Name"])
pt.align = 'l'
[ pt.add_row((ml,)) for ml in my_likes ]
print "My likes"
print pt

# Use the set intersection as represented by the ampersand
# operator to find common likes.

common_likes = list(set(my_likes) & set(friends_likes))

pt = PrettyTable(field_names=["Name"])
pt.align = 'l'
[ pt.add_row((cl,)) for cl in common_likes ]
print
```

---

5. Remember, the *ego* of a social network is its logical center or basis. In this case, the ego of the network is the author of this book—that is, the person whose social network we are examining.

```
print "My common likes with friends"
print pt
```

Here's the abbreviated output containing the results of the overlapping likes that are in common for this social network:

```
My likes
+------------------------------+
| Name                         |
+------------------------------+
| Snatch (weightlifting)       |
| First Blood                  |
| Robinson Crusoe              |
| The Godfather                |
| The Godfather                |
|          ...                 |
| The Art of Manliness         |
| USA Triathlon                |
| CrossFit                     |
| Mining the Social Web        |
+------------------------------+

My common likes with friends
+------------------------------+
| Name                         |
+------------------------------+
| www.SEALFIT.com              |
| Rich Froning Jr. Fan Site    |
| CrossFit                     |
| The Great Courses            |
| The Art of Manliness         |
| Dan Carlin - Hardcore History|
| Mining the Social Web        |
| Crossfit Cool Springs        |
+------------------------------+
```

Coming back full circle, it's perhaps not too surprising that the common theme of sports/exercise once again emerges (but with additional detail this time), as do some topics related to Christianity.[6] There are many more engaging questions to ask (and answer), but let's wrap up this section by completing the second half of this query, which is to now find the particular friends that share the common interests with the ego in the network. Example 2-12 shows how to do this by iterating over the friendships with a double list comprehension and processing the results. It also reminds us that we have full access to the plotting capabilities from matplotlib that were introduced in Section 1.4.5 on page 37.

---

6. Rich Froning Jr. is a well-known (and outspokenly Christian) CrossFit athlete.

If you are using the virtual machine, your IPython Notebooks should be configured to use plotting capabilities out of the box. If you are running on your own local environment, be sure to have started IPython Notebook with PyLab (*http://bit.ly/1a1l6BN*) enabled as follows: ipython notebook --pylab=inline.

Example 2-12. Calculating the friends most similar to an ego in a social network

```
# Which of your friends like things that you like?

similar_friends = [ (friend, friend_like['name'])
                        for friend, friend_likes in likes.items()
                          for friend_like in friend_likes
                            if friend_like.get('name') in common_likes ]


# Filter out any possible duplicates that could occur

ranked_friends = Counter([ friend for (friend, like) in list(set(similar_friends)) ])


pt = PrettyTable(field_names=["Friend", "Common Likes"])
pt.align["Friend"], pt.align["Common Likes"] = 'l', 'r'
[ pt.add_row(rf)
  for rf in sorted(ranked_friends.items(),
                 key=itemgetter(1),
                 reverse=True) ]
print "My similar friends (ranked)"
print pt

# Also keep in mind that you have the full range of plotting
# capabilities available to you. A quick histogram that shows
# how many friends.

plt.hist(ranked_friends.values())
plt.xlabel('Bins (number of friends with shared likes)')
plt.ylabel('Number of shared likes in each bin')

# Keep in mind that you can customize the binning
# as desired. See http://matplotlib.org/api/pyplot_api.html

# For example...

plt.figure() # Display the previous plot
plt.hist(ranked_friends.values(),
         bins=arange(1,max(ranked_friends.values()),1))
plt.xlabel('Bins (number of friends with shared likes)')
plt.ylabel('Number of shared likes in each bin')
plt.figure() # Display the working plot
```

By now, you should be familiar with the processing. We've simply iterated over the variables we've built up so far to build a list of expanded tuples of the form *(friend, friend's like)* and then used it to compute a frequency distribution to determine which friends have the most common likes. Sample results for this query in tabular form follow, and Figure 2-7 displays the same results as a histogram:

```
My similar friends (ranked)
+----------+--------------+
| Friend   | Common Likes |
+----------+--------------+
| Derek    |            7 |
| Jamie    |            4 |
| Joshua   |            3 |
| Heather  |            3 |
| ...      |          ... |
| Patrick  |            1 |
+----------+--------------+
```

As you are probably thinking, there is an abundance of questions that can be investigated with just a small sliver of data from your Facebook friends. We've just scratched the surface, but hopefully these exercises have been helpful in terms of framing some good starting points that can be further explored. It doesn't take much imagination to continue down this road or to pick up with a different angle and start down an entirely different one. To illustrate just one possibility, let's take just a moment to check out a nifty way to visualize some of your Facebook friends' data that's along a different line of thinking before closing out this chapter.

2.3.2.2. Analyzing mutual friendships with directed graphs

Unlike Twitter, which is an inherently open network in which you can crawl "friend-ships" over an extended period of time and build a large graph for any given starting point, Facebook data is much richer and rife with personally identifiable and sensitive properties about people, so the privacy and access controls make it much more closed. While you can use the Graph API to access data for the authenticating user and the authenticating user's friends, you cannot access data for arbitrary users beyond those boundaries unless it is exposed as publicly available. One Graph API operation of particular interest is the ability to get the mutual friendships (available through the mutualfriends (*http://bit.ly/1a1lK29*) API and documented as part of the User object (*http://bit.ly/1a1lHU1*)) that exist within your social network (or the social network of the authenticating user). (In other words, which of your friends are also friends with one another?) From a graph analytics perspective, analysis of an ego graph for mutual friendships can very naturally be formulated as a *clique* (*http://bit.ly/1a1lKiG*) detection problem.

For example, if Abe is friends with Bob, Carol, and Dale, and Bob and Carol are also friends, the largest ("maximum") clique in the graph exists among Abe, Bob, and Carol. If Abe, Bob, Carol, and Dale were all mutual friends, however, the graph would be fully

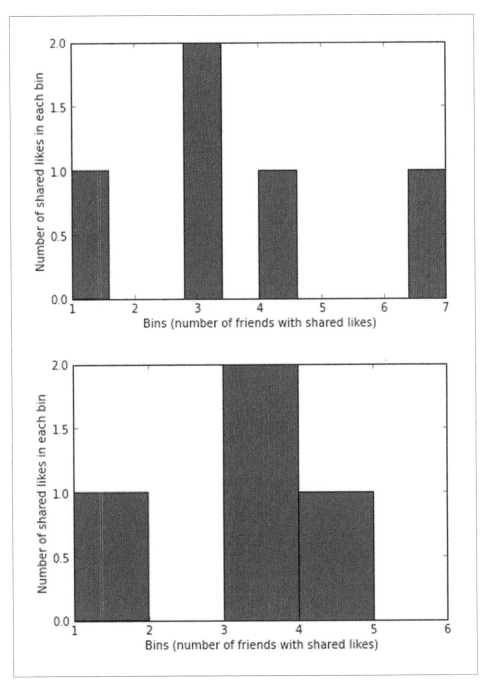

Figure 2-7. Histograms displaying data from Example 2-12

connected, and the maximum clique would be of size 4. Adding nodes to the graph might create additional cliques, but it would not necessarily affect the size of the maximum clique in the graph. In the context of the social web, the maximum clique is interesting because it indicates the largest set of common friendships in the graph. Given two social networks, comparing the sizes of the maximum friendship cliques might provide a good starting point for analysis about various aspects of group dynamics, such as teamwork, trust, and productivity. Figure 2-8 illustrates a sample graph with the maximum clique highlighted. This graph would be said to have a *clique number* of size 4.

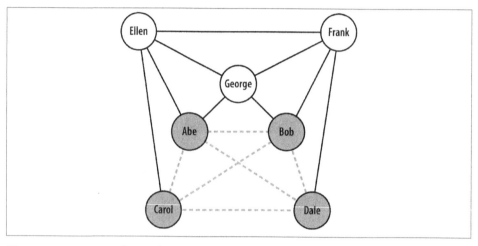

Figure 2-8. An example graph containing a maximum clique of size 4

 Technically speaking, there is a subtle difference between a *maximal* clique and a *maximum* clique. The maximum clique is the largest clique in the graph (or cliques in the graph, if they have the same size). A maximal clique, on the other hand, is one that is not a *subgraph* of another clique. Figure 2-8, for example, illustrates a maximum clique of size 4, but there are several other maximal cliques of size 3 in the graph as well.

Finding cliques is an NP-complete problem (implying an exponential runtime (*http:// bit.ly/1a1lKz9*)), but there is an amazing Python package called NetworkX (pronounced either "networks" or "network x") that provides extensive graph analytics functionality, including a find_cliques (*http://1.usa.gov/1a1lKzk*) method that delivers a solid implementation of this difficult problem. Just be advised that it might take a long time to run as graphs get beyond a reasonably small size (hence, the aforementioned exponential runtime). Examples 2-13 and 2-14 demonstrate how to use Facebook data to construct a graph of mutual friendships and then use NetworkX to analyze the cliques within the graph. You can install NetworkX with the predictable **pip install net workx** from a terminal.

Example 2-13. Constructing a graph of mutual friendships

```
import networkx as nx # pip install networkx
import requests # pip install requests

friends = [ (friend['id'], friend['name'],)
               for friend in g.get_connections('me', 'friends')['data'] ]

url = 'https://graph.facebook.com/me/mutualfriends/%s?access_token=%s'

mutual_friends = {}

# This loop spawns a separate request for each iteration, so
# it may take a while. Optimization with a thread pool or similar
# technique would be possible.
for friend_id, friend_name in friends:
    r = requests.get(url % (friend_id, ACCESS_TOKEN,) )
    response_data = json.loads(r.content)['data']
    mutual_friends[friend_name] = [ data['name']
                                       for data in response_data ]

nxg = nx.Graph()

[ nxg.add_edge('me', mf) for mf in mutual_friends ]

[ nxg.add_edge(f1, f2)
  for f1 in mutual_friends
      for f2 in mutual_friends[f1] ]

# Explore what's possible to do with the graph by
# typing nxg.<tab> or executing a new cell with
# the following value in it to see some pydoc on nxg
print nxg
```

Example 2-14. Finding and analyzing cliques in a graph of mutual friendships

```
# Finding cliques is a hard problem, so this could
# take a while for large graphs.
# See http://en.wikipedia.org/wiki/NP-complete and
# http://en.wikipedia.org/wiki/Clique_problem.

cliques = [c for c in nx.find_cliques(nxg)]

num_cliques = len(cliques)

clique_sizes = [len(c) for c in cliques]
max_clique_size = max(clique_sizes)
avg_clique_size = sum(clique_sizes) / num_cliques
```

```
max_cliques = [c for c in cliques if len(c) == max_clique_size]

num_max_cliques = len(max_cliques)

max_clique_sets = [set(c) for c in max_cliques]
friends_in_all_max_cliques = list(reduce(lambda x, y: x.intersection(y),
                                   max_clique_sets))

print 'Num cliques:', num_cliques
print 'Avg clique size:', avg_clique_size
print 'Max clique size:', max_clique_size
print 'Num max cliques:', num_max_cliques
print
print 'Friends in all max cliques:'
print json.dumps(friends_in_all_max_cliques, indent=1)
print
print 'Max cliques:'
print json.dumps(max_cliques, indent=1)
```

Sample output for Example 2-14 follows and illustrates that there are four cliques of size 4, with the ego ("me") and one other person being common to the sample social network. Although the other person in common to all of the cliques is not guaranteed to be the second most highly connected person in the network, this person is likely to be among the most influential because of the relationships in common:

```
Num cliques: 6
Avg clique size: 3
Max clique size: 4
Num max cliques: 4

Friends in all max cliques:
[
 "me",
 "Bas"
]

Max cliques:
[
 [
  "me",
  "Bas",
  "Joshua",
  "Heather"
 ],
 [
  "me",
  "Bas",
  "Ray",
  "Patrick"
 ],
 [
```

```
    "me",
    "Bas",
    "Ray",
    "Rick"
  ],
  [
    "me",
    "Bas",
    "Jamie",
    "Heather"
  ]
]
```

Example 2-14 could be modified in any number of ways, and clearly, there's much more we could do than just detect the cliques. Plotting the locations of people involved in cliques on a map to see whether there's any correlation between tightly connected networks of people and geographic locale and analyzing information in their profile data and the content in their posts might be a couple of good starting points. In the next section, we'll learn how to put together a concise but effective visualization of mutual friendships in an intuitive graphical format.

2.3.2.3. Visualizing directed graphs of mutual friendships

D3.js (*http://bit.ly/1a1kGvo*) is a truly state-of-the-art JavaScript toolkit that can render some beautiful visualizations in the browser with an intuitive approach that involves manipulating objects with a series of data-driven transformations. If you haven't already encountered D3, then you really should take a few moments to browse the example gallery (*http://bit.ly/1a1lMal*) to get a feel for what is possible. You will be impressed.

A tutorial of how to use D3 is well outside the scope of this book, and there are numerous tutorials (*http://bit.ly/1a1lMHg*) and discussions online about how to use many of its exciting visualizations. What we'll do in this section before rounding out the chapter is render an interactive visualization for the mutual friendship graph introduced in the previous section. Abstractly, a graph is just a mathematical construct and doesn't have a visual representation, but a number of *layout algorithms* are available that can render the graph in two-dimensional space so that it displays rather nicely (although you may need to tweak some of the layout parameters from time to time to get things just right).

NetworkX can emit a format that is directly consumable by D3, and very little work is necessary to visualize the graph since IPython Notebook can serve and render local content with an inline frame by prepending *files* to the path. Example 2-15 demonstrates how to serialize out the graph for rendering, and Example 2-16 uses IPython Notebook to serve up a web page displaying an interactive graph like the one shown in Figure 2-9. The HTML that embeds the necessary style and scripts is included with the IPython Notebook for this chapter in a subfolder of its resources called *viz*.

You can access files for reading or writing with IPython Notebook by using relative or absolute paths; however, serving files as web pages requires you to prepend the special cue *files* to the path.

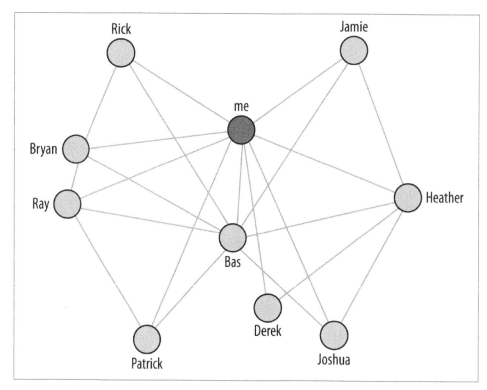

Figure 2-9. A graph of mutual friendships within a Facebook social network—you can generate graphs like this one by following along with the sample code in IPython Notebook

Example 2-15. Serializing a NetworkX graph to a file for consumption by D3

```
from networkx.readwrite import json_graph

nld = json_graph.node_link_data(nxg)

json.dump(nld, open('resources/ch02-facebook/viz/force.json','w'))
```

Example 2-16. Visualizing a mutual friendship graph with D3

```
from IPython.display import IFrame
from IPython.core.display import display
```

```
# IPython Notebook can serve files and display them into
# inline frames. Prepend the path with the 'files' prefix.

viz_file = 'files/resources/ch02-facebook/viz/force.html'

display(IFrame(viz_file, '100%', '600px'))
```

2.4. Closing Remarks

The goal of this chapter was to teach you about the Graph API, how the Open Graph protocol can create connections between arbitrary web pages and Facebook's Social Graph, and how to programmatically query the Social Graph to gain insight into Facebook pages and your own social network. If you've worked through the examples in this chapter, you should have little to no trouble probing the Social Graph for answers to questions that may prove valuable. Keep in mind that as you explore a data set as enormous and interesting as Facebook's Social Graph, you really just need a good starting point. As you investigate answers to an initial query, you'll likely follow a natural course of exploration that will successively refine your understanding of the data and get you closer to the answers that you are looking for.

The possibilities for mining data on Facebook are immense, but be respectful of privacy, and always comply with Facebook's terms of service (*http://on.fb.me/1a1lMXM*) to the best of your ability. Unlike data from Twitter and some other sources that are inherently more open in nature, Facebook data can be quite sensitive, especially if you are analyzing your own social network. Hopefully, this chapter has made it apparent that there are many exciting possibilities for what can be done with social data, and that there's enormous value tucked away on Facebook.

 The source code outlined for this chapter and all other chapters is available at GitHub (*http://bit.ly/1a1kNqy*) in a convenient IPython Notebook format that you're highly encouraged to try out from the comfort of your own web browser.

2.5. Recommended Exercises

- Analyze data from the fan page for something you're interested in on Facebook and attempt to analyze the natural language in the comments stream to gain insights. What are the most common topics being discussed? Can you tell if fans are particularly happy or upset about anything?

- Select two different fan pages that are similar in nature and compare/contrast them. For example, what similarities and differences can you identify between fans of Chipotle Mexican Grill and Taco Bell? Can you find anything surprising?

- Analyze your own friendships and try to determine if your own network has any natural rallying points or common interests. What is the common glue that binds your network together?

- The number of Facebook objects available to the Graph API (*http://bit.ly/1a1lNeg*) is enormous. Can you examine objects such as photos or checkins to discover insights about anyone in your network? For example, who posts the most pictures, and can you tell what are they about based on the comments stream? Where do your friends check in most often?

- Use histograms (introduced in Section 1.4.5 on page 37) to further slice and dice your friends' likes data.

- Use the Graph API to collect other kinds of data and find a suitable D3 visualization for rendering it. For example, can you plot where your friends live or where they grew up on a map? Which of your friends still live in their hometowns?

- Harvest some Twitter data, construct a graph, and analyze/visualize it using the techniques introduced in this chapter.

- Try out some different similarity metrics to compute your most similar friendships. The Jaccard Index (*http://bit.ly/1a1lNuR*) is a good starting point. See Section 4.4.4 on page 167 for some information that may be helpful here.

2.6. Online Resources

The following list of links from this chapter may be useful for review:

- "Bag of words" model (*http://bit.ly/1a1lHDF*)
- D3.js example gallery (*http://bit.ly/1a1lMaI*)
- D3.js tutorials (*http://bit.ly/1a1lMHg*)
- Facebook Developers (*http://bit.ly/1a1lm3Q*)
- Facebook Developers pagination documentation (*http://bit.ly/1a1ltMP*)
- Facebook Platform Policies (*http://bit.ly/1a1lm3C*)
- FQL field expansion and nesting (*http://bit.ly/1a1lsIE*)
- FQL Reference (*http://bit.ly/1a1lmRd*)
- Getting Started: The Graph API (*http://bit.ly/1a1lobU*)
- Graph API Explorer (*http://bit.ly/1a1lnVv*)
- Graph API Reference (*http://bit.ly/1a1lvEr*)
- Graph cliques (*http://bit.ly/1a1lJLJ*)
- HTML meta elements (*http://bit.ly/1a1lBMa*)

- NetworkX clique algorithms (*http://bit.ly/1a1lWyo*)
- NP-complete problem (*http://bit.ly/1a1lLDd*)
- OAuth (*http://bit.ly/1a1kZWN*)
- Open Graph protocol (*http://bit.ly/1a1lu3m*)
- PyLab (*http://bit.ly/1a1l6BN*)
- Python Requests library (*http://bit.ly/1a1lrEt*)
- RDFa (*http://bit.ly/1a1lujR*)

## CHAPTER 3

Mining LinkedIn: Faceting Job Titles, Clustering Colleagues, and More

This chapter introduces techniques and considerations for mining the troves of data tucked away at LinkedIn, a social networking site focused on professional and business relationships. Although LinkedIn may initially seem like any other social network, the nature of its API data is inherently quite different. If you liken Twitter to a busy public forum like a town square and Facebook to a very large room filled with friends and family chatting about things that are (mostly) appropriate for dinner conversation, then you might liken LinkedIn to a private event with a semiformal dress code where everyone is on their best behavior and trying to convey the specific value and expertise that they could bring to the professional marketplace.

Given the somewhat sensitive nature of the data that's tucked away at LinkedIn, its API has its own nuances that make it a bit different from many of the others we've looked at in this book. People who join LinkedIn are principally interested in the business opportunities that it provides as opposed to arbitrary socializing and will necessarily be providing sensitive details about business relationships, job histories, and more. For example, while you can generally access all of the details about *your* LinkedIn connections' educational histories and previous work positions, you cannot determine whether two arbitrary people are "mutually connected" as you could with Facebook. The absence of such an API method is *intentional*. The API doesn't lend itself to being modeled as a social graph like Facebook or Twitter, therefore requiring that you ask different types of questions about the data that's available to you.

The remainder of this chapter gets you set up to access data with the LinkedIn API and introduces some fundamental data mining techniques that can help you cluster colleagues according to a similarity measurement in order to answer the following kinds of queries:

- Which of your connections are the most similar based upon a criterion like job title?
- Which of your connections have worked in companies you want to work for?
- Where do most of your connections reside geographically?

In all cases, the pattern for analysis with a clustering technique is essentially the same: extract some features from data in a colleague's profile, define a similarity measurement to compare the features from each profile, and use a clustering technique to group together colleagues that are "similar enough." The approach works well for LinkedIn data, and you can apply these same techniques to just about any kind of other data that you'll ever encounter.

 Always get the latest bug-fixed source code for this chapter (and every other chapter) online at *http://bit.ly/MiningTheSocialWeb2E*. Be sure to also take advantage of this book's virtual machine experience, as described in Appendix A, to maximize your enjoyment of the sample code.

3.1. Overview

This chapter introduces content that is foundational in machine learning and, in general, is a bit more advanced than the two chapters before it. It is recommended that you have a firm grasp on the previous two chapters before working through the material presented here. In this chapter, you'll learn about:

- LinkedIn's Developer Platform and making API requests
- Three common types of clustering, a fundamental machine-learning topic that applies to nearly any problem domain
- Data cleansing and normalization
- Geocoding, a means of arriving at a set of coordinates from a textual reference to a location
- Visualizing geographic data with Google Earth and with cartograms

3.2. Exploring the LinkedIn API

You'll need a LinkedIn account and a handful of colleagues in your professional network to follow along with this chapter's examples in a meaningful way. If you don't have a LinkedIn account, you can still apply the fundamental clustering techniques that you'll learn about to other domains, but this chapter won't be quite as engaging since you can't follow along with the examples without your own LinkedIn data. Start developing a LinkedIn professional network if you don't already have one as a worthwhile investment in your professional life.

Although most of the analysis in this chapter is performed against a comma-separated values (CSV) file of your LinkedIn connections that you can download, this section maintains continuity with other chapters in the book by providing an overview of the LinkedIn API. If you're not interested in learning about the LinkedIn API and would like to jump straight into the analysis, skip ahead to Section 3.2.2 on page 96 and come back to the details about making API requests at a later time.

3.2.1. Making LinkedIn API Requests

As is the case with other social web properties, such as Twitter and Facebook (discussed in the preceding chapters), the first step involved in gaining API access to LinkedIn is to create an application. You'll be able to create a sample application at *https://www.link edin.com/secure/developer*; you will want to take note of your application's API Key, Secret Key, OAuth User Token, and OAuth User Secret credentials, which you'll use to programmatically access the API. Figure 3-1 illustrates the form that you'll see once you have created an application.

Figure 3-1. To access the LinkedIn API, create an application at https://www.linke din.com/secure/developer and take note of the four OAuth credentials (shown here as blurred values) that are available from the application details page

With the necessary OAuth credentials in hand, the process for obtaining API access to your own personal data is much like that of Twitter in that you'll provide these credentials to a library that will take care of the details involved in making API requests. If you're not taking advantage of the book's virtual machine experience, you'll need to install it by typing **pip install python-linkedin** in a terminal.

> See Appendix B for details on implementing an OAuth 2.0 flow, which you will need to build an application that requires an arbitrary user to authorize it to access account data.

Example 3-1 illustrates a sample script that uses your LinkedIn credentials to ultimately create an instance of a `LinkedInApplication` class that can access your account data. Notice that the final line of the script retrieves your basic profile information, which includes your name and headline. Before going too much further, you should take a moment to read about what LinkedIn API operations are available to you as a developer by browsing its REST documentation (*http://linkd.in/1a1lZuj*), which provides a broad overview of what you can do. Although we'll be accessing the API through a Python package that abstracts the HTTP requests that are involved, the core API documentation is always your definitive reference, and most good libraries mimic its style.

> Should you need to revoke account access from your application or any other OAuth application, you can do so in your account settings (*http://linkd.in/1a1lZKN*).

Example 3-1. Using LinkedIn OAuth credentials to receive an access token suitable for development and accessing your own data

```
from linkedin import linkedin # pip install python-linkedin

# Define CONSUMER_KEY, CONSUMER_SECRET,
# USER_TOKEN, and USER_SECRET from the credentials
# provided in your LinkedIn application

CONSUMER_KEY = ''
CONSUMER_SECRET = ''
USER_TOKEN = ''
USER_SECRET = ''

RETURN_URL = '' # Not required for developer authentication

# Instantiate the developer authentication class

auth = linkedin.LinkedInDeveloperAuthentication(CONSUMER_KEY, CONSUMER_SECRET,
                           USER_TOKEN, USER_SECRET,
```

```
                              RETURN_URL,
                              permissions=linkedin.PERMISSIONS.enums.values())
```

```
# Pass it in to the app...
```

```
app = linkedin.LinkedInApplication(auth)
```

```
# Use the app...
```

```
app.get_profile()
```

In short, the calls available to you through an instance of `LinkedInApplication` are the same as those available through the REST API (*http://linkd.in/1a1lZuj*), and the `python-linkedin` documentation (*http://bit.ly/1a1m2Gk*) on GitHub provides a number of queries to get you started. A couple of APIs of particular interest are the Connections API and the Search API. You'll recall from our introductory discussion that you cannot get "friends of friends" ("connections of connections," in LinkedIn parlance), but the Connections API returns a list of your connections, which provides a jumping-off point for obtaining profile information. The Search API provides a means of querying for people, companies, or jobs that are available on LinkedIn.

Additional APIs are available, and it's worth your while to take a moment and familiarize yourself with them. The quality of the data available about your professional network is quite remarkable, as it can potentially contain full job histories, company details, geographic information about the location of positions, and more.

Example 3-2 shows you how to use `app`, an instance of your `LinkedInApplication`, to retrieve extended profile information for your connections[1] and save this data to a file so as to avoid making any unnecessary API requests that will count against your rate-throttling limits (*http://linkd.in/1a1m2WP*), which are similar to those of Twitter's API.

 Be careful when tinkering around with LinkedIn's API: the rate limits don't reset until midnight UTC, and one buggy loop could potentially blow your plans for the next 24 hours if you aren't careful.

Example 3-2. Retrieving your LinkedIn connections and storing them to disk

```
import json
```

```
connections = app.get_connections()
```

```
connections_data = 'resources/ch03-linkedin/linkedin_connections.json'
```

---

1. If any of your connections have opted out of LinkedIn API access, their first and last names will appear as "private" and additional details will not be available.

```
f = open(conections_data, 'w')
f.write(json.dumps(connections, indent=1))
f.close()

# You can reuse the data without using the API later like this...
# connections = json.loads(open(connections_data).read())
```

For an initial step in reviewing your connections' data, let's use the `prettytable` package as introduced in previous chapters to display a nicely formatted table of your connections and where they are each located, as shown in Example 3-3. If you're not taking advantage of this book's preconfigured virtual machine, you'll need to type **pip install prettytable** from a terminal for most of the examples in this chapter to work; it's a package that produces nicely formatted, tabular output.

Example 3-3. Pretty-printing your LinkedIn connections' data

```
from prettytable import PrettyTable # pip install prettytable

pt = PrettyTable(field_names=['Name', 'Location'])
pt.align = 'l'

[ pt.add_row((c['firstName'] + ' ' + c['lastName'], c['location']['name']))
  for c in connections['values']
      if c.has_key('location')]

print pt
```

Sample (anonymized) results follow and display your connections and where they are currently located according to their profiles.

```
+--------------------------------+--------------------------------------------+
| Name                           | Location                                   |
+--------------------------------+--------------------------------------------+
| Laurel A.                      | Greater Boston Area                        |
| Eve A.                         | Greater Chicago Area                       |
| Jim A.                         | Washington D.C. Metro Area                 |
| Tom A.                         | San Francisco Bay Area                     |
|   ...                          |            ...                             |
+--------------------------------+--------------------------------------------+
```

A full scan of the profile information returned from the Connections API reveals that it's pretty spartan, but you can use field selectors as outlined in the Profile Fields online documentation (*http://linkd.in/1a1m3ds*) to retrieve additional details, if available. For example, Example 3-4 shows how to fetch a connection's job position history.

Example 3-4. Displaying job position history for your profile and a connection's profile

```
import json

# See http://developer.linkedin.com/documents/profile-fields#fullprofile
# for details on additional field selectors that can be passed in for
# retrieving additional profile information.

# Display your own positions...

my_positions = app.get_profile(selectors=['positions'])
print json.dumps(my_positions, indent=1)

# Display positions for someone in your network...

# Get an id for a connection. We'll just pick the first one.
connection_id = connections['values'][0]['id']
connection_positions = app.get_profile(member_id=connection_id,
                                       selectors=['positions'])
print json.dumps(connection_positions, indent=1)
```

Sample output reveals a number of interesting details about each position, including the company name, industry, summary of efforts, and employment dates:

```
{
 "positions": {
  "_total": 10,
  "values": [
   {
    "startDate": {
     "year": 2013,
     "month": 2
    },
    "title": "Chief Technology Officer",
    "company": {
     "industry": "Computer Software",
     "name": "Digital Reasoning Systems"
    },
    "summary": "I lead strategic technology efforts...",
    "isCurrent": true,
    "id": 370675000
   },
   {
    "startDate": {
     "year": 2009,
     "month": 10
    }
    ...
   }
  ]
 }
}
```

As might be expected, some API responses may not necessarily contain all of the information that you want to know, and some responses may contain more information than you need. Instead of making multiple API calls to piece together information or potentially stripping out information you don't want to keep, you could take advantage of the field selector syntax (*http://linkd.in/1a1m3tV*) to customize the response details. Example 3-5 shows how you can retrieve only the name, industry, and id fields for companies as part of a response for profile positions.

Example 3-5. Using field selector syntax to request additional details for APIs

```
# See http://developer.linkedin.com/documents/understanding-field-selectors
# for more information on the field selector syntax

my_positions = app.get_profile(selectors=['positions:(company:(name,industry,id))'])
print json.dumps(my_positions, indent=1)
```

Once you're familiar with the basic APIs that are available to you, have a few handy pieces of documentation bookmarked, and have made a few API calls to familiarize yourself with the basics, you're up and running with LinkedIn.

3.2.2. Downloading LinkedIn Connections as a CSV File

While using the API provides programmatic access to everything that would be visible to you as an authenticated user browsing profiles at *http://linkedin.com*, you can get all of the job title details you'll need for much of this chapter by exporting your LinkedIn connections as address book data in a CSV file format. To initiate the export, select the Connections menu item from the Contacts menu to navigate to your LinkedIn connections (*http://linkd.in/1a1m415*) page, and then select the "Export connections" link from within your LinkedIn account. Alternatively, you can navigate directly to the Export LinkedIn Connections dialog (*http://linkd.in/1a1m4ho*) illustrated in Figure 3-2.

Later in this chapter, we'll be using the csv module that's part of Python's standard library to parse the exported data, so in order to ensure compatibility with the upcoming code listing, choose the Outlook CSV option from the available choices.

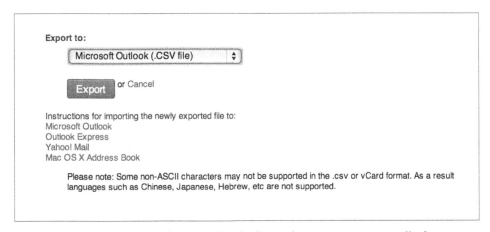

Export to:

Microsoft Outlook (.CSV file) ↕

Export or Cancel

Instructions for importing the newly exported file to:
Microsoft Outlook
Outlook Express
Yahoo! Mail
Mac OS X Address Book

Please note: Some non-ASCII characters may not be supported in the .csv or vCard format. As a result languages such as Chinese, Japanese, Hebrew, etc are not supported.

Figure 3-2. A lesser-known feature of LinkedIn is that you can export all of your connections in a convenient and portable CSV format at http://www.linkedin.com/people/export-settings

3.3. Crash Course on Clustering Data

Now that you have a basic understanding of how to access LinkedIn's API, let's dig into some more specific analysis with what will turn out to be a fairly thorough discussion of *clustering*,[2] an unsupervised machine-learning technique that is a staple in any data mining toolkit. Clustering involves taking a collection of items and partitioning them into smaller collections (clusters) according to some heuristic that is usually designed to compare items in the collection.

Clustering is a fundamental data mining technique, and as part of a proper introduction to it, this chapter includes some footnotes and interlaced discussion of a somewhat mathematical nature that undergirds the problem. Although you should strive to eventually understand these details, you don't need to grasp all of the finer points to successfully employ clustering techniques, and you certainly shouldn't feel any pressure to understand them the first time that you encounter them. It may take a little bit of reflection to digest some of the discussion, especially if you don't have a mathematical background.

---

2. Without splitting hairs over technical nuances, it's also commonly referred to as *approximate matching, fuzzy matching*, and/or *deduplication*, among many other names.

For example, if you were considering a geographic relocation, you might find it useful to cluster your LinkedIn connections into some number of geographic regions in order to better understand the economic opportunities available. We'll revisit this concept momentarily, but first let's take a moment to briefly discuss some nuances associated with clustering.

When implementing solutions to problems that lend themselves to clustering on LinkedIn or elsewhere, you'll repeatedly encounter at least two primary themes (see the sidebar "The Role of Dimensionality Reduction in Clustering" on page 98 for a discussion of a third) as part of a clustering analysis:

Data normalization

> Even when you're retrieving data from a nice API, it's usually not the case that the data will be provided to you in exactly the format you'd like—it often takes more than a little bit of munging to get the data into a form suitable for analysis. For example, LinkedIn members can enter in text that describes their job titles, so you won't always end up with perfectly normalized job titles. One executive might choose the title "Chief Technology Officer," while another may opt for the more ambiguous "CTO," and still others may choose other variations of the same role. We'll revisit the data normalization problem and implement a pattern for handling certain aspects of it for LinkedIn data momentarily.

Similarity computation

> Assuming you have reasonably well-normalized items, you'll need to measure similarity between any two of them, whether they're job titles, company names, professional interests, geographic labels, or any other field you can enter in as variable-free text, so you'll need to define a heuristic that can approximate the similarity between any two values. In some situations computing a similarity heuristic can be quite obvious, but in others it can be tricky. For example, comparing the combined years of career experience for two people might be as simple as some addition operations, but comparing a broad professional element such as "leadership aptitude" in a fully automated manner could be quite a challenge.

The Role of Dimensionality Reduction in Clustering

Although data normalization and similarity computation are two overarching themes that you'll encounter in clustering at an abstract level, dimensionality reduction is a third theme that soon emerges once the scale of the data you are working with becomes nontrivial. To cluster all of the items in a set using a similarity metric, you would ideally compare every member to every other member. Thus, for a set of n members in a collection, you would perform somewhere on the order of n^2 similarity computations in your algorithm for the worst-case scenario because you have to compare each of the n items to $n-1$ other items.

Computer scientists call this predicament an *n-squared problem* and generally use the nomenclature $O(n^2)$ to describe it; conversationally, you'd say it's a "Big-*O* of *n*-squared" problem. $O(n^2)$ problems become intractable for very large values of *n*, and most of the time, the use of the term *intractable* means you'd have to wait "too long" for a solution to be computed. "Too long" might be minutes, years, or eons, depending on the nature of the problem and its constraints.

An exploration of dimensionality reduction techniques is beyond the scope of the current discussion, but suffice it to say that a typical dimensionality reduction technique involves using a function to organize "similar enough" items into a fixed number of bins so that the items within each bin can then be more exhaustively compared to one another. Dimensionality reduction is often as much art as it is science, and is frequently considered proprietary information or a trade secret by organizations that successfully employ it to gain a competitive advantage.

Techniques for clustering are a fundamental part of any legitimate data miner's tool belt, because in nearly any sector of any industry—ranging from defense intelligence to fraud detection at a bank to landscaping—there can be a truly immense amount of semi-standardized relational data that needs to be analyzed, and the rise of data scientist job opportunities over the previous years has been a testament to this.

What generally happens is that a company establishes a database for collecting some kind of information, but not every field is enumerated into some predefined universe of valid answers. Whether it's because the application's user interface logic wasn't designed properly, because some fields just don't lend themselves to having static predetermined values, or because it was critical to the user experience that users be allowed to enter whatever they'd like into a text box, the result is always the same: you eventually end up with a lot of semi-standardized data, or "dirty records." While there might be a total of *N* distinct string values for a particular field, some number of these string values will actually relate the same concept. Duplicates can occur for various reasons—for example, misspellings, abbreviations or shorthand, and differences in the case of words.

Although it may not be obvious, this is exactly one of the classic situations we're faced with in mining LinkedIn data: LinkedIn members are able to enter in their professional information as free text, which results in a certain amount of unavoidable variation. For example, if you wanted to examine your professional network and try to determine where most of your connections work, you'd need to consider common variations in company names. Even the simplest of company names has a few common variations you'll almost certainly encounter. For example, it should be obvious to most people that "Google" is an abbreviated form of "Google, Inc.," but even these kinds of simple variations in naming conventions must be explicitly accounted for during standardization efforts. In standardizing company names, a good starting point is to first consider suffixes such as LLC and Inc.

3.3.1. Clustering Enhances User Experiences

Simple clustering techniques can create incredibly compelling user experiences by leveraging results even as simple as the job title ones we just produced. Figure 3-3 demonstrates a powerful alternative view of your data via a simple tree widget that could be used as part of a navigation pane or faceted display for filtering search criteria. Assuming that the underlying similarity metrics you've chosen have produced meaningful clusters, a simple hierarchical display that presents data in logical groups with a count of each group's items can streamline the process of finding information and power intuitive workflows for almost any application where a lot of skimming would otherwise be required to find the results.

 The code for creating a faceted display from your LinkedIn connections is included as a turnkey example with the IPython Notebook for this chapter.

Figure 3-3. Intelligently clustered data lends itself to faceted displays and compelling user experiences

The code to create a simple navigational display can be surprisingly simple, given the maturity of Ajax toolkits and other UI libraries, and there's incredible value in being able to create user experiences that present data in intuitive ways that power workflows. Something as simple as an intelligently crafted hierarchical display can inadvertently motivate users to spend more time on a site, discover more information than they normally would, and ultimately realize more value in the services the site offers.

3.3.2. Normalizing Data to Enable Analysis

As a necessary and helpful interlude toward building a working knowledge of clustering algorithms, let's explore a few of the common situations you may face in normalizing LinkedIn data. In this section, we'll implement a common pattern for normalizing company names and job titles. As a more advanced exercise, we'll also briefly divert and discuss the problem of disambiguating and geocoding geographic references from LinkedIn profile information. (In other words, we'll attempt to convert labels from LinkedIn profiles such as "Greater Nashville Area" to coordinates that can be plotted on a map.)

The chief artifact of data normalization efforts is that you can count and analyze important features of the data and enable advanced data mining techniques such as clustering. In the case of LinkedIn data, we'll be examining entities such as companies' job titles and geographic locations.

3.3.2.1. Normalizing and counting companies

Let's take a stab at standardizing company names from your professional network. Recall that the two primary ways you can access your LinkedIn data are either by using the LinkedIn API to programmatically retrieve the relevant fields or by employing a slightly lesser-known mechanism that allows you to export your professional network as address book data, which includes basic information such as name, job title, company, and contact information.

Assuming you have a CSV file of contacts that you've exported from LinkedIn, you could normalize and display selected entities from a histogram, as illustrated in Example 3-6.

As you'll notice in the opening comments of code listings such as Example 3-6, you'll need to copy and rename the CSV file of your LinkedIn connections that you exported to a particular directory in your source code checkout, per the guidance provided in Section 3.2.2 on page 96.

Example 3-6. Simple normalization of company suffixes from address book data

```
import os
import csv
from collections import Counter
from operator import itemgetter
from prettytable import PrettyTable
```

```
# XXX: Place your "Outlook CSV" formatted file of connections from
# http://www.linkedin.com/people/export-settings at the following
# location: resources/ch03-linkedin/my_connections.csv

CSV_FILE = os.path.join("resources", "ch03-linkedin", 'my_connections.csv')

# Define a set of transforms that converts the first item
# to the second item. Here, we're simply handling some
# commonly known abbreviations, stripping off common suffixes,
# etc.

transforms = [(', Inc.', ''), (', Inc', ''), (', LLC', ''), (', LLP', ''),
              (' LLC', ''), (' Inc.', ''), (' Inc', '')]

csvReader = csv.DictReader(open(CSV_FILE), delimiter=',', quotechar='"')
contacts = [row for row in csvReader]
companies = [c['Company'].strip() for c in contacts if c['Company'].strip() != '']

for i, _ in enumerate(companies):
    for transform in transforms:
        companies[i] = companies[i].replace(*transform)

pt = PrettyTable(field_names=['Company', 'Freq'])
pt.align = 'l'
c = Counter(companies)
[pt.add_row([company, freq])
 for (company, freq) in sorted(c.items(), key=itemgetter(1), reverse=True)
     if freq > 1]
print pt
```

The following illustrates typical results for frequency analysis:

```
+--------------------------------+------+
| Company                        | Freq |
+--------------------------------+------+
| Digital Reasoning Systems      | 31   |
| O'Reilly Media                 | 19   |
| Google                         | 18   |
| Novetta Solutions              | 9    |
| Mozilla Corporation            | 9    |
| Booz Allen Hamilton            | 8    |
| ...                            | ...  |
+--------------------------------+------+
```

 Python allows you to pass arguments to a function by *dereferencing* a list and dictionary as parameters, which is sometimes convenient, as illustrated in Example 3-6. For example, calling f(*args, **kw) is equivalent to calling f(1,7, x=23) so long as args is defined as [1,7] and kw is defined as {'x' : 23}. See Appendix C for more Python tips.

Keep in mind that you'll need to get a little more sophisticated to handle more complex situations, such as the various manifestations of company names—like O'Reilly Media —that have evolved over the years. For example, you might see this company's name represented as O'Reilly & Associates, O'Reilly Media, O'Reilly, Inc., or just O'Reilly.[3]

3.3.2.2. Normalizing and counting job titles

As might be expected, the same problem that occurs with normalizing company names presents itself when considering job titles, except that it can get a lot messier because job titles are so much more variable. Table 3-1 lists a few job titles you're likely to encounter in a software company that include a certain amount of natural variation. How many distinct roles do you see for the 10 distinct titles that are listed?

Table 3-1. Example job titles for the technology industry

Job title
Chief Executive Officer
President/CEO
President & CEO
CEO
Developer
Software Developer
Software Engineer
Chief Technical Officer
President
Senior Software Engineer

While it's certainly possible to define a list of aliases or abbreviations that equate titles like CEO and Chief Executive Officer, it may not be practical to manually define lists that equate titles such as Software Engineer and Developer for the general case in all possible domains. However, for even the messiest of fields in a worst-case scenario, it shouldn't be too difficult to implement a solution that condenses the data to the point that it's manageable for an expert to review it and then feed it back into a program that can apply it in much the same way that the expert would have done. More times than not, this is actually the approach that organizations prefer since it allows humans to briefly insert themselves into the loop to perform quality control.

---

3. If you think this is starting to sound complicated, just consider the work taken on by Dun & Bradstreet (*http://bit.ly/1a1m4Om*), the "Who's Who" of company information, blessed with the challenge of maintaining a worldwide directory that identifies companies spanning multiple languages from all over the globe.

Recall that one of the most obvious starting points when working with any data set is to count things, and this situation is no different. Let's reuse the same concepts from normalizing company names to implement a pattern for normalizing common job titles and then perform a basic frequency analysis on those titles as an initial basis for clustering. Assuming you have a reasonable number of exported contacts, the minor nuances among job titles that you'll encounter may actually be surprising, but before we get into that, let's introduce some sample code that establishes some patterns for normalizing record data and takes a basic inventory sorted by frequency.

Example 3-7 inspects job titles and prints out frequency information for the titles themselves and for individual tokens that occur in them.

Example 3-7. Standardizing common job titles and computing their frequencies

```
import os
import csv
from operator import itemgetter
from collections import Counter
from prettytable import PrettyTable

# XXX: Place your "Outlook CSV" formatted file of connections from
# http://www.linkedin.com/people/export-settings at the following
# location: resources/ch03-linkedin/my_connections.csv

CSV_FILE = os.path.join("resources", "ch03-linkedin", 'my_connections.csv')

transforms = [
    ('Sr.', 'Senior'),
    ('Sr', 'Senior'),
    ('Jr.', 'Junior'),
    ('Jr', 'Junior'),
    ('CEO', 'Chief Executive Officer'),
    ('COO', 'Chief Operating Officer'),
    ('CTO', 'Chief Technology Officer'),
    ('CFO', 'Chief Finance Officer'),
    ('VP', 'Vice President'),
    ]

csvReader = csv.DictReader(open(CSV_FILE), delimiter=',', quotechar='"')
contacts = [row for row in csvReader]

# Read in a list of titles and split apart
# any combined titles like "President/CEO."
# Other variations could be handled as well, such
# as "President & CEO", "President and CEO", etc.

titles = []
for contact in contacts:
    titles.extend([t.strip() for t in contact['Job Title'].split('/')
                if contact['Job Title'].strip() != ''])
```

```
# Replace common/known abbreviations

for i, _ in enumerate(titles):
    for transform in transforms:
        titles[i] = titles[i].replace(*transform)

# Print out a table of titles sorted by frequency

pt = PrettyTable(field_names=['Title', 'Freq'])
pt.align = 'l'
c = Counter(titles)
[pt.add_row([title, freq])
 for (title, freq) in sorted(c.items(), key=itemgetter(1), reverse=True)
    if freq > 1]
print pt

# Print out a table of tokens sorted by frequency

tokens = []
for title in titles:
    tokens.extend([t.strip(',') for t in title.split()])
pt = PrettyTable(field_names=['Token', 'Freq'])
pt.align = 'l'
c = Counter(tokens)
[pt.add_row([token, freq])
 for (token, freq) in sorted(c.items(), key=itemgetter(1), reverse=True)
    if freq > 1 and len(token) > 2]
print pt
```

In short, the code reads in CSV records and makes a mild attempt at normalizing them by splitting apart combined titles that use the forward slash (like a title of "President/CEO") and replacing known abbreviations. Beyond that, it just displays the results of a frequency distribution of both full job titles and individual tokens contained in the job titles.

This is not all that different from the previous exercise with company names, but it serves as a useful starting template and provides you with some reasonable insight into how the data breaks down.

Sample results follow:

```
+-------------------------------------+------+
| Title                               | Freq |
+-------------------------------------+------+
| Chief Executive Officer             | 19   |
| Senior Software Engineer            | 17   |
| President                           | 12   |
| Founder                             | 9    |
| ...                                 | ...  |
+-------------------------------------+------+
```

```
+----------------+------+
| Token          | Freq |
+----------------+------+
| Engineer       | 43   |
| Chief          | 43   |
| Senior         | 42   |
| Officer        | 37   |
| ...            | ...  |
+----------------+------+
```

One thing that's notable about the sample results is that the most common job title based on exact matches is "Chief Executive Officer," which is closely followed by other senior positions such as "President" and "Founder." Hence, the ego of this professional network has reasonably good access to entrepreneurs and business leaders. The most common tokens from within the job titles are "Engineer" and "Chief." The "Chief" token correlates back to the previous thought about connections to higher-ups in companies, while the token "Engineer" provides a slightly different clue into the nature of the professional network. Although "Engineer" is not a constituent token of the most common job title, it does appear in a large number of job titles such as "Senior Software Engineer" and "Software Engineer," which show up near the top of the job titles list. Therefore, the ego of this network appears to have connections to technical practitioners as well.

In job title or address book data analysis, this is precisely the kind of insight that motivates the need for an approximate matching or clustering algorithm. The next section investigates further.

3.3.2.3. Normalizing and counting locations

Although LinkedIn includes a general geographic region that usually corresponds to a metropolitan area for each of your connections, this label is not specific enough that it can be pinpointed on a map without some additional work. Knowing that someone works in the "Greater Nashville Area" is useful, and as human beings with additional knowledge, we know that this label probably refers to the Nashville, Tennessee metro area. However, writing code to transform "Greater Nashville Area" to a set of coordinates that you could render on a map can be trickier than it sounds, particularly when the human-readable label for a region is especially common.

As a generalized problem, disambiguating geographic references is quite difficult. The population of New York City might be high enough that you can reasonably infer that "New York" refers to New York City, New York, but what about "Smithville"? There are hundreds of Smithvilles in the United States, and with most states having several of them, geographic context beyond the surrounding state is needed to make the right determination. It won't be the case that a highly ambiguous place like "Greater Smithville Area" is something you'll see on LinkedIn, but it serves to illustrate the general problem of disambiguating a geographic reference so that it can be resolved to a specific set of coordinates.

Disambiguating and geocoding the whereabouts of LinkedIn connections is slightly easier than the most generalized form of the problem because most professionals tend to identify with the larger metropolitan area that they're associated with, and there are a relatively finite number of these regions. Although not always the case, you can generally employ the crude assumption that the location referred to in a LinkedIn profile is a relatively well-known location and is likely to be the "most popular" metropolitan region by that name.

You can install a Python package called geopy via **pip install geopy**; it provides a generalized mechanism for passing in labels for locations and getting back lists of coordinates that might match. The geopy package itself is a proxy to multiple web services providers such as Bing and Google that perform the geocoding, and an advantage of using it is that it provides a standardized API for interfacing with various geocoding services so that you don't have to manually craft requests and parse responses. The geopy GitHub code repository (*http://bit.ly/1a1m7Ka*) is a good starting point for reading the documentation that's available online.

Example 3-8 illustrates how to use geopy with Microsoft's Bing, which offers a generous number of API calls for accounts that fall under educational usage guidelines that apply to situations such as learning from as this book. To run the script, you will need to request an API key from Bing (*http://bit.ly/1a1m5lq*).

 Bing is the recommended geocoder for exercises in this book with geopy, because at the time of this writing the Yahoo! geocoding service was not operational due to some changes in product strategy resulting in the creation of a new product called Yahoo! BOSS Geo Services (*http://yhoo.it/1a1m5C4*). Although the Google Maps (v3) API was operational, its maximum number of requests per day seemed less ideal than that offered by Bing.

Example 3-8. Geocoding locations with Microsoft Bing

```
from geopy import geocoders

GEO_APP_KEY = '' # XXX: Get this from https://www.bingmapsportal.com
g = geocoders.Bing(GEO_APP_KEY)
print g.geocode("Nashville", exactly_one=False)
```

The keyword parameter exactly_one=False tells the geocoder not to trigger an error if there is more than one possible result, which is more common than you might imagine. Sample results from this script follow and illustrate the nature of using an ambiguous label like "Nashville" to resolve a set of coordinates:

```
[(u'Nashville, TN, United States', (36.16783905029297, -86.77816009521484)),
    (u'Nashville, AR, United States', (33.94792938232422, -93.84703826904297)),
```

```
(u'Nashville, GA, United States', (31.206039428710938, -83.25031280517578)),
(u'Nashville, IL, United States', (38.34368133544922, -89.38263702392578)),
(u'Nashville, NC, United States', (35.97433090209961, -77.96495056152344))]
```

The Bing geocoding service appears to return the most populous locations first in the list of results, so we'll opt to simply select the first item in the list as our response given that LinkedIn generally exposes locations in profiles as large metropolitan areas. However, before we'll be able to geocode, we'll have to return to the problem of data normalization, because passing in a value such as "Greater Nashville Area" to the geocoder won't return a response to us. (Try it and see for yourself.) As a pattern, we can transform locations such that common prefixes and suffixes are routinely stripped, as illustrated in Example 3-9.

Example 3-9. Geocoding locations of LinkedIn connections with Microsoft Bing

```
from geopy import geocoders

GEO_APP_KEY = '' # XXX: Get this from https://www.bingmapsportal.com
g = geocoders.Bing(GEO_APP_KEY)

transforms = [('Greater ', ''), (' Area', '')]

results = {}
for c in connections['values']:
    if not c.has_key('location'): continue

    transformed_location = c['location']['name']
    for transform in transforms:
        transformed_location = transformed_location.replace(*transform)
    geo = g.geocode(transformed_location, exactly_one=False)
    if geo == []: continue
    results.update({ c['location']['name'] : geo })

print json.dumps(results, indent=1)
```

Sample results from the geocoding exercise follow:

```
{
 "Greater Chicago Area": [
  "Chicago, IL, United States",
  [
   41.884151458740234,
   -87.63240814208984
  ]
 ],
 "Greater Boston Area": [
  "Boston, MA, United States",
  [
   42.3586311340332,
   -71.05670166015625
  ]
 ],
```

```
"Bengaluru Area, India": [
 "Bangalore, Karnataka, India",
 [
  12.966970443725586,
  77.5872802734375
 ]
],
"San Francisco Bay Area": [
 "CA, United States",
 [
  37.71476745605469,
  -122.24223327636719
 ]
],
...
}
```

Later in this chapter, we'll use the coordinates returned from geocoding as part of a clustering algorithm that can be a good way to analyze your professional network. Meanwhile, there's another useful visualization called a *cartogram* that can be interesting for visualizing your network.

3.3.2.4. Visualizing locations with cartograms

A cartogram (*http://bit.ly/1a1m5Ss*) is a visualization that displays a geography by scaling geographic boundaries according to an underlying variable. For example, a map of the United States might scale the size of each state so that it is larger or smaller than it should be based upon a variable such as obesity rate, poverty levels, number of millionaires, or any other variable. The resulting visualization would not necessarily present a fully integrated view of the geography since the individual states would no longer fit together due to their scaling. Still, you'd have an idea about the overall status of the variable that led to the scaling for each state.

A specialized variation of a cartogram called a *Dorling Cartogram* substitutes a shape, such as a circle, for each unit of area on a map in its approximate location and scales the size of the shape according to the value of the underlying variable. Another way to describe a Dorling Cartogram is as a "geographically clustered bubble chart." It's a great visualization tool because it allows you to use your instincts about where information should appear on a 2D mapping surface, and it's able to encode parameters using very intuitive properties of shapes, like area and color.

Given that the Bing geocoding service returns results that include the state for each city that is geocoded, let's take advantage of this information and build a Dorling Cartogram of your professional network where we'll scale the size of each state according to the number of contacts you have there. D3 (*http://bit.ly/1a1kGvo*), the cutting-edge visualization toolkit introduced in Chapter 2, includes most of the machinery for a Dorling Cartogram and provides a highly customizable means of extending the visualization to include other variables if you'd like to do so. D3 also includes several other visualizations that convey geographical information, such as heatmaps, symbol maps, and choropleth maps that should be easily adaptable to the working data.

There's really just one data munging nuance that needs to be performed in order to visualize your contacts by state, and that's the task of parsing the states from the geocoder responses. In general, there can be some slight variation in the text of the response that contains the state, but as a general pattern, the state is always represented by two consecutive uppercase letters, and a regular expression (*http://bit.ly/1a1m6pJ*) is a fine way to parse out that kind of pattern from text.

Example 3-10 illustrates how to use the re package from Python's standard library to parse the geocoder response and write out a JSON file that can be loaded by a D3-powered Dorling Cartogram visualization. Teaching regular expression fundamentals is outside the current scope of our discussion, but the gist of the pattern '.*([A-Z] {2}).*' is that we are looking for exactly two consecutive uppercase letters in the text, which can be preceded or followed by any text at all, as denoted by the .* wildcard. Parentheses are used to capture (or "tag," in regular expression parlance) the *group* that we are interested in so that it can easily be retrieved.

Example 3-10. Parsing out states from Bing geocoder results using a regular expression

```
import re

# Most results contain a response that can be parsed by
# picking out the first two consecutive upper case letters
# as a clue for the state
pattern = re.compile('.*([A-Z]{2}).*')

def parseStateFromBingResult(r):
    result = pattern.search(r[0][0])
    if result == None:
        print "Unresolved match:", r
        return "???"
    elif len(result.groups()) == 1:
        print result.groups()
        return result.groups()[0]
    else:
        print "Unresolved match:", result.groups()
        return "???"


transforms = [('Greater ', ''), (' Area', '')]

results = {}
for c in connections['values']:
    if not c.has_key('location'): continue
    if not c['location']['country']['code'] == 'us': continue

    transformed_location = c['location']['name']
    for transform in transforms:
```

```
        transformed_location = transformed_location.replace(*transform)

    geo = g.geocode(transformed_location, exactly_one=False)
    if geo == []: continue
    parsed_state = parseStateFromBingResult(geo)
    if parsed_state != "???":
        results.update({c['location']['name'] : parsed_state})

print json.dumps(results, indent=1)
```

Sample results follow and illustrate the efficacy of this technique:

```
{
 "Greater Chicago Area": "IL",
 "Greater Boston Area": "MA",
 "Dallas/Fort Worth Area": "TX",
 "San Francisco Bay Area": "CA",
 "Washington D.C. Metro Area": "DC",
 ...
}
```

With the ability to distill reliable state abbreviations from your LinkedIn contacts, we can now compute the frequency at which each state appears, which is all that is needed to drive a turnkey Dorling Cartogram visualization with D3. A sample visualization for a professional network is displayed in Figure 3-4. Note that in many cartograms, Alaska and Hawaii are often displayed in the lower-left corner of the visualization (as is the case with many maps that display them as inlays). Despite the fact that the visualization is just a lot of carefully displayed circles on a map, it's relatively obvious which circles correspond to which states. Hovering over circles produces tool tips that display the name of the state by default, and additional customization would not be difficult to implement by observing standard D3 best practices. The process of generating the final output for consumption by D3 involves little more than generating a frequency distribution by state and serializing it out as JSON.

 Some of the code for creating a Dorling Cartogram from your LinkedIn connections is omitted from this section for brevity, but it is included as a completely turnkey example with the IPython Notebook for this chapter.

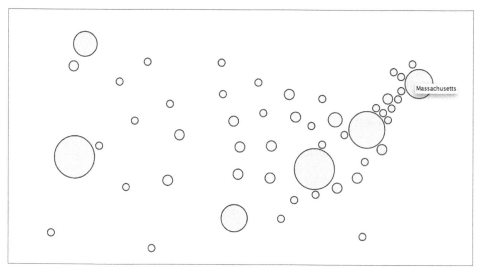

Figure 3-4. A Dorling Cartogram of locations resolved from a LinkedIn professional network—tool tips display the name of each state when the circles are hovered over (in this particular figure, the state of Massachusetts is being hovered over with the mouse)

3.3.3. Measuring Similarity

With an appreciation for some of the subtleties that are required to normalize data, let us now turn our attention to the problem of computing similarity, which is the principal basis of clustering. The most substantive decision we need to make in clustering a set of strings—job titles, in this case—in a useful way is which underlying similarity metric to use. There are myriad string similarity metrics available, and choosing the one that's most appropriate for your situation largely depends on the nature of your objective.

Although these similarity measurements are not difficult to define and compute ourselves, I'll take this opportunity to introduce NLTK (the Natural Language Toolkit) (*http://bit.ly/1a1mc0m*), a Python toolkit that you'll be glad to have in your arsenal for mining the social web. As with other Python packages, simply run **pip install nltk** to install NLTK per the norm.

> Depending on your use of NLTK, you may find that you also need to download some additional data sets that aren't packaged with it by default. If you're not employing the book's virtual machine, running the command nltk.download() downloads all of NLTK's data add-ons. You can read more about it at Installing NLTK Data (*http://bit.ly/1a1mcgV*).

Here are a few of the common similarity metrics that might be helpful in comparing job titles that are implemented in NLTK:

Edit distance

Edit distance, also known as Levenshtein distance (*http://bit.ly/1a1mcNO*), is a simple measure of how many insertions, deletions, and replacements it would take to convert one string into another. For example, the cost of converting *dad* into *bad* would be one replacement operation (substituting the first *d* with a *b*) and would yield a value of 1. NLTK provides an implementation of edit distance via the `nltk.metrics.distance.edit_distance` function.

The actual edit distance between two strings is quite different from the number of operations required to *compute* the edit distance; computation of edit distance is usually on the order of $M*N$ operations for strings of length M and N. In other words, computing edit distance can be a computationally intense operation, so use it wisely on nontrivial amounts of data.

n-gram similarity

An *n*-gram is just a terse way of expressing each possible consecutive sequence of *n* tokens from a text, and it provides the foundational data structure for computing collocations. There are many variations of *n*-gram similarity, but consider the straightforward case of computing all possible bigrams (two-grams) for the tokens of two strings, and scoring the similarity between the strings by counting the number of common bigrams between them, as demonstrated in Example 3-11.

 An extended discussion of *n*-grams and collocations is presented in Section 4.4.4 on page 167.

Example 3-11. Using NLTK to compute bigrams

```
ceo_bigrams = nltk.bigrams("Chief Executive Officer".split(), pad_right=True,
                                                               pad_left=True)
cto_bigrams = nltk.bigrams("Chief Technology Officer".split(), pad_right=True,
                                                               pad_left=True)

print ceo_bigrams
print cto_bigrams
print len(set(ceo_bigrams).intersection(set(cto_bigrams)))
```

The following sample results illustrate the computation of bigrams and the set intersection of bigrams between two different job titles:

```
[(None, 'Chief'), ('Chief', 'Executive'), ('Executive', 'Officer'),
 ('Officer', None)]
[(None, 'Chief'), ('Chief', 'Technology'), ('Technology', 'Officer'),
```

```
('Officer', None)]
2
```

The use of the keyword arguments `pad_right` and `pad_left` intentionally allows for leading and trailing tokens to match. The effect of padding is to allow bigrams such as (`None`, `'Chief'`) to emerge, which are important matches across job titles. NLTK provides a fairly comprehensive array of bigram and trigram (three-gram) scoring functions via the `BigramAssociationMeasures` and `TrigramAssociationMeasures` classes defined in its `nltk.metrics.association` module.

Jaccard distance

More often than not, similarity can be computed between two sets of things, where a *set* is just an unordered collection of items. The Jaccard similarity metric expresses the similarity of two sets and is defined by the intersection of the sets divided by the union of the sets. Mathematically, the Jaccard similarity is written as:

$$\frac{|\ Set1 \cap Set2\ |}{|\ Set1 \cup Set2\ |}$$

which is the number of items in common between the two sets (the cardinality of their set intersection) divided by the total number of distinct items in the two sets (the cardinality of their union). The intuition behind this ratio is that calculating the number of unique items that are common to both sets divided by the number of total unique items is a reasonable way to derive a normalized score for computing similarity. In general, you'll compute Jaccard similarity by using *n*-grams, including unigrams (single tokens), to measure the similarity of two strings.

Given that the Jaccard similarity metric measures how close two sets are to one another, you can measure the dissimilarity between them by subtracting this value from 1.0 to arrive at what is known as the *Jaccard distance*.

> In addition to these handy similarity measurements and among its other numerous utilities, NLTK provides a class you can access as `nltk.FreqDist`. This is a frequency distribution similar to the way that we've been using `collections.Counter` from Python's standard library.

Calculating similarity is a critical aspect of any clustering algorithm, and it's easy enough to try out different similarity heuristics as part of your work in data science once you have a better feel for the data you're mining. The next section works up a script that clusters job titles using Jaccard similarity.

3.3.4. Clustering Algorithms

With the prerequisite appreciation for data normalization and similarity heuristics in place, let's now collect some real-world data from LinkedIn and compute some meaningful clusters to gain a few more insights into the dynamics of your professional network. Whether you want to take an honest look at whether your networking skills have been helping you to meet the "right kinds of people," you want to approach contacts who will most likely fit into a certain socioeconomic bracket with a particular kind of business inquiry or proposition, or you want to determine if there's a better place you could live or open a remote office to drum up business, there's bound to be something valuable in a professional network rich with high-quality data. The remainder of this section illustrates a few different clustering approaches by further considering the problem of grouping together job titles that are similar.

3.3.4.1. Greedy clustering

Given that we have insight suggesting that overlap in titles is important, let's try to cluster job titles by comparing them to one another as an extension of Example 3-7 using Jaccard distance. Example 3-12 clusters similar titles and then displays your contacts accordingly. Skim the code—especially the nested loop invoking the DISTANCE function—and then we'll discuss.

Example 3-12. Clustering job titles using a greedy heuristic

```
import os
import csv
from nltk.metrics.distance import jaccard_distance

# XXX: Place your "Outlook CSV" formatted file of connections from
# http://www.linkedin.com/people/export-settings at the following
# location: resources/ch03-linkedin/my_connections.csv

CSV_FILE = os.path.join("resources", "ch03-linkedin", 'my_connections.csv')

# Tweak this distance threshold and try different distance calculations
# during experimentation
DISTANCE_THRESHOLD = 0.5
DISTANCE = jaccard_distance

def cluster_contacts_by_title(csv_file):

    transforms = [
        ('Sr.', 'Senior'),
        ('Sr', 'Senior'),
        ('Jr.', 'Junior'),
        ('Jr', 'Junior'),
        ('CEO', 'Chief Executive Officer'),
        ('COO', 'Chief Operating Officer'),
        ('CTO', 'Chief Technology Officer'),
        ('CFO', 'Chief Finance Officer'),
```

```
        ('VP', 'Vice President'),
        ]

separators = ['/', 'and', '&']

csvReader = csv.DictReader(open(csv_file), delimiter=',', quotechar='"')
contacts = [row for row in csvReader]

# Normalize and/or replace known abbreviations
# and build up a list of common titles.

all_titles = []
for i, _ in enumerate(contacts):
    if contacts[i]['Job Title'] == '':
        contacts[i]['Job Titles'] = ['']
        continue
    titles = [contacts[i]['Job Title']]
    for title in titles:
        for separator in separators:
            if title.find(separator) >= 0:
                titles.remove(title)
                titles.extend([title.strip() for title in title.split(separator)
                               if title.strip() != ''])

    for transform in transforms:
        titles = [title.replace(*transform) for title in titles]
    contacts[i]['Job Titles'] = titles
    all_titles.extend(titles)

all_titles = list(set(all_titles))

clusters = {}
for title1 in all_titles:
    clusters[title1] = []
    for title2 in all_titles:
        if title2 in clusters[title1] or clusters.has_key(title2) and title1 \
            in clusters[title2]:
            continue
        distance = DISTANCE(set(title1.split()), set(title2.split()))

        if distance < DISTANCE_THRESHOLD:
            clusters[title1].append(title2)

# Flatten out clusters

clusters = [clusters[title] for title in clusters if len(clusters[title]) > 1]

# Round up contacts who are in these clusters and group them together

clustered_contacts = {}
for cluster in clusters:
    clustered_contacts[tuple(cluster)] = []
```

```
            for contact in contacts:
                for title in contact['Job Titles']:
                    if title in cluster:
                        clustered_contacts[tuple(cluster)].append('%s %s'
                                % (contact['First Name'], contact['Last Name']))

    return clustered_contacts


clustered_contacts = cluster_contacts_by_title(CSV_FILE)
print clustered_contacts
for titles in clustered_contacts:
    common_titles_heading = 'Common Titles: ' + ', '.join(titles)

    descriptive_terms = set(titles[0].split())
    for title in titles:
        descriptive_terms.intersection_update(set(title.split()))
    descriptive_terms_heading = 'Descriptive Terms: ' \
        + ', '.join(descriptive_terms)
    print descriptive_terms_heading
    print '-' * max(len(descriptive_terms_heading), len(common_titles_heading))
    print '\n'.join(clustered_contacts[titles])
    print
```

The code listing starts by separating out combined titles using a list of common conjunctions and then normalizes common titles. Then, a nested loop iterates over all of the titles and clusters them together according to a thresholded Jaccard similarity metric as defined by DISTANCE, where the assignment of jaccard_distance to DISTANCE was chosen to make it easy to swap in a different distance calculation for experimentation. This tight loop is where most of the real action happens in the listing: it's where each title is compared to each other title.

If the distance between any two titles as determined by a similarity heuristic is "close enough," we *greedily* group them together. In this context, being "greedy" means that the first time we are able to determine that an item might fit in a cluster, we go ahead and assign it without further considering whether there might be a better fit, or making any attempt to account for such a better fit if one appears later. Although incredibly pragmatic, this approach produces very reasonable results. Clearly, the choice of an effective similarity heuristic is critical to its success, but given the nature of the nested loop, the fewer times we have to invoke the scoring function, the faster the code executes (a principal concern for nontrivial sets of data). More will be said about this consideration in the next section, but do note that we use some conditional logic to try to avoid repeating unnecessary calculations if possible.

The rest of the listing just looks up contacts with a particular job title and groups them for display, but there is one other nuance involved in computing clusters: *you often need to assign each cluster a meaningful label*. The working implementation computes labels by taking the setwise intersection of terms in the job titles for each cluster, which seems reasonable given that it's the most obvious common thread. Your mileage is sure to vary with other approaches.

The types of results you might expect from this code are useful in that they group together individuals who are likely to share common responsibilities in their job duties. As previously noted, this information might be useful for a variety of reasons, whether you're planning an event that includes a "CEO Panel," trying to figure out who can best help you to make your next career move, or trying to determine whether you are *really* well enough connected to other similar professionals given your own job responsibilities and future aspirations. Abridged results for a sample professional network follow:

```
Common Titles: Chief Technology Officer,
               Founder,
               Chief Technology Officer,
               Co-Founder,
               Chief Technology Officer
Descriptive Terms: Chief, Technology, Officer
---------------------------------------------
Damien K.
Andrew O.
Matthias B.
Pete W.
...

Common Titles: Founder,
               Chief Executive Officer,
               Chief Executive Officer
Descriptive Terms: Chief, Executive, Officer
---------------------------------------------
Joseph C.
Janine T.
Kabir K.
Scott S.
Bob B.
Steve S.
John T. H.
...
```

Runtime analysis.

 This section contains a relatively advanced discussion about the computational details of clustering and should be considered optional reading, as it may not appeal to everyone. If this is your first reading of this chapter, feel free to skip this section and peruse it upon encountering it a second time.

In the *worst case*, the nested loop executing the `DISTANCE` calculation from Example 3-12 would require it to be invoked in what we've already mentioned is $O(n^2)$ time complexity —in other words, `len(all_titles)*len(all_titles)` times. A nested loop that compares every single item to every single other item for clustering purposes is *not* a scalable approach for a very large value of *n*, but given that the unique number of titles for your professional network is not likely to be very large, it shouldn't impose a performance constraint. It may not seem like a big deal—after all, it's just a nested loop—but the crux of an $O(n^2)$ algorithm is that the number of comparisons required to process an input set increases exponentially in proportion to the number of items in the set. For example, a small input set of 100 job titles would require only 10,000 scoring operations, while 10,000 job titles would require 100,000,000 scoring operations. The math doesn't work out so well and eventually buckles, even when you have a lot of hardware to throw at it.

Your initial reaction when faced with what seems like a predicament that doesn't scale will probably be to try to reduce the value of *n* as much as possible. But most of the time you won't be able to reduce it enough to make your solution scalable as the size of your input grows, because you still have an $O(n^2)$ algorithm. What you really want to do is come up with an algorithm that's on the order of $O(k^*n)$, where *k* is much smaller than *n* and represents a manageable amount of overhead that grows much more slowly than the rate of *n*'s growth. As with any other engineering decision, there are performance and quality trade-offs to be made in all corners of the real world, and *it can be quite challenging* to strike the right balance. In fact, many data mining companies that have successfully implemented scalable record-matching analytics at a high degree of fidelity consider their specific approaches to be proprietary information (trade secrets), since they result in definite business advantages.

For situations in which an $O(n^2)$ algorithm is simply unacceptable, one variation to the working example that you might try is rewriting the nested loops so that a random sample is selected for the scoring function, which would effectively reduce it to $O(k^*n)$, if *k* were the sample size. As the value of the sample size approaches *n*, however, you'd expect the runtime to begin approaching the $O(n^2)$ runtime. The following amendments to Example 3-12 show how that sampling technique might look in code; the key changes to the previous listing are highlighted in bold. The core takeaway is that for each invocation of the outer loop, we're executing the inner loop a much smaller, fixed number of times:

```
# ... snip ...

all_titles = list(set(all_titles))
clusters = {}
for title1 in all_titles:
    clusters[title1] = []
    for sample in range(SAMPLE_SIZE):
        title2 = all_titles[random.randint(0, len(all_titles)-1)]
        if title2 in clusters[title1] or clusters.has_key(title2) and title1 \
            in clusters[title2]:
```

```
        continue
    distance = DISTANCE(set(title1.split()), set(title2.split()))
    if distance < DISTANCE_THRESHOLD:
        clusters[title1].append(title2)

# ... snip ...
```

Another approach you might consider is to randomly sample the data into n bins (where n is some number that's generally less than or equal to the square root of the number of items in your set), perform clustering within each of those individual bins, and then optionally merge the output. For example, if you had 1 million items, an $O(n^2)$ algorithm would take a trillion logical operations, whereas binning the 1 million items into 1,000 bins containing 1,000 items each and clustering each individual bin would require only a billion operations. (That's 1,000*1,000 comparisons for each bin for all 1,000 bins.) A billion is still a large number, but it's three orders of magnitude smaller than a trillion, and that's a substantial improvement (although it still may not be enough in some situations).

There are many other approaches in the literature besides sampling or binning that could be far better at reducing the dimensionality of a problem. For example, you'd ideally compare every item in a set, and at the end of the day, the particular technique you'll end up using to avoid an $O(n^2)$ situation for a large value of n will vary based upon real-world constraints and insights you're likely to gain through experimentation and domain-specific knowledge. As you consider the possibilities, keep in mind that the field of machine learning offers many techniques that are designed to combat exactly these types of scale problems by using various sorts of probabilistic models and sophisticated sampling techniques. In Section 3.3.4.3 on page 124, you'll be introduced to a fairly intuitive and well-known clustering algorithm called k-means, which is a general-purpose unsupervised approach for clustering a multidimensional space. We'll be using this technique later to cluster your contacts by geographic location.

3.3.4.2. Hierarchical clustering

Example 3-12 introduced an intuitive, greedy approach to clustering, principally as part of an exercise to teach you about the underlying aspects of the problem. With a proper appreciation for the fundamentals now in place, it's time to introduce you to two common clustering algorithms that you'll routinely encounter throughout your data mining career and apply in a variety of situations: hierarchical clustering and k-means clustering.

Hierarchical clustering is superficially similar to the greedy heuristic we have been using, while k-means clustering is radically different. We'll primarily focus on k-means throughout the rest of this chapter, but it's worthwhile to briefly introduce the theory behind both of these approaches since you're very likely to encounter them during literature review and research. An excellent implementation of both of these approaches is available via the cluster module that you can install via **pip install cluster**.

Hierarchical clustering is a deterministic technique in that it computes the full matrix[4] of distances between all items and then walks through the matrix clustering items that meet a minimum distance threshold. It's *hierarchical* in that walking over the matrix and clustering items together produces a tree structure that expresses the relative distances between items. In the literature, you may see this technique called *agglomerative* because it constructs a tree by arranging individual data items into clusters, which hierarchically merge into other clusters until the entire data set is clustered at the top of the tree. The leaf nodes on the tree represent the data items that are being clustered, while intermediate nodes in the tree hierarchically agglomerate these items into clusters.

To conceptualize the idea of agglomeration, take a look ahead at Figure 3-5 and observe that people such as "Andrew O." and "Matthias B." are leaves on the tree that are clustered, while nodes such as "Chief, Technology, Officer" agglomerate these leaves into a cluster. Although the tree in the dendogram is only two levels deep, it's not hard to imagine an additional level of agglomeration that conceptualizes something along the lines of a business executive with a label like "Chief, Officer" and agglomerates the "Chief, Technology, Officer" and "Chief, Executive, Officer" nodes.

Agglomeration is a technique that is similar to but not fundamentally the same as the approach used in Example 3-12, which uses a greedy heuristic to cluster items instead of successively building up a hierarchy. As such, the amount of time it takes for the code to run for hierarchical clustering may be considerably longer, and you may need to tweak your scoring function and distance threshold accordingly.[5] Oftentimes, agglomerative clustering is not appropriate for large data sets because of its impractical runtimes.

If we were to rewrite Example 3-12 to use the cluster package, the nested loop performing the clustering DISTANCE computation would be replaced with something like the following code:

```
# ... snip ...

# Define a scoring function
def score(title1, title2):
    return DISTANCE(set(title1.split()), set(title2.split()))
```

4. The computation of a full matrix implies a polynomial runtime. For agglomerative clustering, the runtime is often on the order of $O(n^3)$.

5. The use of dynamic programming (*http://bit.ly/1a1maFO*) and other clever bookkeeping techniques can result in substantial savings in execution time, and one of the advantages of using a well-implemented toolkit is that these clever optimizations often are already implemented for you. For example, given that the distance between two items such as job titles is almost certainly going to be symmetric, you should have to compute only one-half of the distance matrix instead of the full matrix. Therefore, even though the time complexity of the algorithm as a whole is still $O(n^2)$, only $n^2/2$ units of work are being performed instead of n^2 units of work.

```
# Feed the class your data and the scoring function
hc = HierarchicalClustering(all_titles, score)

# Cluster the data according to a distance threshold
clusters = hc.getlevel(DISTANCE_THRESHOLD)

# Remove singleton clusters
clusters = [c for c in clusters if len(c) > 1]

# ... snip ...
```

If you're interested in variations on hierarchical clustering, be sure to check out the `HierarchicalClustering` class's `setLinkageMethod` method, which provides some subtle variations on how the class can compute distances between clusters. For example, you can specify whether distances between clusters should be determined by calculating the shortest, longest, or average distance between any two clusters. Depending on the distribution of your data, choosing a different linkage method can potentially produce quite different results.

Figures 3-5 and 3-6 display a slice from a professional network as a dendogram and a node-link tree layout, respectively, using D3 (*http://bit.ly/1a1kGvo*), the state-of-the-art visualization toolkit introduced earlier. The node-link tree layout is more space-efficient and probably a better choice for this particular data set, while a dendogram (*http://bit.ly/1a1md4B*) would be a great choice if you needed to easily find correlations between each level in the tree (which would correspond to each level of agglomeration in hierarchical clustering) for a more complex set of data. If the hierarchical layout were deeper, the dendogram would have obvious benefits, but the current clustering approach is just a couple of levels deep, so the particular advantages of one layout versus the other may be mostly aesthetic for this particular data set. Keep in mind that both of the visualizations presented here are essentially just incarnations of the interactive tree widget from Figure 3-3. As these visualizations show, an amazing amount of information becomes apparent when you are able to look at a simple image of your professional network.

 The code for creating node-link tree and dendogram visualizations with D3 is omitted from this section for brevity but is included as a completely turnkey example with the IPython Notebook for this chapter.

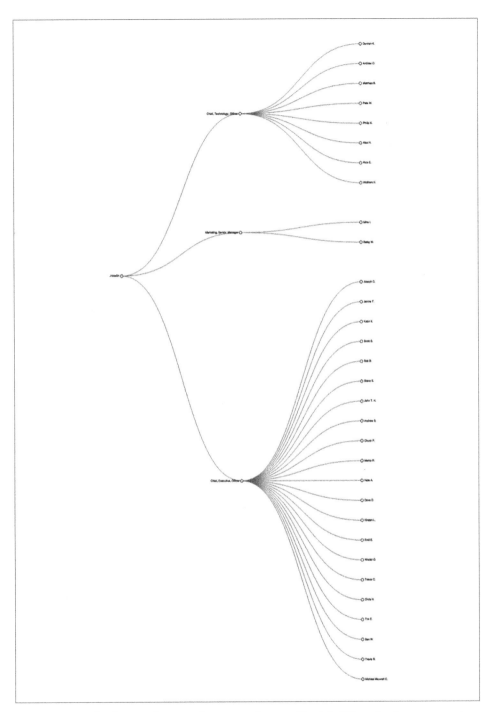

Figure 3-5. A dendogram layout of contacts clustered by job title—dendograms are typically presented in an explicitly hierarchical manner

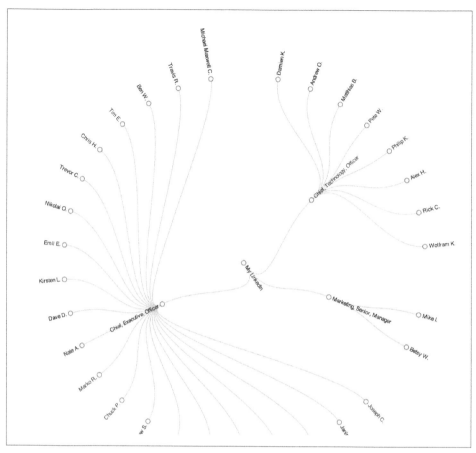

Figure 3-6. A node-link tree layout of contacts clustered by job title that conveys the same information as the dendogram in Figure 3-5—node-link trees tend to provide a more aesthetically pleasing layout when compared to dendograms

3.3.4.3. k-means clustering

Whereas hierarchical clustering is a deterministic technique that exhausts the possibilities and is often an expensive computation on the order of $O(n^3)$, k-means clustering generally executes on the order of $O(k*n)$ times. For even small values of k, the savings are substantial. The savings in performance come at the expense of results that are approximate, but they still have the potential to be quite good. The idea is that you generally have a multidimensional space containing n points, which you cluster into k clusters through the following series of steps:

1. Randomly pick k points in the data space as initial values that will be used to compute the k clusters: $K_1, K_2, ..., K_k$.

2. Assign each of the n points to a cluster by finding the nearest K_n—effectively creating k clusters and requiring $k*n$ comparisons.

3. For each of the k clusters, calculate the *centroid (http://bit.ly/1a1mbcW)*, or the mean of the cluster, and reassign its K_i value to be that value. (Hence, you're computing "k-means" during each iteration of the algorithm.)

4. Repeat steps 2–3 until the members of the clusters do not change between iterations. Generally speaking, relatively few iterations are required for convergence.

Because k-means may not be all that intuitive at first glance, Figure 3-7 displays each step of the algorithm as presented in the online "Tutorial on Clustering Algorithms," (*http://bit.ly/1a1mbtp*) which features an interactive Java applet. The sample parameters used involve 100 data points and a value of 3 for the parameter k, which means that the algorithm will produce three clusters. The important thing to note at each step is the location of the squares, and which points are included in each of those three clusters as the algorithm progresses. The algorithm takes only nine steps to complete.

Although you could run k-means on points in two dimensions or two thousand dimensions, the most common range is usually somewhere on the order of tens of dimensions, with the most common cases being two or three dimensions. When the dimensionality of the space you're working in is relatively small, k-means can be an effective clustering technique because it executes fairly quickly and is capable of producing very reasonable results. You do, however, need to pick an appropriate value for k, which is not always obvious.

The remainder of this section demonstrates how to geographically cluster and visualize your professional network by applying k-means and rendering the output with Google Maps (*http://bit.ly/1a1mdRV*) or Google Earth (*http://bit.ly/1a1meFC*).

Figure 3-7. Progression of k-means for k=3 with 100 points—notice how quickly the clusters emerge in the first few steps of the algorithm, with the remaining steps primarily affecting the data points around the edges of the clusters

3.3.4.4. Visualizing geographic clusters with Google Earth

A worthwhile exercise to see *k*-means in action is to use it to visualize and cluster your professional LinkedIn network by plotting it in two-dimensional space. In addition to the insight gained by visualizing how your contacts are spread out and noting any patterns or anomalies, you can analyze clusters by using your contacts, the distinct employers of your contacts, or the distinct metro areas in which your contacts reside as a basis. All three approaches might yield results that are useful for different purposes.

Recalling that through the LinkedIn API you can fetch location information that describes the major metropolitan area, such as "Greater Nashville Area," we'll be able to geocode the locations into coordinates and emit them in an appropriate format (such as KML (*http://bit.ly/1a1meWb*)) that we can plot in a tool like Google Earth, which provides an interactive user experience.

> Google's new Maps Engine also provides various means of uploading data (*http://bit.ly/1a1mep1*) for visualization purposes.

The primary things that you must do in order to convert your LinkedIn contacts to a format such as KML include parsing out the geographic location from each of your connections' profiles and constructing the KML for a visualization such as Google Earth. Example 3-9 demonstrated how to geocode profile information and provides a working foundation for gathering the data we'll need. The KMeansClustering class of the cluster package can calculate clusters for us, so all that's really left is to munge the data and clustering results into KML, which is a relatively rote exercise with XML tools.

As in Example 3-12, most of the work involved in getting to the point where the results can be visualized is data-processing boilerplate. The most interesting details are tucked away inside of KMeansClustering's getclusters method call, toward the end of Example 3-13, which illustrates *k*-means clustering. The approach demonstrated groups your contacts by location, clusters them, and then uses the results of the clustering algorithm to compute the centroids. Figure 3-8 illustrates sample results from running the code in Example 3-13.

> The linkedin__kml_utility that provides the createKML function in Example 3-13 is a rote exercise that is omitted for brevity here, but it's included with the IPython Notebook for this chapter as a turnkey example.

Example 3-13. Clustering your LinkedIn professional network based upon the locations of your connections and emitting KML output for visualization with Google Earth

```
import os
import sys
import json
from urllib2 import HTTPError
from geopy import geocoders
from cluster import KMeansClustering, centroid

# A helper function to munge data and build up an XML tree.
# It references some code tucked away in another directory, so we have to
# add that directory to the PYTHONPATH for it to be picked up.
sys.path.append(os.path.join(os.getcwd(), "resources", "ch03-linkedin"))
from linkedin__kml_utility import createKML

# XXX: Try different values for K to see the difference in clusters that emerge

K = 3

# XXX: Get an API key and pass it in here. See https://www.bingmapsportal.com.
GEO_API_KEY = ''
g = geocoders.Bing(GEO_API_KEY)

# Load this data from where you've previously stored it

CONNECTIONS_DATA = 'resources/ch03-linkedin/linkedin_connections.json'

OUT_FILE = "resources/ch03-linkedin/viz/linkedin_clusters_kmeans.kml"

# Open up your saved connections with extended profile information
# or fetch them again from LinkedIn if you prefer

connections = json.loads(open(CONNECTIONS_DATA).read())['values']

locations = [c['location']['name'] for c in connections if c.has_key('location')]

# Some basic transforms may be necessary for geocoding services to function properly
# Here are a couple that seem to help.

transforms = [('Greater ', ''), (' Area', '')]

# Step 1 - Tally the frequency of each location

coords_freqs = {}
for location in locations:

    if not c.has_key('location'): continue

    # Avoid unnecessary I/O and geo requests by building up a cache

    if coords_freqs.has_key(location):
```

```
                coords_freqs[location][1] += 1
                continue
        transformed_location = location

        for transform in transforms:
            transformed_location = transformed_location.replace(*transform)

            # Handle potential I/O errors with a retry pattern...

            while True:
                num_errors = 0
                try:
                    results = g.geocode(transformed_location, exactly_one=False)
                    break
                except HTTPError, e:
                    num_errors += 1
                    if num_errors >= 3:
                        sys.exit()
                    print >> sys.stderr, e
                    print >> sys.stderr, 'Encountered an urllib2 error. Trying again...'

            for result in results:
                # Each result is of the form ("Description", (X,Y))
                coords_freqs[location] = [result[1], 1]
                break # Disambiguation strategy is "pick first"

# Step 2 - Build up data structure for converting locations to KML

# Here, you could optionally segment locations by continent or country
# so as to avoid potentially finding a mean in the middle of the ocean.
# The k-means algorithm will expect distinct points for each contact, so
# build out an expanded list to pass it.

expanded_coords = []
for label in coords_freqs:
    # Flip lat/lon for Google Earth
    ((lat, lon), f) = coords_freqs[label]
    expanded_coords.append((label, [(lon, lat)] * f))

# No need to clutter the map with unnecessary placemarks...

kml_items = [{'label': label, 'coords': '%s,%s' % coords[0]} for (label,
            coords) in expanded_coords]

# It would also be helpful to include names of your contacts on the map

for item in kml_items:
    item['contacts'] = '\n'.join(['%s %s.' % (c['firstName'], c['lastName'])
        for c in connections if c.has_key('location') and
                        c['location']['name'] == item['label']])

# Step 3 - Cluster locations and extend the KML data structure with centroids
```

```
cl = KMeansClustering([coords for (label, coords_list) in expanded_coords
                                for coords in coords_list])

centroids = [{'label': 'CENTROID', 'coords': '%s,%s' % centroid(c)} for c in
                cl.getclusters(K)]

kml_items.extend(centroids)

# Step 4 - Create the final KML output and write it to a file

kml = createKML(kml_items)

f = open(OUT_FILE, 'w')
f.write(kml)
f.close()

print 'Data written to ' + OUT
```

Just visualizing your network can provide previously unknown insight, but computing the geographic centroids of your professional network can also open up some intriguing possibilities. For example, you might want to compute candidate locations for a series of regional workshops or conferences. Alternatively, if you're in the consulting business and have a hectic travel schedule, you might want to plot out some good locations for renting a little home away from home. Or maybe you want to map out professionals in your network according to their job duties, or the socioeconomic bracket they're likely to fit into based on their job titles and experience. Beyond the numerous options opened up by visualizing your professional network's location data, geographic clustering lends itself to many other possibilities, such as supply chain management and travelling salesman (*http://bit.ly/1a1mhkF*) types of problems in which it is necessary to minimize the expenses involved in travelling or moving goods from point to point.

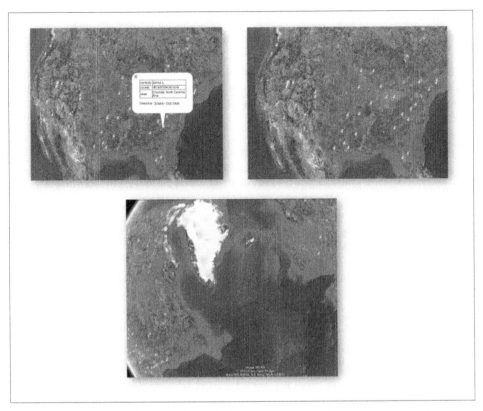

Figure 3-8. Clockwise from top-left: 1) clustering contacts by location so that you can easily see who lives/works in what city; 2) finding the centroids of three clusters computed by k-means; 3) don't forget that clusters could span countries or even continents when trying to find an ideal meeting location!

3.4. Closing Remarks

This chapter covered some serious ground, introducing the fundamental concept of clustering and demonstrating a variety of ways to apply it to your professional network data on LinkedIn. This chapter was without a doubt more advanced than the preceding chapters in terms of core content, in that it began to address common problems such as normalization of (somewhat) messy data, similarity computation on normalized data, and concerns related to the computational efficiency of approaches for a common data mining technique. Although it might be difficult to absorb all of the material in a single reading, don't be discouraged if you feel a bit overwhelmed. It may take a couple of readings to fully absorb the details introduced in this chapter.

Also keep in mind that a working knowledge of how to employ clustering doesn't necessarily require an advanced understanding of the theory behind it, although in general you should strive to understand the fundamentals that undergird the techniques you employ when mining the social web. As in the other chapters, you could easily make the case that we've just barely touched the tip of the iceberg; there are many other interesting things that you can do with your LinkedIn data that were not introduced in this chapter, many of which involve basic frequency analysis and do not require clustering at all. That said, you do have a pretty nice power tool in your belt now.

 The source code outlined for this chapter and all other chapters is available at GitHub (*http://bit.ly/1a1kNqy*) in a convenient IPython Notebook format that you're highly encouraged to try out from the comfort of your own web browser.

3.5. Recommended Exercises

- Take some time to explore the extended profile information that you have available. It could be fun to try to correlate where people work versus where they went to school and/or to analyze whether people tend to relocate into and out of certain areas.

- Try employing an alternative visualization from D3, such as a choropleth map (*http://bit.ly/1a1mg0a*), to visualize your professional network.

- Read up on new and exciting GeoJSON specification (*http://bit.ly/1a1mggF*) and how you can easily create interactive visualizations at GitHub by generating GeoJSON data. Try to apply this technique to your professional network as an alternative to using Google Earth.

- Visualize your LinkedIn network with the LinkedIn Labs InMaps (*http://bit.ly/1a1mgx2*). It constructs a graphical representation of your network using some additional information that isn't directly available to you through the API and produces a compelling visualization.

- Take a look at `geodict` (*http://bit.ly/1a1mgxd*) and some of the other geo utilities in the Data Science Toolkit (*http://bit.ly/1a1mgNK*). Can you extract locations from arbitrary prose and visualize them in a meaningful way to gain insight into what's happening in the data without having to read through all of it?

- Mine Twitter or Facebook profiles for geo information and visualize it in a meaningful way. Tweets and Facebook posts often contain geocodes as part of their structured metadata.

- The LinkedIn API provides a means of retrieving a connection's Twitter handle. How many of your LinkedIn connections have Twitter accounts associated with their professional profiles? How active are their accounts? How *professional* are their online Twitter personalities from the perspective of a potential employer?

- Apply clustering techniques from this chapter to tweets. Given a user's tweets, can you extract meaningful tweet entities, define a meaningful similarity computation, and cluster tweets in a meaningful way?

- Apply clustering techniques from this chapter to Facebook data such as likes or posts. Given a collection of Facebook likes for a friend, can you define a meaningful similarity computation, and cluster the likes in a meaningful way? Given all of the likes for all of your friends, can you cluster the likes (or your friends) in a meaningful way?

3.6. Online Resources

The following list of links from this chapter may be useful for review:

- Bing maps portal (*http://bit.ly/1a1m5lq*)
- Centroid (*http://bit.ly/1a1mbcW*)
- D3.js examples gallery (*http://bit.ly/1a1lMal*)
- Data Science Toolkit (*http://bit.ly/1a1mgNK*)
- Dendogram (*http://bit.ly/1a1md4B*)
- Export LinkedIn Connections (*http://linkd.in/1a1m4ho*)
- geopy GitHub code repository (*http://bit.ly/1a1m7Ka*)
- Keyhole Markup Language (KML) (*http://bit.ly/1a1meWb*)
- Levenshtein distance (*http://bit.ly/1a1mcNO*)
- LinkedIn API rate-throttling limits (*http://linkd.in/1a1m2WP*)
- LinkedIn API field selector syntax (*http://linkd.in/1a1m3tV*)
- LinkedIn Developers (*http://linkd.in/1a1lZuj*)
- LinkedIn InMaps (*http://bit.ly/1a1mgx2*)
- Mapping GeoJSON files on GitHub (*http://bit.ly/1a1mp3J*)
- python-linkedin GitHub code repository (*http://bit.ly/1a1m2Gk*)
- Travelling salesman problem (*http://bit.ly/1a1mhkF*)
- Tutorial on Clustering Algorithms (*http://bit.ly/1a1mbtp*)

## CHAPTER 4

Mining Google+: Computing Document Similarity, Extracting Collocations, and More

This chapter introduces some fundamental concepts from text mining[1] and is somewhat of an inflection point in this book. Whereas we started the book with basic frequency analyses of Twitter data and gradually worked up to more sophisticated clustering analyses of messier data from LinkedIn profiles, this chapter begins munging and making sense of textual information in documents by introducing information retrieval (IR) theory fundamentals such as TF-IDF, cosine similarity, and collocation detection. Accordingly, its content is a bit more complex than that of the chapters before it, and it may be helpful to have worked through those chapters before picking up here.

Google+ (*http://bit.ly/1a1mqES*) initially serves as our primary source of data for this chapter because it's inherently social, features content that's often expressed as longer-form notes that resemble blog entries, and is now an established staple in the social web. It's not hard to make a case that Google+ *activities* (notes) fill a niche somewhere between Twitter and blogs. The concepts from previous chapters could equally be applied to the data behind Google+'s diverse and powerful API, although we'll opt to leave regurgitations of those examples (mostly) as exercises for the motivated reader.

Wherever possible we won't reinvent the wheel and implement analysis tools from scratch, but we will take a couple of "deep dives" when particularly foundational topics come up that are essential to an understanding of text mining. The Natural Language Toolkit (NLTK) is a powerful technology that you may recall from Chapter 3; it provides

---

1. This book avoids splitting hairs over exactly what differences could be implied by common phrases such as *text mining*, *unstructured data analytics* (UDA), or *information retrieval*, and simply treats them as essentially the same thing.

many of the tools we'll use in this chapter. Its rich suites of APIs can be a bit over-whelming at first, but don't worry: while text analytics is an incredibly diverse and complex field of study, there are lots of powerful fundamentals that can take you a long way without too significant of an investment. This chapter and the chapters after it aim to hone in on those fundamentals. (A full-blown introduction to NLTK is outside the scope of this book, but you can review the full text of *Natural Language Processing with Python: Analyzing Text with the Natural Language Toolkit* [O'Reilly] at the NLTK web-site (*http://bit.ly/1a1mtAk*).)

 Always get the latest bug-fixed source code for this chapter (and every other chapter) online at *http://bit.ly/MiningTheSocialWeb2E*. Be sure to also take advantage of this book's virtual machine experience, as described in Appendix A, to maximize your enjoyment of the sample code.

4.1. Overview

This chapter uses Google+ to begin our journey in analyzing human language data. In this chapter you'll learn about:

- The Google+ API and making API requests
- TF-IDF (Term Frequency–Inverse Document Frequency), a fundamental technique for analyzing words in documents
- How to apply NLTK to the problem of understanding human language
- How to apply cosine similarity to common problems such as querying documents by keyword
- How to extract meaningful phrases from human language data by detecting collocation patterns

4.2. Exploring the Google+ API

Anyone with a Gmail account can trivially create a Google+ account and start collaborating with friends. From a product standpoint, Google+ has evolved rapidly and used some of the most compelling features of existing social network platforms such as Twitter and Facebook in carving out its own set of unique capabilities. As with the other social websites featured in this book, a full overview of Google+ isn't in scope for this chapter, but you can easily read about it (or sign up) online. The best way to learn is by creating an account and spending some time exploring. For the most part, where there's a feature in the user interface, there's an API that provides that feature that you can tap into. Suffice it to say that Google+ has leveraged tried-and-true features of existing social networks, such as marking content with hashtags and maintaining a profile according to customizable privacy settings, with additional novelties such as a fresh take on content sharing called *circles*, video chats called *hangouts*, and extensive integration with other Google services such as Gmail contacts. In Google+ API (*http://bit.ly/1a1mtR0*) parlance, social interactions are framed in terms of people, activities, comments, and moments.

The API documentation that's available online is always the definitive source of guidance, but a brief overview may be helpful to get you thinking about how Google+ compares to another platform such as Twitter or Facebook:

People (http://bit.ly/1a1mu7B)

> People are Google+ users. Programmatically, you'll either discover users by using the search API, look them up by a personalized URL (*http://bit.ly/1a1muEo*) if they're a celebrity type,[2] or strip their Google+ IDs out of the URLs that appear in your web browser and use them for exploring their profiles. Later in this chapter, we'll use the search API to find users on Google+.

Activities (http://bit.ly/1a1muV4)

> Activities are the things that people do on Google+. An activity is essentially a note and can be as long or short as the author likes: it can be as long as a blog post, or it can be devoid of any real textual meaning (e.g., just used to share links or multimedia content). Given a Google+ user, you can easily retrieve a list of that person's activities, and we'll do that later in this chapter. Like a tweet, an activity contains a lot of fascinating metadata , such as the number of times the activity has been reshared.

Comments (http://bit.ly/1a1mvrX)

> Leaving comments is the way Google+ users interact with one another. Simple statistical analysis of comments on Google+ could be very interesting and potentially reveal a lot of insights into a person's social circles or the virality of content. For example, which other Google+ users most frequently comment on activities? Which activities have the highest numbers of comments (and why)?

Moments (http://bit.ly/1a1mvIx)

> Moments are a relatively recent addition to Google+ and represent a way of capturing interactions between a user and a Google+ application. Moments are similar to Facebook's social graph stories (*http://bit.ly/1a1my7k*) in that they are designed to capture and create opportunities for user interaction with an application that can be displayed on a timeline. For example, if you were to make a purchase in an application, upload a photo, or watch a YouTube video, it could be captured as a

---

2. Google+ only offered personalized URLs such as *https://plus.google.com/+TimOReilly* to well-known individuals at the outset, but is in the process of making them available to all users. Until you are either selected by Google or eligible to apply, you'll have to continue using your more arcane URL with a numeric identifier in it (such as *https://plus.google.com/107033731246200681024*).

moment (something you did in time) and displayed in a history of your actions or shared with friends in an activity stream by the application.

For the purposes of this chapter, we'll be focusing on harvesting and analyzing Google+ activity data that is textual and intended to convey the same kind of meaning that you might encounter in a tweet, blog post, or Facebook status update. In other words, we'll be trying to analyze human language data. If you haven't signed up for Google+ yet, it's worth taking the time to do so, as well as spending a few moments to familiarize yourself with a Google+ profile. One of the easiest ways to find specific users on Google+ is to just search for them at *http://plus.google.com*, and explore the platform from there.

As you explore Google+, bear in mind that it has a unique set of capabilities and is a little awkward to compare directly to other social web properties. If you're expecting it to be a straightforward comparison, you might find yourself a bit surprised. It's similar to Twitter in that it provides a "following" model where you can add individuals to one of your Google+ circles and keep up with their happenings without any approval on their part, but the Google+ platform also offers rich integration with other Google web properties, sports a powerful feature for videoconferencing (hangouts), and has an API similar to Facebook's in the way that users share content and interact. Without further ado, let's get busy exploring the API and work toward mining some data.

4.2.1. Making Google+ API Requests

From a software development standpoint, Google+ leverages OAuth like the rest of the social web to enable an application that you'll build to access data on a user's behalf, so you'll need to register an application to get appropriate credentials for accessing the Google+ platform. The Google API Console (*http://bit.ly/1a1mwMP*) provides a means of registering an application (called a *project* in the Google API Console) to get OAuth credentials but also exposes an API key that you can use for "simple API access." This API key is what we'll use in this chapter to programmatically access the Google+ platform and just about every other Google service.

Once you've created an application, you'll also need to specifically enable it to use Google+ as a separate step. Figure 4-1 provides a screenshot of the Google+ API Console as well as a view that demonstrates what it looks like when you have enabled your application for Google+ API access.

Figure 4-1. Registering an application with the Google API Console to gain API access to Google services; don't forget to enable Google+ API access as one of the service options

You can install a Python package called `google-api-python-client` for accessing Google's API via **pip install google-api-python-client**. This is one of the standard Python-based options for accessing Google+ data. The online documentation for `google-api-python-client` (*http://bit.ly/1a1mzYI*) is marginally helpful in familiarizing yourself with the capabilities of what it offers, but in general, you'll just be plugging parameters from the official Google+ API documents into some predictable access patterns with the Python package. Once you've walked through a couple of exercises, it's a relatively straightforward process.

 Don't forget that `pydoc` can be helpful for gathering clues about a package, class, or method in a terminal as you are learning it. The `help` function in a standard Python interpreter is also useful. Recall that appending ? to a method name in IPython is a shortcut for displaying its docstring.

As an initial exercise, let's consider the problem of locating a person on Google+. Like any other social web API, the Google+ API offers a means of searching, and in particular we'll be interested in the People: search API (*http://bit.ly/1a1mzrQ*). Example 4-1 illustrates how to search for a person with the Google+ API. Since Tim O'Reilly is a well-known personality with an active and compelling Google+ account, let's look him up.

The basic pattern that you'll repeatedly use with the Python client is to create an instance of a service that's parameterized for Google+ access with your API key that you can then instantiate for particular platform services. Here, we create a connection to the People API by invoking `service.people()` and then chaining on some additional API operations deduced from reviewing the API documentation online. In a moment we'll query for activity data, and you'll see that the same basic pattern holds.

Example 4-1. Searching for a person with the Google+ API

```
import httplib2
import json
import apiclient.discovery # pip install google-api-python-client

# XXX: Enter any person's name
Q = "Tim O'Reilly"

# XXX: Enter in your API key from  https://code.google.com/apis/console
API_KEY = ''

service = apiclient.discovery.build('plus', 'v1', http=httplib2.Http(),
                                    developerKey=API_KEY)

people_feed = service.people().search(query=Q).execute()

print json.dumps(people_feed['items'], indent=1)
```

Following are sample results for searching for Tim O'Reilly:

```
[
 {
  "kind": "plus#person",
  "displayName": "Tim O'Reilly",
  "url": "https://plus.google.com/+TimOReilly",
  "image": {
   "url": "https://lh4.googleusercontent.com/-J8..."
  },
  "etag": "\"WIBkkymG3C8dXBjiaEVMpCLNTTs/wwgOCMn...\"",
  "id": "107033731246200681024",
  "objectType": "person"
 },
 {
  "kind": "plus#person",
  "displayName": "Tim O'Reilly",
  "url": "https://plus.google.com/11566571170551...",
  "image": {
   "url": "https://lh3.googleusercontent.com/-yka..."
  },
  "etag": "\"WIBkkymG3C8dXBjiaEVMpCLNTTs/0z-EwRK7...\"",
  "id": "115665711705516993369",
  "objectType": "person"
 },
 ...
]
```

The results do indeed return a list of people named Tim O'Reilly, but how can we tell which one of these results refers to the well-known Tim O'Reilly of technology fame that we are looking for? One option would be to request profile or activity information for each of these results and try to disambiguate them manually. Another option is to render the avatars included in each of the results, which is trivial to do by rendering the avatars as images within IPython Notebook. Example 4-2 illustrates how to display avatars and the corresponding ID values for each search result by generating HTML and rendering it inline as a result in the notebook.

Example 4-2. Displaying Google+ avatars in IPython Notebook provides a quick way to disambiguate the search results and discover the person you are looking for

```
from IPython.core.display import HTML

html = []

for p in people_feed['items']:
    html += ['<p><img src="%s" /> %s: %s</p>' % \
            (p['image']['url'], p['id'], p['displayName'])]

HTML(''.join(html))
```

Sample results are displayed in Figure 4-2 and provide the "quick fix" that we're looking for in our search for the particular Tim O'Reilly of O'Reilly Media.

```
In [4]:  from IPython.core.display import HTML

         html = []

         for p in people_feed['items']:
             html += ['<p><img src="%s" /> %s: %s</p>' % \
                         (p['image']['url'], p['id'], p['displayName'])]

         HTML(''.join(html))

Out[4]:

         107033731246200681024: Tim O'Reilly


         107415629896108700526: Timothy O'Reilly


         115665711705516993369: Tim O'Reilly


         104189405442379396369: Timothy O'Reilly


         102994447097932477991: Timothy O'Reilly
```

Figure 4-2. Rendering Google+ avatars as images allows you to quickly scan the search results to disambiguate the person you are looking for

Although there's a multiplicity of things we could do with the People API, our focus in this chapter is on an analysis of the textual content in accounts, so let's turn our attention to the task of retrieving *activities* associated with this account. As you're about to find out, Google+ activities are the linchpin of Google+ content, containing a variety of rich content associated with the account and providing logical pivots to other platform objects such as *comments*. To get some activities, we'll need to tweak the design pattern we applied for searching for people, as illustrated in Example 4-3.

Example 4-3. Fetching recent activities for a particular Google+ user

```
import httplib2
import json
import apiclient.discovery

USER_ID = '107033731246200681024' # Tim O'Reilly
```

```
# XXX: Re-enter your API_KEY from  https://code.google.com/apis/console
# if not currently set
# API_KEY = ''

service = apiclient.discovery.build('plus', 'v1', http=httplib2.Http(),
                                    developerKey=API_KEY)

activity_feed = service.activities().list(
  userId=USER_ID,
  collection='public',
  maxResults='100' # Max allowed per API
).execute()

print json.dumps(activity_feed, indent=1)
```

Sample results for the first item in the results (`activity_feed['items'][0]`) follow and illustrate the basic nature of a Google+ activity:

```
{
 "kind": "plus#activity",
 "provider": {
  "title": "Google+"
 },
 "title": "This is the best piece about privacy that I've read in a ...",
 "url": "https://plus.google.com/107033731246200681024/posts/78UeZ1jdRsQ",
 "object": {
  "resharers": {
   "totalItems": 191,
   "selfLink": "https://www.googleapis.com/plus/v1/activities/z125xvy..."
  },
  "attachments": [
   {
    "content": "Many governments (including our own, here in the US) ...",
    "url": "http://www.zdziarski.com/blog/?p=2155",
    "displayName": "On Expectation of Privacy | Jonathan Zdziarski's Domain",
    "objectType": "article"
   }
  ],
  "url": "https://plus.google.com/107033731246200681024/posts/78UeZ1jdRsQ",
  "content": "This is the best piece about privacy that I&#39;ve read ...",
  "plusoners": {
   "totalItems": 356,
   "selfLink": "https://www.googleapis.com/plus/v1/activities/z125xvyid..."
  },
  "replies": {
   "totalItems": 48,
   "selfLink": "https://www.googleapis.com/plus/v1/activities/z125xvyid..."
  },
  "objectType": "note"
 },
 "updated": "2013-04-25T14:46:16.908Z",
 "actor": {
```

```
      "url": "https://plus.google.com/107033731246200681024",
      "image": {
       "url": "https://lh4.googleusercontent.com/-J8nmMwIhpiA/AAAAAAAAAAI/A..."
      },
      "displayName": "Tim O'Reilly",
      "id": "107033731246200681024"
     },
     "access": {
      "items": [
       {
         "type": "public"
       }
      ],
      "kind": "plus#acl",
      "description": "Public"
     },
     "verb": "post",
     "etag": "\"WIBkkymG3C8dXBjiaEVMpCLNTTs/d-ppAzuVZpXrW_YeLXc5ctstsCM\"",
     "published": "2013-04-25T14:46:16.908Z",
     "id": "z125xvyidpqjdtol423gcxizetybvpydh"
    }
```

Each activity object follows a three-tuple pattern of the form *(actor, verb, object)*. In this post, the tuple *(Tim O'Reilly, post, note)* tells us that this particular item in the results is a *note*, which is essentially just a status update with some textual content. A closer look at the result reveals that the content is something that Tim O'Reilly feels strongly about as indicated by the title "This is the best piece about privacy that I've read in a long time!" and hints that the note is active as evidenced by the number of reshares and comments.

If you reviewed the output carefully, you may have noticed that the content field for the activity contains HTML markup, as evidenced by the HTML entity I've that appears. In general, you should assume that the textual data exposed as Google+ activities contains some basic markup—such as <br /> tags and escaped HTML entities for apostrophes—so as a best practice we need to do a little bit of additional filtering to clean it up. Example 4-4 provides an example of how to distill plain text from the content field of a note by introducing a function called cleanHtml. It takes advantage of a clean_html function provided by NLTK and another handy package for manipulating HTML, called BeautifulSoup, that converts HTML entities back to plain text. If you haven't already encountered BeautifulSoup, it's a package that you won't want to live without once you've added it to your toolbox—it has the ability to process HTML in a reasonable way even if it is invalid and violates standards or other reasonable expectations (à la web data). You should install these packages via **pip install nltk beauti fulsoup4** if you haven't already.

Example 4-4. Cleaning HTML in Google+ content by stripping out HTML tags and converting HTML entities back to plain-text representations

```
from nltk import clean_html
from BeautifulSoup import BeautifulStoneSoup

# clean_html removes tags and
# BeautifulStoneSoup converts HTML entities

def cleanHtml(html):
  if html == "": return ""

  return BeautifulStoneSoup(clean_html(html),
        convertEntities=BeautifulStoneSoup.HTML_ENTITIES).contents[0]

print activity_feed['items'][0]['object']['content']
print
print cleanHtml(activity_feed['items'][0]['object']['content'])
```

The output from the note's content, once cleansed with `cleanHtml`, is very clean text that can be processed without additional concerns about noise in the content. As we'll learn in this chapter and follow-on chapters about text mining, reduction of noise in text content is a critical aspect of improving accuracy. The before and after content follows.

Here's the raw content in `activity_feed['items'][0]['object']['content']`:

```
This is the best piece about privacy that I&#39;ve read in a long time!
If it doesn&#39;t change how you think about the privacy issue, I&#39;ll be
surprised.  It opens:<br /><br />&quot;Many governments (including our own,
here in the US) would have its citizens believe that privacy is a switch (that
is, you either reasonably expect it, or you don't). This has been demonstrated
in many legal tests, and abused in many circumstances ranging from spying
on electronic mail, to drones in our airspace monitoring the movements of
private citizens. But privacy doesn't work like a switch - at least it shouldn't
for a country that recognizes that privacy is an inherent right. In fact,
privacy, like other components to security, works in layers...&quot;<br /><br />
Please read!
```

And here's the content rendered after cleansing with `cleanHtml(activity _feed['items'][0]['object']['content'])`:

```
This is the best piece about privacy that I've read in a long time!  If it
doesn't change how you think about the privacy issue, I'll be surprised.  It
opens: "Many governments (including our own, here in the US) would have its
citizens believe that privacy is a switch (that is, you either reasonably expect it,
or you don't). This has been demonstrated in many legal tests, and abused
in many circumstances ranging from spying on electronic mail, to drones in our
airspace monitoring the movements of private citizens. But privacy doesn't work like
a switch - at least it shouldn't for a country that recognizes that privacy is an
inherent right. In fact, privacy, like other components to security, works in
layers..." Please read!
```

The ability to query out clean text from Google+ is the basis for the remainder of the text mining exercises in this chapter, but one additional consideration that you may find useful before we focus our attention elsewhere is a pattern for fetching multiple pages of content.

Whereas the previous example fetched 100 activities, the maximum number of results for a query, it may be the case that you'll want to iterate over an activities feed and retrieve more than the maximum number of activities per page. The pattern for pagination is outlined in the HTTP API Overview (*http://bit.ly/1a1mAfm*), and the Python client wrapper takes care of most of the hassle.

Example 4-5 shows how to fetch multiple pages of activities and distill the text from them if they are notes and have meaningful content.

Example 4-5. Looping over multiple pages of Google+ activities and distilling clean text from notes

```python
import os
import httplib2
import json
import apiclient.discovery
from BeautifulSoup import BeautifulStoneSoup
from nltk import clean_html

USER_ID = '107033731246200681024' # Tim O'Reilly

# XXX: Re-enter your API_KEY from  https://code.google.com/apis/console
# if not currently set
# API_KEY = ''

MAX_RESULTS = 200 # Will require multiple requests

def cleanHtml(html):
  if html == "": return ""

  return BeautifulStoneSoup(clean_html(html),
          convertEntities=BeautifulStoneSoup.HTML_ENTITIES).contents[0]

service = apiclient.discovery.build('plus', 'v1', http=httplib2.Http(),
                                    developerKey=API_KEY)

activity_feed = service.activities().list(
  userId=USER_ID,
  collection='public',
  maxResults='100' # Max allowed per request
)

activity_results = []

while activity_feed != None and len(activity_results) < MAX_RESULTS:
```

```
activities = activity_feed.execute()

if 'items' in activities:

    for activity in activities['items']:

        if activity['object']['objectType'] == 'note' and \
            activity['object']['content'] != '':

            activity['title'] = cleanHtml(activity['title'])
            activity['object']['content'] = cleanHtml(activity['object']['content'])
            activity_results += [activity]

    # list_next requires the previous request and response objects
    activity_feed = service.activities().list_next(activity_feed, activities)

# Write the output to a file for convenience

f = open(os.path.join('resources', 'ch04-googleplus', USER_ID + '.json'), 'w')
f.write(json.dumps(activity_results, indent=1))
f.close()

print str(len(activity_results)), "activities written to", f.name
```

With the know-how to explore the Google+ API and fetch some interesting human language data from activities' content, let's now turn our attention to the problem of analyzing the content.

4.3. A Whiz-Bang Introduction to TF-IDF

Although rigorous approaches to natural language processing (NLP) that include such things as sentence segmentation, tokenization, word chunking, and entity detection are necessary in order to achieve the deepest possible understanding of textual data, it's helpful to first introduce some fundamentals from information retrieval theory. The remainder of this chapter introduces some of its more foundational aspects, including TF-IDF, the cosine similarity metric, and some of the theory behind collocation detection. Chapter 5 provides a deeper discussion of NLP as a logical continuation of this discussion.

 If you want to dig deeper into IR theory, the full text of Christopher Manning, Prabhakar Raghavan, and Hinrich Schütze's *Introduction to Information Retrieval* (Cambridge University Press) is available on-line (*http://stanford.io/1a1mAvP*) and provides more information than you could (probably) ever want to know about the field.

Information retrieval is an extensive field with many specialties. This discussion narrows in on TF-IDF, one of the most fundamental techniques for retrieving relevant documents from a corpus (collection). TF-IDF stands for *term frequency-inverse document frequency* and can be used to query a corpus by calculating normalized scores that express the relative importance of terms in the documents.

Mathematically, TF-IDF is expressed as the product of the term frequency and the inverse document frequency, *tf_idf = tf*idf*, where the term *tf* represents the importance of a term in a specific document, and *idf* represents the importance of a term relative to the entire corpus. Multiplying these terms together produces a score that accounts for both factors and has been an integral part of every major search engine at some point in its existence. To get a more intuitive idea of how TF-IDF works, let's walk through each of the calculations involved in computing the overall score.

4.3.1. Term Frequency

For simplicity in illustration, suppose you have a corpus containing three sample documents and terms are calculated by simply breaking on whitespace, as illustrated in Example 4-6 as ordinary Python code.

Example 4-6. Sample data structures used in illustrations for the rest of this chapter

```
corpus = {
 'a' : "Mr. Green killed Colonel Mustard in the study with the candlestick. \
Mr. Green is not a very nice fellow.",
 'b' : "Professor Plum has a green plant in his study.",
 'c' : "Miss Scarlett watered Professor Plum's green plant while he was away \
from his office last week."
}
terms = {
 'a' : [ i.lower() for i in corpus['a'].split() ],
 'b' : [ i.lower() for i in corpus['b'].split() ],
 'c' : [ i.lower() for i in corpus['c'].split() ]
 }
```

A term's frequency could simply be represented as the number of times it occurs in the text, but it is more commonly the case that you normalize it by taking into account the total number of terms in the text, so that the overall score accounts for document length relative to a term's frequency. For example, "green" (once normalized to lowercase) occurs twice in corpus['a'] and only once in corpus['b'], so corpus['a'] would produce a higher score if frequency were the only scoring criterion. However, if you normalize for document length, corpus['b'] would have a slightly higher term frequency score for "green" (1/9) than corpus['a'] (2/19), because corpus['b'] is shorter than corpus['a']—even though "green" occurs more frequently in corpus['a']. A common technique for scoring a compound query such as "Mr. Green" is to sum the term frequency scores for each of the query terms in each document, and return the documents ranked by the summed term frequency score.

Let's illustrate how term frequency works by querying our sample corpus for "Mr. Green," which would produce the normalized scores reported in Table 4-1 for each document.

Table 4-1. Sample term frequency scores for "Mr. Green"

Document	tf(mr.)	tf(green)	Sum
corpus['a']	2/19	2/19	4/19 (0.2105)
corpus['b']	0	1/9	1/9 (0.1111)
corpus['c']	0	1/16	1/16 (0.0625)

For this contrived example, a cumulative term frequency scoring scheme works out and returns corpus['a'] (the document that we'd expect it to return), since corpus['a'] is the only one that contains the compound token "Mr. Green." However, a number of problems could have emerged, because the term frequency scoring model looks at each document as an unordered collection of words. For example, queries for "Green Mr." or "Green Mr. Foo" would have returned the exact same scores as the query for "Mr. Green," even though neither of those phrases appears in the sample sentences. Additionally, there are a number of scenarios that we could easily contrive to illustrate fairly poor results from the term frequency ranking technique given that trailing punctuation is not handled properly, and that the context around tokens of interest is not taken into account by the calculations.

Considering term frequency alone turns out to be a common source of problems when scoring on a document-by-document basis, because it doesn't account for very frequent words, called stopwords,[3] that are common across many documents. In other words, all terms are weighted equally, regardless of their actual importance. For example, "the green plant" contains the stopword "the," which skews overall term frequency scores in favor of corpus['a'] because "the" appears twice in that document, as does "green." In contrast, in corpus['c'] "green" and "plant" each appear only once.

Consequently, the scores would break down as shown in Table 4-2, with corpus['a'] ranked as more relevant than corpus['c'], even though intuition might lead you to believe that ideal query results probably shouldn't have turned out that way. (Fortunately, however, corpus['b'] still ranks highest.)

---

3. *Stopwords* are words that appear frequently in text but usually relay little information. Common examples of stopwords are *a*, *an*, *the*, and other determinants.

Table 4-2. Sample term frequency scores for "the green plant"

Document	tf(the)	tf(green)	tf(plant)	Sum
corpus['a']	2/19	2/19	0	4/19 (0.2105)
corpus['b']	0	1/9	1/9	2/9 (0.2222)
corpus['c']	0	1/16	1/16	1/8 (0.125)

4.3.2. Inverse Document Frequency

Toolkits such as NLTK provide lists of stopwords that can be used to filter out terms such as *and*, *a*, and *the*, but keep in mind that there may be terms that evade even the best stopword lists and yet still are quite common to specialized domains. Although you can certainly customize a list of stopwords with domain knowledge, the inverse document frequency metric is a calculation that provides a generic normalization metric for a corpus. It works in the general case by accounting for the appearance of common terms across a set of documents by considering the total number of documents in which a query term ever appears.

The intuition behind this metric is that it produces a higher value if a term is somewhat uncommon across the corpus than if it is common, which helps to account for the problem with stopwords we just investigated. For example, a query for "green" in the corpus of sample documents should return a lower inverse document frequency score than a query for "candlestick," because "green" appears in every document while "candlestick" appears in only one. Mathematically, the only nuance of interest for the inverse document frequency calculation is that a logarithm is used to reduce the result into a compressed range, since its usual application is in multiplying it against term frequency as a scaling factor. For reference, a logarithm function is shown in Figure 4-3; as you can see, the logarithm function grows very slowly as values for its domain increase, effectively "squashing" its input.

Figure 4-3. The logarithm function "squashes" a large range of values into a more compressed space—notice how slowly the y-values grow as the values of x-increase

Table 4-3 provides inverse document frequency scores that correspond to the term frequency scores for in the previous section. Example 4-7 in the next section presents source code that shows how to compute these scores. In the meantime, you can notionally think of the IDF score for a term as the logarithm of a quotient that is defined by the number of documents in the corpus divided by the number of texts in the corpus that contain the term. When viewing these tables, keep in mind that whereas a term frequency score is calculated on a per-document basis, an inverse document frequency score is computed on the basis of the entire corpus. Hopefully this makes sense given that its purpose is to act as a normalizer for common words across the entire corpus.

Table 4-3. Sample inverse document frequency scores for terms appearing in "mr. green" and "the green plant"

idf(mr.)	idf(green)	idf(the)	idf(plant)
$1 + \log(3/1) = 2.0986$	$1 + \log(3/3) = 1.0$	$1 + \log(3/1) = 2.0986$	$1 + \log(3/2) = 1.4055$

4.3.3. TF-IDF

At this point, we've come full circle and devised a way to compute a score for a multiterm query that accounts for the frequency of terms appearing in a document, the length of the document in which any particular term appears, and the overall uniqueness of the terms across documents in the entire corpus. We can combine the concepts behind term frequency and inverse document frequency into a single score by multiplying them together, so that *TF–IDF = TF*IDF*. Example 4-7 is a naive implementation of this discussion that should help solidify the concepts described. Take a moment to review it, and then we'll discuss a few sample queries.

Example 4-7. Running TF-IDF on sample data

```
from math import log

# XXX: Enter in a query term from the corpus variable
QUERY_TERMS = ['mr.', 'green']

def tf(term, doc, normalize=True):
    doc = doc.lower().split()
    if normalize:
        return doc.count(term.lower()) / float(len(doc))
    else:
        return doc.count(term.lower()) / 1.0


def idf(term, corpus):
    num_texts_with_term = len([True for text in corpus if term.lower()
                              in text.lower().split()])

    # tf-idf calc involves multiplying against a tf value less than 0, so it's
    # necessary to return a value greater than 1 for consistent scoring.
```

```
    # (Multiplying two values less than 1 returns a value less than each of
    # them.)

    try:
        return 1.0 + log(float(len(corpus)) / num_texts_with_term)
    except ZeroDivisionError:
        return 1.0


def tf_idf(term, doc, corpus):
    return tf(term, doc) * idf(term, corpus)


corpus = \
    {'a': 'Mr. Green killed Colonel Mustard in the study with the candlestick. \
Mr. Green is not a very nice fellow.',
     'b': 'Professor Plum has a green plant in his study.',
     'c': "Miss Scarlett watered Professor Plum's green plant while he was away \
from his office last week."}

for (k, v) in sorted(corpus.items()):
    print k, ':', v
print

# Score queries by calculating cumulative tf_idf score for each term in query

query_scores = {'a': 0, 'b': 0, 'c': 0}
for term in [t.lower() for t in QUERY_TERMS]:
    for doc in sorted(corpus):
        print 'TF(%s): %s' % (doc, term), tf(term, corpus[doc])
    print 'IDF: %s' % (term, ), idf(term, corpus.values())
    print

    for doc in sorted(corpus):
        score = tf_idf(term, corpus[doc], corpus.values())
        print 'TF-IDF(%s): %s' % (doc, term), score
        query_scores[doc] += score
    print

print "Overall TF-IDF scores for query '%s'" % (' '.join(QUERY_TERMS), )
for (doc, score) in sorted(query_scores.items()):
    print doc, score
```

Sample output follows:

```
    a : Mr. Green killed Colonel Mustard in the study...
    b : Professor Plum has a green plant in his study.
    c : Miss Scarlett watered Professor Plum's green...

    TF(a): mr. 0.105263157895
    TF(b): mr. 0.0
    TF(c): mr. 0.0
    IDF: mr. 2.09861228867
```

```
TF-IDF(a): mr. 0.220906556702
TF-IDF(b): mr. 0.0
TF-IDF(c): mr. 0.0

TF(a): green 0.105263157895
TF(b): green 0.111111111111
TF(c): green 0.0625
IDF: green 1.0

TF-IDF(a): green 0.105263157895
TF-IDF(b): green 0.111111111111
TF-IDF(c): green 0.0625

Overall TF-IDF scores for query 'mr. green'
a 0.326169714597
b 0.111111111111
c 0.0625
```

Although we're working on a trivially small scale, the calculations involved work the same for larger data sets. Table 4-4 is a consolidated adaptation of the program's output for three sample queries that involve four distinct terms:

- "green"
- "mr. green"
- "the green plant"

Even though the IDF calculations for terms are computed on the basis of the entire corpus, they are displayed on a per-document basis so that you can easily verify TF-IDF scores by skimming a single row and multiplying two numbers. *As you work through the query results, you'll find that it's remarkable just how powerful TF-IDF is, given that it doesn't account for the proximity or ordering of words in a document.*

Table 4-4. Calculations involved in TF-IDF sample queries, as computed by Example 4-7

Document	tf(mr.)	tf(green)	tf(the)	tf(plant)
corpus['a']	0.1053	0.1053	0.1053	0
corpus['b']	0	0.1111	0	0.1111
corpus['c']	0	0.0625	0	0.0625

idf(mr.)	idf(green)	idf(the)	idf(plant)
2.0986	1.0	2.099	1.4055

	tf-idf(mr.)	tf-idf(green)	tf-idf(the)	tf-idf(plant)
corpus['a']	0.1053*2.0986 = 0.2209	0.1053*1.0 = 0.1053	0.1053*2.099 = 0.2209	0*1.4055 = 0
corpus['b']	0*2.0986 = 0	0.1111*1.0 = 0.1111	0*2.099 = 0	0.1111*1.4055 = 0.1562
corpus['c']	0*2.0986 = 0	0.0625*1.0 = 0.0625	0*2.099 = 0	0.0625*1.4055 = 0.0878

The same results for each query are shown in Table 4-5, with the TF-IDF values summed on a per-document basis.

Table 4-5. Summed TF-IDF values for sample queries as computed by Example 4-7 (values in bold are the maximum scores for each of the three queries)

Query	corpus['a']	corpus['b']	corpus['c']
green	0.1053	**0.1111**	0.0625
Mr. Green	0.2209 + 0.1053 = **0.3262**	0 + 0.1111 = 0.1111	0 + 0.0625 = 0.0625
the green plant	0.2209 + 0.1053 + 0 = **0.3262**	0 + 0.1111 + 0.1562 = 0.2673	0 + 0.0625 + 0.0878 = 0.1503

From a qualitative standpoint, the query results are quite reasonable. The corpus['b'] document is the winner for the query "green," with corpus['a'] just a hair behind. In this case, the deciding factor was the length of corpus['b'] being much smaller than that of corpus['a']—the normalized TF score tipped the results in favor of corpus['b'] for its one occurrence of "green," even though "Green" appeared in corpus['a'] two times. Since "green" appears in all three documents, the net effect of the IDF term in the calculations was a wash.

Do note, however, that if we had returned 0.0 instead of 1.0 for "green," as is done in some IDF implementations, the TF-IDF scores for "green" would have been 0.0 for all three documents due the effect of multiplying the TF score by zero. Depending on the particular situation, it may be better to return 0.0 for the IDF scores rather than 1.0. For example, if you had 100,000 documents and "green" appeared in all of them, you'd almost certainly consider it to be a stopword and want to remove its effects in a query entirely.

For the query "Mr. Green," the clear and appropriate winner is the corpus['a'] document. However, this document also comes out on top for the query "the green plant." A worthwhile exercise is to consider why corpus['a'] scored highest for this query as opposed to corpus['b'], which at first blush might have seemed a little more obvious.

A final nuanced point to observe is that the sample implementation provided in Example 4-7 adjusts the IDF score by adding a value of 1.0 to the logarithm calculation, for the purposes of illustration and because we're dealing with a trivial document set. Without the 1.0 adjustment in the calculation, it would be possible to have the idf function return values that are less than 1.0, which would result in two fractions being multiplied in the TF-IDF calculation. Since multiplying two fractions together results in a value smaller than either of them, this turns out to be an easily overlooked edge case in the TF-IDF calculation. Recall that the intuition behind the TF-IDF calculation is that we'd like to be able to multiply two terms in a way that consistently produces larger TF-IDF scores for more relevant queries than for less relevant queries.

4.4. Querying Human Language Data with TF-IDF

Let's take the theory that you just learned about in the previous section and put it to work. In this section, you'll get officially introduced to NLTK, a powerful toolkit for processing natural language, and use it to support the analysis of human language data that we'll fetch from Google+.

4.4.1. Introducing the Natural Language Toolkit

NLTK is written such that you can explore data easily and begin to form some impressions without a lot of upfront investment. Before skipping ahead, though, consider following along with the interpreter session in Example 4-8 to get a feel for some of the powerful functionality that NLTK provides right out of the box. Since you may not have done much work with NLTK before, don't forget that you can use the built-in help function to get more information whenever you need it. For example, help(nltk) would provide documentation on the NLTK package in an interpreter session.

Not all of the functionality from NLTK is intended for incorporation into production software, since output is written to the console and not capturable into a data structure such as a list. In that regard, methods such as nltk.text.concordance are considered "demo functionality." Speaking of which, many of NLTK's modules have a demo function that you can call to get some idea of how to use the functionality they provide, and the source code for these demos is a great starting point for learning how to use new APIs. For example, you could run nltk.text.demo() in the interpreter to get some additional insight into the capabilities provided by the nltk.text module.

Example 4-8 demonstrates some good starting points for exploring the data with sample output included as part of an interactive interpreter session, and the same commands to explore the data are included in the IPython Notebook for this chapter. Please follow along with this example and examine the outputs of each step along the way. Are you able to follow along and understand the investigative flow of the interpreter session? Take a look, and we'll discuss some of the details after the example.

 The next example includes stopwords, which—as noted earlier—are words that appear frequently in text but usually relay very little information (e.g., *a*, *an*, *the*, and other determinants).

Example 4-8. Exploring Google+ data with NLTK

```
# Explore some of NLTK's functionality by exploring the data.
# Here are some suggestions for an interactive interpreter session.

import nltk

# Download ancillary nltk packages if not already installed
nltk.download('stopwords')

all_content = " ".join([ a['object']['content'] for a in activity_results ])

# Approximate bytes of text
print len(all_content)

tokens = all_content.split()
text = nltk.Text(tokens)

# Examples of the appearance of the word "open"
text.concordance("open")

# Frequent collocations in the text (usually meaningful phrases)
text.collocations()

# Frequency analysis for words of interest
fdist = text.vocab()
fdist["open"]
fdist["source"]
fdist["web"]
fdist["2.0"]

# Number of words in the text
len(tokens)

# Number of unique words in the text

len(fdist.keys())

# Common words that aren't stopwords
[w for w in fdist.keys()[:100] \
    if w.lower() not in nltk.corpus.stopwords.words('english')]

# Long words that aren't URLs
[w for w in fdist.keys() if len(w) > 15 and not w.startswith("http")]

# Number of URLs
len([w for w in fdist.keys() if w.startswith("http")])

# Enumerate the frequency distribution
for rank, word in enumerate(fdist):
    print rank, word, fdist[word]
```

The examples throughout this chapter, including the prior example, use the split method to tokenize text. Tokenization isn't quite as simple as splitting on whitespace, however, and Chapter 5 introduces more sophisticated approaches for tokenization that work better for the general case.

The last command in the interpreter session lists the words from the frequency distribution, sorted by frequency. Not surprisingly, stopwords like *the, to*, and *of* are the most frequently occurring, but there's a steep decline and the distribution has a very long tail. We're working with a small sample of text data, but this same property will hold true for any frequency analysis of natural language.

Zipf's law (*http://bit.ly/1a1mCUD*), a well-known empirical law of natural language, asserts that a word's frequency within a corpus is inversely proportional to its rank in the frequency table. What this means is that if the most frequently occurring term in a corpus accounts for N% of the total words, the second most frequently occurring term in the corpus should account for $(N/2)$% of the words, the third most frequent term for $(N/3)$% of the words, and so on. When graphed, such a distribution (even for a small sample of data) shows a curve that hugs each axis, as you can see in Figure 4-4.

Though perhaps not initially obvious, most of the area in such a distribution lies in its tail and for a corpus large enough to span a reasonable sample of a language, the tail is always quite long. If you were to plot this kind of distribution on a chart where each axis was scaled by a logarithm, the curve would approach a straight line for a representative sample size.

Zipf's law gives you insight into what a frequency distribution for words appearing in a corpus should look like, and it provides some rules of thumb that can be useful in estimating frequency. For example, if you know that there are a million (nonunique) words in a corpus, and you assume that the most frequently used word (usually *the*, in English) accounts for 7% of the words,[4] you could derive the total number of logical calculations an algorithm performs if you were to consider a particular slice of the terms from the frequency distribution. Sometimes this kind of simple, back-of-the-napkin arithmetic is all that it takes to sanity-check assumptions about a long-running wall-clock time, or confirm whether certain computations on a large enough data set are even tractable.

---

4. The word *the* accounts for 7% of the tokens in the Brown Corpus (*http://bit.ly/1a1mB2X*) and provides a reasonable starting point for a corpus if you don't know anything else about it.

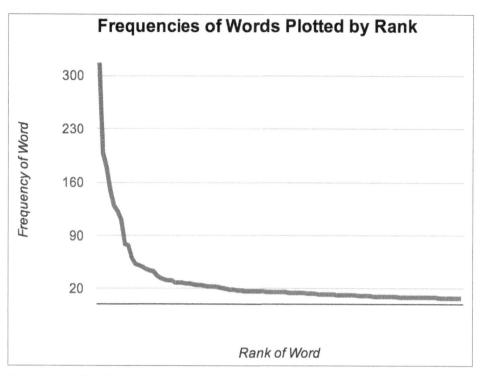

Frequencies of Words Plotted by Rank

Figure 4-4. The frequency distribution for terms appearing in a small sample of Google+ data "hugs" each axis closely; plotting it on a log-log scale would render it as something much closer to a straight line with a negative slope

Can you graph the same kind of curve shown in Figure 4-4 for the content from a few hundred Google+ activities using the techniques introduced in this chapter combined with IPython's plotting functionality, as introduced in Chapter 1?

4.4.2. Applying TF-IDF to Human Language

Let's apply TF-IDF to the Google+ data we collected earlier and see how it works out as a tool for querying the data. NLTK provides some abstractions that we can use instead of rolling our own, so there's actually very little to do now that you understand the underlying theory. The listing in Example 4-9 assumes you saved the working Google+ data from earlier in this chapter as a JSON file, and it allows you to pass in multiple query terms that are used to score the documents by relevance.

Example 4-9. Querying Google+ data with TF-IDF

```
import json
import nltk
```

```
# Load in human language data from wherever you've saved it

DATA = 'resources/ch04-googleplus/107033731246200681024.json'
data = json.loads(open(DATA).read())

# XXX: Provide your own query terms here

QUERY_TERMS = ['SOPA']

activities = [activity['object']['content'].lower().split() \
              for activity in data \
                if activity['object']['content'] != ""]

# TextCollection provides tf, idf, and tf_idf abstractions so
# that we don't have to maintain/compute them ourselves

tc = nltk.TextCollection(activities)

relevant_activities = []

for idx in range(len(activities)):
    score = 0
    for term in [t.lower() for t in QUERY_TERMS]:
        score += tc.tf_idf(term, activities[idx])
    if score > 0:
        relevant_activities.append({'score': score, 'title': data[idx]['title'],
                                    'url': data[idx]['url']})

# Sort by score and display results

relevant_activities = sorted(relevant_activities,
                             key=lambda p: p['score'], reverse=True)
for activity in relevant_activities:
    print activity['title']
    print '\tLink: %s' % (activity['url'], )
    print '\tScore: %s' % (activity['score'], )
    print
```

Sample query results for "SOPA," a controversial piece of proposed legislation, on Tim O'Reilly's Google+ data are as follows:

```
I think the key point of this piece by +Mike Loukides, that PIPA and SOPA provide
a "right of ext...
    Link: https://plus.google.com/107033731246200681024/posts/ULi4RYpvQGT
    Score: 0.0805961208217

Learn to Be a Better Activist During the SOPA Blackouts +Clay Johnson has put
together an awesome...
    Link: https://plus.google.com/107033731246200681024/posts/hrC5aj7gS6v
    Score: 0.0255051015259
```

```
SOPA and PIPA are bad industrial policy There are many arguments against SOPA
and PIPA that are b...
    Link: https://plus.google.com/107033731246200681024/posts/LZs8TekXK2T
    Score: 0.0227351539694

Further thoughts on SOPA, and why Congress shouldn't listen to lobbyists
Colleen Taylor of GigaOM...
    Link: https://plus.google.com/107033731246200681024/posts/5Xd3VjFR8gx
    Score: 0.0112879721039


    ...
```

Given a search term, being able to zero in on three Google+ content items ranked by
relevance is of tremendous benefit when analyzing unstructured text data. Try out some
other queries and qualitatively review the results to see for yourself how well the TF-
IDF metric works, keeping in mind that the absolute values of the scores aren't really
important—it's the ability to find and sort documents by relevance that matters. Then,
begin to ponder the countless ways that you could tune or augment this metric to be
even more effective. One obvious improvement that's left as an exercise for the reader
is to stem verbs so that variations in elements such as tense and grammatical role resolve
to the same stem and can be more accurately accounted for in similarity calculations.
The `nltk.stem` module provides easy-to-use implementations for several common
stemming algorithms.

Now let's take our new tools and apply them to the foundational problem of finding
similar documents. After all, once you've zeroed in on a document of interest, the next
natural step is to discover other content that might be of interest.

4.4.3. Finding Similar Documents

Once you've queried and discovered documents of interest, one of the next things you
might want to do is find similar documents. Whereas TF-IDF can provide the means
to narrow down a corpus based on search terms, cosine similarity is one of the most
common techniques for comparing documents to one another, which is the essence of
finding a similar document. An understanding of cosine similarity requires a brief introduction to vector space models, which is the topic of the next section.

4.4.3.1. The theory behind vector space models and cosine similarity

While it has been emphasized that TF-IDF models documents as unordered collections
of words, another convenient way to model documents is with a model called a *vector
space*. The basic theory behind a vector space model is that you have a large multidimensional space that contains one vector for each document, and the distance between
any two vectors indicates the similarity of the corresponding documents. One of the
most beautiful things about vector space models is that you can also represent a query
as a vector and discover the most relevant documents for the query by finding the
document vectors with the shortest distance to the query vector.

Although it's virtually impossible to do this subject justice in a short section, it's important to have a basic understanding of vector space models if you have any interest at all in text mining or the IR field. If you're not interested in the background theory and want to jump straight into implementation details on good faith, feel free to skip ahead to the next section.

 This section assumes a basic understanding of trigonometry. If your trigonometry skills are a little rusty, consider this section a great opportunity to brush up on high school math. If you're not feeling up to it, just skim this section and rest assured that there is some mathematical rigor that backs the similarity computation we'll be employing to find similar documents.

First, it might be helpful to clarify exactly what is meant by the term *vector*, since there are so many subtle variations associated with it across various fields of study. Generally speaking, a vector is a list of numbers that expresses both a direction relative to an origin and a magnitude, which is the distance from that origin. A vector can naturally be represented as a line segment drawn between the origin and a point in an *N*-dimensional space.

To illustrate, imagine a document that is defined by only two terms ("Open" and "Web"), with a corresponding vector of (*0.45, 0.67*), where the values in the vector are values such as TF-IDF scores for the terms. In a vector space, this document could be represented in two dimensions by a line segment extending from the origin at (*0, 0*) to the point at (*0.45, 0.67*). In reference to an x/y plane, the x-axis would represent "Open," the y-axis would represent "Web," and the vector from (*0, 0*) to (*0.45, 0.67*) would represent the document in question. Nontrivial documents generally contain hundreds of terms at a minimum, but the same fundamentals apply for modeling documents in these higher-dimensional spaces; it's just harder to visualize.

Try making the transition from visualizing a document represented by a vector with two components to a document represented by three dimensions, such as ("Open," "Web," and "Government"). Then consider taking a leap of faith and accepting that although it's hard to visualize, it is still possible to have a vector represent additional dimensions that you can't easily sketch out or see. If you're able to do that, you should have no problem believing that the same vector operations that can be applied to a 2-dimensional space can be applied equally well to a 10-dimensional space or a 367-dimensional space. Figure 4-5 shows an example vector in 3-dimensional space.

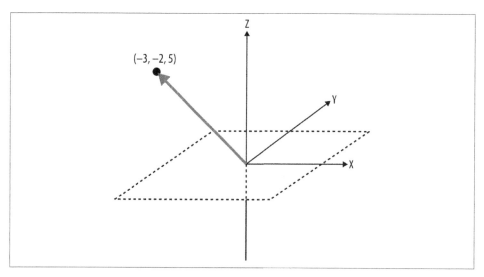

Figure 4-5. An example vector with the value (–3, –2, 5) plotted in 3D space; from the origin, move to the left three units, move down two units, and move up five units to arrive at the point

Given that it's possible to model documents as term-centric vectors, with each term in the document represented by its corresponding TF-IDF score, the task is to determine what metric best represents the similarity between two documents. As it turns out, the cosine of the angle between any two vectors is a valid metric for comparing them and is known as the *cosine similarity* of the vectors. Although it's perhaps not yet intuitive, years of scientific research have demonstrated that computing the cosine similarity of documents represented as term vectors is a very effective metric. (It does suffer from many of the same problems as TF-IDF, though; see Section 4.5 on page 178 for a brief synopsis.) Building up a rigorous proof of the details behind the cosine similarity metric would be beyond the scope of this book, but the gist is that the cosine of the angle between any two vectors indicates the similarity between them and is equivalent to the dot product (*http://bit.ly/1a1mBjn*) of their unit vectors.

Intuitively, it might be helpful to consider that the closer two vectors are to one another, the smaller the angle between them will be, and thus the larger the cosine of the angle between them will be. Two identical vectors would have an angle of 0 degrees and a similarity metric of 1.0, while two vectors that are orthogonal to one another would have an angle of 90 degrees and a similarity metric of 0.0. The following sketch attempts to demonstrate:

$\vec{doc1} \cdot \vec{doc2} = \|doc1\| \cdot \|doc2\| \cdot \cos\Theta$	Given (by trigonometry)
$\dfrac{\vec{doc1} \cdot \vec{doc2}}{\|doc1\| \cdot \|doc2\|} = \cos\Theta$	By division
$\hat{doc1} \cdot \hat{doc2} = \cos\Theta$	By definition of "unit vector"
$\hat{doc1} \cdot \hat{doc2} = \text{Similarity (doc1, doc2)}$	By substitution (assume: $\cos\Theta$ = Similarity (doc1, doc2))

Recalling that a unit vector has a length of 1.0 (by definition), you can see that the beauty of computing document similarity with unit vectors is that they're already normalized against what might be substantial variations in length. We'll put all of this newly found knowledge to work in the next section.

4.4.3.2. Clustering posts with cosine similarity

One of the most important points to internalize from the previous discussion is that *to compute the similarity between two documents, you really just need to produce a term vector for each document and compute the dot product of the unit vectors for those documents.* Conveniently, NLTK exposes the `nltk.cluster.util.cosine_dis tance(v1,v2)` function for computing cosine similarity, so it really is pretty straightforward to compare documents. As the upcoming Example 4-10 shows, all of the work involved is in producing the appropriate term vectors; in short, it computes term vectors for a given pair of documents by assigning TF-IDF scores to each component in the vectors. Because the exact vocabularies of the two documents are probably not identical, however, placeholders with a value of 0.0 must be left in each vector for words that are missing from the document at hand but present in the other one. The net effect is that you end up with two vectors of identical length with components ordered identically that can be used to perform the vector operations.

For example, suppose *document1* contained the terms *(A, B, C)* and had the corresponding vector of TF-IDF weights *(0.10, 0.15, 0.12)*, while *document2* contained the terms *(C, D, E)* with the corresponding vector of TF-IDF weights *(0.05, 0.10, 0.09)*. The derived vector for *document1* would be *(0.10, 0.15, 0.12, 0.0, 0.0)*, and the derived vector for *document2* would be *(0.0, 0.0, 0.05, 0.10, 0.09)*. Each of these vectors could be passed into NLTK's `cosine_distance` function, which yields the cosine similarity. Internally, `cosine_distance` uses the `numpy` module to *very* efficiently compute the dot product of the unit vectors, and that's the result. Although the code in this section reuses the TF-IDF calculations that were introduced previously, the exact scoring function could be any useful metric. TF-IDF (or some variation thereof), however, is quite common for many implementations and provides a great starting point.

Example 4-10 illustrates an approach for using cosine similarity to find the most similar document to each document in a corpus of Google+ data. It should apply equally well to any other type of human language data, such as blog posts or books.

Example 4-10. Finding similar documents using cosine similarity

```python
import json
import nltk

# Load in human language data from wherever you've saved it

DATA = 'resources/ch04-googleplus/107033731246200681024.json'
data = json.loads(open(DATA).read())

# Only consider content that's ~1000+ words.
data = [ post for post in json.loads(open(DATA).read())
         if len(post['object']['content']) > 1000 ]

all_posts = [post['object']['content'].lower().split()
             for post in data ]


# Provides tf, idf, and tf_idf abstractions for scoring

tc = nltk.TextCollection(all_posts)

# Compute a term-document matrix such that td_matrix[doc_title][term]
# returns a tf-idf score for the term in the document

td_matrix = {}
for idx in range(len(all_posts)):
    post = all_posts[idx]
    fdist = nltk.FreqDist(post)

    doc_title = data[idx]['title']
    url = data[idx]['url']
    td_matrix[(doc_title, url)] = {}

    for term in fdist.iterkeys():
        td_matrix[(doc_title, url)][term] = tc.tf_idf(term, post)

# Build vectors such that term scores are in the same positions...

distances = {}
for (title1, url1) in td_matrix.keys():

    distances[(title1, url1)] = {}
    (min_dist, most_similar) = (1.0, ('', ''))

    for (title2, url2) in td_matrix.keys():

        # Take care not to mutate the original data structures
```

```
# since we're in a loop and need the originals multiple times

terms1 = td_matrix[(title1, url1)].copy()
terms2 = td_matrix[(title2, url2)].copy()

# Fill in "gaps" in each map so vectors of the same length can be computed

for term1 in terms1:
    if term1 not in terms2:
        terms2[term1] = 0

for term2 in terms2:
    if term2 not in terms1:
        terms1[term2] = 0

# Create vectors from term maps

v1 = [score for (term, score) in sorted(terms1.items())]
v2 = [score for (term, score) in sorted(terms2.items())]

# Compute similarity amongst documents

distances[(title1, url1)][(title2, url2)] = \
    nltk.cluster.util.cosine_distance(v1, v2)

if url1 == url2:
    #print distances[(title1, url1)][(title2, url2)]
    continue

if distances[(title1, url1)][(title2, url2)] < min_dist:
    (min_dist, most_similar) = (distances[(title1, url1)][(title2,
                                url2)], (title2, url2))

    print '''Most similar to %s (%s)
\t%s (%s)
\tscore %f
''' % (title1, url1,
        most_similar[0], most_similar[1], 1-min_dist)
```

If you've found this discussion of cosine similarity interesting, it might at first seem almost magical when you realize that *the best part is that querying a vector space is the same operation as computing the similarity between documents, except that instead of comparing just document vectors, you compare your query vector and the document vectors.* Take a moment to think about it: it's a rather profound insight that the mathematics work out that way.

In terms of implementing a program to compute similarity across an entire corpus, however, take note that the naive approach means constructing a vector containing your query terms and comparing it to every single document in the corpus. Clearly, the approach of directly comparing a query vector to every possible document vector is not a good idea for even a corpus of modest size, and you'd need to make some good engineering decisions involving the appropriate use of indexes to achieve a scalable solution. We briefly touched upon the fundamental problem of needing a dimensionality reduction as a common staple in clustering in Chapter 3, and here we see the same concept emerge. *Any time you encounter a similarity computation, you will almost imminently encounter the need for a dimensionality reduction to make the computation tractable.*

4.4.3.3. Visualizing document similarity with a matrix diagram

The approach for visualizing similarity between items as introduced in this section is by using use graph-like structures, where a link between documents encodes a measure of the similarity between them. This situation presents an excellent opportunity to introduce more visualizations from D3 (*http://bit.ly/1a1kGvo*), the state-of-the-art visualization toolkit introduced in Chapter 2. D3 is specifically designed with the interests of data scientists in mind, offers a familiar declarative syntax, and achieves a nice middle ground between high-level and low-level interfaces.

A minimal adaptation to Example 4-10 is all that's needed to emit a collection of nodes and edges that can be used to produce visualizations similar to those in the D3 examples gallery (*http://bit.ly/1a1lMal*). A nested loop can compute the similarity between the documents in our sample corpus of Google+ data from earlier in this chapter, and linkages between items may be determined based upon a simple statistical thresholding criterion.

 The details associated with munging the data and producing the output required to power the visualizations won't be presented here, but the turnkey example code is provided in the IPython Notebook for this chapter.

The code produces the matrix diagram in Figure 4-6. Although the text labels are not readily viewable as printed in this image, you could look at the cells in the matrix for patterns and view the labels in your browser with an interactive visualization. For example, hovering over a cell might display a tool tip with each label.

An advantage of a matrix diagram versus a graph-based layout is that there's no potential for messy overlap between edges that represent linkages, so you avoid the proverbial "hairball" problem with your display. However, the ordering of rows and columns affects the intuition about the patterns that may be present in the matrix, so careful thought should be given to the best ordering for the rows and columns. Usually, rows and columns have additional properties that could be used to order them such that it's easier to pinpoint patterns in the data. A recommended exercise for this chapter is to spend some time enhancing the capabilities of this matrix diagram.

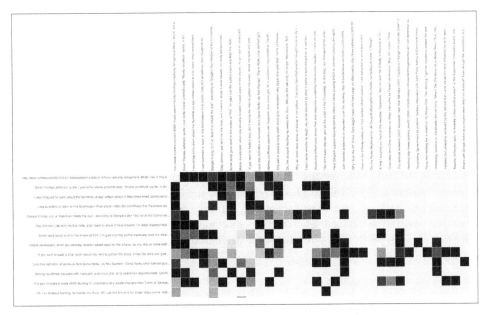

Figure 4-6. A matrix diagram displaying linkages between Google+ activities

4.4.4. Analyzing Bigrams in Human Language

As previously mentioned, one issue that is frequently overlooked in unstructured text processing is the tremendous amount of information gained when you're able to look at more than one token at a time, because so many concepts we express are phrases and not just single words. For example, if someone were to tell you that a few of the most common terms in a post are "open," "source," and "government," could you necessarily say that the text is probably about "open source," "open government," both, or neither? If you had a priori knowledge of the author or content, you could probably make a good guess, but if you were relying totally on a machine to try to *classify* a document as being about collaborative software development or transformational government, you'd need to go back to the text and somehow determine which of the other two words most frequently occurs after "open"—that is, you'd like to find the *collocations* that start with the token "open."

Recall from Chapter 3 that an *n*-gram is just a terse way of expressing each possible consecutive sequence of *n* tokens from a text, and it provides the foundational data structure for computing collocations. There are always (*n*–1) *n*-grams for any value of *n*, and if you were to consider all of the bigrams (two grams) for the sequence of tokens ["Mr.", "Green", "killed", "Colonel", "Mustard"], you'd have four possibilities: [("Mr.", "Green"), ("Green", "killed"), ("killed", "Colonel"), ("Colonel", "Mustard")]. You'd need a larger sample of text than just our sample sentence to determine collocations, but assuming you had background knowledge or additional text, the next step would be to statistically analyze the bigrams in order to determine which of them are likely to be collocations.

Storage Requirements for N-Grams

It's worth noting that the storage necessary for persisting an n-gram model requires space for $(T–1)*n$ tokens (which is practically $T*n$), where T is the number of tokens in question and n is defined by the size of the desired n-gram. As an example, assume a document contains 1,000 tokens and requires around 8 KB of storage. Storing all bigrams for the text would require roughly double the original storage, or 16 KB, as you would be storing 999*2 tokens plus overhead. Storing all trigrams for the text (998*3 tokens plus overhead) would require roughly triple the original storage, or 24 KB. Thus, without devising specialized data structures or compression schemes, the storage costs for n-grams can be estimated as n times the original storage requirement for any value of n.

---

n-grams are very simple yet very powerful as a technique for clustering commonly co-occurring words. If you compute all of the n-grams for even a small value of n, you're likely to discover that some interesting patterns emerge from the text itself with no additional work required. (Typically, bigrams and trigrams are what you'll often see used in practice for data mining exercises.) For example, in considering the bigrams for a sufficiently long text, you're likely to discover the proper names, such as "Mr. Green" and "Colonel Mustard," concepts such as "open source" or "open government," and so forth. In fact, computing bigrams in this way produces essentially the same results as the collocations function that you ran earlier, except that some additional statistical analysis takes into account the use of rare words. Similar patterns emerge when you consider frequent trigrams and n-grams for values of n slightly larger than three. As you already know from Example 4-8, NLTK takes care of most of the effort in computing n-grams, discovering collocations in a text, discovering the context in which a token has been used, and more. Example 4-11 demonstrates.

Example 4-11. Using NLTK to compute bigrams and collocations for a sentence

```
import nltk

sentence = "Mr. Green killed Colonel Mustard in the study with the " + \
           "candlestick. Mr. Green is not a very nice fellow."

print nltk.ngrams(sentence.split(), 2)
txt = nltk.Text(sentence.split())

txt.collocations()
```

A drawback to using built-in "demo" functionality such as `nltk.Text.collocations` is that these functions don't usually return data structures that you can store and

---

manipulate. Whenever you run into such a situation, just take a look at the underlying source code, which is usually pretty easy to learn from and adapt for your own purposes. Example 4-12 illustrates how you could compute the collocations and concordance indexes for a collection of tokens and maintain control of the results.

 In a Python interpreter, you can usually find the source directory for a package on disk by accessing the package's __file__ attribute. For example, try printing out the value of nltk.__file__ to find where NLTK's source is at on disk. In IPython or IPython Notebook, you could use "double question mark magic" function to preview the source code on the spot by executing nltk??.

Example 4-12. Using NLTK to compute collocations in a similar manner to the nltk.Text.collocations demo functionality

```
import json
import nltk

# Load in human language data from wherever you've saved it

DATA = 'resources/ch04-googleplus/107033731246200681024.json'
data = json.loads(open(DATA).read())

# Number of collocations to find

N = 25

all_tokens = [token for activity in data for token in activity['object']['content'
            ].lower().split()]

finder = nltk.BigramCollocationFinder.from_words(all_tokens)
finder.apply_freq_filter(2)
finder.apply_word_filter(lambda w: w in nltk.corpus.stopwords.words('english'))
scorer = nltk.metrics.BigramAssocMeasures.jaccard
collocations = finder.nbest(scorer, N)

for collocation in collocations:
    c = ' '.join(collocation)
    print c
```

In short, the implementation loosely follows NLTK's collocations demo function. It filters out bigrams that don't appear more than a minimum number of times (two, in this case) and then applies a scoring metric to rank the results. In this instance, the scoring function is the well-known *Jaccard Index* we discussed in Chapter 3, as defined by nltk.metrics.BigramAssocMeasures.jaccard. A *contingency table* is used by the BigramAssocMeasures class to rank the co-occurrence of terms in any given bigram as compared to the possibilities of other words that could have appeared in the bigram. Conceptually, the Jaccard Index measures similarity of sets, and in this case, the sample sets are specific comparisons of bigrams that appeared in the text.

The details of how contingency tables and Jaccard values are calculated is arguably an advanced topic, but the next section, Section 4.4.4.1 on page 172, provides an extended discussion of those details since they're foundational to a deeper understanding of collocation detection.

In the meantime, though, let's examine some output from Tim O'Reilly's Google+ data that makes it pretty apparent that returning scored bigrams is immensely more powerful than returning only tokens, because of the additional context that grounds the terms in meaning:

```
ada lovelace
jennifer pahlka
hod lipson
pine nuts
safe, welcoming
1st floor,
5 southampton
7ha cost:
bcs, 1st
borrow 42
broadcom masters
building, 5
date: friday
disaster relief
dissolvable sugar
do-it-yourself festival,
dot com
fabric samples
finance protection
london, wc2e
maximizing shareholder
patron profiles
portable disaster
rural co
vat tickets:
```

Keeping in mind that no special heuristics or tactics that could have inspected the text for proper names based on Title Case were employed, it's actually quite amazing that so many proper names and common phrases were sifted out of the data. For example, Ada Lovelace is a fairly well-known historical figure that Mr. O'Reilly is known to write about from time to time (given her affiliation with computing), and Jennifer Pahlka is popular for her "Code for America" work that Mr. O'Reilly closely follows. Hod Lipson is an accomplished robotics professor at Cornell University. Although you could have read through the content and picked those names out for yourself, it's remarkable that a machine could do it for you as a means of bootstrapping your own more focused analysis.

There's still a certain amount of inevitable noise in the results because we have not yet made any effort to clean punctuation from the tokens, but for the small amount of work we've put in, the results are really quite good. This might be the right time to mention that even if reasonably good natural language processing capabilities were employed, it might still be difficult to eliminate all the noise from the results of textual analysis. Getting comfortable with the noise and finding heuristics to control it is a good idea until you get to the point where you're willing to make a significant investment in obtaining the perfect results that a well-educated human would be able to pick out from the text.

Hopefully, the primary observation you're making at this point is that with very little effort and time invested, we've been able to use another basic technique to draw out some powerful meaning from some free text data, and *the results seem to be pretty representative of what we already suspect should be true.* This is encouraging, because it suggests that applying the same technique to anyone else's Google+ data (or any other kind of unstructured text, for that matter) would potentially be just as informative, giving you a quick glimpse into key items that are being discussed. And just as importantly, while the data in this case probably confirms a few things you may already know about Tim O'Reilly, you may have learned a couple of new things, as evidenced by the people who showed up at the top of the collocations list. While it would be easy enough to use the concordance, a regular expression, or even the Python string type's built-in find method to find posts relevant to "ada lovelace," let's instead take advantage of the code we developed in Example 4-9 and use TF-IDF to query for "ada lovelace." Here's what comes back:

```
I just got an email from +Suw Charman about Ada Lovelace Day,
and thought I'd share it here, sinc...
    Link: https://plus.google.com/107033731246200681024/posts/1XSAkDs9b44
    Score: 0.198150014715
```

And there you have it: the "ada lovelace" query leads us to some content about Ada Lovelace Day. You've effectively started with a nominal (if that) understanding of the text, zeroed in on some interesting topics using collocation analysis, and searched the text for one of those topics using TF-IDF. There's no reason you couldn't also use cosine similarity at this point to find the most similar post to the one about the lovely Ada Lovelace (or whatever it is that you're keen to investigate).

4.4.4.1. Contingency tables and scoring functions

 This section dives into some of the more technical details of how BigramCollocationFinder—the Jaccard scoring function from Example 4-12—works. If this is your first reading of the chapter or you're not interested in these details, feel free to skip this section and come back to it later. It's arguably an advanced topic, and you don't need to fully understand it to effectively employ the techniques from this chapter.

A common data structure that's used to compute metrics related to bigrams is the *contingency table*. The purpose of a contingency table is to compactly express the frequencies associated with the various possibilities for the appearance of different terms of a bigram. Take a look at the bold entries in Table 4-6, where *token1* expresses the existence of *token1* in the bigram, and *~token1* expresses that *token1* does not exist in the bigram.

Table 4-6. Contingency table example—values in italics represent "marginals," and values in bold represent frequency counts of bigram variations

	token1	~token1	
token2	**frequency(token1, token2)**	**frequency(~token1, token2)**	*frequency(*, token2)*
~token2	**frequency(token1, ~token2)**	**frequency(~token1, ~token2)**	
	frequency(token1, *)		*frequency(*, *)*

Although there are a few details associated with which cells are significant for which calculations, hopefully it's not difficult to see that the four middle cells in the table express the frequencies associated with the appearance of various tokens in the bigram. The values in these cells can compute different similarity metrics that can be used to score and rank bigrams in order of likely significance, as was the case with the previously introduced Jaccard Index, which we'll dissect in just a moment. First, however, let's briefly discuss how the terms for the contingency table are computed.

The way that the various entries in the contingency table are computed is directly tied to which data structures you have precomputed or otherwise have available. If you assume that you have available only a frequency distribution for the various bigrams in the text, the way to calculate *frequency(token1, token2)* is a direct lookup, but what about *frequency(~token1, token2)*? With no other information available, you'd need to scan *every single bigram* for the appearance of *token2* in the second slot and subtract *frequency(token1, token2)* from that value. (Take a moment to convince yourself that this is true if it isn't obvious.)

However, if you assume that you have a frequency distribution available that counts the occurrences of each individual token in the text (the text's unigrams) in addition to a frequency distribution of the bigrams, there's a *much less expensive* shortcut you can take that involves two lookups and an arithmetic operation. Subtract the number of times that *token2* appeared as a unigram from the number of times the bigram *(token1, token2)* appeared, and you're left with the number of times the bigram *(~token1, token2)* appeared. For example, if the bigram *("mr.", "green")* appeared three times and the unigram *("green")* appeared seven times, it must be the case that the bigram *(~"mr.", "green")* appeared four times (where *~"mr."* literally means "any token other than *'mr.'"). In Table 4-6, the expression *frequency(*, token2)* represents the unigram *token2* and is referred to as a *marginal* because it's noted in the margin of the table as a shortcut. The value for *frequency(token1, *)* works the same way in helping to compute *frequency(token1, ~token2)*, and the expression *frequency(*, *)* refers to any possible unigram and is equivalent to the total number of tokens in the text. Given *frequency(token1, token2)*, *frequency(token1, ~token2)*, and *frequency(~token1, token2)*, the value of *frequency(*, *)* is necessary to calculate *frequency(~token1, ~token2)*.

Although this discussion of contingency tables may seem somewhat tangential, it's an important foundation for understanding different scoring functions. For example, consider the Jaccard Index as introduced back in Chapter 3. Conceptually, it expresses the similarity of two sets and is defined by:

$$\frac{|Set1 \cap Set2|}{|Set1 \cup Set2|}$$

In other words, that's the number of items in common between the two sets divided by the total number of distinct items in the combined sets. It's worth taking a moment to ponder this simple yet effective calculation. If *Set1* and *Set2* were identical, the union and the intersection of the two sets would be equivalent to one another, resulting in a ratio of 1.0. If both sets were completely different, the numerator of the ratio would be 0, resulting in a value of 0.0. Then there's everything else in between.

The Jaccard Index as applied to a particular bigram expresses the ratio between the frequency of a particular bigram and the sum of the frequencies with which any bigram containing a term in the bigram of interest appears. One interpretation of that metric might be that the higher the ratio is, the more likely it is that *(token1, token2)* appears in the text, and hence the more likely it is that the collocation "token1 token2" expresses a meaningful concept.

The selection of the most appropriate scoring function is usually determined based upon knowledge about the characteristics of the underlying data, some intuition, and sometimes a bit of luck. Most of the association metrics defined in `nltk.metrics.associa tions` are discussed in Chapter 5 of Christopher Manning and Hinrich Schütze's *Foundations of Statistical Natural Language Processing* (MIT Press), which is conveniently available online (*http://stanford.io/1a1mBQy*) and serves as a useful reference for the descriptions that follow.

Is Being "Normal" Important?

One of the most fundamental concepts in statistics is a normal distribution. A normal distribution, often referred to as a *bell curve* because of its shape, is called a "normal" distribution because it is often the basis (or norm) against which other distributions are compared. It is a symmetric distribution that is perhaps the most widely used in statistics. One reason that its significance is so profound is because it provides a model for the variation that is regularly encountered in many natural phenomena in the world, ranging from physical characteristics of populations to defects in manufacturing processes and the rolling of dice.

A rule of thumb that shows why the normal distribution can be so useful is the so-called *68-95-99.7 rule* (*http://bit.ly/1a1mEf0*), a handy heuristic that can be used to answer many questions about approximately normal distributions.. For a normal distribution, it turns out that virtually all (99.7%) of the data lies within three standard deviations of the mean, 95% of it lies within two standard deviations, and 68% of it lies within one standard deviation. Thus, if you know that a distribution that explains some real-world phenomenon is approximately normal for some characteristic and its mean and standard deviation are defined, you can reason about it to answer many useful questions. Figure 4-7 illustrates the 68-95-99.7 rule.

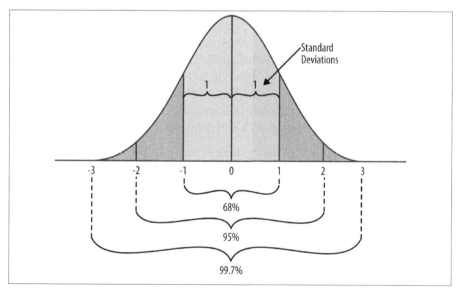

Figure 4-7. The normal distribution is a staple in statistical mathematics because it models variance in so many natural phenomena

---

The Khan Academy's "Introduction to the Normal Distribution" (*http://bit.ly/1a1mCnm*) provides an excellent 30-minute overview of the normal distribution; you might also enjoy the 10-minute segment on the central limit theorem (*http://bit.ly/1a1mCnA*), which is an equally profound concept in statistics in which the normal distribution emerges in a surprising (and amazing) way.

A thorough discussion of these metrics is outside the scope of this book, but the promotional chapter just mentioned provides a detailed account with in-depth examples. The Jaccard Index, Dice's coefficient, and the likelihood ratio are good starting points if you find yourself needing to build your own collocation detector. They are described, along with some other key terms, in the list that follows:

Raw frequency
As its name implies, raw frequency is the ratio expressing the frequency of a particular *n*-gram divided by the frequency of all *n*-grams. It is useful for examining the overall frequency of a particular collocation in a text.

Jaccard Index
The Jaccard Index is a ratio that measures the similarity between sets. As applied to collocations, it is defined as the frequency of a particular collocation divided by the total number of collocations that contain at least one term in the collocation of interest. It is useful for determining the likelihood of whether the given terms actually form a collocation, as well as ranking the likelihood of probable collocations. Using notation consistent with previous explanations, this formulation would be mathematically defined as:

$$\frac{freq(term1,\ term2)}{freq(term1,\ term2) + freq(\sim term1,\ term2) + freq(term1,\ \sim term2)}$$

Dice's coefficient
Dice's coefficient is extremely similar to the Jaccard Index. The fundamental difference is that it weights agreements among the sets twice as heavily as Jaccard. It is defined mathematically as:

$$\frac{2 * freq(term1,\ term2)}{freq(*,\ term2) + freq(term1,\ *)}$$

Mathematically, it can be shown fairly easily that:

$$Dice = \frac{2 * Jaccard}{1 + Jaccard}$$

You'd likely choose to use this metric instead of the Jaccard Index when you'd like to boost the score to favor overlap between sets, which may be handy when one or more of the differences between the sets are high. The reason is that a Jaccard score inherently diminishes as the cardinality of the set differences increases in size, since the union of the set is in the denominator of the Jaccard score.

Student's t-score

Traditionally, Student's t-score has been used for hypothesis testing, and as applied to *n*-gram analysis, t-scores can be used for testing the hypothesis of whether two terms are collocations. The statistical procedure for this calculation uses a standard distribution per the norm for t-testing. An advantage of the t-score values as opposed to raw frequencies is that a t-score takes into account the frequency of a bigram relative to its constituent components. This characteristic facilitates ranking the strengths of collocations. A criticism of the t-test is that it necessarily assumes that the underlying probability distribution for collocations is normal, which is not often the case.

Chi-square

Like Student's t-score, this metric is commonly used for testing independence between two variables and can be used to measure whether two tokens are collocations based upon Pearson's chi-square test of statistical significance. Generally speaking, the differences obtained from applying the t-test and chi-square test are not substantial. The advantage of chi-square testing is that unlike t-testing, it does not assume an underlying normal distribution; for this reason, chi-square testing is more commonly used.

Likelihood ratio

This metric is yet another approach to hypothesis testing that is used to measure the independence between terms that may form a collocation. It's been shown to be a more appropriate approach for collocation discovery than the chi-square test in the general case, and it works well on data that includes many infrequent collocations. The particular calculations involved in computing likelihood estimates for collocations as implemented by NLTK assume a binomial distribution (*http://bit.ly/1a1mEMj*), where the parameters governing the distribution are calculated based upon the number of occurrences of collocations and constituent terms.

Pointwise Mutual Information

Pointwise Mutual Information (PMI) is a measure of how much information is gained about a particular word if you also know the value of a neighboring word. To put it another way, it refers to how much one word can tell you about another. Ironically (in the context of the current discussion), the calculations involved in computing the PMI lead it to score high-frequency words lower than low-frequency words, which is the opposite of the desired effect. Therefore, it is a good measure of independence but not a good measure of dependence (i.e., it's a less-than-ideal choice for scoring collocations). It has also been shown that sparse data is a particular stumbling block for PMI scoring, and that other techniques such as the likelihood ratio tend to outperform it.

Evaluating and determining the best method to apply in any particular situation is often as much art as science. Some problems are fairly well studied and provide a foundation that guides additional work, while some circumstances often require more novel research and experimentation. For most nontrivial problems, you'll want to consider exploring the latest scientific literature (whether it be a textbook or a white paper from academia that you find with Google Scholar (*http://bit.ly/1a1mHYk*)) to determine if a particular problem you are trying to solve has been well studied.

4.4.5. Reflections on Analyzing Human Language Data

This chapter has introduced a variety of tools and processes for analyzing human language data, and some closing reflections may be helpful in synthesizing its content:

Context drives meaning

While TF-IDF is a powerful tool that's easy to use, our specific implementation of it has a few important limitations that we've conveniently overlooked but that you should consider. One of the most fundamental is that it treats a document as a "bag of words," which means that the order of terms in both the document and the query itself does not matter. For example, querying for "Green Mr." would return the same results as "Mr. Green" if we didn't implement logic to take the query term order into account or interpret the query as a phrase as opposed to a pair of independent terms. But obviously, the order in which terms appear is very important.

In performing an *n*-gram analysis to account for collocations and term ordering, we still face the underlying issue that TF-IDF assumes that all tokens with the same text value mean the same thing. Clearly, however, this need not be the case. A homonym (*http://bit.ly/1a1mFzJ*) is a word that has identical spellings and pronunciations to another word but whose meaning is driven entirely by context, and any homonym of your choice is a counterexample. Homonyms such as *book*, *match*, *cave*, and *cool* are a few examples that should illustrate the importance of context in determining the meaning of a word.

Cosine similarity suffers from many of the same flaws as TF-IDF. It does not take into account the context of the document or the term order from the *n*-gram analysis, and it assumes that terms appearing close to one another in vector space are necessarily similar, which is certainly not always the case. As with TF-IDF, the obvious counterexample is homonyms. Our particular implementation of cosine similarity also hinges on TF-IDF scoring as its means of computing the relative importance of words in documents, so the TF-IDF errors have a cascading effect.

Human language is overloaded with context

You've probably noticed that there can be a lot of pesky details that have to be managed in analyzing unstructured text, and these details turn out to be pretty important for competitive implementations. For example, string comparisons are case-sensitive, so it's important to normalize terms so that frequencies can be calculated as accurately as possible. However, blindly normalizing to lowercase can also complicate the situation since the case used in certain words and phrases can be important.

"Mr. Green" and "Web 2.0" are two examples worth considering. In the case of "Mr. Green," maintaining the title case in "Green" could potentially be advantageous since it could provide a useful clue to a query algorithm that this term is not referring to an adjective and is likely part of a noun phrase. We'll briefly touch on this topic again in Chapter 5 when NLP is discussed, since it's ultimately the *context* in which "Green" is being used that is lost with the bag-of-words approach, whereas more advanced parsing with NLP has the potential to preserve that context.

Parsing context from human language isn't easy

Another consideration that's rooted more in our particular implementation than a general characteristic of TF-IDF itself is that our use of `split` to tokenize the text may leave trailing punctuation on tokens that can affect tabulating frequencies. For example, in Example 4-6, `corpus['b']` ends with the token "study."; this is not the same as the token "study" that appears in `corpus['a']` (the token that someone would probably be more likely to query). In this instance, the trailing period on the token affects both the TF and the IDF calculations. Something as seemingly simple as a period signaling the end of a sentence is context that our brain processes trivially, but it's much more difficult for a machine to do this with the same level of accuracy.

Writing software to help machines better understand the context of words as they appear in human language data is a very active area of research and has tremendous potential for the future of search technology and the Web.

4.5. Closing Remarks

This chapter introduced the Google+ API and how to collect and cleanse human language data as part of an exercise in querying for a person's Google+ activities. We then spent some time learning about a few of the fundamentals of IR theory, TF-IDF, cosine similarity, and collocations as the means of analyzing the data we collect. Eventually we worked up to the point where we were considering some of the same problems that any search engine provider has had to consider to build a successful technology product. However, even though I hope this chapter has given you some good insight into how to extract useful information from unstructured text, it's barely scratched the surface of the most fundamental concepts, both in terms of theory and engineering considerations.

Information retrieval is literally a multibillion-dollar industry, so you can only imagine the amount of combined investment that goes into both the theory and implementations that work at scale to power search engines such as Google and Bing.

Given the immense power of search providers like Google, it's easy to forget that these foundational search techniques even exist. However, understanding them yields insight into the assumptions and limitations of the commonly accepted status quo for search, while also clearly differentiating the state-of-the-art, entity-centric techniques that are emerging. Chapter 5 introduces a fundamental paradigm shift away from some of the techniques in this chapter. There are lots of exciting opportunities for technology-driven companies that can effectively analyze human language data.

 The source code outlined for this chapter and all other chapters is available at GitHub (*http://bit.ly/1a1kNqy*) in a convenient IPython Notebook format that you're highly encouraged to try out from the comfort of your own web browser.

4.6. Recommended Exercises

- Take advantage of IPython Notebook's plotting features, introduced in Chapter 1, to graph Zipf's curve for the tokens from a corpus.

- Mine the comments feed and try to identify trends based on frequency of commenting. For example, who are the most frequent commenters across a few hundred activities for a popular Google+ user like Tim O'Reilly?

- Mine Google+ activities to discover which activities are the most popular. A suitable starting point might be the number of comments and number of times a post is reshared.

- Fetch the content from links that are referenced in Google+ activities and adapt the cleanHtml function from this chapter to extract the text across the web pages in a user's activity stream for analysis. Are there any common themes in links that are shared? What are the most frequent words that appear in the text?

- If you'd like to try applying the techniques from this chapter to the Web (in general), you might want to check out Scrapy (*http://bit.ly/1a1mG6P*), an easy-to-use and mature web scraping and crawling framework that can help you to harvest web pages.

- Spend some time and add interactive capabilities to the matrix diagram presented in this chapter. Can you add event handlers to automatically take you to the post when text is clicked on? Can you conceive of any meaningful ways to order the rows and columns so that it's easier to identify patterns?

- Update the code that emits the JSON that drives the matrix diagram so that it computes similarity differently and thus correlates documents differently from the default implementation.

- What additional features from the text can you think of that would make computing similarity across documents more accurate?

- Spend some time really digging into the theory presented in this chapter for the underlying IR concepts that were presented.

4.7. Online Resources

The following list of links from this chapter may be useful for review:

- 68-95-99.7 rule (*http://bit.ly/1a1mEf0*)
- Binomial distribution (*http://bit.ly/1a1mEMj*)
- Brown Corpus (*http://bit.ly/1a1mB2X*)
- Central Limit Theorem (*http://bit.ly/1a1mCnA*)
- D3.js examples gallery (*http://bit.ly/1a1lMaI*)
- Google API Console (*http://bit.ly/1a1mwMP*)
- `google-api-python-client` (*http://bit.ly/1a1mzYI*)
- Google+ API Reference (*http://bit.ly/1a1mtR0*)
- HTTP API Overview (*http://bit.ly/1a1mAfm*)
- Introduction to Information Retrieval (*http://stanford.io/1a1mAvP*)
- Introduction to the Normal Distribution (*http://bit.ly/1a1mCnm*)
- Manning and Schütze (Chapter 5: Collocations) (*http://stanford.io/1a1mBQy*)
- NLTK online book (*http://bit.ly/1a1mtAk*)
- Scrapy (*http://bit.ly/1a1mG6P*)
- Social graph stories (*http://bit.ly/1a1my7k*)
- Zipf's Law (*http://bit.ly/1a1mCUD*)

Mining Web Pages: Using Natural Language Processing to Understand Human Language, Summarize Blog Posts, and More

This chapter follows closely on the heels of the chapter before it and is a modest attempt to introduce natural language processing (NLP) and apply it to the vast source of human language[1] data that you'll encounter on the social web (or elsewhere). The previous chapter introduced some foundational techniques from information retrieval (IR) theory, which generally treats text as document-centric "bags of words" (unordered collections of words) that can be modeled and manipulated as vectors. Although these models often perform remarkably well in many circumstances, a recurring shortcoming is that they do not maximize cues from the immediate context that ground words in meaning.

This chapter employs different techniques that are more context-driven and delves deeper into the semantics of human language data. Social web APIs that return data conforming to a well-defined schema are essential, but the most basic currency of human communication is natural language data such as the words that you are reading on this page, Facebook posts, web pages linked into tweets, and so forth. Human language is by far the most ubiquitous kind of data available to us, and the future of data-driven innovation depends largely upon our ability to effectively harness machines to understand digital forms of human communication.

---

1. Throughout this chapter, the phrase *human language data* refers to the object of natural language processing and is intended to convey the same meaning as *natural language data* or *unstructured data*. No particular distinction is intended to be drawn by this choice of words other than its precision in describing the data itself.

It is highly recommended that you have a good working knowledge of the content in the previous chapter before you dive into this chapter. A good understanding of NLP presupposes an appreciation and working knowledge of some of the fundamental strengths and weaknesses of TF-IDF, vector space models, and so on. In that regard, this chapter and the one before it have a somewhat tighter coupling than most other chapters in this book.

In the spirit of the prior chapters, we'll attempt to cover the minimal level of detail required to empower you with a solid general understanding of an inherently complex topic, while also providing enough of a technical drill-down that you'll be able to immediately get to work mining some data. While continuing to cut corners and attempting to give you the crucial 20% of the skills that you can use to do 80% of the work (no single chapter out of any book—or small multivolume set of books, for that matter—could possibly do the topic of NLP justice), the content in this chapter is a pragmatic introduction that'll give you enough information to do some pretty amazing things with the human language data that you'll find all over the social web. Although we'll be focused on extracting human language data from web pages and feeds, keep in mind that just about every social website with an API is going to return human language, so these techniques generalize to just about any social website.

 Always get the latest bug-fixed source code for this chapter (and every other chapter) online at *http://bit.ly/MiningTheSocialWeb2E*. Be sure to also take advantage of this book's virtual machine experience, as described in Appendix A, to maximize your enjoyment of the sample code.

5.1. Overview

This chapter continues our journey in analyzing human language data and uses arbitrary web pages and feeds as a basis. In this chapter you'll learn about:

- Fetching web pages and extracting the human language data from them
- Leveraging NLTK for completing fundamental tasks in natural language processing
- Contextually driven analysis in NLP
- Using NLP to complete analytical tasks such as generating document abstracts
- Metrics for measuring quality for domains that involve predictive analysis

5.2. Scraping, Parsing, and Crawling the Web

Although it's trivial to use a programming language or terminal utility such as curl or wget to fetch an arbitrary web page, extracting the isolated text that you want from the page isn't quite as trivial. Although the text is certainly in the page, so is lots of other *boilerplate* content such as navigation bars, headers, footers, advertisements, and other sources of noise that you probably don't care about. Hence, the bad news is that the problem isn't quite as simple as just stripping out the HTML tags and processing the text that is left behind, because the removal of HTML tags would have done nothing to remove the boilerplate itself. In some cases, there may actually be more boilerplate in the page that contributes noise than the signal you were looking for in the first place.

The good news is that the tools for helping to identify the content you're interested in have continued to mature over the years, and there are some excellent options for isolating the material that you'd want for text-mining purposes. Additionally, the relative ubiquity of feeds such as RSS and Atom can often aid the process of retrieving clean text without all of the cruft that's typically in web pages, if you have the foresight to fetch the feeds while they are available.

It's often the case that feeds are published only for "recent" content, so you may sometimes have to process web pages even if feeds are available. If given the choice, you'll probably want to prefer the feeds over arbitrary web pages, but you'll need to be prepared for both.

One excellent tool for *web scraping* (the process of extracting text from a web page) is the Java-based boilerpipe (*http://bit.ly/1a1mMLA*) library, which is designed to identify and remove the boilerplate from web pages. The boilerpipe library is based on a published paper entitled "Boilerplate Detection Using Shallow Text Features," (*http://bit.ly/1a1mN21*) which explains the efficacy of using supervised machine learning (*http://bit.ly/1a1mPHr*) techniques to bifurcate the boilerplate and the content of the page. Supervised machine learning techniques involve a process that creates a predictive model from training samples that are representative of its domain, and thus, boilerpipe is customizable should you desire to tweak it for increased accuracy.

Even though the library is Java-based, it's useful and popular enough that a Python package wrapper called python-boilerpipe (*http://bit.ly/1a1mSD4*) is available.. Installation of this package is predictable: use **pip install boilerpipe**. Assuming you have a relatively recent version of Java on your system, that's all that should be required to use boilerpipe.

Example 5-1 demonstrates a sample script that illustrates its rather straightforward usage for the task of extracting the body content of an article, as denoted by the Arti cleExtractor parameter that's passed into the Extractor constructor. You can also try out a hosted version of boilerpipe (*http://bit.ly/1a1mSTF*) online to see the difference between some of its other provided extractors, such as the `LargestContentExtrac` `tor` or `DefaultExtractor`.

There's a default extractor that works for the general case, an extractor that has been trained for web pages containing articles, and an extractor that is trained to extract the largest body of text on a page, which might be suitable for web pages that tend to have just one large block of text. In any case, there may still be some light post-processing required on the text, depending on what other features you can identify that may be noise or require attention, but employing boilerpipe to do the heavy lifting is just about as easy as it should be.

Example 5-1. Using boilerpipe to extract the text from a web page

```
from boilerpipe.extract import Extractor

URL='http://radar.oreilly.com/2010/07/louvre-industrial-age-henry-ford.html'

extractor = Extractor(extractor='ArticleExtractor', url=URL)

print extractor.getText()
```

Although web scraping used to be the only way to fetch content from websites, there's potentially an easier way to harvest content, especially if it's content that's coming from a news source, blog, or other syndicated source. But before we get into that, let's take a quick trip down memory lane.

If you've been using the Web long enough, you may remember a time in the late 1990s when news readers didn't exist. Back then, if you wanted to know what the latest changes to a website were, you just had to go to the site and see if anything had changed. As a result, syndication formats took advantage of the self-publishing movement with blogs and formats such as RSS (Really Simple Syndication) and Atom built upon the evolving XML (*http://bit.ly/18RFKaW*) specifications that were growing in popularity to handle content providers publishing content and consumers subscribing to it. Parsing feeds is an easier problem to solve since the feeds are well-formed (*http://bit.ly/1a1mQLr*) XML data that validates (*http://bit.ly/1a1mTqE*) to a published schema, whereas web pages may or may not be well formed, be valid, or even conform to best practices.

A commonly used Python package for processing feed, appropriately named `feed` `parser`, is an essential utility to have on hand for parsing feeds. You can install it with `pip` using the standard **pip install feedparser** approach in a terminal, and Example 5-2 illustrates minimal usage to extract the text, title, and source URL for an entry in an RSS feed.

Example 5-2. Using feedparser to extract the text (and other fields) from an RSS or Atom feed

```
import feedparser

FEED_URL='http://feeds.feedburner.com/oreilly/radar/atom'

fp = feedparser.parse(FEED_URL)

for e in fp.entries:
    print e.title
    print e.links[0].href
    print e.content[0].value
```

HTML, XML, and XHTML

As the early Web evolved, the difficulty of separating the content in a page from its presentation quickly became recognized as a problem, and XML was (in part) a solution. The idea was that content creators could publish data in an XML format and use a stylesheet to transform it into XHTML for presentation to an end user. XHTML is essentially just HTML that is written as well-formed XML: each tag is defined in low-ercase, tags are properly nested as a tree structure, and tags are either self-closing (such as <br />), or each opening tag (e.g., <p>) has a corresponding closing tag (</p>).

In the context of web scraping, these conventions have the added benefit of making each web page much easier to process with a parser, and in terms of design, it appeared that XHTML was exactly what the Web needed. There was a lot to gain and virtually nothing to lose from the proposition: *well-formed* XHTML content could be proven *valid* against an XML schema and enjoy all of the other perks of XML, such as custom attributes using namespaces (a device that semantic web technologies such as RDFa rely upon).

The problem is that it just didn't catch on. As a result, we now live in a world where semantic markup based on the HTML 4.01 standard that's over a decade old continues to thrive, while XHTML and XHTML-based technologies such as RDFa remain on the fringe. (In fact, libraries such as BeautifulSoup (*http://bit.ly/1a1mRit*) are designed with the specific intent of being able to reasonably process HTML that probably isn't well-formed or even sane.) Most of the web development world is holding its breath and hoping that HTML5 (*http://bit.ly/1a1mRz5*) will indeed create a long-overdue conver-gence as technologies like microdata (*http://bit.ly/1a1mRPA*) catch on and publishing tools modernize. The HTML article on Wikipedia (*http://bit.ly/1a1mS66*) is worth reading if you find this kind of history interesting.

Crawling websites is a logical extension of the same concepts already presented in this section: it typically consists of fetching a page, extracting the hyperlinks in the page, and then systematically fetching all of those pages that are hyperlinked. This process is re-peated to an arbitrary depth, depending on your objective. This very process is the way that the earliest search engines used to work, and the way most search engines that index the Web still continue to work today. Although a crawl of the Web is far outside our scope, it is helpful to have a working knowledge of the problem, so let's briefly think about the computational complexity of harvesting all of those pages.

In terms of implementing your own web crawl, should you ever desire to do so, Scrapy (*http://bit.ly/1a1mG6P*) is a Python-based framework for web scraping that serves as an excellent resource if your endeavors entail web crawling. The actual exercise of performing a web crawl is just outside the scope of this chapter, but the Scrapy documentation online is excellent and includes all of the tutelage you'll need to get a targeted web crawl going with little effort up front. The next section is a brief aside that discusses the computational complexity of how web crawls are typically implemented so that you can better appreciate what you may be getting yourself into.

Nowadays, you can get a periodically updated crawl of the Web that's suitable for most research purposes from a source such as Amazon's Common Crawl Corpus (*http://amzn.to/1a1mXXb*), which features more than 5 billion web pages and checks in at over 81 terabytes of data!

5.2.1. Breadth-First Search in Web Crawling

This section contains some detailed content and analysis about how web crawls can be implemented and is not essential to your understanding of the content in this chapter (although you will likely find it interesting and edifying). If this is your first reading of the chapter, feel free to save it for next time.

The basic algorithm for a web crawl can be framed as a *breadth-first search* (*http://bit.ly/1a1mYdG*), which is a fundamental technique for exploring a space that's typically modeled as a tree or a graph given a starting node and no other known information except a set of possibilities. In our web crawl scenario, our starting node would be the initial web page and the set of neighboring nodes would be the other pages that are hyperlinked.

There are alternative ways to search the space, with a depth-first search (*http://bit.ly/1a1mVPd*) being a common alternative to a breadth-first search. The particular choice of one technique versus another often depends on available computing resources, specific domain knowledge, and even theoretical considerations. A breadth-first search is a reasonable approach for exploring a sliver of the Web. Example 5-3 presents some pseudocode that illustrates how it works, and Figure 5-1 provides some visual insight into how the search would look if you were to draw it out on the back of a napkin.

Example 5-3. Pseudocode for a breadth-first search

```
Create an empty graph
Create an empty queue to keep track of nodes that need to be processed

Add the starting point to the graph as the root node
Add the root node to a queue for processing

Repeat until some maximum depth is reached or the queue is empty:
  Remove a node from the queue
  For each of the node's neighbors:
    If the neighbor hasn't already been processed:
      Add it to the queue
      Add it to the graph
      Create an edge in the graph that connects the node and its neighbor
```

We generally haven't taken quite this long of a pause to analyze an approach, but breadth-first search is a fundamental tool you'll want to have in your belt and understand well. In general, there are two criteria for examination that you should always consider for an algorithm: efficiency and effectiveness (or, to put it another way: performance and quality).

Standard performance analysis of any algorithm generally involves examining its worst-case time and space complexity—in other words, the amount of time it would take the program to execute, and the amount of memory required for execution over a very large data set. The breadth-first approach we've used to frame a web crawl is essentially a breadth-first search, except that we're not actually searching for anything in particular because there are no exit criteria beyond expanding the graph out either to a maximum depth or until we run out of nodes. If we were searching for something specific instead of just crawling links indefinitely, that would be considered an actual breadth-first search. Thus, a more common variation of a breadth-first search is called a *bounded breadth-first* search, which imposes a limit on the maximum depth of the search just as we do in this example.

For a breadth-first search (or breadth-first crawl), both the time and space complexity can be bounded in the worst case by b^d, where b is the branching factor of the graph and d is the depth. If you sketch out an example on paper, as in Figure 5-1, and think about it, this analysis quickly becomes more apparent.

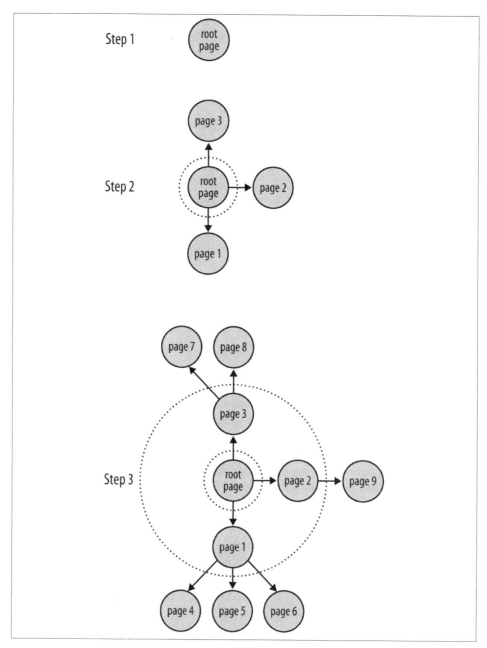

Figure 5-1. In a breadth-first search, each step of the search expands the depth by one level until a maximum depth or some other termination criterion is reached

If every node in a graph had five neighbors, and you only went out to a depth of one, you'd end up with six nodes in all: the root node and its five neighbors. If all five of those neighbors had five neighbors too and you expanded out another level, you'd end up with 31 nodes in all: the root node, the root node's five neighbors, and five neighbors for each of the root node's neighbors. Table 5-1 provides an overview of how b^d grows for a few sizes of b and d.

Table 5-1. Example branching factor calculations for graphs of varying depths

Branching factor	Nodes for depth = 1	Nodes for depth = 2	Nodes for depth = 3	Nodes for depth = 4	Nodes for depth = 5
2	3	7	15	31	63
3	4	13	40	121	364
4	5	21	85	341	1,365
5	6	31	156	781	3,906
6	7	43	259	1,555	9,331

Figure 5-2 provides a visual for the values displayed in Table 5-1.

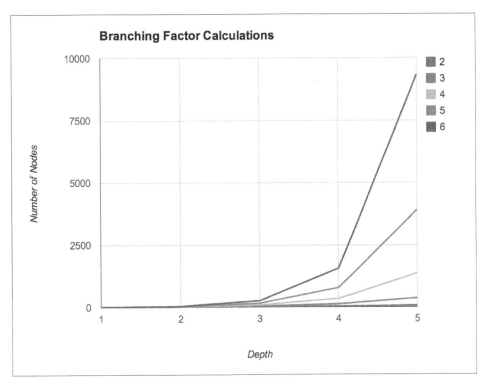

Figure 5-2. The growth in the number of nodes as the depth of a breadth-first search increases

While the previous comments pertain primarily to the theoretical bounds of the algorithm, one final consideration worth noting is the practical performance of the algorithm for a data set of a fixed size. Mild profiling of a breadth-first implementation that fetches web pages would likely reveal that the code is primarily *I/O bound* from the standpoint that the vast majority of time is spent waiting for a library call to return content to be processed. In situations in which you are I/O bound, a thread pool (*http://bit.ly/1a1mW5M*) is a common technique for increasing performance.

5.3. Discovering Semantics by Decoding Syntax

You may recall from the previous chapter that perhaps the most fundamental weaknesses of TF-IDF and cosine similarity are that these models inherently don't leverage a deep *semantic* understanding of the data and throw away a lot of critical context. Quite the contrary, the examples in that chapter took advantage of very basic syntax that separated tokens by whitespace to break an otherwise opaque document into a bag of words (*http://bit.ly/1a1lHDF*) and used frequency and simple statistical similarity metrics to determine which tokens were likely to be important in the data. Although you can do some really amazing things with these techniques, they don't really give you any notion of what any given token means in the context in which it appears in the document. Look no further than a sentence containing a homograph (*http://bit.ly/1a1mWCL*)[2] such as *fish*, *bear*, or even *google* as a case in point; either one could be a noun or a verb.

NLP is inherently complex and difficult to do even reasonably well, and completely nailing it for a large set of commonly spoken languages may well be the problem of the century. However, despite what many believe, it's far from being a solved problem, and it is already the case that we are starting to see a rising interest in a "deeper understanding" of the Web with initiatives such as Google's Knowledge Graph (*http://bit.ly/1a1mZyk*), which is being promoted as "the future of search." After all, a complete mastery of NLP is essentially a plausible strategy for acing the Turing Test (*http://bit.ly/1a1mZON*), and to the most careful observer, a computer program that achieves this level of "understanding" demonstrates an uncanny amount of human-like intelligence even if it is through a brain that's mathematically modeled in software as opposed to a biological one.

Whereas structured or semistructured sources are essentially collections of records with some presupposed meaning given to each field that can immediately be analyzed, there are more subtle considerations to be handled with human language data for even the seemingly simplest of tasks. For example, let's suppose you're given a document and asked to count the number of sentences in it. It's a trivial task if you're a human and have

---

2. A homonym is a special case of a homograph. Two words are homographs if they have the same spelling. Two words are homonyms if they have the same spelling and the same pronunciation. For some reason, *homonym* seems more common in parlance than *homograph*, even if it's being misused.

---

just a basic understanding of English grammar, but it's another story entirely for a machine, which will require a complex and detailed set of instructions to complete the same task.

The encouraging news is that machines can detect the ends of sentences on relatively well-formed data quickly and with nearly perfect accuracy. Even if you've accurately detected all of the sentences, though, there's still a lot that you probably don't know about the ways that words or phrases are used in those sentences. Look no further than sarcasm or other forms of ironic language as cases in point. Even with perfect information about the structure of a sentence, you often still need additional context outside the sentence to properly interpret it.

Thus, as an overly broad generalization, we can say that NLP is fundamentally about taking an opaque document that consists of an ordered collection of symbols adhering to proper *syntax* and a reasonably well-defined *grammar*, and deducing the *semantics* associated with those symbols.

Let's get back to the task of detecting sentences, the first step in most NLP pipelines, to illustrate some of the complexity involved in NLP. It's deceptively easy to overestimate the utility of simple rule-based heuristics, and it's important to work through an exercise so that you realize what some of the key issues are and don't waste time trying to reinvent the wheel.

Your first attempt at solving the sentence detection problem might be to just count the periods, question marks, and exclamation points in the sentence. That's the most obvious heuristic for starting out, but it's quite crude and has the potential for producing an extremely high margin of error. Consider the following (relatively unambiguous) accusation:

> Mr. Green killed Colonel Mustard in the study with the candlestick. Mr. Green is not a very nice fellow.

Simply tokenizing the sentence by splitting on punctuation (specifically, periods) would produce the following result:

```
>>> txt = "Mr. Green killed Colonel Mustard in the study with the \
... candlestick. Mr. Green is not a very nice fellow."
>>> txt.split(".")
['Mr', 'Green killed Colonel Mustard in the study with the candlestick',
 'Mr', 'Green is not a very nice fellow', '']
```

It should be immediately obvious that performing sentence detection by blindly breaking on periods without incorporating some notion of context or higher-level information is insufficient. In this case, the problem is the use of "Mr.," a valid abbreviation that's commonly used in the English language. Although we already know from the previous chapter that *n*-gram analysis of this sample would likely tell us that "Mr. Green" is really one compound token called a collocation or *chunk*, if we had a larger amount of text to analyze, it's not hard to imagine other edge cases that would be difficult to detect based on the appearance of collocations. Thinking ahead a bit, it's also worth pointing out that finding the key topics in a sentence isn't easy to accomplish with trivial logic either. As an intelligent human, you can easily discern that the key topics in our sample might be "Mr. Green," "Colonel Mustard," "the study," and "the candlestick," but training a machine to tell you the same things without human intervention is a complex task.

 Take a moment to think about how you might write a computer program to solve the problem before continuing in order to get the most out of the remainder of this discussion.

A few obvious possibilities are probably occurring to you, such as doing some "Title Case" detection with a regular expression, constructing a list of common abbreviations to parse out the proper noun phrases, and applying some variation of that logic to the problem of finding end-of-sentence (EOS) boundaries to prevent yourself from getting into trouble on that front. OK, sure. Those things will work for some examples, but what's the margin of error going to be like for *arbitrary* English text? How forgiving is your algorithm for poorly formed English text; highly abbreviated information such as text messages or tweets; or (gasp) other romantic languages, such as Spanish, French, or Italian? There are no simple answers here, and that's why text analytics is such an important topic in an age where the amount of digitally available human language data is literally increasing every second.

5.3.1. Natural Language Processing Illustrated Step-by-Step

Let's prepare to step through a series of examples that illustrate NLP with NLTK. The NLP pipeline we'll examine involves the following steps:

1. EOS detection
2. Tokenization
3. Part-of-speech tagging
4. Chunking
5. Extraction

We'll continue to use the following sample text from the previous chapter for the purposes of illustration: "Mr. Green killed Colonel Mustard in the study with the candlestick. Mr. Green is not a very nice fellow." Remember that even though you have already read the text and understand its underlying grammatical structure, it's merely an opaque string value to a machine at this point. Let's look at the steps we need to work through in more detail.

The following NLP pipeline is presented as though it is unfolding in a Python interpreter session for clarity and ease of illustration in the input and expected output of each step. However, each step of the pipeline is preloaded into this chapter's IPython Notebook so that you can follow along per the norm with all other examples.

The five steps are:

EOS detection

This step breaks a text into a collection of meaningful sentences. Since sentences generally represent logical units of thought, they tend to have a predictable syntax that lends itself well to further analysis. Most NLP pipelines you'll see begin with this step because tokenization (the next step) operates on individual sentences. Breaking the text into paragraphs or sections might add value for certain types of analysis, but it is unlikely to aid in the overall task of EOS detection. In the interpreter, you'd parse out a sentence with NLTK like so:

```
>>> import nltk
>>> txt = "Mr. Green killed Colonel Mustard in the study with the \
... candlestick. Mr. Green is not a very nice fellow."
>>> txt = "Mr. Green killed Colonel Mustard in the study with the \
... candlestick. Mr. Green is not a very nice fellow."
>>> sentences = nltk.tokenize.sent_tokenize(txt)
>>> sentences
['Mr. Green killed Colonel Mustard in the study with the candlestick.',
 'Mr. Green is not a very nice fellow.']
```

We'll talk a little bit more about what is happening under the hood with sent_token ize in the next section. For now, we'll accept at face value that proper sentence detection has occurred for arbitrary text—a clear improvement over breaking on characters that are likely to be punctuation marks.

Tokenization

This step operates on individual sentences, splitting them into tokens. Following along in the example interpreter session, you'd do the following:

```
>>> tokens = [nltk.tokenize.word_tokenize(s) for s in sentences]
>>> tokens
[['Mr.', 'Green', 'killed', 'Colonel', 'Mustard', 'in', 'the', 'study',
  'with', 'the', 'candlestick', '.'],
 ['Mr.', 'Green', 'is', 'not', 'a', 'very', 'nice', 'fellow', '.']]
```

Note that for this simple example, tokenization appeared to do the same thing as splitting on whitespace, with the exception that it tokenized out EOS markers (the periods) correctly. As we'll see in a later section, though, it can do a bit more if we give it the opportunity, and we already know that distinguishing between whether a period is an EOS marker or part of an abbreviation isn't always trivial. As an anecdotal note, some written languages, such as ones that use pictograms as opposed to letters, don't necessarily even require whitespace to separate the tokens in sentences and require the reader (or machine) to distinguish the boundaries.

POS tagging

This step assigns part-of-speech (POS) information to each token. In the example interpreter session, you'd run the tokens through one more step to have them decorated with tags:

```
>>> pos_tagged_tokens = [nltk.pos_tag(t) for t in tokens]
>>> pos_tagged_tokens
[[('Mr.', 'NNP'), ('Green', 'NNP'), ('killed', 'VBD'), ('Colonel', 'NNP'),
  ('Mustard', 'NNP'), ('in', 'IN'), ('the', 'DT'), ('study', 'NN'),
  ('with', 'IN'), ('the', 'DT'), ('candlestick', 'NN'), ('.', '.')],
 [('Mr.', 'NNP'), ('Green', 'NNP'), ('is', 'VBZ'), ('not', 'RB'),
  ('a', 'DT'), ('very', 'RB'), ('nice', 'JJ'), ('fellow', 'JJ'),
  ('.', '.')]]
```

You may not intuitively understand all of these tags, but they do represent POS information. For example, 'NNP' indicates that the token is a noun that is part of a noun phrase, 'VBD' indicates a verb that's in simple past tense, and 'JJ' indicates an adjective. The Penn Treebank Project (*http://bit.ly/1a1mXqf*) provides a full summary (*http://bit.ly/1a1n05o*) of the POS tags that could be returned. With POS tagging completed, it should be getting pretty apparent just how powerful analysis can become. For example, by using the POS tags, we'll be able to chunk together nouns as part of noun phrases and then try to reason about what types of entities they might be (e.g., people, places, or organizations). If you never thought that you'd need to apply those exercises from elementary school regarding parts of speech, think again: it's essential to a proper application of natural language processing.

Chunking

This step involves analyzing each tagged token within a sentence and assembling compound tokens that express logical concepts—quite a different approach than statistically analyzing collocations. It is possible to define a custom grammar through NLTK's chunk.RegexpParser, but that's beyond the scope of this chapter; see Chapter 9 ("Building Feature Based Grammars") of *Natural Language Processing with Python* (O'Reilly) for full details. Besides, NLTK exposes a function that combines chunking with named entity extraction, which is the next step.

Extraction

This step involves analyzing each chunk and further tagging the chunks as named entities, such as people, organizations, locations, etc. The continuing saga of NLP in the interpreter demonstrates:

```
>>> ne_chunks = nltk.batch_ne_chunk(pos_tagged_tokens)
>>> print ne_chunks
[Tree('S', [Tree('PERSON', [('Mr.', 'NNP')]),
 Tree('PERSON', [('Green', 'NNP')]), ('killed', 'VBD'),
 Tree('ORGANIZATION', [('Colonel', 'NNP'), ('Mustard', 'NNP')]),
     ('in', 'IN'), ('the', 'DT'), ('study', 'NN'), ('with', 'IN'),
     ('the', 'DT'), ('candlestick', 'NN'), ('.', '.')]),
 Tree('S', [Tree('PERSON', [('Mr.', 'NNP')]),
                Tree('ORGANIZATION',
                    [('Green', 'NNP')]), ('is', 'VBZ'), ('not', 'RB'),
                    ('a', 'DT'), ('very', 'RB'), ('nice', 'JJ'),
                    ('fellow', 'JJ'), ('.', '.')])]
>>> print ne_chunks[0].pprint() # You can pretty-print each chunk in the tree

(S
  (PERSON Mr./NNP)
  (PERSON Green/NNP)
  killed/VBD
  (ORGANIZATION Colonel/NNP Mustard/NNP)
  in/IN
  the/DT
  study/NN
  with/IN
  the/DT
  candlestick/NN
  ./.)
```

Don't get too wrapped up in trying to decipher exactly what the tree output means just yet. In short, it has chunked together some tokens and attempted to classify them as being certain types of entities. (You may be able to discern that it has identified "Mr. Green" as a person, but unfortunately categorized "Colonel Mustard" as an organization.) Figure 5-3 illustrates output in IPython Notebook.

As worthwhile as it would be to continue exploring natural language with NLTK, that level of engagement isn't really our purpose here. The background in this section is provided to motivate an appreciation for the difficulty of the task and to encourage you to review the NLTK book (*http://bit.ly/1a1mtAk*) or one of the many other plentiful resources available online if you'd like to pursue the topic further.

```
In [5]:  # Downloading nltk packages used in this example
         nltk.download('maxent_ne_chunker')
         nltk.download('words')

         ne_chunks = nltk.batch_ne_chunk(pos_tagged_tokens)
         print ne_chunks
         print ne_chunks[0].pprint() # You can prettyprint each chunk in the tree

[nltk_data] Downloading package 'maxent_ne_chunker' to
[nltk_data]     /usr/share/nltk_data...
[nltk_data]   Package maxent_ne_chunker is already up-to-date!
[nltk_data] Downloading package 'words' to /usr/share/nltk_data...
[nltk_data]   Package words is already up-to-date!
[Tree('S', [Tree('PERSON', [('Mr.', 'NNP')]), Tree('PERSON', [('Green', 'N
('in', 'IN'), ('the', 'DT'), ('study', 'NN'), ('with', 'IN'), ('the', 'DT'
Tree('ORGANIZATION', [('Green', 'NNP')]), ('is', 'VBZ'), ('not', 'RB'), ('
(S
  (PERSON Mr./NNP)
  (PERSON Green/NNP)
  killed/VBD
  (ORGANIZATION Colonel/NNP Mustard/NNP)
  in/IN
  the/DT
  study/NN
  with/IN
  the/DT
  candlestick/NN
  ./.)
```

Figure 5-3. NLTK can interface with drawing toolkits so that you can inspect the chunked output in a more intuitive visual form than the raw text output you see in the interpreter

Given that it's possible to customize certain aspects of NLTK, the remainder of this chapter assumes you'll be using NLTK "as is" unless otherwise noted.

With that brief introduction to NLP concluded, let's get to work mining some blog data.

5.3.2. Sentence Detection in Human Language Data

Given that sentence detection is probably the first task you'll want to ponder when building an NLP stack, it makes sense to start there. Even if you never complete the remaining tasks in the pipeline, it turns out that EOS detection alone yields some powerful possibilities, such as document summarization, which we'll be considering as a follow-up exercise in the next section. But first, we'll need to fetch some clean human language data. Let's use the tried-and-true feedparser package, along with some utilities introduced in the previous chapter that are based on nltk and BeautifulSoup, to clean up HTML formatting that may appear in the content to fetch some posts from the O'Reilly Radar blog (*http://oreil.ly/1a1n3Oz*). The listing in Example 5-4 fetches a few posts and saves them to a local file as JSON.

Example 5-4. Harvesting blog data by parsing feeds

```
import os
import sys
import json
import feedparser
from BeautifulSoup import BeautifulStoneSoup
from nltk import clean_html

FEED_URL = 'http://feeds.feedburner.com/oreilly/radar/atom'

def cleanHtml(html):
    return BeautifulStoneSoup(clean_html(html),
                convertEntities=BeautifulStoneSoup.HTML_ENTITIES).contents[0]

fp = feedparser.parse(FEED_URL)

print "Fetched %s entries from '%s'" % (len(fp.entries[0].title), fp.feed.title)

blog_posts = []
for e in fp.entries:
    blog_posts.append({'title': e.title, 'content'
                        : cleanHtml(e.content[0].value), 'link': e.links[0].href})

out_file = os.path.join('resources', 'ch05-webpages', 'feed.json')
f = open(out_file, 'w')
f.write(json.dumps(blog_posts, indent=1))
f.close()

print 'Wrote output file to %s' % (f.name, )
```

Obtaining human language data from a reputable source affords us the luxury of assuming good English grammar; hopefully this also means that one of NLTK's out-of-the-box sentence detectors will work reasonably well. There's no better way to find out than hacking some code to see what happens, so go ahead and review the code listing in Example 5-5. It introduces the `sent_tokenize` and `word_tokenize` methods, which are aliases for NLTK's currently recommended sentence detector and word tokenizer. A brief discussion of the listing is provided afterward.

Example 5-5. Using NLTK's NLP tools to process human language in blog data

```
import json
import nltk

# Download nltk packages used in this example
nltk.download('stopwords')

BLOG_DATA = "resources/ch05-webpages/feed.json"

blog_data = json.loads(open(BLOG_DATA).read())

# Customize your list of stopwords as needed. Here, we add common
```

```
    # punctuation and contraction artifacts.

stop_words = nltk.corpus.stopwords.words('english') + [
    '.',
    ',',
    '--',
    '\'s',
    '?',
    ')',
    '(',
    ':',
    '\'',
    '\'re',
    '"',
    '-',
    '}',
    '{',
    u'\u2014',
    ]

for post in blog_data:
    sentences = nltk.tokenize.sent_tokenize(post['content'])

    words = [w.lower() for sentence in sentences for w in
                nltk.tokenize.word_tokenize(sentence)]

    fdist = nltk.FreqDist(words)

    # Basic stats

    num_words = sum([i[1] for i in fdist.items()])
    num_unique_words = len(fdist.keys())

    # Hapaxes are words that appear only once

    num_hapaxes = len(fdist.hapaxes())

    top_10_words_sans_stop_words = [w for w in fdist.items() if w[0]
                                    not in stop_words][:10]

    print post['title']
    print '\tNum Sentences:'.ljust(25), len(sentences)
    print '\tNum Words:'.ljust(25), num_words
    print '\tNum Unique Words:'.ljust(25), num_unique_words
    print '\tNum Hapaxes:'.ljust(25), num_hapaxes
    print '\tTop 10 Most Frequent Words (sans stop words):\n\t\t', \
            '\n\t\t'.join(['%s (%s)'
            % (w[0], w[1]) for w in top_10_words_sans_stop_words])
    print
```

The first things you're probably wondering about are the sent_tokenize and word_tokenize calls. NLTK provides several options for tokenization, but it provides "recommendations" as to the best available via these aliases. At the time of this writing (you can double-check this with pydoc or a command like nltk.tokenize.sent_token ize? in IPython or IPython Notebook at any time), the sentence detector is the Punkt SentenceTokenizer and the word tokenizer is the TreebankWordTokenizer. Let's take a brief look at each of these.

Internally, the PunktSentenceTokenizer relies heavily on being able to detect abbreviations as part of collocation patterns, and it uses some regular expressions to try to intelligently parse sentences by taking into account common patterns of punctuation usage. A full explanation of the innards of the PunktSentenceTokenizer's logic is outside the scope of this book, but Tibor Kiss and Jan Strunk's original paper "Unsupervised Multilingual Sentence Boundary Detection" (*http://bit.ly/1a1n3OI*) discusses its approach in a highly readable way, and you should take some time to review it.

As we'll see in a bit, it is possible to instantiate the PunktSentenceTokenizer with sample text that it trains on to try to improve its accuracy. The type of underlying algorithm that's used is an *unsupervised learning algorithm*; it does not require you to explicitly mark up the sample training data in any way. Instead, the algorithm inspects certain *features* that appear in the text itself, such as the use of capitalization and the co-occurrences of tokens, to derive suitable parameters for breaking the text into sentences.

While NLTK's WhitespaceTokenizer, which creates tokens by breaking a piece of text on whitespace, would have been the simplest word tokenizer to introduce, you're already familiar with some of the shortcomings of blindly breaking on whitespace. Instead, NLTK currently recommends the TreebankWordTokenizer, a word tokenizer that operates on sentences and uses the same conventions as the Penn Treebank Project.[3] The one thing that may catch you off guard is that the TreebankWordTokenizer's tokenization (*http://bit.ly/1a1n4ly*) does some less-than-obvious things, such as separately tagging components in contractions and nouns having possessive forms. For example, the parsing for the sentence "I'm hungry" would yield separate components for "I" and "'m," maintaining a distinction between the subject and verb for the two words conjoined in the contraction "I'm." As you might imagine, finely grained access to this kind of grammatical information can be quite valuable when it's time to do advanced analysis that scrutinizes relationships between subjects and verbs in sentences.

Given a sentence tokenizer and a word tokenizer, we can first parse the text into sentences and then parse each sentence into tokens. While this approach is fairly intuitive, its Achilles' heel is that errors produced by the sentence detector propagate forward and

---

3. *Treebank* is a very specific term that refers to a corpus that's been specially tagged with advanced linguistic information. In fact, the reason such a corpus is called a *treebank* is to emphasize that it's a bank (think: collection) of sentences that have been parsed into trees adhering to a particular grammar.

can potentially bound the upper limit of the quality that the rest of the NLP stack can produce. For example, if the sentence tokenizer mistakenly breaks a sentence on the period after "Mr." that appears in a section of text such as "Mr. Green killed Colonel Mustard in the study with the candlestick," it may not be possible to extract the entity "Mr. Green" from the text unless specialized repair logic is in place. Again, it all depends on the sophistication of the full NLP stack and how it accounts for error propagation.

The out-of-the-box PunktSentenceTokenizer is trained on the Penn Treebank corpus and performs quite well. The end goal of the parsing is to instantiate an nltk.FreqDist object (which is like a slightly more sophisticated collections.Counter), which expects a list of tokens. The remainder of the code in Example 5-5 is a straightforward usage of a few of the commonly used NLTK APIs.

 If you have a lot of trouble with advanced word tokenizers such as NLTK's TreebankWordTokenizer or PunktWordTokenizer, it's fine to default to the WhitespaceTokenizer until you decide whether it's worth the investment to use a more advanced tokenizer. In fact, using a more straightforward tokenizer can often be advantageous. For example, using an advanced tokenizer on data that frequently inlines URLs might be a bad idea.

The aim of this section was to familiarize you with the first step involved in building an NLP pipeline. Along the way, we developed a few metrics that make a feeble attempt at characterizing some blog data. Our pipeline doesn't involve part-of-speech tagging or chunking (yet), but it should give you a basic understanding of some concepts and get you thinking about some of the subtler issues involved. While it's true that we could have simply split on whitespace, counted terms, tallied the results, and still gained a lot of information from the data, it won't be long before you'll be glad that you took these initial steps toward a deeper understanding of the data. To illustrate one possible application for what you've just learned, in the next section we'll look at a simple document summarization algorithm that relies on little more than sentence segmentation and frequency analysis.

5.3.3. Document Summarization

Being able to perform reasonably good sentence detection as part of an NLP approach to mining unstructured data can enable some pretty powerful text-mining capabilities, such as crude but very reasonable attempts at document summarization. There are numerous possibilities and approaches, but one of the simplest to get started with dates all the way back to the April 1958 issue of *IBM Journal*. In the seminal article entitled "The Automatic Creation of Literature Abstracts," (*http://bit.ly/1a1n4Cj*) H.P. Luhn describes a technique that essentially boils down to filtering out sentences containing frequently occurring words that appear near one another.

The original paper is easy to understand and rather interesting; Luhn actually describes how he prepared punch cards in order to run various tests with different parameters! It's amazing to think that what we can implement in a few dozen lines of Python on a cheap piece of commodity hardware, he probably labored over for hours and hours to program into a gargantuan mainframe. Example 5-6 provides a basic implementation of Luhn's algorithm for document summarization. A brief analysis of the algorithm appears in the next section. Before skipping ahead to that discussion, first take a moment to trace through the code to learn more about how it works.

 Example 5-6 uses the numpy package (a collection of highly optimized numeric operations), which should have been installed alongside nltk. If for some reason you are not using the virtual machine and need to install it, just use **pip install numpy**.

Example 5-6. A document summarization algorithm based principally upon sentence detection and frequency analysis within sentences

```
import json
import nltk
import numpy

BLOG_DATA = "resources/ch05-webpages/feed.json"

N = 100  # Number of words to consider
CLUSTER_THRESHOLD = 5  # Distance between words to consider
TOP_SENTENCES = 5  # Number of sentences to return for a "top n" summary

# Approach taken from "The Automatic Creation of Literature Abstracts" by H.P. Luhn

def _score_sentences(sentences, important_words):
    scores = []
    sentence_idx = -1

    for s in [nltk.tokenize.word_tokenize(s) for s in sentences]:

        sentence_idx += 1
        word_idx = []

        # For each word in the word list...
        for w in important_words:
            try:
                # Compute an index for where any important words occur in the sentence.

                word_idx.append(s.index(w))
            except ValueError, e: # w not in this particular sentence
```

```
            pass

        word_idx.sort()

        # It is possible that some sentences may not contain any important words at all.
        if len(word_idx)== 0: continue

        # Using the word index, compute clusters by using a max distance threshold
        # for any two consecutive words.

        clusters = []
        cluster = [word_idx[0]]
        i = 1
        while i < len(word_idx):
            if word_idx[i] - word_idx[i - 1] < CLUSTER_THRESHOLD:
                cluster.append(word_idx[i])
            else:
                clusters.append(cluster[:])
                cluster = [word_idx[i]]
            i += 1
        clusters.append(cluster)

        # Score each cluster. The max score for any given cluster is the score
        # for the sentence.

        max_cluster_score = 0
        for c in clusters:
            significant_words_in_cluster = len(c)
            total_words_in_cluster = c[-1] - c[0] + 1
            score = 1.0 * significant_words_in_cluster \
                * significant_words_in_cluster / total_words_in_cluster

            if score > max_cluster_score:
                max_cluster_score = score

        scores.append((sentence_idx, score))

    return scores

def summarize(txt):
    sentences = [s for s in nltk.tokenize.sent_tokenize(txt)]
    normalized_sentences = [s.lower() for s in sentences]

    words = [w.lower() for sentence in normalized_sentences for w in
            nltk.tokenize.word_tokenize(sentence)]

    fdist = nltk.FreqDist(words)

    top_n_words = [w[0] for w in fdist.items()
            if w[0] not in nltk.corpus.stopwords.words('english')][:N]

    scored_sentences = _score_sentences(normalized_sentences, top_n_words)
```

```
    # Summarization Approach 1:
    # Filter out nonsignificant sentences by using the average score plus a
    # fraction of the std dev as a filter

    avg = numpy.mean([s[1] for s in scored_sentences])
    std = numpy.std([s[1] for s in scored_sentences])
    mean_scored = [(sent_idx, score) for (sent_idx, score) in scored_sentences
                   if score > avg + 0.5 * std]

    # Summarization Approach 2:
    # Another approach would be to return only the top N ranked sentences

    top_n_scored = sorted(scored_sentences, key=lambda s: s[1])[-TOP_SENTENCES:]
    top_n_scored = sorted(top_n_scored, key=lambda s: s[0])

    # Decorate the post object with summaries

    return dict(top_n_summary=[sentences[idx] for (idx, score) in top_n_scored],
                mean_scored_summary=[sentences[idx] for (idx, score) in mean_scored])

blog_data = json.loads(open(BLOG_DATA).read())

for post in blog_data:

    post.update(summarize(post['content']))

    print post['title']
    print '=' * len(post['title'])
    print
    print 'Top N Summary'
    print '-------------'
    print ' '.join(post['top_n_summary'])
    print
    print 'Mean Scored Summary'
    print '-------------------'
    print ' '.join(post['mean_scored_summary'])
    print
```

As example input/output, we'll use Tim O'Reilly's Radar post, "The Louvre of the Industrial Age" (*http://oreil.ly/1a1n4SO*). It's around 460 words long and is reprinted here so that you can compare the sample output from the two summarization attempts in the listing:

> This morning I had the chance to get a tour of The Henry Ford Museum in Dearborn, MI, along with Dale Dougherty, creator of Make: and Makerfaire, and Marc Greuther, the chief curator of the museum. I had expected a museum dedicated to the auto industry, but it's so much more than that. As I wrote in my first stunned tweet, "it's the Louvre of the Industrial Age."
>
> When we first entered, Marc took us to what he said may be his favorite artifact in the museum, a block of concrete that contains Luther Burbank's shovel, and Thomas Edison's

signature and footprints. Luther Burbank was, of course, the great agricultural inventor who created such treasures as the nectarine and the Santa Rosa plum. Ford was a farm boy who became an industrialist; Thomas Edison was his friend and mentor. The museum, opened in 1929, was Ford's personal homage to the transformation of the world that he was so much a part of. This museum chronicles that transformation.

The machines are astonishing—steam engines and coal-fired electric generators as big as houses, the first lathes capable of making other precision lathes (the makerbot of the 19th century), a ribbon glass machine that is one of five that in the 1970s made virtually all of the incandescent lightbulbs in the world, combine harvesters, railroad locomotives, cars, airplanes, even motels, gas stations, an early McDonalds' restaurant and other epiphenomena of the automobile era.

Under Marc's eye, we also saw the transformation of the machines from purely functional objects to things of beauty. We saw the advances in engineering—the materials, the workmanship, the design, over a hundred years of innovation. Visiting The Henry Ford, as they call it, is a truly humbling experience. I would never in a hundred years have thought of making a visit to Detroit just to visit this museum, but knowing what I know now, I will tell you confidently that it is as worth your while as a visit to Paris just to see the Louvre, to Rome for the Vatican Museum, to Florence for the Uffizi Gallery, to St. Petersburg for the Hermitage, or to Berlin for the Pergamon Museum. This is truly one of the world's great museums, and the world that it chronicles is our own.

I am truly humbled that the Museum has partnered with us to hold Makerfaire Detroit on their grounds. If you are anywhere in reach of Detroit this weekend, I heartily recommend that you plan to spend both days there. You can easily spend a day at Makerfaire, and you could easily spend a day at The Henry Ford. P.S. Here are some of my photos from my visit. (More to come soon. Can't upload many as I'm currently on a plane.)

Filtering sentences using an average score and standard deviation yields a summary of around 170 words:

This morning I had the chance to get a tour of The Henry Ford Museum in Dearborn, MI, along with Dale Dougherty, creator of Make: and Makerfaire, and Marc Greuther, the chief curator of the museum. I had expected a museum dedicated to the auto industry, but it's so much more than that. As I wrote in my first stunned tweet, "it's the Louvre of the Industrial Age. This museum chronicles that transformation. The machines are astonishing - steam engines and coal fired electric generators as big as houses, the first lathes capable of making other precision lathes (the makerbot of the 19th century), a ribbon glass machine that is one of five that in the 1970s made virtually all of the incandescent lightbulbs in the world, combine harvesters, railroad locomotives, cars, airplanes, even motels, gas stations, an early McDonalds' restaurant and other epiphenomena of the automobile era. You can easily spend a day at Makerfaire, and you could easily spend a day at The Henry Ford.

An alternative summarization approach, which considers only the top N sentences (where N = 5 in this case), produces a slightly more abridged result of around 90 words. It's even more succinct, but arguably still a pretty informative distillation:

This morning I had the chance to get a tour of The Henry Ford Museum in Dearborn, MI, along with Dale Dougherty, creator of Make: and Makerfaire, and Marc Greuther, the chief curator of the museum. I had expected a museum dedicated to the auto industry, but it's so much more than that. As I wrote in my first stunned tweet, "it's the Louvre of the Industrial Age. This museum chronicles that transformation. You can easily spend a day at Makerfaire, and you could easily spend a day at The Henry Ford.

As in any other situation involving analysis, there's a lot of insight to be gained from visually inspecting the summarizations in relation to the full text.

Outputting a simple markup format that can be opened by virtually any web browser is as simple as adjusting the final portion of the script that performs the output to do some string substitution. Example 5-7 illustrates one possibility for visualizing the output of document summarization by presenting the full text of the article with the sentences that are included as part of the summary in bold so that it's easy to see what was included in the summary and what wasn't. The script saves a collection of HTML files to disk that you can view within your IPython Notebook session or open in a browser without the need for a web server.

Example 5-7. Visualizing document summarization results with HTML output

```
import os
import json
import nltk
import numpy
from IPython.display import IFrame
from IPython.core.display import display

BLOG_DATA = "resources/ch05-webpages/feed.json"

HTML_TEMPLATE = """<html>
    <head>
        <title>%s</title>
        <meta http-equiv="Content-Type" content="text/html; charset=UTF-8"/>
    </head>
    <body>%s</body>
</html>"""

blog_data = json.loads(open(BLOG_DATA).read())

for post in blog_data:

    # Uses previously defined summarize function.
    post.update(summarize(post['content']))

    # You could also store a version of the full post with key sentences marked up
    # for analysis with simple string replacement...

    for summary_type in ['top_n_summary', 'mean_scored_summary']:
        post[summary_type + '_marked_up'] = '<p>%s</p>' % (post['content'], )
        for s in post[summary_type]:
```

```
        post[summary_type + '_marked_up'] = \
        post[summary_type + '_marked_up'].replace(s, '<strong>%s</strong>' % (s, ))

    filename = post['title'].replace("?", "") + '.summary.' + summary_type + '.html'
    f = open(os.path.join('resources', 'ch05-webpages', filename), 'w')
    html = HTML_TEMPLATE % (post['title'] + \
      ' Summary', post[summary_type + '_marked_up'],)

    f.write(html.encode('utf-8'))
    f.close()

    print "Data written to", f.name

# Display any of these files with an inline frame. This displays the
# last file processed by using the last value of f.name...

print "Displaying %s:" % f.name
display(IFrame('files/%s' % f.name, '100%', '600px'))
```

The resulting output is the full text of the document with sentences composing the summary highlighted in bold, as displayed in Figure 5-4. As you explore alternative techniques for summarization, a quick glance between browser tabs can give you an intuitive feel for the similarity between the summarization techniques. The primary difference illustrated here is a fairly long (and descriptive) sentence near the middle of the document, beginning with the words "The machines are astonishing."

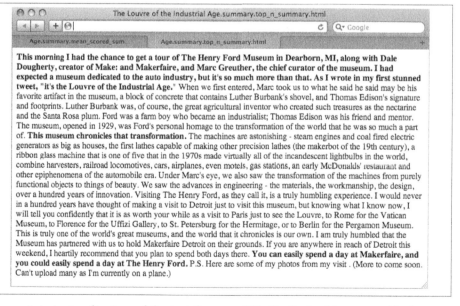

Figure 5-4. A visualization of the text from an O'Reilly Radar blog post with the most important sentences as determined by a summarization algorithm conveyed in bold

The next section presents a brief discussion of Luhn's document summarization approach.

5.3.3.1. Analysis of Luhn's summarization algorithm

 This section provides an analysis of Luhn's summarization algorithm. It aims to broaden your understanding of techniques in processing human language data but is certainly not a requirement for mining the social web. If you find yourself getting lost in the details, feel free to skip this section and return to it at a later time.

The basic premise behind Luhn's algorithm is that the important sentences in a document will be the ones that contain frequently occurring words. However, there are a few details worth pointing out. First, not all frequently occurring words are important; generally speaking, stopwords are filler and are hardly ever of interest for analysis. Keep in mind that although we do filter out common stopwords in the sample implementation, it may be possible to create a custom list of stopwords for any given blog or domain with additional a priori knowledge, which might further bolster the strength of this algorithm or any other algorithm that assumes stopwords have been filtered. For example, a blog written exclusively about baseball might so commonly use the word *baseball* that you should consider adding it to a stopword list, even though it's not a general-purpose stopword. (As a side note, it would be interesting to incorporate TF-IDF into the scoring function for a particular data source as a means of accounting for common words in the parlance of the domain.)

Assuming that a reasonable attempt to eliminate stopwords has been made, the next step in the algorithm is to choose a reasonable value for N and choose the top N words as the basis of analysis. The latent assumption behind this algorithm is that these top N words are sufficiently descriptive to characterize the nature of the document, and that for any two sentences in the document, the sentence that contains more of these words will be considered more descriptive. All that's left after determining the "important words" in the document is to apply a heuristic to each sentence and filter out some subset of sentences to use as a summarization or abstract of the document. Scoring each sentence takes place in the function `score_sentences`. This is where most of the action happens in the listing.

In order to score each sentence, the algorithm in `score_sentences` applies a simple distance threshold to cluster tokens, and scores each cluster according to the following formula:

$$\frac{(significant\ words\ in\ cluster)^2}{total\ words\ in\ cluster}$$

The final score for each sentence is equal to the highest score for any cluster appearing in the sentence. Let's consider the high-level steps involved in score_sentences for an example sentence to see how this approach works in practice:

Input: Sample sentence
```
['Mr.', 'Green', 'killed', 'Colonel', 'Mustard', 'in', 'the',
'study', 'with', 'the', 'candlestick', '.']
```

Input: List of important words
```
['Mr.', 'Green', 'Colonel', 'Mustard', 'candlestick']
```

Input/assumption: Cluster threshold (distance)
```
3
```

Intermediate computation: Clusters detected
```
[ ['Mr.', 'Green', 'killed', 'Colonel', 'Mustard'], ['candlestick'] ]
```

Intermediate computation: Cluster scores
```
[ 3.2, 1 ] # Computation: [ (4*4)/5, (1*1)/1]
```

Output: Sentence score
```
3.2 # max([3.2, 1])
```

The actual work done in score_sentences is just bookkeeping to detect the *clusters* in the sentence. A cluster is defined as a sequence of words containing two or more important words, where each important word is within a distance threshold of its nearest neighbor. While Luhn's paper suggests a value of 4 or 5 for the distance threshold, we used a value of 3 for simplicity in this example; thus, the distance between 'Green' and 'Colonel' was sufficiently bridged, and the first cluster detected consisted of the first five words in the sentence. Had the word *study* also appeared in the list of important words, the entire sentence (except the final punctuation) would have emerged as a cluster.

Once each sentence has been scored, all that's left is to determine which sentences to return as a summary. The sample implementation provides two approaches. The first approach uses a statistical threshold to filter out sentences by computing the mean and standard deviation for the scores obtained, while the latter simply returns the top *N* sentences. Depending on the nature of the data, your mileage will vary, but you should be able to tune the parameters to achieve reasonable results with either. One nice thing about using the top *N* sentences is that you have a pretty good idea about the maximum length of the summary. Using the mean and standard deviation could potentially return more sentences than you'd prefer, if a lot of sentences contain scores that are relatively close to one another.

Luhn's algorithm is simple to implement and plays to the usual strength of frequently appearing words being descriptive of the overall document. However, keep in mind that like many of the approaches based on the classic information retrieval concepts we explored in the previous chapter, Luhn's algorithm itself makes no attempt to understand the data at a deeper semantic level—although it does depend on more than just a "bag of words." It directly computes summarizations as a function of frequently occurring words, and it isn't terribly sophisticated in how it scores sentences, but (as was the case with TF-IDF), this just makes it all the more amazing that it can perform as well as it seems to perform on randomly selected blog data.

When you're weighing the pros and cons of implementing a much more complicated approach, it's worth reflecting on the effort that would be required to improve upon a reasonable summarization such as that produced by Luhn's algorithm. Sometimes, a crude heuristic is all you really need to accomplish your goal. At other times, however, you may need something more cutting-edge. The tricky part is computing the cost-benefit analysis of migrating from the crude heuristic to the state-of-the-art solution. Many of us tend to be overly optimistic about the relative effort involved.

5.4. Entity-Centric Analysis: A Paradigm Shift

Throughout this chapter, it's been implied that analytic approaches that exhibit a deeper understanding of the data can be dramatically more powerful than approaches that simply treat each token as an opaque symbol. But what does a "deeper understanding" of the data really mean?

One interpretation is being able to detect the entities in documents and using those entities as the basis of analysis, as opposed to doing document-centric analysis involving keyword searches or interpreting a search input as a particular type of entity and customizing the results accordingly. Although you may not have thought about it in those terms, this is precisely what emerging technologies such as WolframAlpha do at the presentation layer. For example, a search for "tim o'reilly" in WolframAlpha returns results that imply an understanding that the entity being searched for is a person; you don't just get back a list of documents containing the keywords (see Figure 5-5). Regardless of the internal technique that's used to accomplish this end, the resulting user experience is dramatically more powerful because the results conform to a format that more closely satisfies the user's expectations.

Although we can't ponder all of the various possibilities of entity-centric analysis in the current discussion, it's well within our reach and quite appropriate to present a means of extracting the entities from a document, which can then be used for various analytic purposes. Assuming the sample flow of an NLP pipeline as presented earlier in this chapter, you could simply extract all the nouns and noun phrases from the document and index them as entities appearing in the documents—the important underlying assumption being that nouns and noun phrases (or some carefully constructed subset thereof) qualify as entities of interest. This is actually a fair assumption to make and a good starting point for entity-centric analysis, as the following sample listing demonstrates. Note that for results annotated according to Penn Treebank conventions, any

tag beginning with `'NN'` is some form of a noun or noun phrase. A full listing of the
Penn Treebank tags (*http://bit.ly/1a1n59j*) is available online.

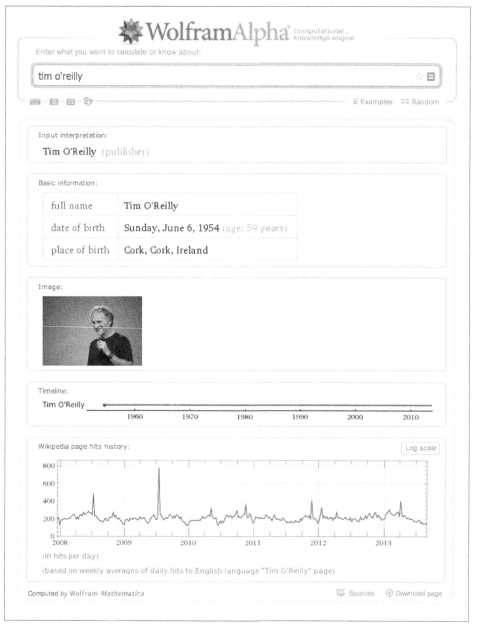

Figure 5-5. Sample results for a "tim o'reilly" query with WolframAlpha

Example 5-8 analyzes the part-of-speech tags that are applied to tokens, and identifies nouns and noun phrases as entities. In data mining parlance, finding the entities in a text is called *entity extraction* or *named entity recognition*, depending on the nuances of exactly what you are trying to accomplish.

Example 5-8. Extracting entities from a text with NLTK

```python
import nltk
import json

BLOG_DATA = "resources/ch05-webpages/feed.json"

blog_data = json.loads(open(BLOG_DATA).read())

for post in blog_data:

    sentences = nltk.tokenize.sent_tokenize(post['content'])
    tokens = [nltk.tokenize.word_tokenize(s) for s in sentences]
    pos_tagged_tokens = [nltk.pos_tag(t) for t in tokens]

    # Flatten the list since we're not using sentence structure
    # and sentences are guaranteed to be separated by a special
    # POS tuple such as ('.', '.')

    pos_tagged_tokens = [token for sent in pos_tagged_tokens for token in sent]

    all_entity_chunks = []
    previous_pos = None
    current_entity_chunk = []
    for (token, pos) in pos_tagged_tokens:

        if pos == previous_pos and pos.startswith('NN'):
            current_entity_chunk.append(token)
        elif pos.startswith('NN'):
            if current_entity_chunk != []:

                # Note that current_entity_chunk could be a duplicate when appended,
                # so frequency analysis again becomes a consideration

                all_entity_chunks.append((' '.join(current_entity_chunk), pos))
            current_entity_chunk = [token]

        previous_pos = pos

    # Store the chunks as an index for the document
    # and account for frequency while we're at it...

    post['entities'] = {}
    for c in all_entity_chunks:
        post['entities'][c] = post['entities'].get(c, 0) + 1

    # For example, we could display just the title-cased entities
```

```
print post['title']
print '-' * len(post['title'])
proper_nouns = []
for (entity, pos) in post['entities']:
    if entity.istitle():
        print '\t%s (%s)' % (entity, post['entities'][(entity, pos)])
print
```

 You may recall from the description of "extraction" in Section 5.3.1 on page 192 that NLTK provides an nltk.batch_ne_chunk function that attempts to extract named entities from POS-tagged tokens. You're welcome to use this capability directly, but you may find that your mileage varies with the out-of-the-box models provided with the NLTK implementation.

Sample output for the listing is presented next and conveys results that are quite meaningful and could be used in a variety of ways. For example, they would make great suggestions for tagging posts by an intelligent blogging platform like a WordPress plugin:

```
The Louvre of the Industrial Age
--------------------------------
    Paris (1)
    Henry Ford Museum (1)
    Vatican Museum (1)
    Museum (1)
    Thomas Edison (2)
    Hermitage (1)
    Uffizi Gallery (1)
    Ford (2)
    Santa Rosa (1)
    Dearborn (1)
    Makerfaire (1)
    Berlin (1)
    Marc (2)
    Makerfaire (1)
    Rome (1)
    Henry Ford (1)
    Ca (1)
    Louvre (1)
    Detroit (2)
    St. Petersburg (1)
    Florence (1)
    Marc Greuther (1)
    Makerfaire Detroit (1)
    Luther Burbank (2)
    Make (1)
```

```
Dale Dougherty (1)
Louvre (1)
```

Statistical artifacts often have different purposes and consumers. A text summary is meant to be read, whereas a list of extracted entities like the preceding one lends itself to being scanned quickly for patterns. For a larger corpus than we're working with in this example, a tag cloud (*http://bit.ly/1a1n5pO*) could be an obvious candidate for visualizing the data.

 Try reproducing these results by scraping the text from the web page *http://oreil.ly/1a1n4SO*.

Could we have discovered the same list of terms by more blindly analyzing the lexical characteristics (such as use of capitalization) of the sentence? Perhaps, but keep in mind that this technique can also capture nouns and noun phrases that are not indicated by title case. Case is indeed an important feature of the text that can generally be exploited to great benefit, but there are other intriguing entities in the sample text that are all lowercase (for example, "chief curator," "locomotives," and "lightbulbs").

Although the list of entities certainly doesn't convey the overall meaning of the text as effectively as the summary we computed earlier, identifying these entities can be extremely valuable for analysis since *they have meaning at a semantic level and are not just frequently occurring words*. In fact, the frequencies of most of the terms displayed in the sample output are quite low. Nevertheless, they're important because they have a grounded meaning in the text—namely, they're people, places, things, or ideas, which are generally the substantive information in the data.

5.4.1. Gisting Human Language Data

It's not much of a leap at this point to think that it would be another major step forward to take into account the verbs and compute triples of the form subject-verb-object so that you know which entities are interacting with which other entities, and the nature of those interactions. Such triples would lend themselves to visualizing object graphs of documents, which we could potentially skim much faster than we could read the documents themselves. Better yet, imagine taking multiple object graphs derived from a set of documents and merging them to get the gist of the larger corpus. This exact technique is an area of active research and has tremendous applicability for virtually any situation suffering from the information-overload problem. But as will be illustrated, it's an excruciating problem for the general case and not for the faint of heart.

Assuming a part-of-speech tagger has identified the parts of speech from a sentence and emitted output such as [('Mr.', 'NNP'), ('Green', 'NNP'), ('killed', 'VBD'), ('Colonel', 'NNP'), ('Mustard', 'NNP'), ...], an index storing subject-predicate-object tuples of the form (`'Mr. Green'`, `'killed'`, `'Colonel Mustard'`) would be easy to compute. However, the reality of the situation is that you're unlikely to run across actual POS-tagged data with that level of simplicity—unless you're planning to mine children's books (not actually a bad starting point for testing toy ideas). For example, consider the tagging emitted from NLTK for the first sentence from the blog post printed earlier in this chapter as an arbitrary and realistic piece of data you might like to translate into an object graph:

> This morning I had the chance to get a tour of The Henry Ford Museum in Dearborn, MI, along with Dale Dougherty, creator of Make: and Makerfaire, and Marc Greuther, the chief curator of the museum.

The simplest possible triple that you might expect to distill from that sentence is (`'I'`, `'get'`, `'tour'`), but even if you got that back, it wouldn't convey that Dale Dougherty also got the tour, or that Marc Greuther was involved. The POS-tagged data should make it pretty clear that it's not quite so straightforward to arrive at any of those interpretations, either, because the sentence has a very rich structure:

```
[(u'This', 'DT'), (u'morning', 'NN'), (u'I', 'PRP'), (u'had', 'VBD'),
(u'the', 'DT'), (u'chance', 'NN'), (u'to', 'TO'), (u'get', 'VB'),
(u'a', 'DT'), (u'tour', 'NN'), (u'of', 'IN'), (u'The', 'DT'),
(u'Henry', 'NNP'), (u'Ford', 'NNP'), (u'Museum', 'NNP'), (u'in', 'IN'),
(u'Dearborn', 'NNP'), (u',', ','), (u'MI', 'NNP'), (u',', ','),
(u'along', 'IN'), (u'with', 'IN'), (u'Dale', 'NNP'), (u'Dougherty', 'NNP'),
(u',', ','), (u'creator', 'NN'), (u'of', 'IN'), (u'Make', 'NNP'), (u':', ':'),
(u'and', 'CC'), (u'Makerfaire', 'NNP'), (u',', ','), (u'and', 'CC'),
(u'Marc', 'NNP'), (u'Greuther', 'NNP'), (u',', ','), (u'the', 'DT'),
(u'chief', 'NN'), (u'curator', 'NN'), (u'of', 'IN'), (u'the', 'DT'),
(u'museum', 'NN'), (u'.', '.')]
```

It's doubtful that a high-quality open source NLP toolkit would be capable of emitting meaningful triples in this case, given the complex nature of the predicate "had a chance to get a tour" and that the other actors involved in the tour are listed in a phrase appended to the end of the sentence.

 If you'd like to pursue strategies for constructing these triples, you should be able to use reasonably accurate POS tagging information to take a good initial stab at it. Advanced tasks in manipulating human language data can be a lot of work, but the results are satisfying and have the potential to be quite disruptive (in a good way).

The good news is that you can actually do a lot of fun things by distilling just the entities from text and using them as the basis of analysis, as demonstrated earlier. You can easily produce triples from text on a per-sentence basis, where the "predicate" of each triple is a notion of a generic relationship signifying that the subject and object "interacted" with each other. Example 5-9 is a refactoring of Example 5-8 that collects entities on a per-sentence basis, which could be quite useful for computing the interactions between entities using a sentence as a context window.

Example 5-9. Discovering interactions between entities

```
import nltk
import json

BLOG_DATA = "resources/ch05-webpages/feed.json"

def extract_interactions(txt):
    sentences = nltk.tokenize.sent_tokenize(txt)
    tokens = [nltk.tokenize.word_tokenize(s) for s in sentences]
    pos_tagged_tokens = [nltk.pos_tag(t) for t in tokens]

    entity_interactions = []
    for sentence in pos_tagged_tokens:

        all_entity_chunks = []
        previous_pos = None
        current_entity_chunk = []

        for (token, pos) in sentence:

            if pos == previous_pos and pos.startswith('NN'):
                current_entity_chunk.append(token)
            elif pos.startswith('NN'):
                if current_entity_chunk != []:
                    all_entity_chunks.append((' '.join(current_entity_chunk),
                            pos))
                current_entity_chunk = [token]

            previous_pos = pos

        if len(all_entity_chunks) > 1:
            entity_interactions.append(all_entity_chunks)
        else:
            entity_interactions.append([])

    assert len(entity_interactions) == len(sentences)

    return dict(entity_interactions=entity_interactions,
                sentences=sentences)

blog_data = json.loads(open(BLOG_DATA).read())

# Display selected interactions on a per-sentence basis

for post in blog_data:

    post.update(extract_interactions(post['content']))
```

```
print post['title']
print '-' * len(post['title'])
for interactions in post['entity_interactions']:
    print '; '.join([i[0] for i in interactions])
print
```

The following results from this listing highlight something important about the nature of unstructured data analysis: it's messy!

```
The Louvre of the Industrial Age
--------------------------------
morning; chance; tour; Henry Ford Museum; Dearborn; MI; Dale Dougherty; creator;
Make; Makerfaire; Marc Greuther; chief curator

tweet; Louvre

"; Marc; artifact; museum; block; contains; Luther Burbank; shovel; Thomas Edison

Luther Burbank; course; inventor; treasures; nectarine; Santa Rosa

Ford; farm boy; industrialist; Thomas Edison; friend

museum; Ford; homage; transformation; world

machines; steam; engines; coal; generators; houses; lathes; precision; lathes;
makerbot; century; ribbon glass machine; incandescent; lightbulbs; world; combine;
harvesters; railroad; locomotives; cars; airplanes; gas; stations; McDonalds;
restaurant; epiphenomena

Marc; eye; transformation; machines; objects; things

advances; engineering; materials; workmanship; design; years

years; visit; Detroit; museum; visit; Paris; Louvre; Rome; Vatican Museum;
Florence; Uffizi Gallery; St. Petersburg; Hermitage; Berlin

world; museums

Museum; Makerfaire Detroit

reach; Detroit; weekend

day; Makerfaire; day
```

A certain amount of noise in the results is almost inevitable, but realizing results that are highly intelligible and useful—even if they do contain a manageable amount of noise—is a worthy aim. The amount of effort required to achieve pristine results that are nearly noise-free can be immense. In fact, in most situations, this is downright impossible because of the inherent complexity involved in natural language and the limitations of most currently available toolkits, including NLTK. If you are able to make certain assumptions about the domain of the data or have expert knowledge of the nature of the noise, you may be able to devise heuristics that are effective without risking an unacceptable amount of information loss—but it's a fairly difficult proposition.

Still, the interactions do provide a certain amount of "gist" that's valuable. For example, how closely would your interpretation of "morning; chance; tour; Henry Ford Museum; Dearborn; MI; Dale Dougherty; creator; Make; Makerfaire; Marc Greuther; chief curator" align with the meaning in the original sentence?

As was the case with our previous adventure in summarization, displaying markup that can be visually skimmed for inspection is also quite handy. A simple modification to Example 5-9 output, as shown in Example 5-10, is all that's necessary to produce the results shown in Figure 5-6.

Example 5-10. Visualizing interactions between entities with HTML output

```
import os
import json
import nltk
from IPython.display import IFrame
from IPython.core.display import display

BLOG_DATA = "resources/ch05-webpages/feed.json"

HTML_TEMPLATE = """"<html>
    <head>
        <title>%s</title>
        <meta http-equiv="Content-Type" content="text/html; charset=UTF-8"/>
    </head>
    <body>%s</body>
</html>"""

blog_data = json.loads(open(BLOG_DATA).read())

for post in blog_data:

    post.update(extract_interactions(post['content']))

    # Display output as markup with entities presented in bold text

    post['markup'] = []

    for sentence_idx in range(len(post['sentences'])):

        s = post['sentences'][sentence_idx]
        for (term, _) in post['entity_interactions'][sentence_idx]:
            s = s.replace(term, '<strong>%s</strong>' % (term, ))

        post['markup'] += [s]

    filename = post['title'].replace("?", "") + '.entity_interactions.html'
    f = open(os.path.join('resources', 'ch05-webpages', filename), 'w')
```

```
html = HTML_TEMPLATE % (post['title'] + ' Interactions',
                        ' '.join(post['markup']),)
f.write(html.encode('utf-8'))
f.close()

print "Data written to", f.name

# Display any of these files with an inline frame. This displays the
# last file processed by using the last value of f.name...

print "Displaying %s:" % f.name
display(IFrame('files/%s' % f.name, '100%', '600px'))
```

Figure 5-6. *Sample HTML output that displays entities identified in the text in bold so that it's easy to visually skim the content for its key concepts*

It could also be fruitful to perform additional analyses to identify the sets of interactions for a larger body of text and to find and visualize co-occurrences in the interactions. The code involving force-directed graphs illustrated in Section 2.3.2.3 on page 83 would make a good starting template for visualization, but even without knowing the specific nature of the interaction, there's still a lot of value in just knowing the subject and the object. If you're feeling ambitious, you should attempt to complete the tuples with the missing verbs.

5.5. Quality of Analytics for Processing Human Language Data

When you've done even a modest amount of text mining, you'll eventually want to start quantifying the quality of your analytics. How accurate is your end-of-sentence detector? How accurate is your part-of-speech tagger? For example, if you began customizing the basic algorithm for extracting the entities from unstructured text, how would you know whether your algorithm was getting more or less performant with respect to the quality of the results? While you could manually inspect the results for a small corpus and tune the algorithm until you were satisfied with them, you'd still have a devil of a time determining whether your analytics would perform well on a much larger corpus or a different class of document altogether—hence, the need for a more automated process.

An obvious starting point is to randomly sample some documents and create a "golden set" of entities that you believe are absolutely crucial for a good algorithm to extract from them, and then use this list as the basis of evaluation. Depending on how rigorous you'd like to be, you might even be able to compute the sample error and use a statistical device called a *confidence interval* (*http://bit.ly/1a1n8BW*) to predict the true error with a sufficient degree of confidence for your needs. However, what exactly is the calculation you should be computing based on the results of your extractor and golden set in order to compute accuracy? A very common calculation for measuring accuracy is called the *F1 score*, which is defined in terms of two concepts called *precision* and *recall*[4] as:

$$F = 2 * \frac{precision * recall}{precision + recall}$$

where:

$$precision = \frac{TP}{TP + FP}$$

---

4. More precisely, F1 is said to be the *harmonic mean* of precision and recall, where the harmonic mean of any two numbers *x* and *y* is defined as:

$$H = 2 * \frac{x * y}{x + y}$$

You can read more about why it's the "harmonic" mean by reviewing the definition of a *harmonic number* (*http://bit.ly/1a1n6tJ*).

---

and:

$$recall = \frac{TP}{TP + FN}$$

In the current context, precision is a measure of exactness that reflects false positives, and recall is a measure of completeness that reflects true positives. The following list clarifies the meaning of these terms in relation to the current discussion in case they're unfamiliar or confusing:

True positives (TP)
    Terms that were correctly identified as entities

False positives (FP)
    Terms that were identified as entities but should not have been

True negatives (TN)
    Terms that were not identified as entities and should not have been

False negatives (FN)
    Terms that were not identified as entities but should have been

Given that precision is a measure of exactness that quantifies false positives, it is defined as *TP / (TP + FP)*. Intuitively, if the number of false positives is zero, the exactness of the algorithm is perfect and the precision yields a value of 1.0. Conversely, if the number of false positives is high and begins to approach or surpass the value of true positives, precision is poor and the ratio approaches zero. As a measure of completeness, recall is defined as *TP / (TP + FN)* and yields a value of 1.0, indicating perfect recall, if the number of false negatives is zero. As the number of false negatives increases, recall approaches zero. By definition, F1 yields a value of 1.0 when precision and recall are both perfect, and approaches zero when both precision and recall are poor.

Of course, what you'll find out in the wild is that it's a trade-off as to whether you want to boost precision or recall, because it's difficult to have both. If you think about it, this makes sense because of the trade-offs involved with false positives and false negatives (see Figure 5-7).

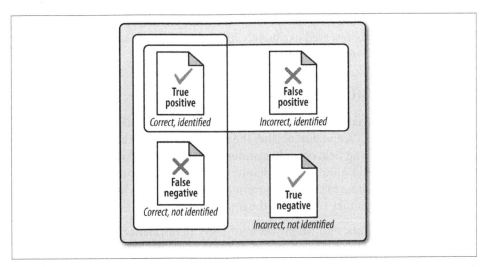

Figure 5-7. The intuition behind true positives, false positives, true negatives, and false negatives from the standpoint of predictive analytics

To put all of this into perspective, let's consider the sentence "Mr. Green killed Colonel Mustard in the study with the candlestick" one last time and assume that an expert has determined that the key entities in the sentence are "Mr. Green," "Colonel Mustard," "study," and "candlestick." Assuming your algorithm identified these four terms and only these four terms, you'd have four true positives, zero false positives, five true negatives ("killed," "with," "the," "in," "the"), and zero false negatives. That's perfect precision and perfect recall, which yields an F1 score of 1.0. Substituting various values into the precision and recall formulas is straightforward and a worthwhile exercise if this is your first time encountering these terms.

 What would the precision, recall, and F1 score have been if your algorithm had identified "Mr. Green," "Colonel," "Mustard," and "candlestick"?

Many of the most compelling technology stacks used by commercial businesses in the NLP space use advanced statistical models to process natural language according to supervised learning algorithms. Given our discussion earlier in this chapter, you know that a *supervised learning algorithm* is essentially an approach in which you provide training samples that comprise inputs and expected outputs such that the model is able to predict the tuples with reasonable accuracy. The tricky part is ensuring that the trained model generalizes well to inputs that have not yet been encountered. If the model performs well for training data but poorly on unseen samples, it's usually said to suffer from the problem of *overfitting* the training data. A common approach for measuring the efficacy of a model is called *cross-validation*. With this approach, a portion of the training data (say, one-third) is reserved exclusively for the purpose of testing the model, and only the remainder is used for training the model.

5.6. Closing Remarks

This chapter introduced the fundamentals of unstructured data analytics, and demonstrated how to use NLTK and put together the rest of an NLP pipeline to extract entities from text. The emerging field of understanding human language data is incredibly interdisciplinary and still quite nascent despite our collective attempts, and nailing the problem of NLP for most of the world's most commonly spoken languages is arguably the problem of this century (or at least the first half of it).

Push NLTK to its limits, and when you need more performance or quality, consider rolling up your sleeves and digging into some of the academic literature. It's admittedly a daunting task at first, but a truly worthy problem if you are interested in tackling it. There's only so much that one chapter out of any book can teach you, but the possibilities are vast, open source toolkits are a good starting point, and there's a bright future ahead for those who can master the science and art of processing human language data.

 The source code outlined for this chapter and all other chapters is available at GitHub (*http://bit.ly/1a1kNqy*) in a convenient IPython Notebook format that you're highly encouraged to try out from the comfort of your own web browser.

5.7. Recommended Exercises

- Adapt the code from this chapter to collect a few hundred high-quality articles or blog posts from the Web and summarize the content.

- Build a hosted web app with a toolkit such as Google App Engine to build an online summarization tool. (Given that Yahoo! recently acquired a company called Summly (*http://tcrn.ch/1a1n70L*) that summarizes news for readers, you may find this exercise particularly inspiring.)

- Consider using NLTK's word-stemming tools to try to compute (*entity, stemmed predicate, entity*) tuples, building upon the code in Example 5-9.

- Look into WordNet (*http://bit.ly/1a1n7hj*), a tool that you'll undoubtedly run into sooner rather than later, to discover additional meaning about predicate phrases you will encounter during NLP.

- Visualize entities extracted from text with a tag cloud (*http://bit.ly/1a1n5pO*).

  Try writing your own end-of-sentence detector as a deterministic parser based upon logic you can encode as rules in if-then statements and compare it to the facilities in NLTK. Is it appropriate to try to model language with deterministic rules?

- Use Scrapy to crawl a small sample of news articles or blog posts and extract the text for processing.

- Explore NLTK's Bayesian classifier (*http://bit.ly/1a1n9Wt*), a supervised learning technique that can be used to label training samples such as documents. Can you train a classifier to label documents as "sports," "editorial," and "other" from a small crawl with Scrapy? Measure your accuracy as an F1 score.

- Are there situations in which a harmonic mean between precision and recall is not desirable? When might you want higher precision at the cost of recall? When might you want higher recall at the cost of precision?

- Can you apply the techniques from this chapter to Twitter data? The GATE Twitter part-of-speech tagger (*http://bit.ly/1a1nad2*) and Carnegie Mellon's Twitter NLP and Part-of-Speech Tagging (*http://bit.ly/1a1n84Y*) libraries make a great starting point.

5.8. Online Resources

The following list of links from this chapter may be useful for review:

- The Automatic Creation of Literature Abstracts (*http://bit.ly/1a1n4Cj*)
- "Bag of words" model (*http://bit.ly/1a1lHDF*)
- Bayesian classifier (*http://bit.ly/1a1n9Wt*)
- BeautifulSoup (*http://bit.ly/1a1mRit*)
- Boilerplate Detection Using Shallow Text Features (*http://bit.ly/1a1mN21*)
- Breadth-first search (*http://bit.ly/1a1mYdG*)
- Carnegie Mellon's Twitter NLP and part-of-speech tagger (*http://bit.ly/1a1n84Y*)
- Common Crawl Corpus (*http://amzn.to/1a1mXXb*)
- Confidence interval (*http://bit.ly/1a1n8BW*)
- d3-cloud GitHub repository (*http://bit.ly/1a1n5pO*)
- Depth-first search (*http://bit.ly/1a1mVPd*)
- GATE Twitter part-of-speech tagger (*http://bit.ly/1a1nad2*)
- Hosted version of boilerpipe (*http://bit.ly/1a1mSTF*)
- HTML5 (*http://bit.ly/1a1mRz5*)

- Microdata (*http://bit.ly/1a1mRPA*)
- NLTK book (*http://bit.ly/1a1mtAk*)
- Penn Treebank Project (*http://bit.ly/1a1mXqf*)
- python-boilerpipe (*http://bit.ly/1a1mSD4*)
- Scrapy (*http://bit.ly/1a1mG6P*)
- Supervised machine learning (*http://bit.ly/1a1mPHr*)
- Thread pool (*http://bit.ly/1a1mW5M*)
- Turing Test (*http://bit.ly/1a1mZON*)
- Unsupervised Multilingual Sentence Boundary Detection (*http://bit.ly/1a1n3OI*)
- WordNet (*http://bit.ly/1a1n7hj*)

## CHAPTER 6

Mining Mailboxes: Analyzing Who's Talking to Whom About What, How Often, and More

Mail archives are arguably the ultimate kind of social web data and the basis of the earliest online social networks. Mail data is ubiquitous, and each message is inherently social, involving conversations and interactions among two or more people. Furthermore, each message consists of human language data that's inherently expressive, and is laced with structured metadata fields that anchor the human language data in particular timespans and unambiguous identities. Mining mailboxes certainly provides an opportunity to synthesize all of the concepts you've learned in previous chapters and opens up incredible opportunities for discovering valuable insights.

Whether you are the CIO of a corporation and want to analyze corporate communications for trends and patterns, you have keen interest in mining online mailing lists for insights, or you'd simply like to explore your own mailbox for patterns as part of quantifying yourself (*http://bit.ly/1a1niJw*), the following discussion provides a primer to help you get started. This chapter introduces some fundamental tools and techniques for exploring mailboxes to answer questions such as:

- Who sends mail to whom (and how much/often)?
- Is there a particular time of the day (or day of the week) when the most mail chatter happens?
- Which people send the most messages to one another?
- What are the subjects of the liveliest discussion threads?

Although social media sites are racking up petabytes of near-real-time social data, there is still the significant drawback that social networking data is centrally managed by a service provider that gets to create the rules about exactly how you can access it and what you can and can't do with it. Mail archives, on the other hand, are decentralized and scattered across the Web in the form of rich mailing list discussions about a litany of topics, as well as the many thousands of messages that people have tucked away in their own accounts. When you take a moment to think about it, it seems as though being able to effectively mine mail archives could be one of the most essential capabilities in your data mining toolbox.

Although it's not always easy to find realistic social data sets for purposes of illustration, this chapter showcases the fairly well-studied Enron corpus (*http://bit.ly/1a1nj01*) as its basis in order to maximize the opportunity for analysis without introducing any legal[1] or privacy concerns. We'll standardize the data set into the well-known Unix mailbox (mbox) format so that we can employ a common set of tools to process it. Finally, although we could just opt to process the data in a JSON format that we store in a flat file, we'll take advantage of the inherently document-centric nature of a mail message and learn how to use MongoDB (*http://bit.ly/1a1nlVK*) to store and analyze the data in a number of powerful and interesting ways, including various types of frequency analysis and keyword search.

As a general-purpose database for storing and querying arbitrary JSON data, MongoDB is hard to beat, and it's a powerful and versatile tool that you'll want to have on hand for a variety of circumstances. (Although we've opted to avoid the use of external dependencies such as databases until this chapter, when it has all but become a necessity given the nature of our subject matter here, you'll soon realize that you could use MongoDB to store any of the social web data we've been retrieving and accessing as flat JSON files.)

 Always get the latest bug-fixed source code for this chapter (and every other chapter) online at *http://bit.ly/MiningTheSocial Web2E*. Be sure to also take advantage of this book's virtual machine experience, as described in Appendix A, to maximize your enjoyment of the sample code.

6.1. Overview

Mail data is incredibly rich and presents opportunities for analysis involving everything you've learned about so far in this book. In this chapter you'll learn about:

---

1. Should you want to analyze mailing list data, be advised that most service providers (such as Google and Yahoo!) restrict your use of mailing list data if you retrieve it using their APIs, but you can easily enough collect and archive mailing list data yourself by subscribing to a list and waiting for your mailbox to start filling up. You might also be able to ask the list owner or members of the list to provide you with an archive as another option.

- The process of standardizing mail data to a convenient and portable format
- MongoDB, a powerful document-oriented database that is ideal for storing mail and other forms of social web data
- The Enron corpus, a public data set consisting of the contents of employee mailboxes from around the time of the Enron scandal
- Using MongoDB to query the Enron corpus in arbitrary ways
- Tools for accessing and exporting your own mailbox data for analysis

6.2. Obtaining and Processing a Mail Corpus

This section illustrates how to obtain a mail corpus, convert it into a standardized mbox, and then import the mbox into MongoDB, which will serve as a general-purpose API for storing and querying the data. We'll start out by analyzing a small fictitious mailbox and then proceed to processing the Enron corpus.

6.2.1. A Primer on Unix Mailboxes

An mbox is really just a large text file of concatenated mail messages that are easily accessible by text-based tools. Mail tools and protocols have long since evolved beyond mboxes, but it's usually the case that you can use this format as a lowest common denominator to easily process the data and feel confident that if you share or distribute the data it'll be just as easy for someone else to process it. In fact, most mail clients provide an "export" or "save as" option to export data to this format (even though the verbiage may vary), as illustrated in Figure 6-2 in the section Section 6.5 on page 268.

In terms of specification, the beginning of each message in an mbox is signaled by a special *From* line formatted to the pattern "From *user@example.com asctime*", where asctime (*http://bit.ly/1a1nmcl*) is a standardized fixed-width representation of a timestamp in the form Fri Dec 25 00:06:42 2009. The boundary between messages is determined by a *From_* line preceded (except for the first occurrence) by exactly two new line characters. (Visually, as shown below, this appears as though there is a single blank line that precedes the *From_* line.) A small slice from a fictitious mbox containing two messages follows:

```
From santa@northpole.example.org Fri Dec 25 00:06:42 2009
Message-ID: <16159836.1075855377439@mail.northpole.example.org>
References: <88364590.8837464573838@mail.northpole.example.org>
In-Reply-To: <194756537.0293874783209@mail.northpole.example.org>
Date: Fri, 25 Dec 2001 00:06:42 -0000 (GMT)
From: St. Nick <santa@northpole.example.org>
To: rudolph@northpole.example.org
Subject: RE: FWD: Tonight
Mime-Version: 1.0
```

```
Content-Type: text/plain; charset=us-ascii
Content-Transfer-Encoding: 7bit

Sounds good. See you at the usual location.

Thanks,
-S

  -----Original Message-----
From:    Rudolph
Sent:    Friday, December 25, 2009 12:04 AM
To: Claus, Santa
Subject:    FWD: Tonight

Santa -

Running a bit late. Will come grab you shortly. Standby.

Rudy

Begin forwarded message:

> Last batch of toys was just loaded onto sleigh.
>
> Please proceed per the norm.
>
> Regards,
> Buddy
>
> --
> Buddy the Elf
> Chief Elf
> Workshop Operations
> North Pole
> buddy.the.elf@northpole.example.org

From buddy.the.elf@northpole.example.org Fri Dec 25 00:03:34 2009
Message-ID: <88364590.8837464573838@mail.northpole.example.org>
Date: Fri, 25 Dec 2001 00:03:34 -0000 (GMT)
From: Buddy <buddy.the.elf@northpole.example.org>
To: workshop@northpole.example.org
Subject: Tonight
Mime-Version: 1.0
Content-Type: text/plain; charset=us-ascii
Content-Transfer-Encoding: 7bit

Last batch of toys was just loaded onto sleigh.

Please proceed per the norm.

Regards,
Buddy
```

```
--
Buddy the Elf
Chief Elf
Workshop Operations
North Pole
buddy.the.elf@northpole.example.org
```

In the preceding sample mailbox we see two messages, although there is evidence of at least one other message that was replied to that might exist elsewhere in the mbox. Chronologically, the first message was authored by a fellow named Buddy and was sent out to *workshop@northpole.example.org* to announce that the toys had just been loaded. The other message in the mbox is a reply from Santa to Rudolph. Not shown in the sample mbox is an intermediate message in which Rudolph forwarded Buddy's message to Santa with the note saying that he was running late. Although we could infer these things by reading the text of the messages themselves as humans with contextualized knowledge, the Message-ID, References, and In-Reply-To headers also provide important clues that can be analyzed.

These headers are pretty intuitive and provide the basis for algorithms that display threaded discussions and things of that nature. We'll look at a well-known algorithm that uses these fields to thread messages a bit later, but the gist is that each message has a unique message ID, contains a reference to the exact message that is being replied to in the case of it being a reply, and can reference multiple other messages in the reply chain that are part of the larger discussion thread at hand.

 Because we'll be employing some Python modules to do much of the tedious work for us, we won't need to digress into discussions concerning the nuances of email messages, such as multipart content, MIME types (*http://bit.ly/1a1nmsJ*), and 7-bit content transfer encoding.

These headers are vitally important. Even with this simple example, you can already see how things can get quite messy when you're parsing the actual body of a message: Rudolph's client quoted forwarded content with > characters, while the mail client Santa used to reply apparently didn't quote anything, but instead included a human-readable message header.

Most mail clients have an option to display extended mail headers beyond the ones you normally see, if you're interested in a technique that's a little more accessible than digging into raw storage when you want to view this kind of information; Figure 6-1 shows sample headers as displayed by Apple Mail.

From:	Matthew Russell
Subject:	**Message to self**
Date:	September 28, 2010 9:31:01 PM CDT
To:	Matthew Russell
Return-Path:	<matthew@zaffra.com>
X-Spam-Checker-Version:	SpamAssassin 3.1.9 (2007-02-13) on mail2.webfaction.com
X-Spam-Level:	
X-Spam-Status:	No, score=-2.6 required=5.0 tests=BAYES_00 autolearn=ham version=3.1.9
Received:	from smtp.webfaction.com (mail6.webfaction.com [74.55.86.74]) by mail2.webfaction.com (8.13.1/8.13.3) with ESMTP id o8T2V254026699 for <matthew@zaffra.com>; Tue, 28 Sep 2010 21:31:02 -0500
Received:	from [192.168.1.67] (99-0-32-163.lightspeed.nsvltn.sbcglobal.net [99.0.32.163]) by smtp.webfaction.com (Postfix) with ESMTP id 9CE61324B7D for <matthew@zaffra.com>; Tue, 28 Sep 2010 21:31:02 -0500 (CDT)
Message-Id:	<D9A2277D-A6A1-4CD2-B891-C0A1E4C6C6CD@zaffra.com>
Content-Type:	text/plain; charset=US-ASCII; format=flowed
Content-Transfer-Encoding:	7bit
Mime-Version:	1.0 (Apple Message framework v936)
X-Mailer:	Apple Mail (2.936)

Hello Matthew!

Regards - Matthew

---
http://www.linkedin.com/in/ptwobrussell

Figure 6-1. Most mail clients allow you to view the extended headers through an options menu

Luckily for us, there's a lot you can do without having to essentially reimplement a mail client. Besides, if all you wanted to do was browse the mailbox, you'd simply import it into a mail client and browse away, right?

 It's worth taking a moment to explore whether your mail client has an option to import/export data in the mbox format so that you can use the tools in this chapter to manipulate it.

To get the ball rolling on some data processing, Example 6-1 illustrates a routine that makes numerous simplifying assumptions about an mbox to introduce the mailbox and email packages that are part of Python's standard library.

Example 6-1. Converting a toy mailbox to JSON

```
import mailbox
import email
import json

MBOX = 'resources/ch06-mailboxes/data/northpole.mbox'
```

```
# A routine that makes a ton of simplifying assumptions
# about converting an mbox message into a Python object
# given the nature of the northpole.mbox file in order
# to demonstrate the basic parsing of an mbox with mail
# utilities

def objectify_message(msg):

    # Map in fields from the message
    o_msg = dict([ (k, v) for (k,v) in msg.items() ])

    # Assume one part to the message and get its content
    # and its content type

    part = [p for p in msg.walk()][0]
    o_msg['contentType'] = part.get_content_type()
    o_msg['content'] = part.get_payload()

    return o_msg

# Create an mbox that can be iterated over and transform each of its
# messages to a convenient JSON representation

mbox = mailbox.UnixMailbox(open(MBOX, 'rb'), email.message_from_file)

messages = []

while 1:
    msg = mbox.next()

    if msg is None: break

    messages.append(objectify_message(msg))

print json.dumps(messages, indent=1)
```

Although this little script for processing an mbox file seems pretty clean and produces reasonable results, trying to parse arbitrary mail data or determine the exact flow of a conversation from mailbox data for the general case can be a tricky enterprise. Many factors contribute to this, such as the ambiguity involved and the variation that can occur in how humans embed replies and comments into reply chains, how different mail clients handle messages and replies, etc.

Table 6-1 illustrates the message flow and explicitly includes the third message that was referenced but not present in the *northpole.mbox* to highlight this point. Truncated sample output from the script follows:

```
[
 {
  "From": "St. Nick <santa@northpole.example.org>",
  "Content-Transfer-Encoding": "7bit",
```

```
        "content": "Sounds good. See you at the usual location.\n\nThanks,...",
        "To": "rudolph@northpole.example.org",
        "References": "<88364590.8837464573838@mail.northpole.example.org>",
        "Mime-Version": "1.0",
        "In-Reply-To": "<194756537.0293874783209@mail.northpole.example.org>",
        "Date": "Fri, 25 Dec 2001 00:06:42 -0000 (GMT)",
        "contentType": "text/plain",
        "Message-ID": "<16159836.1075855377439@mail.northpole.example.org>",
        "Content-Type": "text/plain; charset=us-ascii",
        "Subject": "RE: FWD: Tonight"
    },
    {
        "From": "Buddy <buddy.the.elf@northpole.example.org>",
        "Subject": "Tonight",
        "Content-Transfer-Encoding": "7bit",
        "content": "Last batch of toys was just loaded onto sleigh. \n\nPlease...",
        "To": "workshop@northpole.example.org",
        "Date": "Fri, 25 Dec 2001 00:03:34 -0000 (GMT)",
        "contentType": "text/plain",
        "Message-ID": "<88364590.8837464573838@mail.northpole.example.org>",
        "Content-Type": "text/plain; charset=us-ascii",
        "Mime-Version": "1.0"
    }
]
```

Table 6-1. Message flow from northpole.mbox

Date	Message activity
Fri, 25 Dec 2001 00:03:34 -0000 (GMT)	Buddy sends a message to the workshop
Friday, December 25, 2009 12:04 AM	Rudolph forwards Buddy's message to Santa with an additional note
Fri, 25 Dec 2001 00:06:42 -0000 (GMT)	Santa replies to Rudolph

With a basic appreciation for mailboxes in place, let's now shift our attention to converting the Enron corpus (*http://bit.ly/1a1nmsU*) to an mbox so that we can leverage Python's standard library as much as possible.

6.2.2. Getting the Enron Data

A downloadable form of the full Enron data set (*http://bit.ly/1a1nmsU*) in a raw form is available in multiple formats requiring various amounts of processing. We'll opt to start with the original raw form of the data set, which is essentially a set of folders that organizes a collection of mailboxes by person and folder. Data standardization and cleansing is a routine problem, and this section should give you some perspective and some appreciation for it.

If you are taking advantage of the virtual machine experience for this book, the IPython Notebook for this chapter provides a script that downloads the data to the proper working location for you to seamlessly follow along with these examples. The full Enron corpus is approximately 450 MB in the compressed form in which you would download it to follow along with these exercises. It may take upward of 10 minutes to download and decompress if you have a reasonable Internet connection speed and a relatively new computer.

Unfortunately, if you are using the virtual machine, the time that it takes for Vagrant to synchronize the thousands of files that are unarchived back to the host machine can be upward of two hours. If time is a significant factor and you can't let this script run at an opportune time, you could opt to skip the download and initial processing steps since the refined version of the data, as produced from Example 6-3, is checked in with the source code and available at *ipynb/resources/ch06-mailboxes/data/enron.mbox* *.json.bz2*. See the notes in the IPython Notebook for this chapter for more details.

The download and decompression of the file is relatively fast compared to the time that it takes for Vagrant to synchronize the high number of files that decompress with the host machine, and at the time of this writing, there isn't a known workaround that will speed this up for all platforms. It may take longer than a hour for Vagrant to synchronize the thousands of files that decompress.

The output from the following terminal session illustrates the basic structure of the corpus once you've downloaded and unarchived it. It's worthwhile to explore the data in a terminal session for a few minutes once you've downloaded it to familiarize yourself with what's there and learn how to navigate through it.

If you are working on a Windows system or are not comfortable working in a terminal, you can poke around in the *ipynb/resources/ ch06-mailboxes/data* folder, which will be synchronized onto your host machine if you are taking advantage of the virtual machine experience for this book.

```
$ cd enron_mail_20110402/maildir # Go into the mail directory

maildir $ ls # Show folders/files in the current directory

    allen-p         crandell-s      gay-r           horton-s
    lokey-t         nemec-g         rogers-b        slinger-r
    tycholiz-b      arnold-j        cuilla-m        geaccone-t
    hyatt-k         love-p          panus-s         ruscitti-k
    smith-m         ward-k          arora-h         dasovich-j
    germany-c       hyvl-d          lucci-p         parks-j
    sager-e         solberg-g       watson-k        badeer-r
    corman-s        gang-l          holst-k         lokay-m
```

```
                 ...directory listing truncated...

   neal-s         rodrique-r     skilling-j      townsend-j

   $ cd allen-p/ # Go into the allen-p folder

   allen-p $ ls # Show files in the current directory

   _sent_mail       contacts         discussion_threads notes_inbox
   sent_items       all_documents    deleted_items      inbox
   sent             straw

   allen-p $ cd inbox/ # Go into the inbox for allen-p

   inbox $ ls # Show the files in the inbox for allen-p

   1.  11. 13. 15. 17. 19. 20. 22. 24. 26. 28. 3.  31. 33. 35. 37. 39. 40.
   42. 44. 5.  62. 64. 66. 68. 7.  71. 73. 75. 79. 83. 85. 87. 10. 12. 14.
   16. 18. 2.  21. 23. 25. 27. 29. 30. 32. 34. 36. 38. 4.  41. 43. 45. 6.
   63. 65. 67. 69. 70. 72. 74. 78. 8.  84. 86. 9.

   inbox $ head -20 1. # Show the first 20 lines of the file named "1."

   Message-ID: <16159836.1075855377439.JavaMail.evans@thyme>
   Date: Fri, 7 Dec 2001 10:06:42 -0800 (PST)
   From: heather.dunton@enron.com
   To: k..allen@enron.com
   Subject: RE: West Position
   Mime-Version: 1.0
   Content-Type: text/plain; charset=us-ascii
   Content-Transfer-Encoding: 7bit
   X-From: Dunton, Heather </O=ENRON/OU=NA/CN=RECIPIENTS/CN=HDUNTON>
   X-To: Allen, Phillip K. </O=ENRON/OU=NA/CN=RECIPIENTS/CN=Pallen>
   X-cc:
   X-bcc:
   X-Folder: \Phillip_Allen_Jan2002_1\Allen, Phillip K.\Inbox
   X-Origin: Allen-P
   X-FileName: pallen (Non-Privileged).pst


   Please let me know if you still need Curve Shift.

   Thanks,
```

The final command in the terminal session shows that mail messages are organized into files and contain metadata in the form of headers that can be processed along with the content of the data itself. The data is in a fairly consistent format, but not necessarily a well-known format with great tools for processing it. So, let's do some preprocessing on the data and convert a portion of it to the well-known Unix mbox format in order to illustrate the general process of standardizing a mail corpus to a format that is widely known and well tooled.

6.2.3. Converting a Mail Corpus to a Unix Mailbox

Example 6-2 illustrates an approach that searches the directory structure of the Enron corpus for folders named "inbox" and adds messages contained in them to a single output file that's written out as *enron.mbox*. To run this script, you will need to download the Enron corpus and unarchive it to the path specified by MAILDIR in the script.

The script takes advantage of a package called dateutil to handle the parsing of dates into a standard format. We didn't do this earlier, and it's slightly trickier than it may sound given the room for variation in the general case. You can install this package with **pip install python_dateutil**. (In this particular instance, the package name that pip tries to install is slightly different than what you import in your code.) Otherwise, the script is just using some tools from Python's standard library to munge the data into an mbox. Although not analytically interesting, the script provides reminders of how to use regular expressions, uses the email package that we'll continue to see, and illustrates some other concepts that may be useful for general data processing. Be sure that you understand how the script works to broaden your overall working knowledge and data mining toolchain.

> This script may take 10–15 minutes to run on the entire Enron corpus, depending on your hardware. IPython Notebook will indicate that it is still processing data by displaying a "Kernel Busy" message in the upper-right corner of the user interface.

Example 6-2. Converting the Enron corpus to a standardized mbox format

```
import re
import email
from time import asctime
import os
import sys
from dateutil.parser import parse # pip install python_dateutil

# XXX: Download the Enron corpus to resources/ch06-mailboxes/data
# and unarchive it there.

MAILDIR = 'resources/ch06-mailboxes/data/enron_mail_20110402/' + \
          'enron_data/maildir'

# Where to write the converted mbox
MBOX = 'resources/ch06-mailboxes/data/enron.mbox'

# Create a file handle that we'll be writing into...
mbox = open(MBOX, 'w')

# Walk the directories and process any folder named 'inbox'

for (root, dirs, file_names) in os.walk(MAILDIR):
```

```
    if root.split(os.sep)[-1].lower() != 'inbox':
        continue

    # Process each message in 'inbox'

    for file_name in file_names:
        file_path = os.path.join(root, file_name)
        message_text = open(file_path).read()

        # Compute fields for the From_ line in a traditional mbox message

        _from = re.search(r"From: ([^\r]+)", message_text).groups()[0]
        _date = re.search(r"Date: ([^\r]+)", message_text).groups()[0]

        # Convert _date to the asctime representation for the From_ line

        _date = asctime(parse(_date).timetuple())

        msg = email.message_from_string(message_text)
        msg.set_unixfrom('From %s %s' % (_from, _date))

        mbox.write(msg.as_string(unixfrom=True) + "\n\n")

mbox.close()
```

If you peek at the mbox file that we've just created, you'll see that it looks quite similar to the mail format we saw earlier, except that it now conforms to well-known specifications and is a single file.

 Keep in mind that you could just as easily create separate mbox files for each individual person or a particular group of people if you preferred to analyze a more focused subset of the Enron corpus.

6.2.4. Converting Unix Mailboxes to JSON

Having an mbox file is especially convenient because of the variety of tools available to process it across computing platforms and programming languages. In this section we'll look at eliminating many of the simplifying assumptions from Example 6-1, to the point that we can robustly process the Enron mailbox and take into account several of the common issues that you'll likely encounter with mailbox data from the wild. Python's tooling for mboxes is included in its standard library, and the script in Example 6-3 introduces a means of converting mbox data to a line-delimited JSON format that can be imported into a document-oriented database such as MongoDB (*http://bit.ly/1a1nlVK*). We'll talk more about MongoDB and why it's such a great fit for storing content such as mail data in a moment, but for now, it's sufficient to know that it stores data in what's conceptually a JSON-like format and provides some powerful capabilities for indexing and manipulating the data.

One additional accommodation that we make for MongoDB is that we normalize the date of each message to a standard *epoch* format that's the number of milliseconds since January 1, 1970, and pass it in with a special hint so that MongoDB can interpret each date field in a standardized way. Although we could have done this after we loaded the data into MongoDB, this chore falls into the "data cleansing" category and enables us to run some queries that use the *Date* field of each mail message in a consistent way immediately after the data is loaded.

Finally, in order to actually get the data to import into MongoDB, we need to write out a file in which each line contains a single JSON object, per MongoDB's documentation. Once again, although not interesting from the standpoint of analysis, this script illustrates some additional realities in data cleansing and processing—namely, that mail data may not be in a particular encoding like UTF-8 and may contain HTML formatting that needs to be stripped out.

 Example 6-3 includes the decode('utf-8', 'ignore') function in several places. When you're working with text-based data such as emails or web pages, it's not at all uncommon to run into the infamous UnicodeDecodeError because of unexpected character encodings, and it's not always immediately obvious what's going on or how to fix the problem. You can run the decode function on any string value and pass it a second argument that specifies what to do in the event of a UnicodeDecodeError. The default value is 'strict', which results in the exception being raised, but you can use 'ignore' or 're place' instead, depending on your needs.

Example 6-3. Converting an mbox to a JSON structure suitable for import into MongoDB

```
import sys
import mailbox
import email
import quopri
import json
import time
from BeautifulSoup import BeautifulSoup
from dateutil.parser import parse

MBOX = 'resources/ch06-mailboxes/data/enron.mbox'
OUT_FILE = 'resources/ch06-mailboxes/data/enron.mbox.json'

def cleanContent(msg):

    # Decode message from "quoted printable" format
```

```
        msg = quopri.decodestring(msg)

        # Strip out HTML tags, if any are present.
        # Bail on unknown encodings if errors happen in BeautifulSoup.
        try:
            soup = BeautifulSoup(msg)
        except:
            return ''
        return ''.join(soup.findAll(text=True))

# There's a lot of data to process, and the Pythonic way to do it is with a
# generator. See http://wiki.python.org/moin/Generators.
# Using a generator requires a trivial encoder to be passed to json for object
# serialization.

class Encoder(json.JSONEncoder):
    def default(self, o): return  list(o)

# The generator itself...
def gen_json_msgs(mb):
    while 1:
        msg = mb.next()
        if msg is None:
            break
        yield jsonifyMessage(msg)

def jsonifyMessage(msg):
    json_msg = {'parts': []}
    for (k, v) in msg.items():
        json_msg[k] = v.decode('utf-8', 'ignore')

    # The To, Cc, and Bcc fields, if present, could have multiple items.
    # Note that not all of these fields are necessarily defined.

    for k in ['To', 'Cc', 'Bcc']:
        if not json_msg.get(k):
            continue
        json_msg[k] = json_msg[k].replace('\n', '').replace('\t', '').replace('\r', '')\
                        .replace(' ', '').decode('utf-8', 'ignore').split(',')

    for part in msg.walk():
        json_part = {}
        if part.get_content_maintype() == 'multipart':
            continue

        json_part['contentType'] = part.get_content_type()
        content = part.get_payload(decode=False).decode('utf-8', 'ignore')
        json_part['content'] = cleanContent(content)

        json_msg['parts'].append(json_part)

    # Finally, convert date from asctime to milliseconds since epoch using the
```

```
# $date descriptor so it imports "natively" as an ISODate object in MongoDB
then = parse(json_msg['Date'])
millis = int(time.mktime(then.timetuple())*1000 + then.microsecond/1000)
json_msg['Date'] = {'$date' : millis}

return json_msg

mbox = mailbox.UnixMailbox(open(MBOX, 'rb'), email.message_from_file)

# Write each message out as a JSON object on a separate line
# for easy import into MongoDB via mongoimport

f = open(OUT_FILE, 'w')
for msg in gen_json_msgs(mbox):
    if msg != None:
        f.write(json.dumps(msg, cls=Encoder) + '\n')
f.close()
```

There's always more data cleansing that we could do, but we've addressed some of the most common issues, including a primitive mechanism for decoding quoted-printable text and stripping out HTML tags. (The quopri package is used to handle the quoted-printable format, an encoding used to transfer 8-bit content over a 7-bit channel.[2]) Following is one line of pretty-printed sample output from running Example 6-3 on the Enron mbox file, to demonstrate the basic form of the output:

```
{
    "Content-Transfer-Encoding": "7bit",
    "Content-Type": "text/plain; charset=us-ascii",
    "Date": {
        "$date": 988145040000
    },
    "From": "craig_estes@enron.com",
    "Message-ID": "<24537021.1075840152262.JavaMail.evans@thyme>",
    "Mime-Version": "1.0",
    "Subject": "Parent Child Mountain Adventure, July 21-25, 2001",
    "X-FileName": "jskillin.pst",
    "X-Folder": "\\jskillin\\Inbox",
    "X-From": "Craig_Estes",
    "X-Origin": "SKILLING-J",
    "X-To": "",
    "X-bcc": "",
    "X-cc": "",
    "parts": [
        {
            "content": "Please respond to Keith_Williams...",
            "contentType": "text/plain"
        }
```

---

2. See Wikipedia (*http://bit.ly/1a1nngg*) for an overview, or RFC 2045 (*http://bit.ly/1a1nnNp*) if you are interested in the nuts and bolts of how this works.

```
        ]
    }
```

This short script does a pretty decent job of removing some of the noise, parsing out the most pertinent information from an email, and constructing a data file that we can now trivially import into MongoDB. This is where the real fun begins. With your new-found ability to cleanse and process mail data into an accessible format, the urge to start analyzing it is only natural. In the next section, we'll import the data into MongoDB and begin the data analysis.

 If you opted not to download the original Enron data and follow along with the preprocessing steps, you can still produce the output from Example 6-3 by following along with the notes in the IPython Note-book for this chapter and proceed from here per the standard discussion that continues.

6.2.5. Importing a JSONified Mail Corpus into MongoDB

Using the right tool for the job can significantly streamline the effort involved in analyzing data, and although Python is a language that would make it fairly simple to process JSON data, it still wouldn't be nearly as easy as storing the JSON data in a document-oriented database like MongoDB.

For all practical purposes, think of MongoDB as a database that makes storing and manipulating JSON just about as easy as it should be. You can organize it into collections, iterate over it and query it in efficient ways, full-text index it, and much more. In the current context of analyzing the Enron corpus, MongoDB provides a natural API into the data since it allows us to create indexes and query on arbitrary fields of the JSON documents, even performing a full-text search if desired.

For our exercises, you'll just be running an instance of MongoDB on your local machine, but you can also scale MongoDB across a cluster of machines as your data grows. It comes with great administration utilities, and it's backed by a professional services company should you need pro support. A full-blown discussion about MongoDB is outside the scope of this book, but it should be straightforward enough to follow along with this section even if you've never heard of MongoDB until reading this chapter. Its online documentation and tutorials (*http://bit.ly/1a1nlVK*) are superb, so take a moment to bookmark them since they make such a handy reference.

Regardless of your operating system, should you choose to install MongoDB instead of using the virtual machine, you should be able to follow the instructions online (*http://bit.ly/1a1nqc9*) easily enough; nice packaging for all major platforms is available. Just make sure that you are using version 2.4 or higher since some of the exercises in this chapter rely on full-text indexing, which is a new beta feature introduced in version 2.4.

For reference, the MongoDB that is preinstalled with the virtual machine is installed and managed as a service (*http://bit.ly/1a1nokx*) with no particular customization aside from setting a parameter in its configuration file (located at */etc/mongodb.conf*) to enable full-text search indexing.

Verify that the Enron data is loaded, full-text indexed, and ready for analysis by executing Examples 6-4, 6-5, and 6-6. These examples take advantage of a lightweight wrapper around the subprocess (*http://bit.ly/1a1nrgb*) package called Envoy (*http://bit.ly/1a1nrwL*), which allows you to easily execute terminal commands from a Python program and get the standard output and standard error. Per the standard protocol, you can install envoy with **pip install envoy** from a terminal.

Example 6-4. Getting the options for the mongoimport command from IPython Notebook

```
import envoy # pip install envoy

r = envoy.run('mongoimport')
print r.std_out
print r.std_err
```

Example 6-5. Using mongoimport to load data into MongoDB from IPython Notebook

```
import os
import sys
import envoy

data_file = os.path.join(os.getcwd(), 'resources/ch06-mailboxes/data/enron.mbox.json')

# Run a command just as you would in a terminal on the virtual machine to
# import the data file into MongoDB.
r = envoy.run('mongoimport --db enron --collection mbox ' + \
              '--file %s' % data_file)

# Print its standard output
print r.std_out
print sys.stderr.write(r.std_err)
```

Example 6-6. Simulating a MongoDB shell that you can run from within IPython Notebook

```
# We can even simulate a MongoDB shell using envoy to execute commands.
# For example, let's get some stats out of MongoDB just as though we were working
# in a shell by passing it the command and wrapping it in a printjson function to
# display it for us.

def mongo(db, cmd):
    r = envoy.run("mongo %s --eval 'printjson(%s)'" % (db, cmd,))
    print r.std_out
    if r.std_err: print r.std_err
```

```
mongo('enron', 'db.mbox.stats()')
```

Sample output from Example 6-6 follows and illustrates that it's exactly what you'd see if you were writing commands in the MongoDB shell. Neat!

```
MongoDB shell version: 2.4.3
connecting to: enron
{
  "ns" : "enron.mbox",
  "count" : 41299,
  "size" : 157744000,
  "avgObjSize" : 3819.5597956366983,
  "storageSize" : 185896960,
  "numExtents" : 10,
  "nindexes" : 1,
  "lastExtentSize" : 56438784,
  "paddingFactor" : 1,
  "systemFlags" : 1,
  "userFlags" : 0,
  "totalIndexSize" : 1349040,
  "indexSizes" : {
    "_id_" : 1349040
  },
  "ok" : 1
}
```

 Loading the JSON data through a terminal session on the virtual machine can be accomplished through mongoimport in exactly the same fashion as illustrated in Example 6-5 with the following command:

```
mongoimport --db enron --collection mbox --file
/home/vagrant/share/ipynb/resources/ch06-mailboxes
/data/enron.mbox.json
```

Once MongoDB is installed, the final administrative task you'll need to perform is installing the Python client package pymongo (*http://bit.ly/1a1nqZE*) via the usual **pip install pymongo** command, since we'll soon be using a Python client to connect to MongoDB and access the Enron data.

 Be advised that MongoDB supports only databases of up to 2 GB in size for 32-bit systems (*http://bit.ly/1a1ns3L*). Although this limitation is not likely to be an issue for the Enron data set that we're working with in this chapter, you may want to take note of it in case any of the machines you commonly work on are 32-bit systems.

6.2.5.1. The MongoDB shell

Although we are programmatically using Python for our exercises in this chapter, MongoDB has a shell that can be quite convenient if you are comfortable working in a terminal, and this brief section introduces you to it. If you are taking advantage of the virtual machine experience for this book, you will need to log into the virtual machine over a secure shell session in order to follow along. Typing **vagrant ssh** from inside the top-level checkout folder containing your *Vagrantfile* automatically logs you into the virtual machine.

If you run Mac OS X or Linux, an SSH client will already exist on your system and vagrant ssh will just work. If you are a Windows user and followed the instructions in Appendix A recommending the installation of Git for Windows (*http://bit.ly/1a1nubC*), which provides an SSH client, vagrant ssh will also work so long as you explicitly opt to install the SSH client as part of the installation process. If you are a Windows user and prefer to use PuTTY (*http://bit.ly/1a1nsAG*), typing **vagrant ssh** provides some instructions on how to configure it:

```
$ vagrant ssh

Last login: Sat Jun  1 04:18:57 2013 from 10.0.2.2

vagrant@precise64:~$ mongo
MongoDB shell version: 2.4.3
connecting to: test

> show dbs
enron 0.953125GB
local 0.078125GB

> use enron
switched to db enron

> db.mbox.stats()
{
  "ns" : "enron.mbox",
  "count" : 41300,
  "size" : 157756112,
  "avgObjSize" : 3819.7605811138014,
  "storageSize" : 174727168,
  "numExtents" : 11,
  "nindexes" : 2,
  "lastExtentSize" : 50798592,
  "paddingFactor" : 1,
  "systemFlags" : 0,
  "userFlags" : 1,
  "totalIndexSize" : 221471488,
  "indexSizes" : {
    "_id_" : 1349040,
    "TextIndex" : 220122448
```

```
  },
  "ok" : 1
}

> db.mbox.findOne()
{
  "_id" : ObjectId("51968affaada66efc5694cb7"),
  "X-cc" : "",
  "From" : "heather.dunton@enron.com",
  "X-Folder" : "\\Phillip_Allen_Jan2002_1\\Allen, Phillip K.\\Inbox",
  "Content-Transfer-Encoding" : "7bit",
  "X-bcc" : "",
  "X-Origin" : "Allen-P",
  "To" : [
    "k..allen@enron.com"
  ],
  "parts" : [
    {
      "content" : " \nPlease let me know if you still need...",
        "contentType" : "text/plain"
    }
  ],
  "X-FileName" : "pallen (Non-Privileged).pst",
  "Mime-Version" : "1.0",
  "X-From" : "Dunton, Heather </O=ENRON/OU=NA/CN=RECIPIENTS/CN=HDUNTON>",
  "Date" : ISODate("2001-12-07T16:06:42Z"),
  "X-To" : "Allen, Phillip K. </O=ENRON/OU=NA/CN=RECIPIENTS/CN=Pallen>",
  "Message-ID" : "<16159836.1075855377439.JavaMail.evans@thyme>",
  "Content-Type" : "text/plain; charset=us-ascii",
  "Subject" : "RE: West Position"
}
```

The commands in this shell session showed the available databases, set the working database to enron, displayed the database statistics for enron, and fetched an arbitrary document for display. We won't spend more time in the MongoDB shell in this chapter, but you'll likely find it useful as you work with data, so it seemed appropriate to briefly introduce you to it. See "The Mongo Shell" (*http://bit.ly/1a1nus8*) in MongoDB's online documentation for details about the capabilities of the MongoDB shell.

6.2.6. Programmatically Accessing MongoDB with Python

With MongoDB successfully loaded with the Enron corpus (or any other data, for that matter), you'll want to access and manipulate it with a programming language. MongoDB is sure to please with a broad selection of libraries for many programming languages, including PyMongo (*http://bit.ly/1a1nqZE*), the recommended way to work with MongoDB from Python. A `pip install pymongo` should get PyMongo ready to use; Example 6-7 contains a simple script to show how it works. Queries are serviced by MongoDB's versatile find (*http://bit.ly/1a1nt7Q*) function, which you'll want to get acquainted with since it's the basis of most queries you'll perform with MongoDB.

Example 6-7. Using PyMongo to access MongoDB from Python

```python
import json
import pymongo # pip install pymongo
from bson import json_util # Comes with pymongo

# Connects to the MongoDB server running on
# localhost:27017 by default

client = pymongo.MongoClient()

# Get a reference to the enron database

db = client.enron

# Reference the mbox collection in the Enron database

mbox = db.mbox

# The number of messages in the collection

print "Number of messages in mbox:"
print mbox.count()
print

# Pick a message to look at...

msg = mbox.find_one()

# Display the message as pretty-printed JSON. The use of
# the custom serializer supplied by PyMongo is necessary in order
# to handle the date field that is provided as a datetime.datetime
# tuple.

print "A message:"
print json.dumps(msg, indent=1, default=json_util.default)
```

Abbreviated sample output follows and demonstrates that using PyMongo is just like using the MongoDB shell, with the exception of a couple of special considerations with relation to object serialization:

```
Number of messages in mbox:
41299

A message:
{
 "X-cc": "",
 "From": "craig_estes@enron.com",
 "Content-Transfer-Encoding": "7bit",
 "X-bcc": "",
 "parts": [
```

```
  {
    "content": "Please respond to Keith_Williams\"A YPO International...",
    "contentType": "text/plain"
  }
],
"X-Folder": "\\jskillin\\Inbox",
"X-Origin": "SKILLING-J",
"X-FileName": "jskillin.pst",
"Mime-Version": "1.0",
"Message-ID": "<24537021.1075840152262.JavaMail.evans@thyme>",
"X-From": "Craig_Estes",
"Date": {
 "$date": 988145040000
},
"X-To": "",
"_id": {
 "$oid": "51a983dae391e8ff964bc4c4"
},
"Content-Type": "text/plain; charset=us-ascii",
"Subject": "Parent Child Mountain Adventure, July 21-25, 2001"
}
```

It's been a bit of a journey, but by now you should have a good understanding of how to obtain some mail data, process it into a normalized Unix mailbox format, load the normalized data into MongoDB, and query it. The steps involved in analyzing any real-world data set will be largely similar to the steps that we've followed here (with their own unique twists and turns along the way), so if you've followed along carefully, you have some powerful new tools in your data science toolkit.

Map-Reduce in 30 Seconds

Map-reduce is a computing paradigm that consists of two primary functions: map and reduce. Mapping functions take a collection of documents and map out a new key/value pair for each document, while reduction functions take a collection of documents and reduce them in some way. For example, computing the arithmetic sum of squares, $f(x) = x_1^2 + x_2^2 + ... + x_n^2$, could be expressed as a mapping function that squares each value, producing a one-to-one correspondence for each input value, while the reducer simply sums the output of the mappers and reduces it to a single value. This programming pattern lends itself well to trivially parallelizable problems but is certainly not a good (performant) fit for every problem.

MongoDB and other document-oriented databases such as CouchDB and Riak support map-reduce both on a single machine and in distributed computing environments. If you are interested in working with "big data" or running highly customized queries on MongoDB, you'll want to learn more about map-reduce. At the present time, it is an essential skill in the big data computing paradigm.

6.3. Analyzing the Enron Corpus

Having invested a significant amount of energy and attention in the problem of getting the Enron data into a convenient format that we can query, let's now embark upon a quest to begin understanding the data. As you know from previous chapters, counting things is usually one of the first exploratory tasks you'll want to consider when faced with a new data set of any kind, because it can tell you so much with so little effort. This section investigates a couple of ways you can use MongoDB's versatile `find` operation to query a mailbox for various combinations of fields and criteria with minimal effort required as an extension of the working discussion.

Overview of the Enron Scandal

Although not entirely necessary, you will likely learn more in this chapter if you are notionally familiar with the Enron scandal, which is the subject of the mail data that we'll be analyzing. Following are a few key facts about Enron that will be helpful in understanding the context as we analyze the data for this chapter:

- Enron was a Texas-based energy company that grew to a multibillion-dollar company between its founding in 1985 and the scandal revealed in October 2001.

- Kenneth Lay was the CEO of Enron and the subject of many Enron-related discussions.

- The substance of the Enron scandal involved the use of financial instruments (referred to as *raptors*) to effectively hide accounting losses.

- Arthur Andersen, once a prestigious accounting firm, was responsible for performing the financial audits. It closed shortly after the Enron scandal.

- Soon after the scandal was revealed, Enron filed bankruptcy to the tune of over $60 billion dollars; this was the largest bankruptcy in U.S. history at the time.

The Wikipedia article on the Enron scandal (*http://bit.ly/1a1nuZo*) provides an easy-to-read introduction to the background and key events, and it takes only a few minutes to read enough of it to get the gist of what happened. If you'd like to dig deeper, the documentary film *Enron: The Smartest Guys in the Room* (*http://imdb.to/1a1nvwd*) provides all the background you'll ever need to know about Enron.

 The website *http://www.enron-mail.com* hosts a version of the Enron mail data that you may find helpful as you initially get acquainted with the Enron corpus.

6.3.1. Querying by Date/Time Range

We've taken care to import data into MongoDB so that the Date field of each object is interpreted correctly by the database, making queries by date/time range rather trivial. In fact, Example 6-8 is just a minor extension of the working example from the previous section, in that it sets up a connection to the database and then issues the following find query with some parameters to constrain the query:

```
mbox.find({"Date" :
          {
            "$lt" : end_date,
            "$gt" : start_date
          }
        }).sort("date")
```

The query is saying, "Find me all of the messages that have a Date that's greater than start_date and less than end_date, and when you get those results, return them in sorted order." Field names that start with the dollar sign, such as $lt and $gt, are special operators in MongoDB and in this case refer to "less than" and "greater than," respectively. You can read about all of the other MongoDB operators (*http://bit.ly/1a1nvN1*) in the excellent online documentation.

One other thing to keep in mind about this query is that sorting data usually takes additional time unless it's already indexed to be in the particular sorted order in which you are requesting it. We arrived at the particular date range for the query in Example 6-8 by arbitrarily picking a date based upon the general time range from our previous results from findOne, which showed us that there was data in the mailbox circa 2001.

Example 6-8. Querying MongoDB by date/time range

```
import json
import pymongo # pip install pymongo
from bson import json_util # Comes with pymongo
from datetime import datetime as dt

client = pymongo.MongoClient()

db = client.enron

mbox = db.mbox

# Create a small date range here of one day

start_date = dt(2001, 4, 1) # Year, Month, Day
end_date = dt(2001, 4, 2) # Year, Month, Day

# Query the database with the highly versatile "find" command,
# just like in the MongoDB shell.

msgs = [ msg
```

```
            for msg in mbox.find({"Date" :
                                  {
                                    "$lt" : end_date,
                                    "$gt" : start_date
                                  }
                        }).sort("date")]

# Create a convenience function to make pretty-printing JSON a little
# less cumbersome

def pp(o, indent=1):
    print json.dumps(msgs, indent=indent, default=json_util.default)

print "Messages from a query by date range:"
pp(msgs)
```

The following sample output shows that there was only one message in the data set for this particular date range:

```
Messages from a query by date range:
[
 {
   "X-cc": "",
   "From": "spisano@sprintmail.com",
   "Subject": "House repair bid",
   "To": [
    "kevin.ruscitti@enron.com"
   ],
   "Content-Transfer-Encoding": "7bit",
   "X-bcc": "",
   "parts": [
    {
      "content": "\n \n - RUSCITTI BID.wps \n\n",
      "contentType": "text/plain"
    }
   ],
   "X-Folder": "\\Ruscitti, Kevin\\Ruscitti, Kevin\\Inbox",
   "X-Origin": "RUSCITTI-K",
   "X-FileName": "Ruscitti, Kevin.pst",
   "Message-ID": "<8472651.1075845282216.JavaMail.evans@thyme>",
   "X-From": "Steven Anthony Pisano  <spisano@sprintmail.com>",
   "Date": {
    "$date": 986163540000
   },
   "X-To": "KEVIN.RUSCITTI@ENRON.COM",
   "_id": {
    "$oid": "51a983dfe391e8ff964c5229"
   },
   "Content-Type": "text/plain; charset=us-ascii",
   "Mime-Version": "1.0"
 }
]
```

Since we've carefully imported the data into MongoDB prior to this query, that's basically all that you need to do in order to slice and dice the data by a date and/or time range. Although it may seem like a "freebie," this ease of querying is dependent upon your having thought about the kinds of queries you'll want to run during the munging and import process. Had you not imported the data in a way that took advantage of MongoDB's abilities to respect dates as particular kinds of specialized fields, you'd have had the chore of now doing that work before you could make this query.

The other thing worth noting here is that Python's datetime (*http://bit.ly/1a1nwjM*) function—which was constructed with a year, month, and date—can be extended to include an hour, minute, second, and even microsecond, along with optional time zone information, as additional constraints in the tuple. Hours take values between 0 and 23. For example, a value of (2013, 12, 25, 0, 23, 5) would be December 25, 2013 at 12:23:05 AM. Although not necessarily the most convenient package to work with, datetime is definitely worth exploring since querying data sets by date/time range is among the most common things you might want to do on any given data analysis occasion.

6.3.2. Analyzing Patterns in Sender/Recipient Communications

Other metrics, such as how many messages a given person originally authored or how many direct communications occurred between any given group of people, are highly relevant statistics to consider as part of email analysis. However before you start analyzing who is communicating with whom, you may first want to simply enumerate all of the possible senders and receivers, optionally constraining the query by a criterion such as the domain from which the emails originated or to which they were delivered. As a starting point in this illustration, let's calculate the number of distinct email addresses that sent or received messages, as demonstrated in Example 6-9.

Example 6-9. Enumerating senders and receivers of messages

```
import json
import pymongo # pip install pymongo
from bson import json_util # Comes with pymongo

client = pymongo.MongoClient()
db = client.enron
mbox = db.mbox

senders = [ i for i in mbox.distinct("From") ]

receivers = [ i for i in mbox.distinct("To") ]

cc_receivers = [ i for i in mbox.distinct("Cc") ]

bcc_receivers = [ i for i in mbox.distinct("Bcc") ]
```

```
print "Num Senders:", len(senders)
print "Num Receivers:", len(receivers)
print "Num CC Receivers:", len(cc_receivers)
print "Num BCC Receivers:", len(bcc_receivers)
```

Sample output for the working data set follows:

```
Num Senders: 7665
Num Receivers: 22162
Num CC Receivers: 6561
Num BCC Receivers: 6561
```

Without any other information, these counts of senders and receivers are fairly interesting to consider. On average, each message was sent to three people, with a fairly substantial number of courtesy copies (CCs) and blind courtesy copies (BCCs) on the messages. The next step might be to winnow down the data and use basic set operations (*http://bit.ly/1a1l2Sw*) (as introduced back in Chapter 1) to determine what kind of overlap exists between various combinations of these criteria. To do that, we'll simply need to cast the lists that contain each unique value to **sets** so that we can make various kinds of set comparisons (*http://bit.ly/1a1nxo2*), including intersections, differences, and unions. Table 6-2 illustrates these basic operations over this small universe of senders and receivers to show you how this will work on the data:

```
Senders = {Abe, Bob}, Receivers = {Bob, Carol}
```

Table 6-2. Sample set operations

Operation	Operation name	Result	Comment
Senders ∪ Receivers	Union	Abe, Bob, Carol	All unique senders and receivers of messages
Senders ∩ Receivers	Intersection	Bob	Senders who were also receivers of messages
Senders – Receivers	Difference	Abe	Senders who did not receive messages
Receivers – Senders	Difference	Carol	Receivers who did not send messages

Example 6-10 shows how to employ set operations in Python to compute on data.

Example 6-10. Analyzing senders and receivers with set operations

```
senders = set(senders)
receivers = set(receivers)
cc_receivers = set(cc_receivers)
bcc_receivers = set(bcc_receivers)

# Find the number of senders who were also direct receivers

senders_intersect_receivers = senders.intersection(receivers)

# Find the senders that didn't receive any messages

senders_diff_receivers = senders.difference(receivers)
```

```
# Find the receivers that didn't send any messages

receivers_diff_senders = receivers.difference(senders)

# Find the senders who were any kind of receiver by
# first computing the union of all types of receivers

all_receivers = receivers.union(cc_receivers, bcc_receivers)
senders_all_receivers = senders.intersection(all_receivers)

print "Num senders in common with receivers:", len(senders_intersect_receivers)
print "Num senders who didn't receive:", len(senders_diff_receivers)
print "Num receivers who didn't send:", len(receivers_diff_senders)
print "Num senders in common with *all* receivers:", len(senders_all_receivers)
```

The following sample output from this script reveals some additional insight about the nature of the mailbox data:

```
Num senders in common with receivers: 3220
Num senders who didn't receive: 4445
Num receivers who didn't send: 18942
Num senders in common with all receivers: 3440
```

In this particular case, there were far more receivers than senders, and of the 7,665 senders, only about 3,220 (less than half) of them also received a message. For arbitrary mailbox data, it may at first seem slightly surprising that there were so many recipients of messages who didn't send messages, but keep in mind that we are only analyzing the mailbox data for a small group of individuals from a large corporation. It seems reasonable that lots of employees would receive "email blasts" from senior management or other corporate communications but be unlikely to respond to any of the original senders.

Furthermore, although we have a mailbox that shows us messages that were both outgoing and incoming among a population spanning not just Enron but the entire world, we still have just a small sample of the overall data, considering that we are looking at the mailboxes of only a small group of Enron employees and we don't have access to any of the senders from other domains, such as *bob@example1.com* or *jane@example2.com*.

The tension this latter insight delivers begs an interesting question that is a nice follow-up exercise in our quest to better understand the inbox: let's determine how many senders and recipients were Enron employees, based upon the assumption that an Enron employee would have an email address that ends with *@enron.com*. Example 6-11 shows one way to do it.

Example 6-11. Finding senders and receivers of messages who were Enron employees

```
# In a Mongo shell, you could try this query for the same effect:
# db.mbox.find({"To" : {"$regex" : /.*enron.com.*/i} },
#               {"To" : 1, "_id" : 0})
```

```
senders = [ i
        for i in mbox.distinct("From")
            if i.lower().find("@enron.com") > -1 ]

receivers = [ i
          for i in mbox.distinct("To")
              if i.lower().find("@enron.com") > -1 ]

cc_receivers = [ i
            for i in mbox.distinct("Cc")
                if i.lower().find("@enron.com") > -1 ]

bcc_receivers = [ i
              for i in mbox.distinct("Bcc")
                  if i.lower().find("@enron.com") > -1 ]

print "Num Senders:", len(senders)
print "Num Receivers:", len(receivers)
print "Num CC Receivers:", len(cc_receivers)
print "Num BCC Receivers:", len(bcc_receivers)
```

Sample output from the script follows:

```
Num Senders: 3137
Num Receivers: 16653
Num CC Receivers: 4890
Num BCC Receivers: 4890
```

The new data reveals that 3,137 of the original 7,665 senders were Enron employees, which implies that the remaining senders were from other domains. The data also reveals to us that these approximately 3,000 senders collectively reached out to nearly 17,000 employees. A *USA Today* analysis of Enron, "The Enron scandal by the numbers," (*http://usat.ly/1a1nxEp*) reveals that there were approximately 20,600 employees at Enron at the time, so we have have upward of 80% of those employees here in our database.

At this point, a logical next step might be to take a particular email address and zero in on communications involving it. For example, how many messages in the data set originated with Enron's CEO, Kenneth Lay? From perusing some of the email address nomenclature in the enumerated outputs of our scripts so far, we could guess that his email address might simply have been *kenneth.lay@enron.com*. However, a closer inspection[3] reveals a few additional aliases that we'll also want to consider. Example 6-12 provides a starting template for further investigation and demonstrates how to use MongoDB's $in operator to search for values that exist within a list of possibilities.

---

3. In this particular case, a "closer inspection" was simply a search for "lay@enron" (grep 'lay@enron'* in a Unix or Linux terminal) on the *ipynb/resources/ch06-mailboxes/data/enron_mail_20110402/enron_data/ maildir/lay-k/inbox* directory, which revealed some of the possible email aliases that might have existed.

Example 6-12. Counting sent/received messages for particular email addresses

```python
import json
import pymongo # pip install pymongo
from bson import json_util # Comes with pymongo

client = pymongo.MongoClient()
db = client.enron
mbox = db.mbox

aliases = ["kenneth.lay@enron.com", "ken_lay@enron.com", "ken.lay@enron.com",
           "kenneth_lay@enron.net", "klay@enron.com"] # More possibilities?

to_msgs = [ msg
            for msg in mbox.find({"To" : { "$in" : aliases } })]

from_msgs = [ msg
          for msg in mbox.find({"From" : { "$in" : aliases } })]

print "Number of message sent to:", len(to_msgs)
print "Number of messages sent from:", len(from_msgs)
```

Sample output from the script is a bit surprising. There are virtually no messages in the subset of the corpus that we loaded that were sent from one of the obvious variations of Kenneth Lay's email address:

```
Number of message sent to: 1326
Number of messages sent from: 7
```

It appears as though there is a substantial amount of data in the Enron corpus that was sent *to* the Enron CEO, but few messages that were sent *from* the CEO—or at least, not in the *inbox* folder that we're considering.[4] (Bear in mind that we opted to load only the portion of the Enron data that appeared in an *inbox* folder. Loading more data, such as the messages from *sent items*, is left as an exercise for the reader and an area for further investigation.) The following two considerations are left for readers who are interested in performing intensive analysis of Kenneth Lay's email data:

- Executives in large corporations tend to use assistants who facilitate a lot of communication. Kenneth Lay's assistant was Rosalee Fleming, who had the email address *rosalee.fleming@enron.com*. Try searching for communications that used his assistant as a proxy.

---

4. A search for "kenneth.lay@enron.com" (grep -R "From: kenneth.lay@enron.com" * on a Unix or Linux system), and other email alias variations of this command that may have appeared in mail headers in the *ipynb/resources/ch06-mailboxes/data/enron_mail_20110402/enron_data/maildir/lay-k* folder of the Enron corpus, turned up few results. This suggests that there simply is not a lot of outgoing mail data in the part of the Enron corpus that we are focused on.

- It is possible that the nature of the court case may have resulted in considerable data redactions due to either relevancy or (attorney-client) privilege.

If you are reading along carefully, your mind may be racing with questions by this point, and you probably have the tools at your fingertips to answer many of them—especially if you apply principles from previous chapters. A few questions that might come to mind at this point include:

- What are some of these messages about, based on what the content bodies say?
- What was the maximum number of recipients on a message? (And what was the message about?)
- Which two people exchanged the most messages? (And what were they talking about?)
- How many messages were person-to-person messages? (Single sender to single receiver or single sender to a few receivers would probably imply a more substantive dialogue than "email blasts" containing company announcements and such things.)
- How many messages were in the longest reply chain? (And what was it about?)

The Enron corpus has been and continues to be the subject of numerous academic publications that investigate these questions and many more. With a little creativity and legwork provided primarily by MongoDB's find operator (*http://bit.ly/1a1nt7Q*), its data aggregations framework (*http://bit.ly/1a1nA2Z*), its indexing capabilities (*http://bit.ly/1a1nA3d*), and some of the text mining techniques from previous chapters, you have the tools you need to begin answering many interesting questions. Of course, we'll only be able to do so much analysis here in the working discussion.

6.3.3. Writing Advanced Queries

MongoDB's powerful aggregation framework (*http://bit.ly/1a1nA2Z*) was introduced in version 2.2. It's called an *aggregation* framework because it is designed to allow you to compute powerful aggregates (as opposed to more primitive queries where you're basically filtering over the data) that involve pipelines of groupings, sorts, and more—all entirely within the MongoDB database instead of your having to dispatch and intermediate multiple queries from your Python script. Like any framework, it's not without its own limitations, but the general pattern for querying MongoDB is fairly intuitive once you have worked through an example or two. The aggregation framework lends itself to constructing queries one step at a time since an aggregate query is a sequence of steps, so let's take a look at an example that seeks to discover the recipients of a message sent by a sender. In a MongoDB shell, one possible interpretation of such a query could look like this:

```
> db.mbox.aggregate(
  {"$match" : {"From" : "kenneth.lay@enron.com"} },
```

```
    {"$project" : {"From" : 1, "To" : 1} },
    {"$group" : {"_id" : "$From", "recipients" : {"$addToSet" : "$To" } } }
    )
```

The query consists of a pipeline comprising three steps, where the first involves using the $match (*http://bit.ly/1a1nAA5*) operator to find any message that is sent from a particular email address. Keep in mind that we could have used MongoDB's $in (*http://bit.ly/1a1nAQA*) operator, as in Example 6-12, to provide an expanded list of options for the match. In general, using $match as early as possible in an aggregation pipeline is considered a best practice, because it narrows down the list of possibilities for each stage later in the pipeline, resulting in less overall computation.

The next step of the pipeline involves using $project (*http://bit.ly/1a1nAQO*) to extract only the From and To fields of each message, since our result set requires knowing only the senders and recipients of messages. Also, as we'll observe in the next step, the From field is used as the basis of grouping with the $group operator to effectively collapse the results into a single list.

Finally, the $group (*http://bit.ly/1a1nB7j*) operator, as just alluded to, specifies that the From field should be the basis of grouping and the value of the To field contained in the results of the grouping should be added to a set via the $addToSet operator (*http://bit.ly/ 1a1nCbg*). An abbreviated result set follows to illustrate the final form of the query. Notice that there is only one result object—a single document containing an _id and a recipients field, where the recipients field is a list of lists that describe each set of recipients with whom the sender (identified by the _id) has communicated:

```
{
  "result" : [
    {
      "_id" : "kenneth.lay@enron.com",
      "recipients" : [
        [
          "j..kean@enron.com",
          "john.brindle@enron.com"
        ],
        [
          "e..haedicke@enron.com"
        ],

              ...2 more very large lists...

        [
          "mark.koenig@enron.com",
          "j..kean@enron.com",
          "pr<.palmer@enron.com>",
          "james.derrick@enron.com",
          "elizabeth.tilney@enron.com",
          "greg.whalley@enron.com",
          "jeffrey.mcmahon@enron.com",
          "raymond.bowen@enron.com"
```

```
    ],
    [
      "tim.despain@enron.com"
    ]
   ]
  }
 ],
 "ok" : 1
}
```

The first time you see a query using the aggregation framework, it may feel a bit daunt-ing, but rest assured that a few minutes fiddling around in the MongoDB shell will go a long way toward breeding familiarity with how it works. It is highly recommended that you take the time to try running each stage of the aggregated query to better un-derstand how each step transforms the data from the previous step.

You could easily manipulate the data structure computed by MongoDB with Python, but for now let's consider one other variation for the same query, primarily to introduce an additional operator from the aggregation framework called $unwind:

```
> db.mbox.aggregate(
  {"$match" : {"From" : "kenneth.lay@enron.com"} },
  {"$project" : {"From" : 1, "To" : 1} },
  {"$unwind" : "$To"},
  {"$group" : {"_id" : "From", "recipients" : {"$addToSet" : "$To"}} }
  )
```

Sample results for this query follow:

```
{
  "result" : [
    {
      "_id" : "kenneth.lay@enron.com",
      "recipients" : [
        "john.brindle@enron.com",
        "colleen.sullivan@enron.com",
        "richard.shapiro@enron.com",

            ...many more results...

        "juan.canavati.@enron.com",
        "jody.crook@enron.com"
      ]
    }
  ],
  "ok" : 1
}
```

Whereas our initial query that didn't use $unwind produced groupings that correspon-ded to the particular recipients of each message, $unwind creates an intermediate stage of the following form, which is then passed into the $group operator:

```
{
  "result" : [
    {
      "_id" : ObjectId("51a983dae391e8ff964bc85e"),
      "From" : "kenneth.lay@enron.com",
      "To" : "tim.despain@enron.com"
    },
    {
      "_id" : ObjectId("51a983dae391e8ff964bdbc1"),
      "From" : "kenneth.lay@enron.com",
      "To" : "mark.koenig@enron.com"
    },

        ...many more results...

    {
      "_id" : ObjectId("51a983dde391e8ff964c241b"),
      "From" : "kenneth.lay@enron.com",
      "To" : "john.brindle@enron.com"
    }
  ],
  "ok" : 1
}
```

In effect, $unwind "unwinds" a list by taking each item and coupling it back with the other fields in the document. In this particular case the only other field of note was the From field, which we'd just projected out. After the unwinding, the $group operator is then able to group on the From field and effectively roll all of the recipients into a single list. The list has exactly the same size as the number of results that were passed into it, which means that there could be (and probably are) some duplicates in the final result. However, a subtle but important point is that the $addToSet modifier in the next $group operation eliminates duplicates since it treats the list it constructs as a set; therefore, the results of this query are ultimately a list of the unique recipients. Example 6-13 illustrates these queries with PyMongo as a wrap-up to this brief overview of MongoDB's aggregation framework and how it can help you to analyze data.

Example 6-13. Using MongoDB's data aggregation framework

```
import json
import pymongo # pip install pymongo
from bson import json_util # Comes with pymongo

# The basis of our query
FROM = "kenneth.lay@enron.com"

client = pymongo.MongoClient()
db = client.enron
mbox = db.mbox

# Get the recipient lists for each message
```

```
recipients_per_message = db.mbox.aggregate([
  {"$match" : {"From" : FROM} },
  {"$project" : {"From" : 1, "To" : 1} },
  {"$group" : {"_id" : "$From", "recipients" : {"$addToSet" : "$To" } } }
])['result'][0]['recipients']

# Collapse the lists of recipients into a single list

all_recipients = [recipient
                  for message in recipients_per_message
                    for recipient in message]

# Calculate the number of recipients per sent message and sort

recipients_per_message_totals = \
  sorted([len(recipients)
    for recipients in recipients_per_message])

# Demonstrate how to use $unwind followed by $group to collapse
# the recipient lists into a single list (with no duplicates
# per the $addToSet operator)

unique_recipients = db.mbox.aggregate([
  {"$match" : {"From" : FROM} },
  {"$project" : {"From" : 1, "To" : 1} },
  {"$unwind" : "$To"},
  {"$group" : {"_id" : "From", "recipients" : {"$addToSet" : "$To"}} }
])['result'][0]['recipients']

print "Num total recipients on all messages:", len(all_recipients)
print "Num recipients for each message:", recipients_per_message_totals
print "Num unique recipients", len(unique_recipients)
```

The sample output from this query is a bit surprising and reveals that just a few messages were sent by this individual (as we noted earlier), ranging from a couple of exchanges with a single individual to a rather large email blast to a huge email blast sent to nearly 1,000 people:

```
Num total recipients on all messages: 1043
Num recipients for each message: [1, 1, 2, 8, 85, 946]
Num unique recipients 916
```

Note the peculiarity that the number of total recipients in the largest email blast (946) is higher than the total number of unique recipients (916). Any guesses on what happened here? A closer inspection of the data reveals that the large email blast to 946 people contained 65 duplicate recipients. It's likely the case that the administrative work involved in managing large email lists is prone to error, so the appearance of duplicates isn't all that surprising. Another possibility that could explain the duplicates, however, is that some of the messages may have been sent to multiple mailing lists, and certain individuals may appear on multiple lists.

6.3.4. Searching Emails by Keywords

MongoDB features a number of powerful indexing capabilities (*http://bit.ly/1a1nA3d*), and version 2.4 introduced a new full-text search (*http://bit.ly/1a1nEzO*) feature that provides a simple yet powerful interface for keyword search on indexable fields of its documents. Although it's a new feature that's still in early development as of v2.4 and some caveats still apply, it's nonetheless worthwhile to introduce, because it allows you to search on the content of the mail messages as well as any other field. The virtual machine for this book comes with MongoDB already configured to enable its text search feature, so all that's required to build a text index is to use the `ensureIndex` method on a collection in your database.

In a MongoDB shell, you'd simply type the following two commands to build a single full-text index on all fields and then view the statistics on the database to see that it has indeed been created, and its size. The special $** field simply means "all fields," the type of the index is "text," and its name is "TextIndex." For the mere cost of 220 MB of disk space, we have a full-text index to run any number of queries that can return documents to help us zero in on particular threads of interest:

```
> db.mbox.ensureIndex({"$**" : "text"}, {name : "TextIndex"})
> db.mbox.stats()
{
  "ns" : "enron.mbox",
  "count" : 41299,
  "size" : 157744000,
  "avgObjSize" : 3819.5597956366983,
  "storageSize" : 185896960,
  "numExtents" : 10,
  "nindexes" : 2,
  "lastExtentSize" : 56438784,
  "paddingFactor" : 1,
  "systemFlags" : 0,
  "userFlags" : 1,
  "totalIndexSize" : 221463312,
  "indexSizes" : {
    "_id_" : 1349040,
    "TextIndex" : 220114272
  },
  "ok" : 1
}
```

Creation of the index and querying of the statistics works pretty much just as you'd expect with PyMongo, as shown in Example 6-14, except that the syntax is slightly different between the MongoDB shell's `ensureIndex` and the PyMongo driver's `ensure_index` (*http://bit.ly/1a1nEA3*). Additionally, the way that you'd query a database for statistics or run a query on the text index varies slightly and involves PyMongo's `command` (*http://bit.ly/1a1nCIq*) method. In general, the `command` method takes a command as its first parameter, a collection name as its second parameter, and a list of relevant keyword parameters as additional parameters if you are trying to correlate its syntax back to the MongoDB shell (which provides some syntactic sugar).

Example 6-14. Creating a text index on MongoDB documents with PyMongo

```
import json
import pymongo # pip install pymongo
from bson import json_util # Comes with pymongo

client = pymongo.MongoClient()
db = client.enron
mbox = db.mbox

# Create an index if it doesn't already exist
mbox.ensure_index([("$**", "text")], name="TextIndex")

# Get the collection stats (collstats) on a collection
# named "mbox"
print json.dumps(db.command("collstats", "mbox"), indent=1)

# Use the db.command method to issue a "text" command
# on collection "mbox" with parameters, remembering that
# we need to use json_util to handle serialization of our JSON
print json.dumps(db.command("text", "mbox",
                            search="raptor",
                            limit=1),
                 indent=1, default=json_util.default)
```

MongoDB's full-text search capabilities are quite powerful, and you should review the text search documentation (*http://bit.ly/1a1nDfb*) to appreciate what is possible. You can search for any term out of a list of terms, search for specific phrases, and prohibit the appearance of certain terms in search results. All fields are initially weighted the same, but it is also even possible to weight fields differently (*http://bit.ly/1a1nFDO*) so as to tune the results that may come back from a search.

In our Enron corpus, for example, if you were searching for an email address, you might want to weight the To: and From: fields more heavily than the Cc: or Bcc: fields to improve the ranking of returned results. If you were searching for keywords, you might want to weight the appearance of terms in the subject of the message more heavily than their appearance in the content of the message.

In the context of Enron, *raptors* were financial devices that were used to hide hundreds of millions of dollars in debt, from an accounting standpoint. Following are truncated sample query results for the infamous word *raptor* (*http://bit.ly/1a1nFE6*), produced by running a text query in the MongoDB shell:

```
> db.mbox.runCommand("text", {"search" : "raptor"})
{
  "queryDebugString" : "raptor||||||",
    "language" : "english",
```

```
"results" : [
  {
"score" : 2.0938471502590676,
"obj" : {
  "_id" : ObjectId("51a983dfe391e8ff964c63a7"),
  "Content-Transfer-Encoding" : "7bit",
  "From" : "joel.ephross@enron.com",
  "X-Folder" : "\\SSHACKL (Non-Privileged)\\Shackleton, Sara\\Inbox",
  "Cc" : [
    "mspradling@velaw.com"
  ],
  "X-bcc" : "",
  "X-Origin" : "Shackleton-S",
  "Bcc" : [
    "mspradling@velaw.com"
  ],
  "X-cc" : "'mspradling@velaw.com'",
  "To" : [
    "maricela.trevino@enron.com",
    "sara.shackleton@enron.com",
    "mary.cook@enron.com",
    "george.mckean@enron.com",
    "brent.vasconcellos@enron.com"
  ],
  "parts" : [
    {
      "content" : "Maricela, attached is a draft of one of the...",
      "contentType" : "text/plain"
    }
  ],
  "X-FileName" : "SSHACKL (Non-Privileged).pst",
  "Mime-Version" : "1.0",
  "X-From" : "Ephross, Joel </O=ENRON/OU=NA/CN=RECIPIENTS/CN=JEPHROS>",
  "Date" : ISODate("2001-09-21T12:25:21Z"),
  "X-To" : "Trevino, Maricela </O=ENRON/OU=NA/CN=RECIPIENTS/CN=Mtr...",
  "Message-ID" : "<28660745.1075858812819.JavaMail.evans@thyme>",
  "Content-Type" : "text/plain; charset=us-ascii",
  "Subject" : "Raptor"
},

    ...73 more results...

  {
"score" : 0.5000529829394935,
"obj" : {
  "_id" : ObjectId("51a983dee391e8ff964c363b"),
  "X-cc" : "",
  "From" : "sarah.palmer@enron.com",
  "X-Folder" : "\\ExMerge - Martin, Thomas A.\\Inbox",
  "Content-Transfer-Encoding" : "7bit",
  "X-bcc" : "",
  "X-Origin" : "MARTIN-T",
```

```
        "To" : [
          "sarah.palmer@enron.com"
        ],
        "parts" : [
          {
            "content" : "\nMore than one Enron official warned company...",
            "contentType" : "text/plain"
          }
        ],
        "X-FileName" : "tom martin 6-25-02.PST",
        "Mime-Version" : "1.0",
        "X-From" : "Palmer, Sarah </O=ENRON/OU=NA/CN=RECIPIENTS/CN=SPALME2>",
        "Date" : ISODate("2002-01-18T14:32:00Z"),
        "X-To" : "Palmer, Sarah </O=ENRON/OU=NA/CN=RECIPIENTS/CN=Spalme2>",
        "Message-ID" : "<8664618.1075841171256.JavaMail.evans@thyme>",
        "Content-Type" : "text/plain; charset=ANSI_X3.4-1968",
        "Subject" : "Enron Mentions -- 01/18/02"
      }
    }
  ],
  "stats" : {
    "nscanned" : 75,
    "nscannedObjects" : 0,
    "n" : 75,
    "nfound" : 75,
    "timeMicros" : 230716
  },
  "ok" : 1
}
```

Now that you're familiar with the term *raptor* as it relates to the Enron story, you might find the first few lines of a highly ranked message in the search results helpful as context:

> The quarterly valuations for the assets hedged in the Raptor structure were valued through the normal quarterly revaluation process. The business units, RAC and Arthur Andersen all signed off on the initial valuations for the assets hedged in Raptor. All the investments in Raptor were on the MPR and were monitored by the business units, and we prepared the Raptor position report based upon this information....

If you felt like you were swimming in a collection of thousands of messages and weren't sure where to start looking, that simple keyword search certainly guided you to a good starting point. The subject of the message just quoted is "RE: Raptor Debris." Wouldn't it be fascinating to know who else was in on that discussion thread and other threads about Raptor? You have the tools and the know-how to find out.

B-Trees Are the Bee's Knees?

B-trees are the fundamental underlying data structure for MongoDB and most other database systems, because they exhibit very efficient performance characteristics for core operations (searches, inserts, updates, deletes) over the long haul, even when continually faced with worst-case situations. In computer science terminology, their performance of their core operations is characterized as "logarithmic" and is expressed as $O(\log n)$ in the "Big-O" notation that was introduced in Chapter 3. B-trees necessarily remain balanced and maintain data in sorted order.

These characteristics yield efficient lookups because the underlying implementations require minimal disk reads. Given that disk seeks for traditional platter-based hard drives are still fast (on the order of low-single-digit milliseconds), this means that huge volumes of data as stored by B-trees can be accessed just as quickly. MongoDB heavily utilizes B-trees not only for its secondary indexes (*http://bit.ly/1a1nA3d*), which you can build on particular fields or combinations of fields, but also to back its geospatial indexes (*http://bit.ly/1a1nGrt*) and its text search index (*http://bit.ly/1a1nEzO*), which was just introduced in this section.

In case you're wondering, there's no complete consensus about the etymology of the name *B-tree*, but it's generally accepted that the *B* stands for Bayer, the man who is credited with inventing them. There is more information about B-trees and their common variants online than you'd probably care to read. If you decide to take the deep dive into MongoDB, it's worthwhile to learn something about them at the theoretical and practical implementation levels since they are so integral to MongoDB's design.

6.4. Discovering and Visualizing Time-Series Trends

There are numerous ways to visualize mail data, and that topic has been the subject of many publications and open source projects that you can seek out for inspiration. The visualizations we've used so far in this book would also be good candidates to recycle. As an initial starting point, let's implement a visualization that takes into account the kind of frequency analysis we did earlier in this chapter with MongoDB and use IPython Notebook to render it in a meaningful way. For example, we could count messages by date/time range and present the data as a table or chart to help identify trends, such as the days of the week or times of the day that the most mail transactions happen. Other possibilities might include creating a graphical representation of connections among senders and recipients and filtering by keywords in the content or subject line of the messages, or computing histograms that show deeper insights than the rudimentary counting we accomplished earlier.

Example 6-15 demonstrates an aggregated query that shows how to use MongoDB to count messages for you by date/time components. The query involves three pipelines. The first pipeline deconstructs the date into a subdocument of its components; the second pipeline groups based upon which fields are assigned to its _id and sums the count by using the built-in $sum (*http://bit.ly/1a1nGYq*) function, which is commonly used in conjunction with $group; and the third pipeline sorts by year and month.

Example 6-15. Aggregate querying for counts of messages by date/time range

```python
import json
import pymongo # pip install pymongo
from bson import json_util # Comes with pymongo

client = pymongo.MongoClient()
db = client.enron
mbox = db.mbox

results = mbox.aggregate([
{
  # Create a subdocument called DateBucket with each date component projected
  # so that these fields can be grouped on in the next stage of the pipeline
  "$project" :
  {
    "_id" : 0,
    "DateBucket" :
    {
      "year" : {"$year" : "$Date"},
      "month" : {"$month" : "$Date"},
      "day" : {"$dayOfMonth" : "$Date"},
      "hour" : {"$hour" : "$Date"},
    }
  }
},
{
  "$group" :
  {
    # Group by year and date by using these fields for the key.
    "_id" : {"year" : "$DateBucket.year", "month" : "$DateBucket.month"},

    # Increment the sum for each group by 1 for every document that's in it
    "num_msgs" : {"$sum" : 1}
  }
},
{
  "$sort" : {"_id.year" : 1, "_id.month" : 1}
}
])

print results
```

Sample output for the query, sorted by month and year, follows:

```
{u'ok': 1.0,
 u'result': [{u'_id': {u'month': 1, u'year': 1997}, u'num_msgs': 1},
  {u'_id': {u'month': 1, u'year': 1998}, u'num_msgs': 1},
  {u'_id': {u'month': 12, u'year': 2000}, u'num_msgs': 1},
  {u'_id': {u'month': 1, u'year': 2001}, u'num_msgs': 3},
  {u'_id': {u'month': 2, u'year': 2001}, u'num_msgs': 3},
  {u'_id': {u'month': 3, u'year': 2001}, u'num_msgs': 21},
  {u'_id': {u'month': 4, u'year': 2001}, u'num_msgs': 811},
  {u'_id': {u'month': 5, u'year': 2001}, u'num_msgs': 2118},
  {u'_id': {u'month': 6, u'year': 2001}, u'num_msgs': 1650},
  {u'_id': {u'month': 7, u'year': 2001}, u'num_msgs': 802},
  {u'_id': {u'month': 8, u'year': 2001}, u'num_msgs': 1538},
  {u'_id': {u'month': 9, u'year': 2001}, u'num_msgs': 3538},
  {u'_id': {u'month': 10, u'year': 2001}, u'num_msgs': 10630},
  {u'_id': {u'month': 11, u'year': 2001}, u'num_msgs': 9219},
  {u'_id': {u'month': 12, u'year': 2001}, u'num_msgs': 4541},
  {u'_id': {u'month': 1, u'year': 2002}, u'num_msgs': 3611},
  {u'_id': {u'month': 2, u'year': 2002}, u'num_msgs': 1919},
  {u'_id': {u'month': 3, u'year': 2002}, u'num_msgs': 514},
  {u'_id': {u'month': 4, u'year': 2002}, u'num_msgs': 97},
  {u'_id': {u'month': 5, u'year': 2002}, u'num_msgs': 85},
  {u'_id': {u'month': 6, u'year': 2002}, u'num_msgs': 166},
  {u'_id': {u'month': 10, u'year': 2002}, u'num_msgs': 1},
  {u'_id': {u'month': 12, u'year': 2002}, u'num_msgs': 1},
  {u'_id': {u'month': 2, u'year': 2004}, u'num_msgs': 26},
  {u'_id': {u'month': 12, u'year': 2020}, u'num_msgs': 2}]}
```

As written, this query counts the number of messages for each month and year, but you could easily adapt it in a variety of ways to discover communications patterns. For example, you could include only the $DateBucket.day or $DateBucket.hour to count which days of the week or which hours of the day show the most volume, respectively. You may find ranges of dates or times worth considering as well; you can do this via the $gt and $lt operators.

Another possibility is to use modulo arithmetic to partition numeric values, such as hours of the day, into ranges. For example, consider the following key and value, which could be part of a MongoDB query document as part of the initial projection:

```
"hour" : {"$subtract" : [
                         {"$hour" : "$Date"},
                         {"$mod" : [{"$hour" :"$Date"} , 2]}
                        ]
```

This query partitions hours into two-unit intervals by taking the hour component from the date and subtracting 1 from its value if it does not evenly divide by two. Spend a few minutes with the sample code introduced in this section and see what you discover in the data for yourself. Keep in mind that the beauty of this kind of aggregated query is that MongoDB is doing all of the work for you, as opposed to just returning you data to process yourself.

Perhaps the simplest display of this kind of information is a table. Example 6-16 shows how to use the `prettytable` package, introduced in earlier chapters, to render the data so that it's easy on the eyes.

Example 6-16. Rendering time series results as a nicely displayed table

```
from prettytable import PrettyTable


pt = PrettyTable(field_names=['Year', 'Month', 'Num Msgs'])
pt.align['Num Msgs'], pt.align['Month'] = 'r', 'r'
[ pt.add_row([ result['_id']['year'], result['_id']['month'], result['num_msgs'] ])
  for result in results['result'] ]

print pt
```

A table lends itself to examining the volume of the mail messages on a monthly basis,[5] and it highlights an important anomaly: the volume of mail data for October 2001 was approximately three times higher than for any preceding month! It was in October 2001 when the Enron scandal was revealed, which no doubt triggered an immense amount of communication that didn't begin to taper off until nearly two months later:

```
+------+-------+----------+
| Year | Month | Num Msgs |
+------+-------+----------+
| 1997 |     1 |        1 |
| 1998 |     1 |        1 |
| 2000 |    12 |        1 |
| 2001 |     1 |        3 |
| 2001 |     2 |        3 |
| 2001 |     3 |       21 |
| 2001 |     4 |      811 |
| 2001 |     5 |     2118 |
| 2001 |     6 |     1650 |
| 2001 |     7 |      802 |
| 2001 |     8 |     1538 |
| 2001 |     9 |     3538 |
| 2001 |    10 |    10630 |
| 2001 |    11 |     9219 |
| 2001 |    12 |     4541 |
| 2002 |     1 |     3611 |
| 2002 |     2 |     1919 |
| 2002 |     3 |      514 |
| 2002 |     4 |       97 |
| 2002 |     5 |       85 |
| 2002 |     6 |      166 |
| 2002 |    10 |        1 |
```

5. The two messages that appear to have been authored in the year 2020 are the result of bugs in the original export of the mail data that are beyond our control.

```
| 2002 |    12 |        1 |
| 2004 |     2 |       26 |
| 2020 |    12 |        2 |
+------+-------+----------+
```

Applying techniques for analyzing the human language data (as introduced in previous chapters) for the months of October and November 2001 reveals some fundamentally different patterns in communication, both from the standpoint of senders and recipients of messages and from the standpoint of the words used in the language itself.

There are numerous other possibilities for visualizing mail data, as mentioned in the recommended exercises for this chapter. Using IPython Notebook's charting libraries might be among the next steps to consider.

6.5. Analyzing Your Own Mail Data

The Enron mail data makes for great illustrations in a chapter on mail analysis, but you'll probably also want to take a closer look at your own mail data. Fortunately, many popular mail clients provide an "export to mbox" option, which makes it pretty simple to get your mail data into a format that lends itself to analysis by the techniques described in this chapter.

For example, in Apple Mail, you can select some number of messages, pick "Save As…" from the File menu, and then choose "Raw Message Source" as the formatting option to export the messages as an mbox file (see Figure 6-2). A little bit of searching should turn up results for how to do this in most other major clients.

Figure 6-2. Most mail clients provide an option for exporting your mail data to an mbox archive

If you exclusively use an online mail client, you could opt to pull your data down into a mail client and export it, but you might prefer to fully automate the creation of an mbox file by pulling the data directly from the server. Just about any online mail service will support POP3 (Post Office Protocol, version 3), most also support IMAP (Internet

Message Access Protocol), and it's not hard to whip up Python scripts for pulling down your mail.

One particularly robust command-line tool that you can use to pull mail data from just about anywhere is getmail (*http://bit.ly/1a1nKaL*), which turns out to be written in Python. Two modules included in Python's standard library, poplib (*http://bit.ly/1a1nI2G*) and imaplib (*http://bit.ly/1a1nIj5*), provide a terrific foundation, so you're also likely to run across lots of useful scripts if you do a bit of searching online. get mail is particularly easy to get up and running. To retrieve your Gmail inbox data, for example, you just download and install it, then set up a *getmailrc* configuration file.

The following sample settings demonstrate some settings for a *nix environment. Windows users would need to change the [destination] path and [options] mes sage_log values to valid paths, but keep in mind that you could opt to run the script on the virtual machine for this book if you needed a quick fix for a *nix environment:

```
[retriever]
type = SimpleIMAPSSLRetriever
server = imap.gmail.com
username = ptwobrussell
password = xxx

[destination]
type = Mboxrd
path = /tmp/gmail.mbox

[options]
verbose = 2
message_log = ~/.getmail/gmail.log
```

With a configuration in place, simply invoking getmail from a terminal does the rest. Once you have a local mbox on hand, you can analyze it using the techniques you've learned in this chapter. Here's what getmail looks like while it's in action slurping down your mail data:

```
$ getmail
getmail version 4.20.0
Copyright (C) 1998-2009 Charles Cazabon.  Licensed under the GNU GPL version 2.
SimpleIMAPSSLRetriever:ptwobrussell@imap.gmail.com:993:
  msg     1/10972 (4227 bytes) from ... delivered to Mboxrd /tmp/gmail.mbox
  msg     2/10972 (3219 bytes) from ... delivered to Mboxrd /tmp/gmail.mbox
  ...
```

6.5.1. Accessing Your Gmail with OAuth

In early 2010, Google announced OAuth access to IMAP and SMTP in Gmail (*http://bit.ly/1a1nIzH*). This was a significant announcement because it officially opened the door to "Gmail as a platform," enabling third-party developers to build apps that can access your Gmail data without you needing to give them your username and password.

This section won't get into the particular nuances of how Xoauth, Google's particular implementation of OAuth (*http://bit.ly/1a1nKHV*), works (see Appendix B for a terse introduction to OAuth in general); instead, it focuses on getting you up and running so that you can access your Gmail data, which involves just a few simple steps:

1. Select the "Enable IMAP" option under the "Forwarding and POP/IMAP" tab in your Gmail Account Settings.

2. Visit the Google Mail Xoauth Tools wiki page (*http://bit.ly/1a1nKYa*), download the xoauth.py command-line utility, and follow the instructions to generate an OAuth token and secret for an "anonymous" consumer.[6]

3. Install python-oauth2 (*http://bit.ly/1a1nJnh*) via pip install oauth2 and use the template in Example 6-17 to establish a connection.

Example 6-17. Connecting to Gmail with Xoauth

```
import sys
import oauth2 as oauth
import oauth2.clients.imap as imaplib

# See http://code.google.com/p/google-mail-xoauth-tools/wiki/
# XoauthDotPyRunThrough for details on obtaining and
# running xoauth.py to get the credentials

OAUTH_TOKEN = ''  # XXX: Obtained with xoauth.py
OAUTH_TOKEN_SECRET = ''  # XXX: Obtained with xoauth.py
GMAIL_ACCOUNT = ''  # XXX: Your Gmail address - example@gmail.com

url = 'https://mail.google.com/mail/b/%s/imap/' % (GMAIL_ACCOUNT, )

# Standard values for Gmail's Xoauth
consumer = oauth.Consumer('anonymous', 'anonymous')
token = oauth.Token(OAUTH_TOKEN, OAUTH_TOKEN_SECRET)

conn = imaplib.IMAP4_SSL('imap.googlemail.com')
conn.debug = 4  # Set to the desired debug level
conn.authenticate(url, consumer, token)

conn.select('INBOX')

# Access your INBOX data
```

Once you're able to programmatically access your mailbox, the next step is to fetch and parse some message data. The great thing about this is that we'll format and export it

---

6. If you're just hacking your own Gmail data, using the anonymous consumer credentials generated from xoauth.py is just fine; you can always register and create a "trusted" client application (*http://bit.ly/1a1nJ6N*) at a later time should you need to do so.

to exactly the same specification that we've been working with so far in this chapter, so all of your scripts and tools will work on both the Enron corpus and your own mail data!

6.5.2. Fetching and Parsing Email Messages with IMAP

The IMAP protocol is a fairly finicky and complex beast, but the good news is that you don't have to know much of it to search and fetch mail messages. Furthermore, `imaplib`-compliant examples are readily available online (*http://bit.ly/1a1nJDG*).

One of the more common operations you'll want to do is search for messages. There are various ways that you can construct an IMAP query. An example of how you'd search for messages from a particular user is `conn.search(None, '(FROM "me")')`, where `None` is an optional parameter for the character set and `'(FROM "me")'` is a search command to find messages that you've sent yourself (Gmail recognizes "me" as the authenticated user). A command to search for messages containing "foo" in the subject would be `'(SUBJECT "foo")'`, and there are *many* additional possibilities that you can read about in Section 6.4.4 of RFC 3501 (*http://bit.ly/XSB5cQ*), which defines the IMAP specification. `imaplib` returns a search response as a tuple that consists of a status code and a string of space-separated message IDs wrapped in a list, such as (`'OK'`, [`'506 527 566'`]). You can parse out these ID values to fetch RFC 822-compliant (*http://bit.ly/ 1a1nMzx*) mail messages, but alas, there's additional work involved to parse the content of the mail messages into a usable form.

Fortunately, with some minimal adaptation we can reuse the code from Example 6-3, which used the `email` module to parse messages into a more readily usable form, to take care of the uninteresting email-parsing cruft that's necessary to get usable text from each message. Example 6-18 illustrates this.

Example 6-18. Query your Gmail inbox and store the results as JSON

```
import sys
import mailbox
import email
import quopri
import json
import time
from BeautifulSoup import BeautifulSoup
from dateutil.parser import parse

# What you'd like to search for in the subject of your mail.
# See Section 6.4.4 of http://www.faqs.org/rfcs/rfc3501.html
# for more SEARCH options.

Q = "Alaska" # XXX

# Recycle some routines from Example 6-3 so that you arrive at the
# very same data structure you've been using throughout this chapter
```

```
def cleanContent(msg):

    # Decode message from "quoted printable" format
    msg = quopri.decodestring(msg)

    # Strip out HTML tags, if any are present.
    # Bail on unknown encodings if errors happen in BeautifulSoup.
    try:
        soup = BeautifulSoup(msg)
    except:
        return ''
    return ''.join(soup.findAll(text=True))

def jsonifyMessage(msg):
    json_msg = {'parts': []}
    for (k, v) in msg.items():
        json_msg[k] = v.decode('utf-8', 'ignore')

    # The To, Cc, and Bcc fields, if present, could have multiple items.
    # Note that not all of these fields are necessarily defined.

    for k in ['To', 'Cc', 'Bcc']:
        if not json_msg.get(k):
            continue
        json_msg[k] = json_msg[k].replace('\n', '').replace('\t', '')\
                            .replace('\r', '').replace(' ', '')\
                            .decode('utf-8', 'ignore').split(',')

    for part in msg.walk():
        json_part = {}
        if part.get_content_maintype() == 'multipart':
            continue

        json_part['contentType'] = part.get_content_type()
        content = part.get_payload(decode=False).decode('utf-8', 'ignore')
        json_part['content'] = cleanContent(content)

        json_msg['parts'].append(json_part)

    # Finally, convert date from asctime to milliseconds since epoch using the
    # $date descriptor so it imports "natively" as an ISODate object in MongoDB.
    then = parse(json_msg['Date'])
    millis = int(time.mktime(then.timetuple())*1000 + then.microsecond/1000)
    json_msg['Date'] = {'$date' : millis}

    return json_msg

# Consume a query from the user. This example illustrates searching by subject.

(status, data) = conn.search(None, '(SUBJECT "%s")' % (Q, ))
ids = data[0].split()
```

```
messages = []
for i in ids:
    try:
        (status, data) = conn.fetch(i, '(RFC822)')
        messages.append(email.message_from_string(data[0][1]))
    except Exception, e:
        print e
        print 'Print error fetching message %s. Skipping it.' % (i, )

print len(messages)
jsonified_messages = [jsonifyMessage(m) for m in messages]

# Separate out the text content from each message so that it can be analyzed.

content = [p['content'] for m in jsonified_messages for p in m['parts']]

# Content can still be quite messy and contain line breaks and other quirks.

filename = os.path.join('resources/ch06-mailboxes/data',
                        GMAIL_ACCOUNT.split("@")[0] + '.gmail.json')
f = open(filename, 'w')
f.write(json.dumps(jsonified_messages))
f.close()

print >> sys.stderr, "Data written out to", f.name
```

Once you've successfully parsed out the text from the body of a Gmail message, some additional work will be required to cleanse the text to the point that it's suitable for a nice display or advanced NLP, as illustrated in Chapter 5. However, not much effort is required to get it to the point where it's clean enough for collocation analysis. In fact, the results of Example 6-18 can be fed almost directly into Example 4-12 to produce a list of collocations from the search results. A worthwhile visualization exercise would be to create a graph plotting the strength of linkages between messages based on the number of bigrams they have in common, as determined by a custom metric.

6.5.3. Visualizing Patterns in GMail with the "Graph Your Inbox" Chrome Extension

There are several useful toolkits floating around that analyze webmail, and one of the most promising to emerge in recent years is the Graph Your Inbox Chrome extension (*http://bit.ly/1a1nMQ2*). To use this extension, you just install it, authorize it to access your mail data, run some Gmail queries, and let it take care of the rest. You can search for keywords like "pizza," search for time values such as "2010," or run more advanced queries such as "from:matthew@zaffra.com" and "label:Strata". Figure 6-3 shows a sample screenshot.

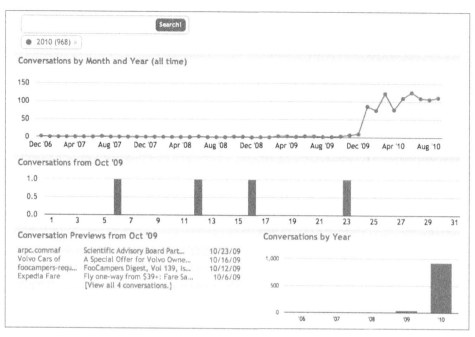

Figure 6-3. The Graph Your Inbox Chrome extension provides a concise summary of your Gmail activity

What's especially remarkable is that you can readily reproduce all of the analytics that this extension provides with the techniques you've learned in this chapter plus some supplemental content from earlier chapters, such as the use of a JavaScript visualization library like D3.js or `matplotlib`'s plotting utilities within IPython Notebook. Your toolbox is full of scripts and techniques that can be readily applied to a data domain to produce a comparable dashboard, whether it be a mailbox, an archive of web pages, or a collection of tweets. You certainly have some careful thinking to do about designing an overall application so that it provides an enjoyable user experience, but the building blocks for the data science and analysis that would be presented to the user are in your grasp.

6.6. Closing Remarks

We've covered a lot of ground in this chapter—arguably far more ground than in any other chapter so far, but that's to be expected. Each chapter has successively built upon previous chapters in an attempt to tell a story about data and analyzing data, and we're more than halfway through the book. Although we've barely begun to scratch the surface of what's possible with mail data, you'll surely be able to take advantage of content in previous chapters to discover amazing insights about your social connections and personal life if you tap into your own mail data, which will add an exciting dimension to the analysis.

Our focus has been on the mbox, a simple and convenient file format that lends itself to high portability and easy analysis by many Python tools and packages, and hopefully you've come to appreciate the value of using a standard and portable format for processing something as complex as a mailbox. There's an incredible amount of open source technology available for mining mboxes, and Python is a terrific language for slicing and dicing them. A small investment in these tools and appropriate storage mediums such as MongoDB will go a long way in allowing you to focus on the problem at hand as opposed to futzing around with the tools themselves.

 The source code outlined for this chapter and all other chapters is available at GitHub (*http://bit.ly/1a1kNqy*) in a convenient IPython Notebook format that you're highly encouraged to try out from the comfort of your own web browser.

6.7. Recommended Exercises

- Identify and hone in on a subset of the original Enron corpus for analysis. For example, do some research on the Enron case by reading about it online or watching a documentary, and then pick 10–15 mailboxes of interest and see what patterns of communication you can identify using the techniques introduced in this chapter.

- Apply text analytics from previous chapters to the content of the mail messages. Can you correlate what people are talking about? What are some of the advantages or disadvantages of using a full-text index compared to the information retrieval concepts from previous chapters?

- Investigate MongoDB's Map-Reduce framework (*http://bit.ly/1a1nN6o*).

- Investigate MongoDB's geospatial indexing (*http://bit.ly/1a1nPuY*). Can you store any of the locations from previous chapters, such as LinkedIn data or geocoordinates from Twitter data, and effectively query it?

- Read about how MongoDB's full-text indexing works internally (*http://bit.ly/1a1nPLr*). In particular, review the Snowball stemmer (*http://bit.ly/1a1nNDk*) that it uses.

- Review an email message threading algorithm (*http://bit.ly/1a1nQ23*) that can be used as an effective heuristic for reconstructing mail conversations from mailboxes. A sample implementation (*http://bit.ly/1a1nQ2e*) is available as part of the (now legacy) source code from *Mining the Social Web, 1st Edition*.

- Use the SIMILE Timeline (*http://bit.ly/1a1nQz3*) project to visualize message threads from the aforementioned email message threading algorithm. There are lots of online demonstrations of Timeline (*http://bit.ly/1a1nOr1*), along with ample documentation. This simple example of plotting mail on Timeline just shows the bare minimum to get you up and running, and it's just the beginning of what's possible.

- Run a search for "Enron" on Google Scholar (*http://bit.ly/1a1nR6c*) and review some of the myriad academic papers and studies that have been written about it. Use some of them as inspiration for your own studies.

6.8. Online Resources

The following list of links from this chapter may be useful for review:

- B-trees (*http://bit.ly/1a1nFUz*)
- Downloadable Enron corpus (*http://bit.ly/1a1nmsU*)
- Enron corpus (*http://bit.ly/1a1nj01*)
- *http://www.enron-mail.com*
- Enron scandal (*http://bit.ly/1a1nuZo*)
- Enron whitepapers on Google Scholar (*http://bit.ly/1a1nR6c*)
- Envoy GitHub repository (*http://bit.ly/1a1nrwL*)
- getmail (*http://bit.ly/1a1nKaL*)
- Google Mail Xoauth Tools wiki page (*http://bit.ly/1a1nKYa*)
- Graph Your Inbox Chrome extension (*http://bit.ly/1a1nMQ2*)
- Git for Windows (*http://bit.ly/1a1nubC*)
- How MongoDB's full-text indexing works internally (*http://bit.ly/1a1nPLr*)
- JWZ email message threading algorithm (*http://bit.ly/1a1nQ23*)
- Map-Reduce (*http://bit.ly/1a1nN6o*)
- MongoDB (*http://bit.ly/1a1nlVK*)
- MongoDB data aggregation framework (*http://bit.ly/1a1nA2Z*)
- MongoDB full-text search (*http://bit.ly/1a1nEzO*)
- MongoDB indexing (*http://bit.ly/1a1nA3d*)
- Online demonstrations of SIMILE Timeline (*http://bit.ly/1a1nOr1*)
- PyMongo documentation (*http://bit.ly/1a1nqZE*)
- RFC 2045 (*http://bit.ly/1a1nnNp*)

- SIMILE Timeline (*http://bit.ly/1a1nQz3*)
- Snowball stemmer (*http://bit.ly/1a1nNDk*)
- subprocess (*http://bit.ly/1a1nrgb*)
- Xoauth (*http://bit.ly/1a1nKHV*)

## CHAPTER 7

Mining GitHub: Inspecting Software Collaboration Habits, Building Interest Graphs, and More

GitHub has rapidly evolved in recent years to become the de facto social coding platform with a deceptively simple premise: provide a top-notch hosted solution for developers to create and maintain open source software projects with an open source distributed version control (*http://bit.ly/1a1o1u8*) system called *Git* (*http://bit.ly/16mhOep*). Unlike version control systems such as CVS (*http://bit.ly/1a1nZCI*) or Subversion (*http://bit.ly/1a1o21g*), with Git there is no canonical copy of the code base, per se. All copies are working copies, and developers can commit local changes on a working copy without needing to be connected to a centralized server.

The distributed version control paradigm lends itself exceptionally well to GitHub's notion of *social coding* because it allows developers who are interested in contributing to a project to *fork* a working copy of its code repository and immediately begin working on it in just the same way that the developer who owns the fork works on it. Git not only keeps track of semantics that allow repositories to be forked arbitrarily but also makes it relatively easy to merge changes from a forked *child* repository back into its *parent* repository. Through the GitHub user interface, this workflow is called a *pull request*.

It is a deceptively simple notion, but the ability for developers to create and collaborate on coding projects with elegant workflows that involve minimal overhead (once you understand some fundamental details about how Git works) has certainly streamlined many of the tedious details that have hindered innovation in open source development, including conveniences that transcend into the visualization of data and interoperability with other systems. In other words, think of GitHub as an enabler of open source software development. In the same way, although developers have collaborated on coding projects for decades, a hosted platform like GitHub supercharges collaboration and enables innovation in unprecedented ways by making it easy to create a project, share out its source code, maintain feedback and an issue tracker, accept patches for improvements and bug fixes, and more. More recently, it even appears that GitHub is increasingly catering to non-developers (*http://bit.ly/1a1o2OZ*)—and becoming one of the hottest social platforms for mainstream collaboration.

Just to be perfectly clear, this chapter does not attempt to provide a tutorial on how to use Git or GitHub as a distributed version control system or even discuss Git software architecture at any level. (See one of the many excellent online Git references, such as *gitscm.com*, for that kind of instruction.) This chapter does, however, attempt to teach you how to mine GitHub's API to discover patterns of social collaboration in the somewhat niche software development space.

 Always get the latest bug-fixed source code for this chapter (and every other chapter) online at *http://bit.ly/MiningTheSocialWeb2E*. Be sure to also take advantage of this book's virtual machine experience, as described in Appendix A, to maximize your enjoyment of the sample code.

7.1. Overview

This chapter provides an introduction to GitHub as a social coding platform and to graph-oriented analysis using NetworkX. In this chapter, you'll learn how to take advantage of GitHub's rich data by constructing a graphical model of the data that can be used in a variety of ways. In particular, we'll treat the relationships between GitHub users, repositories, and programming languages as an interest graph (*http://bit.ly/1a1o3Cu*), which is a way of interpreting the nodes and links in the graph primarily from the vantage point of people and the things in which they are interested. There is a lot of discussion these days amongst hackers, entrepreneurs, and web mavens as to whether or not the future of the Web is largely predicated upon some notion of an interest graph, so now is a fine time to get up to speed on the emerging graph landscape and all that it entails.

In sum, then, this chapter follows the same predictable template as chapters before it and covers:

- GitHub's developer platform and how to make API requests
- Graph schemas and how to model property graphs with NetworkX
- The concept of an interest graph and how to construct an interest graph from GitHub data

- Using NetworkX to query property graphs
- Graph centrality algorithms, including degree, betweenness, and closeness centrality

7.2. Exploring GitHub's API

Like the other social web properties featured in this book, GitHub's developer site (*http://bit.ly/1a1o49k*) offers comprehensive documentation on its APIs, the terms of service governing the use of those APIs, example code, and much more. Although the APIs are fairly rich, we'll be focusing on only the few API calls that we need in order to collect the data for creating some interest graphs that associate software developers, projects, programming languages, and other aspects of software development. The APIs more or less provide you with everything you'd need to build a rich user experience just like *github.com* offers itself, and there is no shortage of compelling and possibly even lucrative applications that you could build with these APIs.

The most fundamental primitives for GitHub are *users* and *projects*. If you are reading this page, you've probably already managed to pull down this book's source code from its GitHub project page (*http://bit.ly/1a1kNqy*), so this discussion assumes that you've at least visited a few GitHub project pages, have poked around a bit, and are familiar with the general notion of what GitHub offers.

A GitHub user has a public profile that generally includes one or more code repositories that have either been created or forked from another GitHub user. For example, the GitHub user ptwobrussell (*http://bit.ly/1a1o4GC*) owns a couple of GitHub repositories, including one called Mining-the-Social-Web (*http://bit.ly/1a1o6Ow*) and another called Mining-the-Social-Web-2nd-Edition (*http://bit.ly/1a1kNqy*). ptwobrussell has also forked a number of repositories in order to capture a particular working snapshot of certain code bases for development purposes, and these forked projects also appear in his public profile.

Part of what makes GitHub so powerful is that ptwobrussell is free to do anything he'd like with any of these forked projects (subject to the terms of their software licenses), in the same way that anyone else could do the same thing to forked projects. When a user forks a code repository, that user effectively owns a working copy of the same repository and can do anything from just fiddle around with it to drastically overhaul and create a long-lived fork of the original project that may never be intended to get merged back into the original parent repository. Although most project forks never materialize into derivative works of their own, the effort involved in creating a derivative work is trivial from the standpoint of source code management. It may be short-lived and manifest as a pull request that is merged back into the parent, or it may be long-lived and become an entirely separate project with its own community. The barrier to entry for open source software contribution and other projects that increasingly find themselves appearing on GitHub is low indeed.

In addition to forking projects on GitHub, a user can also bookmark or *star* a project to become what is known as a *stargazer* of the project. Bookmarking a project is essentially the same thing as bookmarking a web page or a tweet. You are signifying interest in the project, and it'll appear on your list of GitHub bookmarks for quick reference. What you'll generally notice is that far fewer people fork code than bookmark it. Bookmarking is an easy and well-understood notion from over a decade of web surfing, whereas forking the code implies having the intent to modify or contribute to it in some way. Throughout the remainder of this chapter, we'll focus primarily on using the list of stargazers for a project as the basis of constructing an interest graph for it.

7.2.1. Creating a GitHub API Connection

Like other social web properties, GitHub implements OAuth, and the steps to gaining API access involve creating an account followed by one of two possibilities: creating an application to use as the consumer of the API or creating a "personal" access token that will be linked directly to your account. In this chapter, we'll opt to use a personal access token, which is as easy as clicking a button in the Personal Access API Tokens section of your account's Applications (*http://bit.ly/1a1o7lw*) menu, as shown in Figure 7-1. (See Appendix B for a more extensive overview of OAuth.)

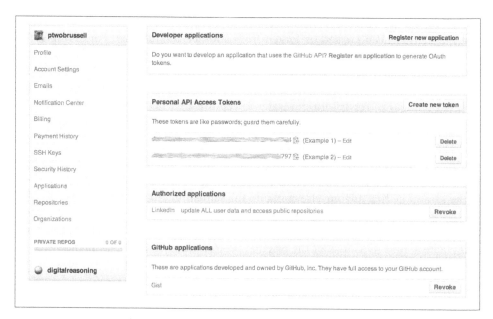

Figure 7-1. Create a "Personal API Access Token" from the Applications menu in your account and provide a meaningful note so that you'll remember its purpose

A programmatic option for obtaining an access token as opposed to creating one within the GitHub user interface is shown in Example 7-1 as an adaptation of "Creating an OAuth token for command-line use" (*http://bit.ly/1a1o7lG*) from GitHub's help site. (If you are not taking advantage of the virtual machine experience for this book, as described in Appendix A, you'll need to type **pip install requests** in a terminal prior to running this example.)

Example 7-1. Programmatically obtaining a personal API access token for accessing GitHub's API

```
import requests
from getpass import getpass
import json

username = '' # Your GitHub username
password = '' # Your GitHub password

# Note that credentials will be transmitted over a secure SSL connection
url = 'https://api.github.com/authorizations'
note = 'Mining the Social Web, 2nd Ed.'
post_data = {'scopes':['repo'],'note': note }

response = requests.post(
    url,
    auth = (username, password),
    data = json.dumps(post_data),
    )

print "API response:", response.text
print
print "Your OAuth token is", response.json()['token']

# Go to https://github.com/settings/applications to revoke this token
```

As is the case with many other social web properties, GitHub's API is built on top of HTTP and accessible through any programming language in which you can make an HTTP request, including command-line tools in a terminal. Following the precedents set by previous chapters, however, we'll opt to take advantage of a Python library so that we can avoid some of the tedious details involved in making requests, parsing responses, and handling pagination. In this particular case, we'll use PyGithub (*http://bit.ly/1a1o7Ca*), which can be installed with the somewhat predictable **pip install PyGithub**. We'll start by taking at a couple of examples of how to make GitHub API requests before transitioning into a discussion of graphical models.

Let's seed an interest graph in this chapter from the Mining-the-Social-Web (*http://bit.ly/1a1o6Ow*) GitHub repository and create connections between it and its stargazers. Listing the stargazers for a repository is possible with the List Stargazers API (*http://bit.ly/1a1o9dd*). You could try out an API request to get an idea of what the response type looks like by copying and pasting the following URL in your web browser: *https://api.github.com/repos/ptwobrussell/Mining-the-Social-Web/stargazers*.

 Although you are reading *Mining the Social Web, 2nd Edition*, at the time of this writing the source code repository for the first edition still has much more activity than the second edition, so the first edition repository will serve as the basis of examples for this chapter. Analysis of any repository, including the repository for the second edition of this book, is easy enough to accomplish by simply changing the name of the initial project as introduced in Example 7-3.

The ability to issue an unauthenticated request in this manner is quite convenient as you are exploring the API, and the rate limit of 60 unauthenticated requests per hour is more than adequate for tinkering and exploring. You could, however, append a query string of the form `?access_token=xxx`, where *xxx* specifies your access token, to make the same request in an authenticated fashion. GitHub's authenticated rate limits are a generous 5,000 requests per hour, as described in the developer documentation for rate limiting (*http://bit.ly/1a1oblo*). Example 7-2 illustrates a sample request and response. (Keep in mind that this is requesting only the first page of results and, as described in the developer documentation for pagination (*http://bit.ly/1a1o9Ki*), metadata information for navigating the pages of results is included in the HTTP headers.)

Example 7-2. Making direct HTTP requests to GitHub's API

```
import json
import requests

# An unauthenticated request that doesn't contain an ?access_token=xxx query string
url = "https://api.github.com/repos/ptwobrussell/Mining-the-Social-Web/stargazers"
response = requests.get(url)

# Display one stargazer

print json.dumps(response.json()[0], indent=1)
print

# Display headers
for (k,v) in response.headers.items():
    print k, "=>", v
```

Sample output follows:

```
{
 "following_url": "https://api.github.com/users/rdempsey/following{/other_user}",
 "events_url": "https://api.github.com/users/rdempsey/events{/privacy}",
 "organizations_url": "https://api.github.com/users/rdempsey/orgs",
 "url": "https://api.github.com/users/rdempsey",
```

```
  "gists_url": "https://api.github.com/users/rdempsey/gists{/gist_id}",
  "html_url": "https://github.com/rdempsey",
  "subscriptions_url": "https://api.github.com/users/rdempsey/subscriptions",
  "avatar_url": "https://1.gravatar.com/avatar/8234a5ea3e56fca09c5549ee...png",
  "repos_url": "https://api.github.com/users/rdempsey/repos",
  "received_events_url": "https://api.github.com/users/rdempsey/received_events",
  "gravatar_id": "8234a5ea3e56fca09c5549ee5e23e3e1",
  "starred_url": "https://api.github.com/users/rdempsey/starred{/owner}{/repo}",
  "login": "rdempsey",
  "type": "User",
  "id": 224,
  "followers_url": "https://api.github.com/users/rdempsey/followers"
}

status => 200 OK
access-control-allow-credentials => true
x-ratelimit-remaining => 58
x-github-media-type => github.beta
x-content-type-options => nosniff
access-control-expose-headers => ETag, Link, X-RateLimit-Limit,
                                 X-RateLimit-Remaining, X-RateLimit-Reset,
                                 X-OAuth-Scopes, X-Accepted-OAuth-Scopes
transfer-encoding => chunked
x-github-request-id => 73f42421-ea0d-448c-9c90-c2d79c5b1fed
content-encoding => gzip
vary => Accept, Accept-Encoding
server => GitHub.com
last-modified => Sun, 08 Sep 2013 17:01:27 GMT
x-ratelimit-limit => 60
link => <https://api.github.com/repositories/1040700/stargazers?page=2>;
            rel="next",
        <https://api.github.com/repositories/1040700/stargazers?page=30>;
            rel="last"
etag => "ca10cd4edc1a44e91f7b28d3fdb05b10"
cache-control => public, max-age=60, s-maxage=60
date => Sun, 08 Sep 2013 19:05:32 GMT
access-control-allow-origin => *
content-type => application/json; charset=utf-8
x-ratelimit-reset => 1378670725
```

As you can see, there's a lot of useful information that GitHub is returning to us that is not in the body of the HTTP response and is instead conveyed as HTTP headers, as outlined in the developer documentation. You should skim and understand what all of the various headers mean, but a few of note include the `status` header, which tells us that the request was OK with a 200 response; headers that involve the rate limit, such as `x-ratelimit-remaining`; and the `link` header, which contains a value such as the following:

```
https://api.github.com/repositories/1040700/stargazers?page=2; rel="next",
https://api.github.com/repositories/1040700/stargazers?page=29; rel="last".
```

The link header's value is giving us a preconstructed URL that could be used to fetch the next page of results as well as an indication of how many total pages of results there are.

7.2.2. Making GitHub API Requests

Although it's not difficult to use a library like requests and make the most of this information by parsing it out ourselves, a library like PyGithub makes it that much easier for us and tackles the abstraction of the implementation details of GitHub's API, leaving us to work with a clean Pythonic API. Better yet, if GitHub changes the underlying implementation of its API, we'll still be able to use PyGithub and our code won't break.

Before making a request with PyGithub, also take a moment to look at the body of the response itself. It contains some rich information, but the piece we're most interested in is a field called login, which is the GitHub username of the user who is stargazing at the repository of interest. This information is the basis of issuing many other queries to other GitHub APIs, such as "List repositories being starred," (*http://bit.ly/1a1oc8X*) an API that returns a list of all repositories a user has starred. This is a powerful pivot because after we have started with an arbitrary repository and queried it for a list of users who are interested in it, we are then able to query those users for additional repositories of interest and potentially discover any patterns that might emerge.

For example, wouldn't it be interesting to know what is the next-most-bookmarked repository among all of the users who have bookmarked Mining-the-Social-Web? The answer to that question could be the basis of an intelligent recommendation that GitHub users would appreciate, and it doesn't take much creativity to imagine different domains in which intelligent recommendations could (and often do) provide enhanced user experiences in applications, as is the case with Amazon and Netflix. At its core, an interest graph inherently lends itself to making such intelligent recommendations, and that's one of the reasons that interest graphs have become such a conversation topic in certain niche circles of late.

Example 7-3 provides an example of how you could use PyGithub to retrieve all of the stargazers for a repository to seed an interest graph.

Example 7-3. Using PyGithub to query for stargazers of a particular repository

```
from github import Github

# XXX: Specify your own access token here

ACCESS_TOKEN = ''

# Specify a username and repository of interest for that user.

USER = 'ptwobrussell'
REPO = 'Mining-the-Social-Web'
```

```
client = Github(ACCESS_TOKEN, per_page=100)
user = client.get_user(USER)
repo = user.get_repo(REPO)

# Get a list of people who have bookmarked the repo.
# Since you'll get a lazy iterator back, you have to traverse
# it if you want to get the total number of stargazers.

stargazers = [ s for s in repo.get_stargazers() ]
print "Number of stargazers", len(stargazers)
```

Behind the scenes, PyGithub takes care of the API implementation details for you and simply exposes some convenient objects for query. In this case, we create a connection to GitHub and use the per_page keyword parameter to tell it that we'd like to receive the maximum number of results (100) as opposed to the default number (30) in each page of data that comes back. Then, we get a repository for a particular user and query for that repository's stargazers. It is possible for users to have repositories with identical names, so there is not an unambiguous way to query by just a repository's name. Since usernames and repository names could overlap, you need to take special care to specify the kind of object that you are working with when using GitHub's API if using one of these names as an identifier. We'll account for this as we create graphs with node names that may be ambiguous if we do not qualify them as repositories or users.

Finally, PyGithub generally provides "lazy iterators" as results, which in this case means that it does not attempt to fetch all 29 pages of results when the query is issued. Instead, it waits until a particular page is requested when iterating over the data before it retrieves that page. For this reason, we need to exhaust the lazy iterator with a list comprehension in order to actually count the number of stargazers with the API if we want to get an exact count.

PyGithub's documentation (*http://bit.ly/1a1odd3*) is helpful, its API generally mimics the GitHub API in a predictable way, and you'll usually be able to use its pydoc, such as through the dir() and help() functions in a Python interpreter. Alternatively, tab completion and "question mark magic" in IPython or IPython Notebook will get you to the same place in figuring out what methods are available to call on what objects. It would be worthwhile to poke around at the GitHub API a bit with PyGithub to better familiarize yourself with some of the possibilities before continuing further. As an exercise to test your skills, can you iterate over Mining-the-Social-Web's stargazers (or some subset thereof) and do some basic frequency analysis that determines which other repositories may be of common interest? You will likely find Python's collec tions.Counter or NLTK's nltk.FreqDist essential in easily computing frequency statistics.

7.3. Modeling Data with Property Graphs

You may recall from Section 2.3.2.2 on page 78 that graphs were introduced in passing as a means of representing, analyzing, and visualizing social network data from Facebook. This section provides a more thorough discussion and hopefully serves as a useful primer for graph computing. Even though it is still a bit under the radar, the graph computing landscape is emerging rapidly given that graphs are a very natural abstraction for modeling many phenomena in the real world. Graphs offer a flexibility in data representation that is especially hard to beat during data experimentation and analysis when compared to other options, such as relational databases. Graph-centric analyses are certainly not a panacea for every problem, but an understanding of how to model your data with graphical structures is a powerful addition to your toolkit.

A general introduction to graph theory is beyond the scope of this chapter, and the discussion that follows simply attempts to provide a gentle introduction to key concepts as they arise. You may enjoy the short YouTube video "Graph Theory—An Introduction!" (*http://bit.ly/1a1odto*) if you'd like to accumulate some general background knowledge before proceeding.

The remainder of this section introduces a common kind of graph called a *property graph* for the purpose of modeling GitHub data as an interest graph by way of a Python package called NetworkX (*http://bit.ly/1a1ocFV*). A property graph is a data structure that represents entities with *nodes* and relationships between the entities with *edges*. Each vertex has a unique identifier, a map of properties that are defined as key/value pairs, and a collection of edges. Likewise, edges are unique in that they connect nodes, can be uniquely identified, and can contain properties.

Figure 7-2 shows a trivial example of a property graph with two nodes that are uniquely identified by *X* and *Y* with an undescribed relationship between them. This particular graph is called a *digraph* because its edges are directed, which need not be the case unless the directionality of the edge is rooted in meaning for the domain being modeled.

Figure 7-2. A trivial property graph with directed edges

Expressed in code with NetworkX, a trivial property graph could be constructed as shown in Example 7-4. (You can use **pip install networkx** to install this package if you aren't using the book's turnkey virtual machine.)

Example 7-4. Constructing a trivial property graph

```python
import networkx as nx

# Create a directed graph

g = nx.DiGraph()

# Add an edge to the directed graph from X to Y

g.add_edge('X', 'Y')

# Print some statistics about the graph

print nx.info(g)
print

# Get the nodes and edges from the graph

print "Nodes:", g.nodes()
print "Edges:", g.edges()
print

# Get node properties

print "X props:", g.node['X']
print "Y props:", g.node['Y']

# Get edge properties

print "X=>Y props:", g['X']['Y']
print

# Update a node property

g.node['X'].update({'prop1' : 'value1'})
print "X props:", g.node['X']
print

# Update an edge property

g['X']['Y'].update({'label' : 'label1'})
print "X=>Y props:", g['X']['Y']
```

Sample output from the example follows:

```
Name:
Type: DiGraph
Number of nodes: 2
Number of edges: 1
Average in degree:    0.5000
Average out degree:   0.5000
```

```
Nodes: ['Y', 'X']
Edges: [('X', 'Y')]

X props: {}
Y props: {}
X=>Y props: {}

X props: {'prop1': 'value1'}

X=>Y props: {'label': 'label1'}
```

In this particular example, the add_edge method of the digraph adds an edge from a node that's uniquely identified by X to a node that's uniquely identified by Y, resulting in a graph with two nodes and one edge between them. In terms of its unique identifier, this node would be represented by the tuple (X, Y) since both nodes that it connects are uniquely identified themselves. Be aware that adding an edge from Y back to X would create a second edge in the graph, and this second edge could contain its own set of edge properties. In general, you wouldn't want to create this second edge since you can get a node's incoming or outgoing edges and effectively traverse the edge in either direction, but there may be some situations in which it is more convenient to explicitly include the additional edge.

The *degree* of a node in a graph is the number of incident edges to it, and for a directed graph, there is a notion of *in degree* and *out degree* since edges have direction. The average in degree and average out degree values provide a normalized score for the graph that represents the number of nodes that have incoming and outgoing edges. In this particular case, the directed graph has a single directed edge, so there is one node with an outgoing edge and one node with an incoming edge.

The in and out degree of a node is a fundamental concept in graph theory. Assuming you know the number of vertices in the graph, the average degree provides a measure of the graph's *density*: the number of actual edges compared to the number of possible edges if the graph were fully connected. In a fully connected graph, each node is connected to every other node, and in the case of a directed graph, this means that all nodes have incoming edges from all other nodes.

You calculate the average in degree for an entire graph by summing the values of each node's in degree and dividing the total by the number of nodes in the graph, which is 1 divided by 2 in Example 7-4. The average out degree calculation is computed the same way except that the sum of each node's out degree is used as the value to divide by the number of nodes in the graph. When you're considering an entire directed graph, there will always be an equal number of incoming edges and outgoing edges because each edge connects only two nodes,[1] and the average in degree and average out degree values for the entire graph will be the same.

 In the general case, the maximum values for average in and out degree in a graph are one less than the number of nodes in the graph. Take a moment to convince yourself that this is the case by considering the number of edges that are necessary to fully connect all of the nodes in a graph.

In the next section, we'll construct an interest graph using these same property graph primitives and illustrate these additional methods at work on real-world data. First, take a moment to explore by adding some nodes, edges, and properties to the graph. The NetworkX documentation (*http://bit.ly/1a1ocFV*) provides a number of useful introductory examples that you can also explore if this is one of your first encounters with graphs and you'd like some extra instruction as a primer.

The Rise of Big Graph Databases

This chapter introduces property graphs, a versatile data structure that can be used to model complex networks with nodes and edges as simple primitives. We'll be modeling the data according to a flexible graph schema that's based largely on natural intuition, and for a narrowly focused domain, this pragmatic approach is often sufficient. As we'll see throughout the remainder of this chapter, property graphs provide flexibility and versatility in modeling and querying complex data.

NetworkX, the Python-based graph toolkit used throughout this book, provides a powerful toolbox for modeling property graphs. Be aware, however, that NetworkX is an in-memory graph database. The limit of what it can do for you is directly proportional to the amount of working memory that you have on the machine on which you are running it. In many situations, you can work around the memory limitation by constraining the domain to a subset of the data or by using a machine with more working memory. In an increasing number of situations involving "big data" and its burgeoning ecosystem that largely involves Hadoop and NoSQL databases, however, in-memory graphs are simply not an option.

There is a nascent ecosystem of so-called "big graph databases" that leverage NoSQL databases for storage and provide property graph semantics that are worth noting. Titan (*http://bit.ly/1a1og8D*), a promising front-runner, and other big graph databases that adopt the property graph model present an opportunity for a departure from the semantic web stack (*http://bit.ly/1a1oegY*) as we know it, involving technologies such as

---

1. A more abstract version of a graph called a *hypergraph* (*http://bit.ly/1a1ocWm*) contains *hyperedges* that can connect an arbitrary number of vertices.

RDF Schema (*http://bit.ly/1a1ogpe*), OWL (*http://bit.ly/1a1ogFz*), and SPARQL (*http:// bit.ly/1a1ogW5*). The idea behind the technologies involved in the semantic web stack is that they provide a mechanism for representing and consolidating data from more complex domains, thereby making it possible to arrive at a standardized vocabulary that can be meaningfully queried. Unfortunately, there have been litanies of historical challenges involved in applying these technologies at web scale. One of Titan's promising key claims is that it is designed to effectively manage the memory hierarchy in order to scale well.

It will be exciting to see what the future holds as big graph databases based upon NoSQL databases and the property graph model fuse with the ideas and technologies involved in a more traditional semantic web toolchain. The next chapter introduces some current web innovations involving microformats that are a step in the general direction of a more semantic web; it ends with a brief example that demonstrates inferencing on a simple graph with a small subset of technology akin to the semantic web stack.

7.4. Analyzing GitHub Interest Graphs

Now equipped with the tools to both query GitHub's API and model the data that comes back as a graph, let's put our skills to the test and begin constructing and analyzing an interest graph. We'll start with a repository that will represent a common interest among a group of GitHub users and use GitHub's API to discover the stargazers for this repository. From there, we'll be able to use other APIs to model social connections between GitHub users who follow one another and hone in on other interests that these users might share.

We'll also learn about some fundamental techniques for analyzing graphs called *centrality measures*. Although a visual layout of a graph is tremendously useful, many graphs are simply too large or complex for an effective visual inspection, and centrality measures can be helpful in analytically measuring aspects of the network structure. (But don't worry, we will also visualize a graph before closing this chapter.)

7.4.1. Seeding an Interest Graph

Recall that an interest graph and a social graph are not the same thing. Whereas a social graph (*http://bit.ly/1a1ofl4*)'s primary focus is representing connections between people and it generally requires a mutual relationship between the parties involved, an interest graph connects people and interests and involves unidirectional edges. Although the two are by no means totally disjoint concepts, do not confuse the connection between a GitHub user following another GitHub user with a social connection—it is an "interested in" connection because there is not a mutual acceptance criterion involved.

A classic example of a hybridized graphical model that would qualify as a social interest graph is Facebook. It started primarily as a technology platform based upon the concept of a social graph, but the incorporation of the Like button squarely catapulted it into hybrid territory that could be articulated as a social-interest graph. It explicitly represents connections between people as well as connections between people and the things that they are interested in. Twitter has always been some flavor of an interest graph with its asymmetric "following" model, which can be interpreted as a connection between a person and the things (which could be other people) that person is interested in.

Examples 7-5 and 7-6 will introduce code samples to construct the initial "gazes" relationships between users and repositories, demonstrating how to explore the graphical structure that emerges. The graph that is initially constructed can be referred to as an *ego graph* in that there is a central point of focus (an ego) that is the basis for most (in this case, all) of the edges. An ego graph is sometimes called a "hub and spoke graph" or a "star graph" since it resembles a hub with spokes emanating from it and looks like a star when visually rendered visually.

From the standpoint of a graph schema, the graph contains two types of nodes and one type of edge, as is demonstrated in Figure 7-3.

 We'll use the graph schema shown in Figure 7-3 as a starting point and evolve it with modifications throughout the remainder of this chapter.

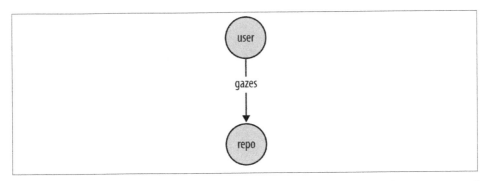

Figure 7-3. The basis of a graph schema that includes GitHub users who are interested in repositories

There is a subtle but important constraint in data modeling that involves the avoidance of naming collisions: usernames and repository names may (and often do) collide with one another. For example, there could be a GitHub user named "ptwobrussell," as well as multiple repositories named "ptwobrussell". Recalling that the add_edge method uses the items passed in as its first two parameters as unique identifiers, we can append either "(user)" or "(repo)" to the items to ensure that all nodes in the graph will be unique. From the standpoint of modeling with NetworkX, appending a type for the node mostly takes care of the problem.

Along the same lines, repositories that are owned by different users can have the same name whether they are forks of the same code base or entirely different code bases. At the moment this particular detail is of no concern to us, but once we begin to add in other repositories that other GitHub users are stargazing at, the possibility of this kind of collision will increase.

Whether to allow these types of collisions or to implement a graph construction strategy that avoids them is a design decision that carries with it certain consequences. For example, it would probably be desirable to have forks of the same repository collapse into the same node in the graph as opposed to representing them all as different repositories, but you would certainly not want completely different projects that shared a name to collapse into the same node.

 Given the limited scope of the problem that we are solving and that it's initially focusing on a particular repository of interest, we'll opt to avoid the complexity that disambiguating repository names introduces.

With that in mind, take a look at Example 7-5, which constructs an ego graph of a repository and its stargazers, and Example 7-6, which introduces some useful graph operations.

Example 7-5. Constructing an ego graph of a repository and its stargazers

```
# Expand the initial graph with (interest) edges pointing each direction for
# additional people interested. Take care to ensure that user and repo nodes
# do not collide by appending their type.

import networkx as nx

g = nx.DiGraph()
g.add_node(repo.name + '(repo)', type='repo', lang=repo.language, owner=user.login)

for sg in stargazers:
    g.add_node(sg.login + '(user)', type='user')
    g.add_edge(sg.login + '(user)', repo.name + '(repo)', type='gazes')
```

Example 7-6. Introducing some handy graph operations

```
# Poke around in the current graph to get a better feel for how NetworkX works

print nx.info(g)
print
print g.node['Mining-the-Social-Web(repo)']
print g.node['ptwobrussell(user)']
print
print g['ptwobrussell(user)']['Mining-the-Social-Web(repo)']
# The next line would throw a KeyError since no such edge exists:
# print g['Mining-the-Social-Web(repo)']['ptwobrussell(user)']
print
print g['ptwobrussell(user)']
print g['Mining-the-Social-Web(repo)']
print
print g.in_edges(['ptwobrussell(user)'])
print g.out_edges(['ptwobrussell(user)'])
print
print g.in_edges(['Mining-the-Social-Web(repo)'])
print g.out_edges(['Mining-the-Social-Web(repo)'])
```

The following sample (abbreviated) output demonstrates some of the possibilities based upon the graph operations just shown:

```
Name:
Type: DiGraph
Number of nodes: 852
Number of edges: 851
Average in degree:   0.9988
Average out degree:   0.9988

{'lang': u'JavaScript', 'owner': u'ptwobrussell', 'type': 'repo'}
{'type': 'user'}

{'type': 'gazes'}

{u'Mining-the-Social-Web(repo)': {'type': 'gazes'}}
{}

[]
[('ptwobrussell(user)', u'Mining-the-Social-Web(repo)')]

[(u'gregmoreno(user)', 'Mining-the-Social-Web(repo)'),
 (u'SathishRaju(user)', 'Mining-the-Social-Web(repo)'),
 ...
 ]
[]
```

With an initial interest graph in place, we can get creative in determining which steps might be most interesting to take next. What we know so far is that there are approximately 850 users who share a common interest in social web mining, as indicated by their stargazing association to ptwobrussell's Mining-the-Social-Web repository. As expected, the number of edges in the graph is one less than the number of nodes. The reason that this is the case is because there is a one-to-one correspondence at this point between the stargazers and the repository (an edge must exist to connect each stargazer to the repository).

If you recall that the average in degree and average out degree metrics yield a normalized value that provides a measure for the density of the graph, the value of 0.9988 should confirm our intuition. We know that we have 851 nodes corresponding to stargazers that each have an out degree equal to 1, and one node corresponding to a repository that has an in degree of 851. In other words, we know that the number of edges in the graph is one less than the number of nodes. The density of edges in the graph is quite low given that the maximum value for the average degree in this case is 851.

It might be tempting to think about the topology of the graph, knowing that it looks like a star if visually rendered, and try to make some kind of connection to the value of 0.9988. It is true that we have one node that is connected to all other nodes in the graph, but it would be a mistake to generalize and try to make some kind of connection to the average degree being approximately 1.0 based on this single node. It could just as easily have been the case that the 851 nodes could have been connected in many other configurations to arrive at a value of 0.9988. To gain insight that would support this kind of conclusion we would need to consider additional analytics, such as the centrality measures introduced in the next section.

7.4.2. Computing Graph Centrality Measures

A centrality measure is a fundamental graph analytic that provides insight into the relative importance of a particular node in a graph. Let's consider the following centrality measures, which will help us more carefully examine graphs to gain insights about networks:

Degree centrality
> The degree centrality of a node in the graph is a measure of the number of incident edges upon it. Think of this centrality measure as a way of tabulating the frequency of incident edges on nodes for the purpose of measuring uniformity among them, finding the nodes with the highest or lowest numbers of incident edges, or otherwise trying to discover patterns that provide insight into the network topology based on number of connections as a primary motivation. The degree centrality of a node is just one facet that is useful in reasoning about its role in a network, and it provides a good starting point for identifying outliers or anomalies with respect to connectedness relative to other nodes in the graph. In aggregate, we also know from our earlier discussion that the average degree centrality tells us something about the density of an overall graph. NetworkX provides `networkx.degree_centrality` as

a built-in function to compute the degree centrality of a graph. It returns a dictionary that maps the ID of each node to its degree centrality.

Betweenness centrality

The betweenness centrality of a node is a measure of how often it connects any other nodes in the graph in the sense of being *in between* other nodes. You might think about betweenness centrality as a measure of how critical a node is in connecting other nodes as a broker or gateway. Although not necessarily the case, the loss of nodes with a high betweenness centrality measure could be quite disruptive to the flow of energy[2] in a graph, and in some circumstances removing nodes with high betweenness centrality can disintegrate a graph into smaller subgraphs. NetworkX provides `networkx.betweenness_centrality` as a built-in function to compute the betweenness centrality of a graph. It returns a dictionary that maps the ID of each node to its betweenness centrality.

Closeness centrality

The closeness centrality of a node is a measure of how highly connected ("close") it is to all other nodes in the graph. This centrality measure is also predicated on the notion of shortest paths in the graph and offers insight into how well connected a particular node is in the graph. Unlike a node's betweenness centrality, which tells you something about how integral it is in connecting nodes as a broker or gateway, a node's closeness centrality accounts more for direct connections. Think of closeness in terms of a node's ability to spread energy to all other nodes in a graph. NetworkX provides `networkx.closeness_centrality` as a built-in function to compute the closeness centrality of a graph. It returns a dictionary that maps the ID of each node to its closeness centrality.

 NetworkX provides a number of powerful centrality measures (*http://1.usa.gov/1a1ofBF*) in its online documentation.

Figure 7-4 shows the Krackhardt kite graph (*http://bit.ly/1a1oixa*), a well-studied graph in social network analysis that illustrates the differences among the centrality measures introduced in this section. It's called a "kite graph" because when rendered visually, it has the appearance of a kite.

---

2. In the current discussion, the term "energy" is used to generically describe flow within an abstract graph.

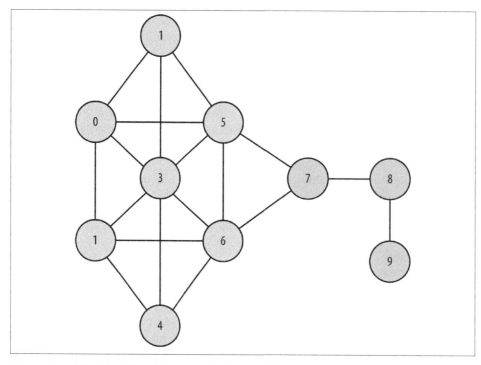

Figure 7-4. The Krackhardt kite graph that will be used to illustrate degree, between-ness, and closeness centrality measures

Example 7-7 shows some code that loads this graph from NetworkX and calculates centrality measures on it, which are reproduced in Table 7-1. Although it has no bearing on the calculations, note that this particular graph is commonly used as a reference in social networking. As such, the edges are not directed since a connection in a social network implies a mutual acceptance criteria. In NetworkX, it is an instance of net workx.Graph as opposed to networkx.DiGraph.

Example 7-7. Calculating degree, betweenness, and closeness centrality measures on the Krackhardt kite graph

```
from operator import itemgetter
from IPython.display import HTML
from IPython.core.display import display

display(HTML('<img src="files/resources/ch07-github/kite-graph.png" width="400px">'))

# The classic Krackhardt kite graph
kkg = nx.generators.small.krackhardt_kite_graph()

print "Degree Centrality"
print sorted(nx.degree_centrality(kkg).items(),
            key=itemgetter(1), reverse=True)
```

```
print

print "Betweenness Centrality"
print sorted(nx.betweenness_centrality(kkg).items(),
             key=itemgetter(1), reverse=True)
print

print "Closeness Centrality"
print sorted(nx.closeness_centrality(kkg).items(),
             key=itemgetter(1), reverse=True)
```

Table 7-1. Degree, betweenness, and closeness centrality measures for the Krackhardt kite graph (maximum values for each column are presented in bold so that you can easily test your intuition against the graph presented in Figure 7-4)

Node	Degree centrality	Betweenness centrality	Closeness centrality
0	0.44	0.02	0.53
1	0.44	0.02	0.53
2	0.33	0.00	0.50
3	**0.67**	0.10	0.60
4	0.33	0	0.50
5	0.55	0.2	**0.64**
6	0.55	0.2	**0.64**
7	0.33	**0.39**	0.60
8	0.22	0.22	0.43
9	0.11	0.00	0.31

Spend a few moments studying the Krackhardt kite graph and the centrality measures associated with it before moving on to the next section. These centrality measures will remain in our toolbox moving forward through this chapter.

7.4.3. Extending the Interest Graph with "Follows" Edges for Users

In addition to stargazing and forking repositories, GitHub also features a Twitter-esque notion of "following" other users. In this section, we'll query GitHub's API and add "follows" relationships to the graph. Based upon our earlier discussions (such the one in Section 1.2 on page 6) about how Twitter is inherently an interest graph, you know that adding these is basically a way of capturing more interest relationships, since a "following" relationship is essentially the same as an "interested in" relationship.

It's a good bet that the owner of a repository is likely to be popular within the community that is stargazing at the repository, but who else might be popular in that community? The answer to this question would certainly be an important insight and provide the basis for a useful pivot into further analysis. Let's answer it by querying GitHub's User

Followers API (*http://bit.ly/1a1oixo*) for the followers of each user in the graph and adding edges to the graph to indicate follows relationships that exist within it. In terms of our graphical model, these additions only insert additional edges into the graph; no new nodes need to be introduced.

While it would be possible to add all follows relationships that we get back from GitHub to the graph, for now we are limiting our analysis to users who have shown an explicit interest in the repository that is the seed of the graph. Example 7-8 illustrates the sample code that adds following edges to the graph, and Figure 7-5 depicts the updated graph schema that now includes following relationships.

 Given GitHub's authenticated rate limit of 5,000 requests per hour, you would need to make more than 80 requests per minute in order to exceed the rate limit. This is somewhat unlikely given the latency incurred with each request, so no special logic is included in this chapter's code samples to cope with the rate limit.

Example 7-8. Adding additional interest edges to the graph through the inclusion of "follows" edges

```
# Add (social) edges from the stargazers' followers. This can take a while
# because of all of the potential API calls to GitHub. The approximate number
# of requests for followers for each iteration of this loop can be calculated as
# math.ceil(sg.get_followers() / 100.0) per the API returning up to 100 items
# at a time.

import sys

for i, sg in enumerate(stargazers):

    # Add "follows" edges between stargazers in the graph if any relationships exist
    try:
        for follower in sg.get_followers():
            if follower.login + '(user)' in g:
                g.add_edge(follower.login + '(user)', sg.login + '(user)',
                           type='follows')
    except Exception, e: #ssl.SSLError
        print >> sys.stderr, "Encountered an error fetching followers for", \
                            sg.login, "Skipping."
        print >> sys.stderr, e

    print "Processed", i+1, " stargazers. Num nodes/edges in graph", \
           g.number_of_nodes(), "/", g.number_of_edges()
    print "Rate limit remaining", client.rate_limiting
```

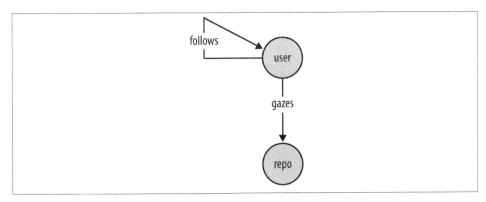

Figure 7-5. The basis of a graph schema that includes GitHub users who are interested in repositories as well as other users

With the incorporation of additional interest data into the graph, the possibilities for analysis become much more interesting. We can now traverse the graph to compute a notion of popularity by counting the number of incoming "follows" edges for a particular user, as demonstrated in Example 7-9. What is so powerful about this analysis is that it enables us to quickly discover who might be the most interesting or influential users to examine for a particular domain of interest.

Given that we seeded the graph with the Mining-the-Social-Web repository, a plausible hypothesis is that users who are interested in this topic may have some affiliation or interest in data mining, and might even have an interest in the Python programming language since its code base is mostly written in Python. Let's explore whether the most popular users, as calculated by Example 7-9, have any affiliation with this programming language.

Example 7-9. Exploring the updated graph's "follows" edges

```
from operator import itemgetter
from collections import Counter

# Let's see how many social edges we added since last time.
print nx.info(g)
print

# The number of "follows" edges is the difference
print len([e for e in g.edges_iter(data=True) if e[2]['type'] == 'follows'])
print

# The repository owner is possibly one of the more popular users in this graph.
print len([e
           for e in g.edges_iter(data=True)
               if e[2]['type'] == 'follows' and e[1] == 'ptwobrussell(user)'])
print
```

```
# Let's examine the number of adjacent edges to each node
print sorted([n for n in g.degree_iter()], key=itemgetter(1), reverse=True)[:10]
print

# Consider the ratio of incoming and outgoing edges for a couple of users with
# high node degrees...

# A user who follows many but is not followed back by many.

print len(g.out_edges('hcilab(user)'))
print len(g.in_edges('hcilab(user)'))
print

# A user who is followed by many but does not follow back.

print len(g.out_edges('ptwobrussell(user)'))
print len(g.in_edges('ptwobrussell(user)'))
print

c = Counter([e[1] for e in g.edges_iter(data=True) if e[2]['type'] == 'follows'])
popular_users = [ (u, f) for (u, f) in c.most_common() if f > 1 ]
print "Number of popular users", len(popular_users)
print "Top 10 popular users:", popular_users[:10]
```

Sample output follows:

```
Name:
Type: DiGraph
Number of nodes: 852
Number of edges: 1417
Average in degree:   1.6631
Average out degree:  1.6631

566

89

[(u'Mining-the-Social-Web(repo)', 851),
 (u'hcilab(user)', 121),
 (u'ptwobrussell(user)', 90),
 (u'kennethreitz(user)', 88),
 (u'equus12(user)', 71),
 (u'hammer(user)', 16),
 (u'necolas(user)', 16),
 (u'japerk(user)', 15),
 (u'douglas(user)', 11),
 (u'jianxioy(user)', 11)]

118
3

1
89
```

```
Number of popular users 95
Top 10 popular users: [(u'ptwobrussell(user)', 89),
                       (u'kennethreitz(user)', 84),
                       (u'necolas(user)', 15),
                       (u'japerk(user)', 14),
                       (u'hammer(user)', 13),
                       (u'isnowfy(user)', 6),
                       (u'kamzilla(user)', 6),
                       (u'acdha(user)', 6),
                       (u'tswicegood(user)', 6),
                       (u'albertsun(user)', 5)]
```

As we might have guessed, the owner of the repository that seeded the original interest graph, ptwobrussell (*http://bit.ly/1a1o4GC*), is the most popular user in the graph, but another user (kennethreitz) is close with 84 followers, and there are several other users in the top 10 with a nontrivial number of followers. Among other things, it turns out that kennethreitz (*http://bit.ly/1a1ojkT*) is the author of the popular `requests` Python package that has been used throughout this book. We also see that hcilab is a user who follows many users but is not followed back by many users. (We'll return to this latter observation in a moment.)

7.4.3.1. Application of centrality measures

Before we do any additional work, let's save a view of our graph so that we have a stable snapshot of our current state in case we'd like to tinker with the graph and recover it later, or in case we'd like to serialize and share the data. Example 7-10 demonstrates how to save and restore graphs using NetworkX's built-in pickling capabilities.

Example 7-10. Snapshotting (pickling) the graph's state to disk

```
# Save your work by serializing out (pickling) the graph
nx.write_gpickle(g, "resources/ch07-github/data/github.gpickle.1")

# How to restore the graph...
# import networkx as nx
# g = nx.read_gpickle("resources/ch07-github/data/github.gpickle.1")
```

With a backup of our work saved out to disk, let's now apply the centrality measures from the previous section to this graph and interpret the results. Since we know that `Mining-the-Social-Web(repo)` is a *supernode* in the graph and connects the majority of the users (all of them in this case), we'll remove it from the graph to get a better view of the network dynamics that might be at play. This leaves behind only GitHub users and the "follows" edges between them. Example 7-11 illustrates some code that provides a starting point for analysis.

Example 7-11. Applying centrality measures to the interest graph

```
from operator import itemgetter

# Create a copy of the graph so that we can iteratively mutate the copy
# as needed for experimentation

h = g.copy()

# Remove the seed of the interest graph, which is a supernode, in order
# to get a better idea of the network dynamics

h.remove_node('Mining-the-Social-Web(repo)')

# XXX: Remove any other nodes that appear to be supernodes.
# Filter any other nodes that you can by threshold
# criteria or heuristics from inspection.

# Display the centrality measures for the top 10 nodes


dc = sorted(nx.degree_centrality(h).items(),
            key=itemgetter(1), reverse=True)

print "Degree Centrality"
print dc[:10]
print

bc = sorted(nx.betweenness_centrality(h).items(),
            key=itemgetter(1), reverse=True)

print "Betweenness Centrality"
print bc[:10]
print

print "Closeness Centrality"
cc = sorted(nx.closeness_centrality(h).items(),
            key=itemgetter(1), reverse=True)
print cc[:10]
```

Sample results follow:

```
    Degree Centrality
    [(u'hcilab(user)', 0.1411764705882353),
     (u'ptwobrussell(user)', 0.10470588235294116),
     (u'kennethreitz(user)', 0.10235294117647058),
     (u'equus12(user)', 0.08235294117647059),
     (u'hammer(user)', 0.01764705882352941),
     (u'necolas(user)', 0.01764705882352941),
     (u'japerk(user)', 0.016470588235294115),
     (u'douglas(user)', 0.011764705882352941),
     (u'jianxioy(user)', 0.011764705882352941),
     (u'mt3(user)', 0.010588235294117647)]
```

```
Betweenness Centrality
[(u'hcilab(user)', 0.0011790110626111459),
 (u'douglas(user)', 0.0006983995011432135),
 (u'kennethreitz(user)', 0.0005637543592230768),
 (u'frac(user)', 0.00023557126030624264),
 (u'equus12(user)', 0.0001768269145113876),
 (u'acdha(user)', 0.00015935702903069354),
 (u'hammer(user)', 6.654723137782793e-05),
 (u'mt3(user)', 4.988567865308668e-05),
 (u'tswicegood(user)', 4.74606803852283e-05),
 (u'stonegao(user)', 4.068058318733853e-05)]

Closeness Centrality
[(u'hcilab(user)', 0.14537589026642048),
 (u'equus12(user)', 0.1161965001054185),
 (u'gawbul(user)', 0.08657147291634332),
 (u'douglas(user)', 0.08576408341114222),
 (u'frac(user)', 0.059923888224421004),
 (u'brunojm(user)', 0.05970317408731448),
 (u'empjustine(user)', 0.04591901349775037),
 (u'jianxioy(user)', 0.012592592592592593),
 (u'nellaivijay(user)', 0.012066365007541477),
 (u'mt3(user)', 0.011029411764705881)]
```

As in our previous analysis, the users ptwobrussell and kennethreitz appear near the top of the list for degree centrality, as expected. However, the hcilab user appears at the top of the chart for all centrality measures. Recalling from our previous analysis that the hcilab user follows lots of other users, a review of this user's public profile at *https:// github.com/hcilab* suggests that this is an account that may be used as part of a data mining process itself! It is named "Account for Github research" and has only logged one day of activity on GitHub in the previous year. Because this user qualifies as a supernode based on our previous analysis, removing it from the graph and rerunning the centrality measures will likely change the network dynamics and add some clarity to the analysis exercise.

Another observation is that the closeness centrality and degree centrality are much higher than the betweenness centrality, which is virtually at a value of zero. In the context of "following" relationships, this means that no user in the graph is effectively acting as a bridge in connecting other users in the graph. This makes sense because the original seed of the graph was a repository, which provided a common interest. While it would have been worthwhile to discover that there was a user whose betweenness had a meaningful value, it is not all that unexpected that this was not the case. Had the basis of the interest graph been a particular *user*, the dynamics might have turned out to be different.

Finally, observe that while ptwobrussell and kennethreitz are popular users in the graph, they do not appear in the top 10 users for closeness centrality. Several other users do appear, have a nontrivial value for closeness, and would be interesting to examine. At the time of this writing in August 2013, the user equus12 has over 400 followers but only two forked repositories and no public activity recently. User gawbul has 44 followers, many active repositories, and a fairly active profile. Further examination of the users with the highest degree and closeness centralities is left as an independent exercise. Keep in mind that the dynamic will vary from community to community.

 A worthwhile exercise would be to compare and contrast the network dynamics of two different communities, such as the Ruby on Rails community and the Django community. You might also try comparing the dynamics of a Microsoft-centric community versus a Linux-oriented community.

7.4.3.2. Adding more repositories to the interest graph

All in all, nothing all that interesting turned up in our analysis of the "follows" edges in the graph, which isn't all that surprising when we recall that the seed of the interest graph was a repository that drew in disparate users from all over the world. What might be worthwhile as a next step would be trying to find additional interests for each user in the graph by iterating over them and adding their starred repositories to the graph. Adding these starred repositories would give us at least two valuable pieces of insight: what other repositories are engaging to this community that is grounded in social web mining (and, to a lesser degree, Python), and what programming languages are popular among this community, given that GitHub attempts to index repositories and determine the programming languages used.

The process of adding repositories and "gazes" edges to the graph is just a simple extension of our previous work in this chapter. GitHub's "List repositories being starred" API (*http://bit.ly/1a1oc8X*) makes it easy enough to get back the list of repositories that a particular user has starred, and we'll just iterate over these results and add the same kinds of nodes and edges to the graph that we added earlier in this chapter. Example 7-12 illustrates the sample code for making this happen. It adds a significant amount of data to the in-memory graph and can take a while to execute. A bit of patience is required if you're working with a repository with more than a few dozen stargazers.

Example 7-12. Adding starred repositories to the graph

```
# Let's add each stargazer's additional starred repos and add edges
# to find additional interests.

MAX_REPOS = 500

for i, sg in enumerate(stargazers):
    print sg.login
    try:
        for starred in sg.get_starred()[:MAX_REPOS]: # Slice to avoid supernodes
            g.add_node(starred.name + '(repo)', type='repo', lang=starred.language, \
```

```
                    owner=starred.owner.login)
         g.add_edge(sg.login + '(user)', starred.name + '(repo)', type='gazes')
    except Exception, e: #ssl.SSLError:
        print "Encountered an error fetching starred repos for", sg.login, "Skipping."

    print "Processed", i+1, "stargazers' starred repos"
    print "Num nodes/edges in graph", g.number_of_nodes(), "/", g.number_of_edges()
    print "Rate limit", client.rate_limiting
```

One subtle concern with constructing this graph is that while most users have starred a "reasonable" number of repositories, some users may have starred an extremely high number of repositories, falling far outside statistical norms and introducing a highly disproportionate number of edges and nodes to the graph. As previously noted, a node with an extreme number of edges that is an outlier by a large margin is called a *super-node*. It is usually not desirable to model graphs (especially in-memory graphs such as the ones implemented by NetworkX) with supernodes because at best they can significantly complicate traversals and other analytics, and at worst they can cause out-of-memory errors. Your particular situation and objectives will determine whether it's appropriate for you to include supernodes.

A reasonable option that we employ to avoid introducing supernodes into the graph with Example 7-12 is to simply cap the number of repositories that we'll consider for a user. In this particular case, we limit the number of repositories under consideration to a fairly high number (500) by slicing the results of the values being iterated over in the for loop as get_starred()[:500]. Later, if we're interested in revisiting the supernodes, we'll need to query our graph only for nodes that have a high number of outgoing edges in order to discover them.

 Python, including the IPython Notebook server kernel, will use as much memory as required as you continue adding data to the graph. If you attempt to create a large enough graph that your operating system can no longer function, a kernel supervisor process may kill the offending Python process. See "Monitoring and Debugging Memory Usage with Vagrant and IPython Notebook" in the online version of Appendix C for some information on how to monitor and increase the memory use of IPython Notebook.

With a graph now constructed that contains additional repositories, we can start having some real fun in querying the graph. There are a number of questions we could now ask and answer beyond the calculation of simple statistics to update us on the overall size of the graph—it might be interesting to zoom in on the user who owns the most repositories that are being watched, for example. Perhaps one of the most pressing questions is what the most popular repositories in the graph are, besides the repository that was used to seed the original interest graph. Example 7-13 demonstrates a sample block of code that answers this question and provides a starting point for further analysis.

 Several other useful properties come back from PyGithub's `get_star` red API call (a wrapper around GitHub's "List repositories being starred" API (*http://bit.ly/1a1oc8X*)) that you might want to consider for future experiments. Be sure to review the API docs so that you don't miss out on anything that might be of use to you in exploring this space.

Example 7-13. Exploring the graph after updates with additional starred repositories

```
# Poke around: how to get users/repos
from operator import itemgetter

print nx.info(g)
print

# Get a list of repositories from the graph.

repos = [n for n in g.nodes_iter() if g.node[n]['type'] == 'repo']

# Most popular repos

print "Popular repositories"
print sorted([(n,d)
            for (n,d) in g.in_degree_iter()
                if g.node[n]['type'] == 'repo'], \
            key=itemgetter(1), reverse=True)[:10]
print

# Projects gazed at by a user

print "Respositories that ptwobrussell has bookmarked"
print [(n,g.node[n]['lang'])
       for n in g['ptwobrussell(user)']
          if g['ptwobrussell(user)'][n]['type'] == 'gazes']
print

# Programming languages for each user

print "Programming languages ptwobrussell is interested in"
print list(set([g.node[n]['lang']
            for n in g['ptwobrussell(user)']
                if g['ptwobrussell(user)'][n]['type'] == 'gazes']))
print

# Find supernodes in the graph by approximating with a high number of
# outgoing edges
```

```
print "Supernode candidates"
print sorted([(n, len(g.out_edges(n)))
                for n in g.nodes_iter()
                    if g.node[n]['type'] == 'user' and len(g.out_edges(n)) > 500], \
             key=itemgetter(1), reverse=True)
```

Sample output follows:

```
Name:
Type: DiGraph
Number of nodes: 48857
Number of edges: 116439
Average in degree:   2.3833
Average out degree:   2.3833

Popular repositories
[(u'Mining-the-Social-Web(repo)', 851),
 (u'bootstrap(repo)', 273),
 (u'd3(repo)', 194),
 (u'dotfiles(repo)', 166),
 (u'node(repo)', 139),
 (u'storm(repo)', 139),
 (u'impress.js(repo)', 125),
 (u'requests(repo)', 122),
 (u'html5-boilerplate(repo)', 114),
 (u'flask(repo)', 106)]

Respositories that ptwobrussell has bookmarked
[(u'Legal-Forms(repo)', u'Python'),
 (u'python-linkedin(repo)', u'Python'),
 (u'ipython(repo)', u'Python'),
 (u'Tweet-Relevance(repo)', u'Python'),
 (u'PyGithub(repo)', u'Python'),
 (u'Recipes-for-Mining-Twitter(repo)', u'JavaScript'),
 (u'wdb(repo)', u'JavaScript'),
 (u'networkx(repo)', u'Python'),
 (u'twitter(repo)', u'Python'),
 (u'envoy(repo)', u'Python'),
 (u'Mining-the-Social-Web(repo)', u'JavaScript'),
 (u'PayPal-APIs-Up-and-Running(repo)', u'Python'),
 (u'storm(repo)', u'Java'),
 (u'PyStratus(repo)', u'Python'),
 (u'Inquire(repo)', u'Python')]

Programming languages ptwobrussell is interested in
[u'Python', u'JavaScript', u'Java']

Supernode candidates
[(u'hcilab(user)', 614),
 (u'equus12(user)', 569),
 (u'jianxioy(user)', 508),
 (u'mcroydon(user)', 503),
 (u'umaar(user)', 502),
```

```
(u'rosco5(user)', 502),
(u'stefaneyr(user)', 502),
(u'aljosa(user)', 502),
(u'miyucy(user)', 501),
(u'zmughal(user)', 501)]
```

An initial observation is that the number of edges in the new graph is three orders of magnitude higher than in the previous graph, and the number of nodes is up well over one order of magnitude. This is where analysis can really get interesting because of the complex network dynamics. However, the complex network dynamics also mean that it will take nontrivial amounts of time for NetworkX to compute global graph statistics. Keep in mind that just because the graph is in memory doesn't mean that all computation will necessarily be fast. This is where a basic working knowledge of some fundamental computing principles can be helpful.

7.4.3.3. Computational Considerations

 This brief section contains a somewhat advanced discussion that involves some of the mathematical complexity involved in running graph algorithms. You are encouraged to read it, though you could opt to revisit this later if this is your first reading of this chapter.

For the three centrality measures being computed, we know that the calculation of degree centrality is relatively simple and should be fast, requiring little more than a single pass over the nodes to compute the number of incident edges. Both betweenness and closeness centralities, however, require computation of the minimum spanning tree (*http://bit.ly/1a1omgr*). The underlying NetworkX minimum spanning tree algorithm (*http://1.usa.gov/1a1omx6*) implements Kruskal's algorithm (*http://bit.ly/1a1on3X*), which is a staple in computer science education. In terms of runtime complexity, it takes on the order of $O(E \log E)$, where E represents the number of edges in the graph. Algorithms of this complexity are generally considered efficient, but 100,000 * log(100,000) is still approximately equal to one million operations, so a full analysis can take some time.

The removal of supernodes is critical in achieving reasonable runtimes for network algorithms, and a targeted exploration in which you extract a subgraph (*http://bit.ly/1a1oo80*) of interest for more thorough analysis is an option to consider. For example, you may want to selectively prune users from the graph based upon filtering criteria such as their number of followers, which could provide a basis for judging their importance to the overall network. You might also consider pruning repositories based upon a threshold for a minimum number of stargazers.

When conducting analyses on large graphs, you are advised to examine each of the centrality measures one at a time so that you can more quickly iterate on the results. It is also critical to remove supernodes from the graph in order to achieve reasonable runtimes, since supernodes can easily dominate computation in network algorithms. Depending on the size of your graph, this may also be a situation in which increasing the amount of memory available to your virtual machine could be beneficial. See Appendix C for details on memory profiling and configuration with Vagrant.

7.4.4. Using Nodes as Pivots for More Efficient Queries

Another characteristic of the data to consider is the popularity of programming languages that are employed by users. It could be the case that users star projects that are implemented in programming languages that they are at least loosely interested in and able to use themselves. Although we have the data and the tools to analyze users and popular programming languages with our existing graph, our schema currently has a shortcoming. Since a programming language is modeled as an attribute on a repository, it is necessary to scan all of the repository nodes and either extract or filter by this attribute in order to answer nontrivial questions.

For example, if we wanted to know which programming languages a user programs in using the current schema, we'd need to look up all of the repositories that user gazes at, extract the lang properties, and compute a frequency distribution. This doesn't seem too cumbersome, but what if we wanted to know how many users program in a particular programming language? Although the answer is computable with the existing schema, it requires a scan of every repository node and a count of all of the incoming "gazes" edges. With a modification to the graph schema, however, answering this question could be as simple as accessing a single node in the graph. The modification would involve creating a node in the graph for each programming language that has incoming programs edges that connect users who program in that language, and outgoing imple ments edges that connect repositories.

Figure 7-6 illustrates our final graph schema, which incorporates programming languages as well as edges between users, repositories, and programming languages. The overall effect of this schema change is that we've taken a property of one node and created an explicit relationship in the graph that was previously implicit. From the standpoint of completeness, there is no new data, but the data that we do have can now be computed on more efficiently for certain queries. Although the schema is fairly simple, the universe of possible graphs adhering to it that could be easily constructed and mined for valuable knowledge is immense.

The nice thing about having a single node in the graph that corresponds to a programming language, as opposed to representing a programming language as a property on many nodes, is that a single node acts as a natural point of aggregation. Central points of aggregation can greatly simplify many kinds of queries, such as finding maximal cliques in the graph, as described in Section 2.3.2.2 on page 78. For example, finding the maximal clique of users who all follow one another and program with a particular language can be more efficiently computed with NetworkX's clique detection algorithms (*http://bit.ly/1a1lWyo*) since the requirement of a particular programming language node in the clique significantly constrains the search.

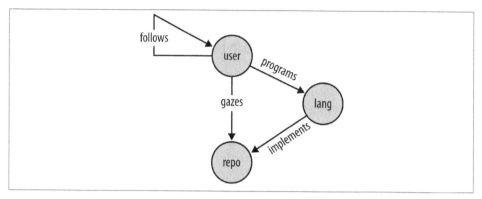

Figure 7-6. A graph schema that includes GitHub users, repositories, and programming languages

Example 7-14 introduces some sample code that constructs the updates as depicted in the final graph schema. Because all of the information that we need to construct the additional nodes and edges is already present in the existing graph (since we have already stored the programming language as a property on the repository nodes), no additional requests to the GitHub API are necessary.

Example 7-14. Updating the graph to include nodes for programming languages

```
# Iterate over all of the repos, and add edges for programming languages
# for each person in the graph. We'll also add edges back to repos so that
# we have a good point to "pivot" upon.

repos = [n
         for n in g.nodes_iter()
             if g.node[n]['type'] == 'repo']

for repo in repos:
    lang = (g.node[repo]['lang'] or "") + "(lang)"

    stargazers = [u
                  for (u, r, d) in g.in_edges_iter(repo, data=True)
                      if d['type'] == 'gazes'
                  ]

    for sg in stargazers:
        g.add_node(lang, type='lang')
        g.add_edge(sg, lang, type='programs')
        g.add_edge(lang, repo, type='implements')
```

Our final graph schema is capable of answering a variety of questions. A few questions that seem ripe for investigation at this point include:

- Which languages do particular users program with?
- How many users program in a particular language?
- Which users program in multiple languages, such as Python and JavaScript?
- Which programmer is the most polyglot (programs with the most languages)?
- Is there a higher correlation between particular languages? (For example, given that a programmer programs in Python, is it more likely that this same programmer also programs in JavaScript or with Go based upon the data in this graph?)

Example 7-15 provides some sample code that is a good starting point for answering most of these questions, and others like them.

Example 7-15. Sample queries for the final graph

```
# Some stats

print nx.info(g)
print

# What languages exist in the graph?

print [n
       for n in g.nodes_iter()
           if g.node[n]['type'] == 'lang']
print

# What languages do users program with?
print [n
       for n in g['ptwobrussell(user)']
           if g['ptwobrussell(user)'][n]['type'] == 'programs']

# What is the most popular programming language?
print "Most popular languages"
print sorted([(n, g.in_degree(n))
 for n in g.nodes_iter()
    if g.node[n]['type'] == 'lang'], key=itemgetter(1), reverse=True)[:10]
print

# How many users program in a particular language?
python_programmers = [u
                     for (u, l) in g.in_edges_iter('Python(lang)')
                         if g.node[u]['type'] == 'user']
print "Number of Python programmers:", len(python_programmers)
print

javascript_programmers = [u for
                          (u, l) in g.in_edges_iter('JavaScript(lang)')
```

```
                              if g.node[u]['type'] == 'user']
print "Number of JavaScript programmers:", len(javascript_programmers)
print

# What users program in both Python and JavaScript?
print "Number of programmers who use JavaScript and Python"
print len(set(python_programmers).intersection(set(javascript_programmers)))

# Programmers who use JavaScript but not Python
print "Number of programmers who use JavaScript but not Python"
print len(set(javascript_programmers).difference(set(python_programmers)))

# XXX: Can you determine who is the most polyglot programmer?
```

Sample output follows:

```
Name:
Type: DiGraph
Number of nodes: 48952
Number of edges: 174180
Average in degree:   3.5582
Average out degree:   3.5582

[u'PHP(lang)', u'Clojure(lang)', u'ActionScript(lang)', u'Logtalk(lang)',
 u'Scilab(lang)', u'Processing(lang)', u'D(lang)', u'Pure Data(lang)',
 u'Java(lang)', u'SuperCollider(lang)', u'Julia(lang)', u'Shell(lang)',
 u'Haxe(lang)', u'Gosu(lang)', u'JavaScript(lang)', u'CLIPS(lang)',
 u'Common Lisp(lang)', u'Visual Basic(lang)', u'Objective-C(lang)',
 u'Delphi(lang)', u'Objective-J(lang)', u'PogoScript(lang)',
 u'Scala(lang)', u'Smalltalk(lang)', u'DCPU-16 ASM(lang)',
 u'FORTRAN(lang)', u'ASP(lang)', u'XML(lang)', u'Ruby(lang)',
 u'VHDL(lang)', u'C++(lang)', u'Python(lang)', u'Perl(lang)',
 u'Assembly(lang)', u'CoffeeScript(lang)', u'Racket(lang)',
 u'Groovy(lang)', u'F#(lang)', u'Opa(lang)', u'Fantom(lang)',
 u'Eiffel(lang)', u'Lua(lang)', u'Puppet(lang)', u'Mirah(lang)',
 u'XSLT(lang)', u'Bro(lang)', u'Ada(lang)', u'OpenEdge ABL(lang)',
 u'Fancy(lang)', u'Rust(lang)', u'C(lang)', '(lang)', u'XQuery(lang)',
 u'Vala(lang)', u'Matlab(lang)', u'Apex(lang)', u'Awk(lang)', u'Lasso(lang)',
 u'OCaml(lang)', u'Arduino(lang)', u'Factor(lang)', u'LiveScript(lang)',
 u'AutoHotkey(lang)', u'Haskell(lang)', u'HaXe(lang)', u'DOT(lang)',
 u'Nu(lang)', u'VimL(lang)', u'Go(lang)', u'ABAP(lang)', u'ooc(lang)',
 u'TypeScript(lang)', u'Standard ML(lang)', u'Turing(lang)', u'Coq(lang)',
 u'ColdFusion(lang)', u'Augeas(lang)', u'Verilog(lang)', u'Tcl(lang)',
 u'Nimrod(lang)', u'Elixir(lang)',u'Ragel in Ruby Host(lang)', u'Monkey(lang)',
 u'Kotlin(lang)', u'C#(lang)',u'Scheme(lang)', u'Dart(lang)', u'Io(lang)',
 u'Prolog(lang)', u'Arc(lang)', u'PowerShell(lang)', u'R(lang)',
 u'AppleScript(lang)', u'Emacs Lisp(lang)', u'Erlang(lang)']

[u'JavaScript(lang)', u'Java(lang)', u'Python(lang)']

Most popular languages
[(u'JavaScript(lang)', 851), (u'Python(lang)', 715), ('(lang)', 642),
 (u'Ruby(lang)', 620), (u'Java(lang)', 573), (u'C(lang)', 556),
```

```
(u'C++(lang)', 508), (u'PHP(lang)', 477), (u'Shell(lang)', 475),
(u'Objective-C(lang)', 435)]

Number of Python programmers: 715

Number of JavaScript programmers: 851

Number of programmers who use JavaScript and Python
715
Number of programmers who use JavaScript but not Python
136
```

Although the graph schema is conceptually simple, the number of edges has increased by nearly 50% because of the additional programming language nodes! As we see from the output for a few sample queries, there are quite a large number of programming languages in use, and JavaScript and Python top the list. The primary source code for the original repository of interest is written in Python, so the emergence of JavaScript as a more popular programming language among users may be indicative of a web development audience. Of course, it is also the case that JavaScript is just a popular programming language, and there is often a high correlation between JavaScript for a client-side language and Python as a server-side language. Ruby is also a popular programming language and is commonly used for server-side web development. It appears fourth in the list. The appearance of '(lang)' as the third most popular language is an indication that there are 642 repositories to which GitHub could not assign a programming language, and in aggregate, they rolled up into this single category.

The possibilities are immense for analyzing a graph that expresses people's interests in other people, open source projects in repositories, and programming languages. Whatever analysis you choose to do, think carefully about the nature of the problem and extract only the relevant data from the graph for analysis—either by zeroing in on a set of nodes to extract with NetworkX graph's subgraph method, or by filtering out nodes by type or frequency threshold.

 A bipartite analysis (*http://bit.ly/1a1oooP*) of users and programming languages would likely be a worthwhile endeavor, given the nature of the relationship between users and programming languages. A bipartite graph involves two disjoint sets of vertices that are connected by edges between the sets. You could easily remove repository nodes from the graph at this point to drastically enhance the efficiency of computing global graph statistics (the number of edges would decrease by over 100,000).

7.4.5. Visualizing Interest Graphs

Although it is exciting to visualize a graph, and a picture really is often worth far more than a thousand words, keep in mind that not all graphs are easily visualized. However, with a little bit of thought you can often extract a subgraph that can be visualized to the extent that it provides some insight or intuition into the problem that you are trying to solve. As you know from our work in this chapter, a graph is just a type of data structure and has no definite visual rendering. To be visualized, a particular type of *layout algorithm* must be applied that maps the nodes and edges to a two- or three-dimensional space for visual consumption.

We'll stick to the core toolkit that we've used throughout the book and lean on NetworkX's ability to export JSON that can be rendered by the JavaScript toolkit D3 (*http://bit.ly/1a1kGvo*), but there are many other toolkits that you could consider when visualizing graphs. Graphviz (*http://bit.ly/1a1ooVG*) is a highly configurable and rather classic tool that can lay out very complex graphs as bitmap images. It has traditionally been used in a terminal setting like other command-line tools, but it also now ships with a user interface for most platforms. Another option is Gephi (*http://bit.ly/1a1opc5*), another popular open source project that provides some powerful interactive possibilities; Gephi has rapidly grown in popularity over the past few years and is an option that's well worth your consideration.

Example 7-16 illustrates a template for extracting a subgraph of the users who gaze at the seed of our original graph (the Mining-the-Social-Web repository) and the "following" connections among them. It extracts the users in the graph with a common interest and visualize the "follows" edges among them. Keep in mind that the entire graph as constructed in this chapter is quite large and contains tens of thousands of nodes and hundreds of thousands of edges, so you'd need to spend some time better understanding it in order to achieve a reasonable visualization with a tool like Gephi.

Example 7-16. Graph visualization of the social network for the original interest graph

```
import os
import json
from IPython.display import IFrame
from IPython.core.display import display
from networkx.readwrite import json_graph

print "Stats on the full graph"
print nx.info(g)
print

# Create a subgraph from a collection of nodes. In this case, the
# collection is all of the users in the original interest graph

mtsw_users = [n for n in g if g.node[n]['type'] == 'user']
h = g.subgraph(mtsw_users)
```

```
print "Stats on the extracted subgraph"
print nx.info(h)

# Visualize the social network of all people from the original interest graph.

d = json_graph.node_link_data(h)
json.dump(d, open('resources/ch07-github/force.json', 'w'))


# IPython Notebook can serve files and display them into
# inline frames. Prepend the path with the 'files' prefix.

# A D3 template for displaying the graph data.
viz_file = 'files/resources/ch07-github/force.html'

# Display the D3 visualization.

display(IFrame(viz_file, '100%', '600px'))
```

Figure 7-7 shows sample results of running this example code.

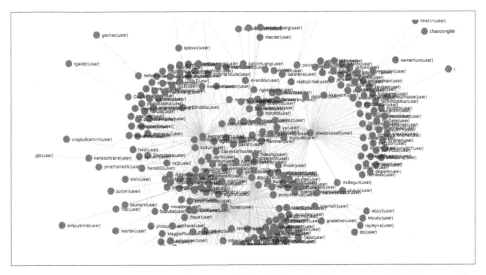

Figure 7-7. An interactive visualization of the "follows" edges among GitHub users for the interest graph—notice the patterns in the visual layout of the graph that correspond to the centrality measures introduced earlier in this chapter

7.5. Closing Remarks

 The source code outlined for this chapter and all other chapters is available at GitHub (*http://bit.ly/1a1kNqy*) in a convenient IPython Notebook format that you're highly encouraged to try out from the comfort of your own web browser.

Although various sorts of graphs have been sprinkled throughout earlier chapters in this book, this chapter provided a more substantial introduction to their use as a flexible data structure for representing a network of GitHub users and their common interests in certain software project repositories and programming languages. GitHub's rich API and NetworkX's easy-to-use API are a nice duo for mining some fascinating and often-overlooked social web data in one of the most overtly "social" web properties that's in widespread use across the globe. The notion of an interest graph isn't an entirely new idea, but its application to the social web is a fairly recent development with exciting implications. Whereas interest graphs (or comparable representations) have been used by advertisers to effectively place ads for some time, they're now being used by entrepreneurs and software developers to more effectively target interests and make intelligent recommendations that enhance a product's relevance to users.

Like most of the other chapters in the book, this chapter has served as merely a primer for graphical modeling, interest graphs, GitHub's API, and what you can do with these technologies. You could just as easily apply the graphical modeling techniques in this chapter to other social web properties such as Twitter or Facebook and achieve compelling analytic results, as well as applying other forms of analysis to the rich data that's available from GitHub's API. The possibilities, as always, are quite vast. My hope first and foremost is that you've enjoyed yourself while working through the exercises in this chapter and learned something new that you can take with you throughout your social web mining journey and beyond.

7.6. Recommended Exercises

- Repeat the exercises in this chapter, but use a different repository as a starting point. Do the findings from this chapter generally hold true, or are the results of your experiments different in any particular way?

- GitHub has published some data regarding correlations between programming languages (*http://bit.ly/1a1or3Y*). Review and explore the data. Is it any different from what you could collect with the GitHub API?

- NetworkX provides an extensive collection of graph traversal algorithms (*http://bit.ly/1a1orkk*). Review the documentation and pick a couple of algorithms to run on the data. Centrality measures, cliques, and bipartite algorithms might make a good starting point for inspiration. Can you compute the largest clique of users in the graph? What about the largest clique that shares a common interest, such as a particular programming language?

- The GitHub Archive (*http://bit.ly/1a1orAK*) provides an extensive amount of data about GitHub activity at a global level. Investigate this data, using some of the recommended "big data" tools to explore it.

- Compare data points across two similar GitHub projects. Given the inextricable links between Mining-the-Social-Web and Mining-the-Social-Web-2nd-Edition, these two projects make for a suitable starting point for analysis. Who has bookmarked or forked one but not the other? How do the interest graphs compare? Can you build and analyze an interest graph that contains all of the users who are interested in both editions?

- Use a similarity measurement such as Jaccard similarity (see `nltk.metrics.jac card_distance`; see also Section 4.4.4.1 on page 172) to compute the similarity of two arbitrary users on GitHub based upon features such as starred repositories in common, programming languages in common, and other features that you can find in GitHub's API.

- Given users and existing interests, can you design an algorithm that recommends interests for other users? Consider adapting the code from Section 4.3 on page 147 that uses cosine similarity as a means of predicting relevance.

- Employ a histogram to gain insight into a facet of the interest graph in this chapter, such as the popularity of programming languages.

- Explore graph visualization tools like Graphviz and Gephi to lay out and render a graph for visual inspection.

- You may have heard that Google discontinued its Google Reader product in mid-2013. One of the ensuing discussions around the perceived void it left is whether a subscription graph (*http://tcrn.ch/1a1opZV*), a more decentralized version of subscription-oriented content based upon "following" mechanics, is already emerging all around us. Do you think that the future of the Web largely involves a technological paradigm shift that makes it easy to unite people with common interests? Is it already happening?

- Explore the Friendster social network and ground-truth communities (*http://stan ford.io/1a1orRr*) data set and use NetworkX algorithms to analyze it.

7.7. Online Resources

The following list of links from this chapter may be useful for review:

- Bipartite graph (*http://bit.ly/1a1oooP*)
- Centrality measures (*http://bit.ly/1a1osEM*)
- Creating a GitHub OAuth token for command-line use (*http://bit.ly/1a1o7lG*)
- D3.js (*http://bit.ly/1a1kGvo*)
- Friendster social network and ground-truth communities (*http://stanford.io/1a1orRr*)
- Gephi (*http://bit.ly/1a1opc5*)
- GitHub Archive (*http://bit.ly/1a1orAK*)
- GitHub Developers (*http://bit.ly/1a1o49k*)
- GitHub developer documentation for pagination (*http://bit.ly/1a1o9Ki*)
- GitHub developer documentation for rate limiting (*http://bit.ly/1a1oblo*)
- gitscm.com (online Git book) (*http://bit.ly/1a1o2hZ*)
- Graph Theory—An Introduction! YouTube video (*http://bit.ly/1a1odto*)
- Graphviz (*http://bit.ly/1a1ooVG*)
- Hypergraph (*http://bit.ly/1a1ocWm*)
- Interest graph (*http://bit.ly/1a1o3Cu*)
- Krackhardt kite graph (*http://bit.ly/1a1oixa*)
- Kruskal's algorithm (*http://bit.ly/1a1on3X*)
- Minimum spanning tree (MST) (*http://bit.ly/1a1omgr*)
- NetworkX (*http://bit.ly/1a1ocFV*)
- NetworkX documentation (*http://bit.ly/1a1ocFV*)
- NetworkX graph traversal algorithms (*http://bit.ly/1a1orkk*)
- PyGithub GitHub repository (*http://bit.ly/1a1o7Ca*)
- Python threads synchronization: Locks, RLocks, Semaphores, Conditions, Events and Queues (*http://bit.ly/1a1oAUQ*)
- Thread pool pattern (*http://bit.ly/1a1mW5M*)
- Thread safety (*http://bit.ly/1a1oE73*)

## CHAPTER 8

Mining the Semantically Marked-Up Web: Extracting Microformats, Inferencing over RDF, and More

While the previous chapters attempted to provide an overview of some popular websites from the social web, this chapter connects that discussion with a highly pragmatic discussion about the semantic web. Think of the *semantic web* as a version of the Web much like the one that you are already experiencing, except that it has evolved to the point that machines are routinely extracting vast amounts of information that they are able to reason over and making automated decisions based upon that information.

The semantic web is a topic worthy of a book in itself, and this chapter is not intended to be any kind of proper technical discussion about it. Rather, it is framed as a technically oriented "cocktail discussion" and attempts to connect the highly pragmatic social web with the more grandiose vision for a semantic web. It is considerably more hypothetical than the chapters before it, but there is still some important technology covered in this chapter.

One of the primary topics that you'll learn about in this chapter from a practitioner's standpoint is *microformats*, a relatively simple technique for embedding unambiguous structured data in web pages that machines can rather trivially parse out and use for various kinds of automated reasoning. As you're about to learn, microformats are an exciting and active chapter in the Web's evolution and are being actively pursued by the IndieWeb (*http://bit.ly/1A5ANScQ*), as well as a number of powerful corporations through an effort called Schema.org. The implications of microformats for social web mining are vast.

Before wrapping up the chapter, we'll bridge the microformats discussion with the more visionary hopes for the semantic web by taking a brief look at some technology for inferencing over collections of facts with inductive logic to answer questions. By the end of the chapter, you should have a pretty good idea of where the mainstream Web stands with respect to embedding semantic metadata into web pages, and how that compares with something a little closer to a state-of-the-art implementation.

 Always get the latest bug-fixed source code for this chapter (and every other chapter) online at *http://bit.ly/MiningTheSocialWeb2E*. Be sure to also take advantage of this book's virtual machine experience, as described in Appendix A, to maximize your enjoyment of the sample code.

8.1. Overview

As mentioned, this chapter is a bit more hypothetical than the chapters before it and provides some perspective that may be helpful as you think about the future of the Web. In this chapter you'll learn about:

- Common types of microformats
- How to identify and manipulate common microformats from web pages
- The currently utility of microformats in the Web
- A brief overview of the semantic web and semantic web technology
- Performing inference on semantic web data with a Python toolkit called FuXi

8.2. Microformats: Easy-to-Implement Metadata

In terms of the Web's ongoing evolution, microformats are quite an important step forward because they provide an effective mechanism for embedding "smarter data" into web pages and are easy for content authors to implement. Put succinctly, micro-formats (*http://bit.ly/1a1oEEd*) are simply conventions for unambiguously embedding metadata into web pages in an entirely value-added way. This chapter begins by briefly introducing the microformats landscape and then digs right into some examples involving specific uses of geo (*http://bit.ly/1a1oFb6*), hRecipe (*http://bit.ly/1a1oHjn*), and hResume (*http://bit.ly/1a1oFIf*) microformats. As we'll see, some of these microformats build upon constructs from other, more fundamental microformats—such as hCard (*http://bit.ly/1a1oFYG*)—that we'll also investigate.

Although it might seem like somewhat of a stretch to call data decorated with micro-formats like geo or hRecipe "social data," it's still interesting and inevitably plays an increased role in social data mashups. At the time the first edition of this book was published back in early 2011, nearly half of all web developers reported some use of microformats (*http://bit.ly/1a1oInm*), the *microformats.org* community had just celebrated its fifth birthday (*http://bit.ly/1a1oJaY*), and Google reported that 94% of the time, microformats were involved in rich snippets (*http://bit.ly/1a1oJaY*). Since then, Google's rich snippets initiative has continued to gain momentum, and Schema.org has emerged to try to ensure a shared vocabulary across vendors implementing semantic markup with comparable technologies such as microformats, HTML5 microdata, and RDFa. Accordingly, you should expect to see continued growth in semantic markup overall, although not all semantic markup initiatives may continue to grow at the same pace. As with almost anything else, market dynamics, corporate politics, and technology trends all play a role.

 Web Data Commons (*http://bit.ly/1a1oJI1*) extracts structured data such as microformats from the Common Crawl (*http://bit.ly/1a1oM6A*) web corpus and makes it available to the public for study and consumption. In particular, the detailed results from the August 2012 corpus (*http://bit.ly/1a1oKf0*) provide some intriguing statistics. It appears that the combined initiatives by Schema.org have been significant.

The story of microformats is largely one of narrowing the gap between a fairly ambiguous Web primarily based on the human-readable HTML 4.01 (*http://bit.ly/1a1oKvt*) standard and a more semantic Web in which information is much less ambiguous and friendlier to machine interpretation. The beauty of microformats is that they provide a way to embed structured data that's related to aspects of life and social activities such as calendaring, résumés, food, products, and product reviews, and they exist within HTML markup *right now* in an entirely backward-compatible way. Table 8-1 provides a synopsis of a few popular microformats and related initiatives you're likely to encounter if you look around on the Web. For more examples, see *http://bit.ly/1a1oKLV*.

Table 8-1. Some popular technologies for embedding structured data into web pages

Technology	Purpose	Popularity	Markup specification	Type
XFN	Representing human-readable relationships in hyperlinks	Widely used by blogging platforms in the early 2000s to implicitly represent social graphs. Rapidly increased in popularity after the retirement of Google's Social Graph API but is now finding new life in IndieWeb's RelMeAuth initiative for web sign-in.	Semantic HTML, XHTML	Microformat
geo	Embedding geocoordinates for people and objects	Widely used, especially by sites such as OpenStreetMap and Wikipedia.	Semantic HTML, XHTML	Microformat

Technology	Purpose	Popularity	Markup specification	Type
hCard	Identifying people, companies, and other contact info	Widely used and included in other popular microformats such as hResume.	Semantic HTML, XHTML	Microformat
hCalendar	Embedding iCalendar data	Continuing to steadily grow (*http://bit.ly/1a1oOeJ*).	Semantic HTML, XHTML	Microformat
hResume	Embedding résumé and CV information	Widely used by sites such as LinkedIn, which presents public résumés in hResume format (*http://bit.ly/1a1oRap*) for its more than 200 million worldwide users (*http://linkd.in/1a1oP2m*).	Semantic HTML, XHTML	Microformat
hRecipe	Identifying recipes	Widely used by niche food sites such as subdomains on *about.com* (e.g., *thaifood.about.com* (*http://abt.cm/1a1oPPX*)).	Semantic HTML, XHTML	Microformat
Microdata	Embedding name/value pairs into web pages authored in HTML5	A technology that emerged as part of HTML5 and has steadily gained traction, especially because of Google's rich snippets initiative and Schema.org.	HTML5	W3C initiative
RDFa	Embedding unambiguous facts into XHTML pages according to specialized vocabularies created by subject-matter experts	The basis of Facebook's Open Graph protocol (*http://bit.ly/1a1lu3m*) and Open Graph concepts, which have rapidly grown in popularity. Otherwise, somewhat hit-or-miss depending on the particular vocabulary.	XHTML[a]	W3C initiative
Open Graph protocol	Embedding profiles of real-world things into XHTML pages	Has seen rapid growth and still has tremendous potential given Facebook's more than 1 billion users (*http://on.wsj.com/1a1oTit*).	XHTML (RDFa-based)	Facebook platform initiative

[a] Embedding RDFa into semantic markup and HTML5 continues to be an active effort at the time of this writing. See the W3C HTML+RDFa 1.1 Working Draft (*http://bit.ly/1a1oSLx*).

If you know much about the short history of the Web, you'll recognize that innovation is rampant and that the highly decentralized way in which the Web operates is not conducive to overnight revolutions; rather, change seems to happen continually, fluidly, and in an evolutionary way. For example, as of mid-2013 XFN (*http://bit.ly/1a1oTyX*) (the XHTML Friends Network) seems to have lost most of its momentum in representing social graphs, due to the declining popularity of blogrolls and because large social web properties such as Facebook, Twitter, and others have not adopted it and instead have pursued their own initiatives for socializing data. Significant technological investments such as Google's Social Graph API used XFN as a foundation and contributed to its overall popularity. However, the retirement of Google's Social Graph API back in early 2012 (*http://bit.ly/1a1oWuI*) seems to have had a comparable dampening effect. It appears that many implementers of social web technologies were building directly on Google's Social Graph API and effectively using it as a proxy for microformats such as XFN rather than building on XFN directly.

Whereas the latter would have been a safer bet looking back, the convenience of the former took priority and somewhat ironically led to a "soft reset" of XFN. However, XFN is now finding a new and exciting life as part of an IndieWeb (*http://bit.ly/ 1a1oWuT*) initiative known as RelMeAuth (*http://bit.ly/1a1oUD4*), the technology behind a web sign-in (*http://bit.ly/1a1oUDd*) that proposes an intriguing open standard for using your own website or other social profiles for authentication.

 In the same way that XFN is fluidly evolving to meet new needs of the Web, microformats in general have evolved to fill the voids of "intelligent data" on the Web and serve as a particularly good example of bridging *existing* technology with *emerging* technology for everyone's mutual benefit.

There are many other microformats that you're likely to encounter. Although a good rule of thumb is to watch what the bigger fish in the pond—such as Google, Yahoo!, Bing, and Facebook—are doing, you should also keep an eye on what is happening in communities that define and shape open standards. The more support a microformat or semantic gets from a player with significant leverage, the more likely it will be to succeed and become useful for data mining, but never underestimate the natural and organic effects of motivated community leaders who genuinely seek to serve the greater good with allegiance to no particular corporate entity. The collaborative efforts of providers involved with Schema.org should be of particular interest to watch over the near term, but so should IndieWeb and W3C initiatives.

 See "HTML, XML, and XHTML" on page 185 for a brief aside about semantic markup as it relates to HTML, XML, and XHTML.

8.2.1. Geocoordinates: A Common Thread for Just About Anything

The implications of using microformats are subtle yet somewhat profound: while a human might be reading an article about a place like Franklin, Tennessee and intuitively know that a dot on a map on the page denotes the town's location, a robot could not reach the same conclusion easily without specialized logic that targets various pattern-matching possibilities. Such page scraping is a messy proposition, and typically just when you think you have all of the possibilities figured out, you find that you've missed one. Embedding proper semantics into the page that effectively tag unstructured data in a way that even Robby the Robot (*http://bit.ly/1a1oXii*) could understand removes ambiguity and lowers the bar for crawlers and developers. It's a win-win situation for the producer and the consumer, and hopefully the net effect is increased innovation for everyone.

Although it's certainly true that standalone geodata isn't particularly social, important but nonobvious relationships often emerge from disparate data sets that are tied together with a common geographic context.

Geodata is ubiquitous. It plays a powerful part in too many social mashups to name, because a particular point in space can be used as the glue for clustering people together. The divide between "real life" and life on the Web continues to close, and just about any kind of data becomes social the moment that it is tied to a particular individual in the real world. For example, there's an awful lot that you might be able to tell about people based on where they live and what kinds of food they like. This section works through some examples of finding, parsing, and visualizing geo-microformatted data.

One of the simplest and most widely used microformats that embeds geolocation information into web pages is appropriately called geo. The specification is inspired by a property with the same name from vCard (*http://bit.ly/1a1oVqL*), which provides a means of specifying a location. There are two possible means of embedding a microformat with geo. The following HTML snippet illustrates the two techniques for describing Franklin, Tennessee (*http://bit.ly/1a1oVHe*):

```
<!-- The multiple class approach -->
<span style="display: none" class="geo">
    <span class="latitude">36.166</span>
    <span class="longitude">-86.784</span>
</span>

<!-- When used as one class, the separator must be a semicolon -->
<span style="display: none" class="geo">36.166; -86.784</span>
```

As you can see, this microformat simply wraps latitude and longitude values in tags with corresponding class names, and packages them both inside a tag with a class of geo. A number of popular sites, including Wikipedia (*http://bit.ly/1a1oVXJ*) and OpenStreet-Map (*http://bit.ly/1a1oYms*), use geo and other microformats to expose structured data in their pages.

A common practice with geo is to hide the information that's encoded from the user. There are two ways that you might do this with traditional CSS: style="display: none" and style="visibility: hidden". The former removes the element's placement on the page entirely so that the layout behaves as though it is not there at all. The latter hides the content but reserves the space it takes up on the page.

Example 8-1 illustrates a simple program that parses geo-microformatted data from a Wikipedia page to show how you could extract coordinates from content implementing the geo microformat. Note that Wikipedia's terms of use define a bot policy (*http://bit.ly/1a1oZ9T*) that you should review prior to attempting to retrieve any content with scripts such as the following. The gist is that you'll need to download data archives that Wikipedia periodically updates as opposed to writing bots to pull nontrivial volumes of data from the live site. (It's fine for us to yank a web page here for educational purposes.)

 As should always be the case, carefully review a website's terms of service to ensure that any scripts you run against it comply with its latest guidelines.

Example 8-1. Extracting geo-microformatted data from a Wikipedia page

```
import requests # pip install requests
from BeautifulSoup import BeautifulSoup # pip install BeautifulSoup

# XXX: Any URL containing a geo microformat...

URL = 'http://en.wikipedia.org/wiki/Franklin,_Tennessee'

# In the case of extracting content from Wikipedia, be sure to
# review its "Bot Policy," which is defined at
# http://meta.wikimedia.org/wiki/Bot_policy#Unacceptable_usage

req = requests.get(URL, headers={'User-Agent' : "Mining the Social Web"})
soup = BeautifulSoup(req.text)

geoTag = soup.find(True, 'geo')

if geoTag and len(geoTag) > 1:
    lat = geoTag.find(True, 'latitude').string
    lon = geoTag.find(True, 'longitude').string
    print 'Location is at', lat, lon
elif geoTag and len(geoTag) == 1:
    (lat, lon) = geoTag.string.split(';')
    (lat, lon) = (lat.strip(), lon.strip())
    print 'Location is at', lat, lon
else:
    print 'No location found'
```

The following sample results illustrate that the output is just a set of coordinates, as expected:

```
Location is at 35.92917 -86.85750
```

To make the output a little bit more interesting, however, you could display the results directly in IPython Notebook with an inline frame, as shown in Example 8-2.

Example 8-2. Displaying geo-microformats with Google Maps in IPython Notebook

```
from IPython.display import IFrame
from IPython.core.display import display

# Google Maps URL template for an iframe

google_maps_url = "http://maps.google.com/maps?q={0}+{1}&" + \
  "ie=UTF8&t=h&z=14&{0},{1}&output=embed".format(lat, lon)

display(IFrame(google_maps_url, '425px', '350px'))
```

Sample results after executing this call in IPython Notebook are shown in Figure 8-1.

Figure 8-1. IPython Notebook's ability to display inline frames can add a lot of interactivity and convenience to your experiments in data analysis

The moment you find a web page with compelling geodata embedded, the first thing you'll want to do is visualize it. For example, consider the "List of National Parks of the United States" Wikipedia article (*http://bit.ly/1a1oYTl*). It displays a nice tabular view of the national parks and marks them up with geoformatting, but wouldn't it be nice to quickly load the data into an interactive tool for visual inspection? A terrific little web service called microform.at (*http://microform.at/*) extracts several types of microformats from a given URL and passes them back in a variety of useful formats. It exposes multiple options for detecting and interacting with microformat data in web pages, as shown in Figure 8-2.

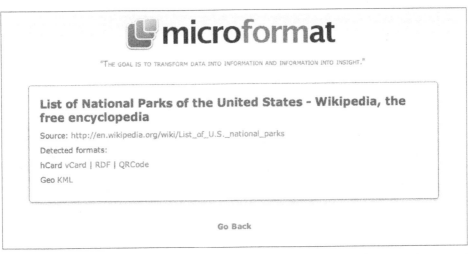

Figure 8-2. microform.at's results for the Wikipedia article entitled "List of National Parks of the United States"

If you're given the option, KML (*http://bit.ly/1a1p1Pb*) (Keyhole Markup Language) output is one of the more ubiquitous ways to visualize geodata. You can either download Google Earth and load the KML file locally, or type a URL containing KML data directly into the Google Maps search bar to bring it up without any additional effort required. In the results displayed for microform.at, clicking on the "KML" link triggers a file download that you can use in Google Earth, but you can copy it to the clipboard via a right-click and pass that to Google Maps.

Figure 8-3 displays the Google Maps visualization for *http://microform.at/? type=geo&url=http%3A%2F%2Fen.wikipedia.org%2Fwiki%2FList_of_U.S._nation al_parks*—the KML results for the aforementioned Wikipedia article, which is just the base URL *http://microform.at* with `type` and `url` query string parameters.

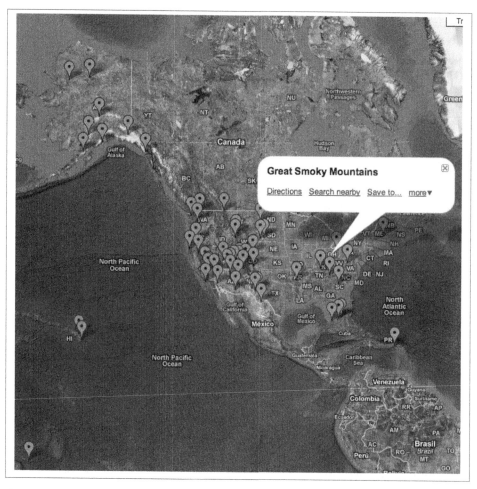

Figure 8-3. Google Maps results that display all of the national parks in the United States when passed KML results from microform.at

The ability to start with a Wikipedia article containing semantic markup such as geodata and trivially visualize it is a powerful analytical capability because it delivers insight quickly for so little effort. Browser extensions such as the Firefox Operator add-on (*http://mzl.la/1a1p2Cy*) aim to minimize the effort even further. Only so much can be said in one chapter, but a neat way to spend an hour or so would be to mash up the national park data from this section with contact information from your LinkedIn professional network to discover how you might be able to have a little bit more fun on your next (possibly contrived) business trip. (See Section 3.3.4.4 on page 127 for an example of how to harvest and analyze geodata by applying the *k*-means technique for finding clusters and computing centroids for those clusters.)

8.2.2. Using Recipe Data to Improve Online Matchmaking

Since Google's rich snippets initiative took off, there's been an ever-increasing awareness of microformats, and many of the most popular foodie websites have made solid progress in exposing recipes and reviews with hRecipe and hReview. Consider the potential for a fictitious online dating service that crawls blogs and other social hubs, attempting to pair people together for dinner dates. One could reasonably expect that having access to enough geo and hRecipe information linked to specific people would make a profound difference in the "success rate" of first dates.

People could be paired according to two criteria: how close they live to each other and what kinds of foods they eat. For example, you might expect a dinner date between two individuals who prefer to cook vegetarian meals with organic ingredients to go a lot better than a date between a BBQ lover and a vegan. Dining preferences and whether specific types of allergens or organic ingredients are used could be useful clues to power the right business idea. While we won't be trying to launch a new online dating service, we'll get the ball rolling in case you decide to take this idea and move forward with it.

About.com (*http://abt.cm/1a1p11C*) is one of the more prevalent online sites that's really embracing microformat initiatives for the betterment of the entire Web, exposing recipe information in the hRecipe microformat and using the hReview microformat for reviews of the recipes; epicurious (*http://epi.us/1a1p1yH*) and many other popular sites have followed suit, due to the benefits afforded by Schema.org initiatives that take advantage of this information for web searches. This section briefly demonstrates how search engines (or you) might parse out the structured data from recipes and reviews contained in web pages for indexing or analyzing. An adaptation of Example 8-1 that parses out hRecipe-formatted data is shown in Example 8-3.

 Although the spec is well defined, microformat implementations may vary subtly. Consider the following code samples that parse web pages more of a starting template than a robust, full-spec parser. A microformats parser implemented in Node.js (*http://bit.ly/1a1p3GL*), however, emerged on GitHub in early 2013 and may be worthy of consideration if you are seeking a more robust solution for parsing web pages with microformats.

Example 8-3. Extracting hRecipe data from a web page

```
import sys
import requests
import json
import BeautifulSoup

# Pass in a URL containing hRecipe...

URL = 'http://britishfood.about.com/od/recipeindex/r/applepie.htm'
```

```python
# Parse out some of the pertinent information for a recipe.
# See http://microformats.org/wiki/hrecipe.


def parse_hrecipe(url):
    req = requests.get(URL)

    soup = BeautifulSoup.BeautifulSoup(req.text)

    hrecipe = soup.find(True, 'hrecipe')

    if hrecipe and len(hrecipe) > 1:
        fn = hrecipe.find(True, 'fn').string
        author = hrecipe.find(True, 'author').find(text=True)
        ingredients = [i.string
                            for i in hrecipe.findAll(True, 'ingredient')
                                if i.string is not None]

        instructions = []
        for i in hrecipe.find(True, 'instructions'):
            if type(i) == BeautifulSoup.Tag:
                s = ''.join(i.findAll(text=True)).strip()
            elif type(i) == BeautifulSoup.NavigableString:
                s = i.string.strip()
            else:
                continue

            if s != '':
                instructions += [s]

        return {
            'name': fn,
            'author': author,
            'ingredients': ingredients,
            'instructions': instructions,
            }
    else:
        return {}


recipe = parse_hrecipe(URL)
print json.dumps(recipe, indent=4)
```

For a sample URL such as a popular apple pie recipe, you should get something like the
following (abbreviated) results:

```
{
    "instructions": [
        "Method",
        "Place the flour, butter and salt into a large clean bowl...",
        "The dough can also be made in a food processor by mixing the flour...",
```

```
            "Heat the oven to 425&#176;F/220&#176;C/gas 7.",
            "Meanwhile simmer the apples with the lemon juice and water..."
        ],
        "ingredients": [
            "Pastry",
            "7 oz/200g all purpose/plain flour",
            "pinch of salt",
            "1 stick/ 110g butter, cubed or an equal mix of butter and lard",
            "2-3 tbsp cold water",
            "Filling",
            "1 &#189; lbs/700g cooking apples, peeled, cored and quartered",
            "2 tbsp lemon juice",
            "&#189; cup/ 100g sugar",
            "4 - 6 tbsp cold water",
            "1 level tsp ground cinnamon ",
            "&#188; stick/25g butter",
            "Milk to glaze"
        ],
        "name": "\t\t\t\t\t\t\tTraditional Apple Pie Recipe\t\t\t\t\t",
        "author": "Elaine Lemm"
    }
```

Aside from space and time, food may be the next most fundamental thing that brings people together, and exploring the opportunities for social analysis and data analytics involving people, food, space, and time could really be quite interesting and lucrative. For example, you might analyze variations of the same recipe to see whether there are any correlations between the appearance or lack of certain ingredients and ratings/reviews for the recipes. You could then try to use this as the basis for better reaching a particular target audience with recommendations for products and services, or possibly even for prototyping that dating site that hypothesizes that a successful first date might highly correlate with a successful first meal together.

Pull down a few different apple pie recipes to determine which ingredients are common to all recipes and which are less common. Can you correlate the appearance or lack of different ingredients to a particular geographic region? Do British apple pies typically contain ingredients that apple pies cooked in the southeast United States do not, and vice versa? How might you use food preferences and geographic information to pair people?

The next section introduces an additional consideration for constructing an online matchmaking service like the one we've discussed.

8.2.2.1. Retrieving recipe reviews

This section concludes our all-too-short survey of microformats by briefly introducing hReview-aggregate (*http://bit.ly/1a1p3Xa*), a variation of the hReview microformat that exposes the aggregate rating about something through structured data that's easily machine parseable. About.com's recipes implement hReview-aggregate (*http://bit.ly/1a1p3Xa*) so that the ratings for recipes can be used to prioritize search results and offer a better experience for users of the site. Example 8-4 demonstrates how to extract hReview information.

Example 8-4. Parsing hReview-aggregate microformat data for a recipe

```
import requests
import json
from BeautifulSoup import BeautifulSoup

# Pass in a URL that contains hReview-aggregate info...

URL = 'http://britishfood.about.com/od/recipeindex/r/applepie.htm'

def parse_hreview_aggregate(url, item_type):

    req = requests.get(URL)

    soup = BeautifulSoup(req.text)

    # Find the hRecipe or whatever other kind of parent item encapsulates
    # the hReview (a required field).

    item_element = soup.find(True, item_type)
    item = item_element.find(True, 'item').find(True, 'fn').text

    # And now parse out the hReview

    hreview = soup.find(True, 'hreview-aggregate')

    # Required field

    rating = hreview.find(True, 'rating').find(True, 'value-title')['title']

    # Optional fields

    try:
        count = hreview.find(True, 'count').text
    except AttributeError: # optional
        count = None
    try:
        votes = hreview.find(True, 'votes').text
    except AttributeError: # optional
        votes = None

    try:
        summary = hreview.find(True, 'summary').text
    except AttributeError: # optional
        summary = None

    return {
        'item': item,
        'rating': rating,
```

```
    'count': count,
    'votes': votes,
    'summary' : summary
}

# Find hReview aggregate information for an hRecipe

reviews = parse_hreview_aggregate(URL, 'hrecipe')

print json.dumps(reviews, indent=4)
```

Here are truncated sample results for Example 8-4:

```
{
    "count": "7",
    "item": "Traditional Apple Pie Recipe",
    "votes": null,
    "summary": null,
    "rating": "4"
}
```

There's no limit to the innovation that can happen when you combine geeks and food data, as evidenced by the popularity of the much-acclaimed *Cooking for Geeks*, also from O'Reilly. As the capabilities of food sites evolve to provide additional APIs, so will the innovations that we see in this space. Figure 8-4 displays a screenshot of the underlying HTML source for a sample web page that displays its hReview-aggregate implementation for those who might be interested in viewing the source of a page.

Figure 8-4. You can view the source of a web page if you're interested in seeing the (often) gory details of its microformats implementation

Most modern browsers now implement CSS query selectors (*http://bit.ly/1a1p5hG*) natively, and you can use `document.querySelector All` to poke around in the developer console for your particular browser to review microformats in JavaScript. For example, run **docu ment.querySelectorAll(".hrecipe")** to query for any nodes that have the `hrecipe` class applied, per the specification.

8.2.3. Accessing LinkedIn's 200 Million Online Résumés

LinkedIn implements hResume (*http://bit.ly/1a1oFIf*) (which itself extensively builds on top of the hCard and hCalendar microformats) for its 200 million users, and this section provides a brief example of the rich data that it makes available for search engines and other machines to consume as structured data. hResume is particularly rich in that you may be able to discover contact information, professional career experience, education, affiliations, and publications, with much of this data being composed as embedded hCalendar and hCard information.

Given that LinkedIn's implementation is rather extensive and that our scope here is not to write a robust microformats parser for the general case, we'll opt to take a look at Google's Structured Data Testing Tool (*http://bit.ly/1a1p5yl*) instead of implementing another Python parser in this short section. Google's tool allows you to plug in any URL, and it'll extract the semantic markup that it finds and even show you a preview of what Google might display in its search results. Depending on the amount of information in the web page, the results can be extensive. For example, a fairly thorough LinkedIn profile (*http://www.linkedin.com/in/ptwobrussell*) produces multiple screen lengths of results that are broken down by all of the aforementioned fields that are available. LinkedIn's hResume implementation is thorough, to be sure, as the sample results in Figure 8-5 illustrate. Given the sample code from earlier in this chapter, you'll have a good starting template to parse out hResume data should you choose to accept this challenge.

You can use Google's Structured Data Testing Tool (*http://bit.ly/1a1p5yl*) on any arbitrary URL to see what structured data may be tucked beneath the surface. In fact, this would be a good first step to take before implementing a parser, and a good help in debugging your implementation, which is part of the underlying intention behind the tool.

+Matthew **Search** Images Maps Play YouTube News Gmail Drive Calendar More

Google   ptwobrussell@gmail.com [5] + Share

Webmaster Tools

Home

Structured Data Testing Tool

Structured Data Markup Helper

Help with:
Troubleshooting
Help Center

Structured Data Testing Tool

| URL | HTML |

linkedin.com/in/ptwobrussell   **PREVIEW**   Examples

Google search results   Google Custom Search

Preview

Matthew Russell | LinkedIn
linkedin.com/in/ptwobrussell
The excerpt from the page will show up here. The reason we can't show text ...
Jan 15, 2011   Popular social networks such ...
Feb 1, 2011   Millions of public Twitter ...
Jun 17, 2008   This book was the first ...

Authorship Testing Result

Page does not contain authorship markup. Learn more

Authorship Email Verification

Please enter a Google+ profile to see if the author has successfully verified an email address on the domain to establish authorship for this webpage. Learn more

http://plus.google.com/NNNNNNNNN   Verify Authorship

Publisher

Page does not contain publisher markup. Learn more

Extracted structured data

hcard

fn:	Matthew Russell
person-name:	
family-name:	Russell
given-name:	Matthew
adr:	
locality:	Greater Nashville Area
title:	Chief Technology Officer at Digital Reasoning Systems
photo:	http://m3.licdn.com/mpr/pub/image-Ce9MPxoTBrWMGrEdWGpExKeo0qVZfU8qC6pXl9_N03hQ8xWCsBXilT0Ts_IUp1yw4l/matthew-russell.jpg

hcalendar

date-start:	2013-02-01
summary:	Digital Reasoning Systems
location:	
	Franklin, TN
duration:	P5M
description:	I lead strategic technology efforts to create software that automates the understanding of unstructured human language data at web scale. Our software transforms data into knowledge by reading...

Warning: Event's start date is in the past.

hcard

org:	
organization-name:	Digital Reasoning Systems
title:	Chief Technology Officer

Warning: This information will not appear as a rich snippet in search results, because it seems to describe an organization. Google does not currently display organization information in rich snippets.
Warning: Missing required field "name (fn)".

hcalendar

date-start:	2009-10-01
summary:	Digital Reasoning Systems
location:	
	Franklin, TN
duration:	P3Y9M

I manage a software development process and lead a team of 20+ talented engineers and

Figure 8-5. Sample results from Google's structured data testing tool that extracts semantic markup from web pages

8.3. From Semantic Markup to Semantic Web: A Brief Interlude

To bring the discussion back full circle before transitioning into coverage of the semantic web, let's briefly reflect on what we've explored so far. Basically, we've learned that there are active initiatives under way that aim to make it possible for machines to extract the structured content in web pages for many ubiquitous things such as résumés, recipes, and geocoordinates. Content authors can feed search engines with machine-readable data that can be used to enhance relevance rankings, provide more informative displays to users, and otherwise reach consumers in increasingly useful ways *right now*. The last two words of the previous sentence are important, because in reality the vision for a more grandiose semantic web as could be defined in a somewhat ungrounded manner and all of the individual initiatives to get there are two quite different things.

For all of the limitations with microformats, the reality is that they are one important step in the Web's evolution. Content authors and consumers are both benefitting from them, and the heightened awareness of both parties is likely to lead to additional evolutions that will surely manifest in even greater things to come.

Although it is quite reasonable to question exactly how scalable this approach is for the longer haul, it is serving a relevant purpose for the current Web as we know it, and we should be grateful that corporate politicos and Open Web advocates have been able to cooperate to the point that the Web continues to evolve in a healthy direction. However, it's quite all right if you are not satisfied with the idea that the future of the Web might depend on small armies of content providers carefully publishing metadata in pages (or writing finely tuned scripts to publish metadata in pages) so that machines can better understand them. It will take many more years to see the fruition of it all, but keep in mind from previous chapters that technologies such as natural language processing (NLP) continue to receive increasing amounts of attention by academia and industry alike.

Eventually, through the gradual evolution of technologies that can understand human language, we'll one day realize a Web filled with robots that can understand human language data in the context in which it is used, and in nonsuperficial ways. In the meantime, contributing efforts of any kind are necessary and important for the Web's continued growth and betterment. A Web in which bots are able to consume human language data that is not laden with gobs of structured metadata that describe it and to effectively coerce it into the kind of structured data that can be reasoned over is one we should all be excited about, but unfortunately, it doesn't exist yet. Hence, it's not difficult to make a strong case that the automated understanding of natural language data is among the worthiest problems of the present time, given the enormous impact it could have on virtually all aspects of life.

8.4. The Semantic Web: An Evolutionary Revolution

Semantic web can mean different things to different people, so let's start out by dissecting the term. Given that the Web is all about sharing information and that a working definition of *semantics* is "enough meaning to result in an action,"[1] it seems reasonable to assert that the semantic web is generally about representing knowledge in a meaningful way—but for whom to consume? Let's take what may seem like a giant leap of faith and not assume that it's a human who is consuming the information that's represented. Let's instead consider the possibilities that could be realized if information were shared in a fully *machine-understandable way*—a way that is unambiguous enough that a reasonably sophisticated user agent like a web robot could extract, interpret, and use the information to make important decisions.

Some steps have been made in this direction: for instance, we discussed how microformats already make this possible for limited contexts earlier in this chapter, and in Chapter 2 we looked at how Facebook is aggressively bootstrapping an explicit graph construct into the Web with its Open Graph protocol (see Section 2.2.2 on page 54). It may be helpful to reflect on how we've arrived at this point.

The Internet is just a network of networks,[2] and what's fascinating about it from a technical standpoint is how layers of increasingly higher-level protocols build on top of lower-level protocols to ultimately produce a fault-tolerant worldwide computing infrastructure. In our online activity, we rely on dozens of protocols every single day, without even thinking about it. However, there is one ubiquitous protocol that is hard not to think about explicitly from time to time: HTTP, the prefix of just about every URL that you type into your browser and the enabling protocol for the extensive universe of hypertext documents (HTML pages) and the links that glue them all together into what we know as the Web. But as you've known for a long time, the Web isn't just about hypertext; it includes various embedded technologies such as JavaScript, Flash, and emerging HTML5 assets such as audio and video streams.

The notion of a cyberworld of documents, platforms, and applications that we can interact with via modern-day browsers (including ones on mobile or tablet devices) over HTTP is admittedly fuzzy, but it's probably pretty close to what most people think of when they hear the term "the Web." To a degree, the motivation behind the Web 2.0 idea that emerged back in 2004 was to more precisely define the increasingly blurry notion of exactly what the Web was and what it was becoming. Along those lines, some folks think of the Web as it existed from its inception until the present era of highly interactive web applications and user collaboration as *Web 1.0*, the era of emergent rich Internet

---

1. As defined in *Programming the Semantic Web* (O'Reilly).

2. *Inter-net* literally implies "mutual or cooperating networks."

applications (RIAs) and collaboration as *Web 2.x*, and the era of semantic karma that's yet to come as *Web 3.0* (see Table 8-2).

At present, there's no real consensus about what Web 3.0 really means, but most discussions of the subject generally include the phrase *semantic web* and the notion of information being consumed and acted upon by machines in ways that are not yet possible at web scale. It's still difficult for machines to extract and make inferences about the facts contained in documents available online. Keyword searching and heuristics can certainly provide listings of relevant search results, but human intelligence is still required to interpret and synthesize the information in the documents themselves. Whether Web 3.0 and the semantic web are really the same thing is open for debate; however, it's generally accepted that the term *semantic web* refers to a web that's much like the one we already know and love, but that has evolved to the point where machines can extract and *act on* the information contained in documents at a granular level.

In that regard, we can look back on the movement with microformats and see how that kind of evolutionary progress really could one day become revolutionary.

Table 8-2. Various manifestations/eras of the Web and their defining characteristics

Manifestation/era	Characteristics
Internet	Application protocols such as SMTP, FTP, BitTorrent, HTTP, etc.
Web 1.0	Mostly static HTML pages and hyperlinks
Web 2.0	Platforms, collaboration, rich user experiences
Social web (Web 2.x)	People and their virtual and real-world social connections and activities
Semantically marked-up web (Web 2.x)	Increasing amounts of machine-readable content such as microformats, RDFa, and microdata
Web 3.0 (the semantic web)	Prolific amounts of machine-understandable content

8.4.1. Man Cannot Live on Facts Alone

The semantic web's fundamental construct for representing knowledge is called a *triple*, which is a highly intuitive and natural way of expressing a fact. As an example, the sentence we've considered on many previous occasions—"Mr. Green killed Colonel Mustard in the study with the candlestick"—expressed as a triple might be something like *(Mr. Green, killed, Colonel Mustard)*, where the constituent pieces of that triple refer to the subject, predicate, and object of the sentence.

The Resource Description Framework (RDF) is the semantic web's model for defining and enabling the exchange of triples. RDF is highly extensible in that while it provides a basic foundation for expressing knowledge, it can also be used to define specialized vocabularies called *ontologies* that provide precise semantics for modeling specific domains. More than a passing mention of specific semantic web technologies such as RDF (*http://bit.ly/1a1p6lR*), RDFa (*http://bit.ly/1a1lujR*), RDF Schema (*http://bit.ly/1a1p8Ky*), and OWL (*http://bit.ly/1a1p9Os*) would be well out of scope here at the eleventh hour, but we will work through a high-level example that attempts to provide some context for the semantic web in general.

As you read through the remainder of this section, keep in mind that RDF is just a way to express knowledge. It may have been manufactured by a nontrivial amount of human labor that has interlaced valuable metadata into web pages, or by a small army of robots (such as web agents) that perform natural language processing and automatically extract tuples of information from human language data. Regardless of the means involved, RDF provides a basis for modeling knowledge, and it lends itself to naturally being expressed as a graph that can be inferenced upon for the purposes of answering questions. We'll illustrate this idea with some working code in the next section.

8.4.1.1. Open-world versus closed-world assumptions

One interesting difference between the way inference works in logic programming languages such as Prolog[3] as opposed to in other technologies, such as the RDF stack, is whether they make *open-world* or *closed-world* assumptions about the universe. Logic programming languages such as Prolog and most traditional database systems assume a closed world, while RDF technology generally assumes an open world.

In a closed world, everything that you haven't been explicitly told about the universe should be considered false, whereas in an open world, everything you don't know is arguably more appropriately handled as being undefined (another way of saying "unknown"). The distinction is that reasoners who assume an open world will *not* rule out interpretations that include facts that are not explicitly stated in a knowledge base, whereas reasoners who assume the closed world of the Prolog programming language or most database systems *will* rule out such facts. Furthermore, in a system that assumes a closed world, merging contradictory knowledge would generally trigger an error, while a system assuming an open world may try to make new inferences that somehow reconcile the contradictory information. As you might imagine, open-world systems are quite flexible and can lead to some conundrums; the potential can become especially pronounced when disparate knowledge bases are merged.

Intuitively, you might think of it like this: systems predicated upon closed-world reasoning assume that the data they are given is complete, and it is typically not the case that every previous fact (explicit or inferred) will still hold when new ones are added. In contrast, open-world systems make no such assumption about the completeness of their data and are monotonic. As you might imagine, there is substantial debate about the merits of making one assumption versus the other. As someone interested in the

---

3. You're highly encouraged to check out a bona fide logic-based programming language like Prolog that's written in a paradigm designed specifically so that you can represent knowledge and deduce new information from existing facts. GNU Prolog (*http://bit.ly/1a1pa53*) is a fine place to start.

semantic web, you should at least be aware of the issue. As the matter specifically relates to RDF, official guidance from the W3C documentation states:[4]

> To facilitate operation at Internet scale, RDF is an open-world framework that allows anyone to make statements about any resource. In general, it is not assumed that complete information about any resource is available. RDF does not prevent anyone from making assertions that are nonsensical or inconsistent with other statements, or the world as people see it. Designers of applications that use RDF should be aware of this and may design their applications to tolerate incomplete or inconsistent sources of information.

You might also check out Peter Patel-Schneider and Ian Horrocks's "Position Paper: A Comparison of Two Modelling Paradigms in the Semantic Web" (*http://bit.ly/1a1p9yb*) if you're interested in pursuing this topic further. Whether or not you decide to dive into this topic right now, keep in mind that the data that's available on the Web is incomplete, and that making a closed-world assumption (i.e., considering all unknown information emphatically false) will entail severe consequences sooner rather than later.

8.4.2. Inferencing About an Open World

Foundational languages such as RDF Schema and OWL are designed so that precise vocabularies can be used to express facts such as the triple (*Mr. Green, killed, Colonel Mustard*) in a machine-readable way, and this is a necessary (but not sufficient) condition for the semantic web to be fully realized. Generally speaking, once you have a set of facts, the next step is to perform *inference* over the facts and draw conclusions that follow from the facts. The concept of formal inference dates back to at least ancient Greece with Aristotle's syllogisms, and the obvious connection to how machines can take advantage of it has not gone unnoticed by researchers interested in artificial intelligence for the past 50 or so years. The Java-based landscape that's filled with enterprise-level options such as Jena (*http://bit.ly/1a1paCa*) and Sesame (*http://bit.ly/1a1pcKf*) certainly seems to be where most of the heavyweight action resides, but fortunately, we do have a couple of solid options to work with in Python.

One of the best Pythonic options capable of inference that you're likely to encounter is FuXi (*http://bit.ly/1a1pb96*). FuXi is a powerful logic-reasoning system for the semantic web that uses a technique called forward chaining (*http://bit.ly/1a1pdh9*) to deduce new information from existing information by starting with a set of facts, deriving new facts from the known facts by applying a set of logical rules, and repeating this process until a particular conclusion can be proved or disproved, or there are no more new facts to derive. The kind of forward chaining that FuXi delivers is said to be both *sound* (because any new facts that are produced are true) and *complete* (because any facts that are true can eventually be proven). A full-blown discussion of propositional and first-order logic

---

4. See *http://www.w3.org/TR/rdf-concepts/*.

could easily fill a book; if you're interested in digging deeper, the now-classic textbook *Artificial Intelligence: A Modern Approach (http://amzn.to/1a1pdhg)*, by Stuart Russell and Peter Norvig (Prentice Hall), is probably the most comprehensive resource.

To demonstrate the kinds of inferencing capabilities a system such as FuXi can provide, let's consider the famous example of Aristotle's syllogism[5] in which you are given a knowledge base that contains the facts "Socrates is a man" and "All men are mortal," which allows you to deduce that "Socrates is mortal." While this problem may seem too trivial, keep in mind that the deterministic algorithms that produce the new fact that "Socrates is mortal" work the same way when there are significantly more facts available —and those new facts may produce additional new facts, which produce additional new facts, and so on. For example, consider a slightly more complex knowledge base containing a few additional facts:

- Socrates is a man.
- All men are mortal.
- Only gods live on Mt. Olympus.
- All mortals drink whisky.
- Chuck Norris lives on Mt. Olympus.

If presented with the given knowledge base and then posed the question, "Does Socrates drink whisky?" you must first infer an intermediate fact before you can definitively answer the question: you would have to deduce that "Socrates is mortal" before you could conclusively affirm the follow-on fact that "Socrates drinks whisky." To illustrate how all of this would work in code, consider the same knowledge base now expressed in Notation3 (*http://bit.ly/1a1pdxO*) (N3), a simple yet powerful syntax that expresses facts and rules in RDF, as shown here:

```
#Assign a namespace for logic predicates
@prefix log: <http://www.w3.org/2000/10/swap/log#> .

#Assign a namespace for the vocabulary defined in this document
@prefix : <MiningTheSocialWeb#> .

#Socrates is a man
:Socrates a :Man.

@forAll :x .

#All men are mortal: Man(x) => Mortal(x)
{ :x a :Man } log:implies { :x a :Mortal } .

#Only gods live at Mt Olympus: Lives(x, MtOlympus) <=> God(x)
```

---

5. In modern parlance, a syllogism is more commonly called an *implication*.

```
{ :x :lives :MtOlympus } log:implies { :x a :god } .
{ :x a :god } log:implies { :x :lives :MtOlympus } .

#All mortals drink whisky: Mortal(x) => Drinks(x, whisky)
{ :x a :Man } log:implies { :x :drinks :whisky } .

#Chuck Norris lives at Mt Olympus: Lives(ChuckNorris, MtOlympus)
:ChuckNorris :lives :MtOlympus .
```

While there are many different formats for expressing RDF, many semantic web tools choose N3 because its readability and expressiveness make it accessible. Skimming down the file, we see some namespaces that are set up to ground the symbols in the vocabulary that is used, and a few assertions that were previously mentioned. Let's see what happens when you run FuXi from the command line and tell it to parse the facts from the sample knowledge base that was just introduced and to accumulate additional facts about it with the following command:

```
$ FuXi --rules=chuck-norris.n3 --ruleFacts --naive
```

 If you are installing FuXi on your own machine for the first time, your simplest and quickest option for installation may be to follow these instructions (*http://bit.ly/1a1pcd2*). Of course, if you are following along with the IPython Notebook as part of the virtual machine experience for this book, this installation dependency (like all others) is already taken care of for you, and the sample code in the corresponding IPython Notebook for this chapter should "just work."

You should see output similar to the following if you run FuXi from the command line against a file named *chuck-norris.n3* containing the preceding N3 knowledge base:

```
('Parsing RDF facts from ', 'chuck-norris.n3')
('Time to calculate closure on working memory: ', '1.66392326355 milli seconds')
<Network: 3 rules, 6 nodes, 3 tokens in working memory, 3 inferred tokens>
@prefix : <file:///.../ipynb/resources/ch08-semanticweb/MiningTheSocialWeb#> .
@prefix iw: <http://inferenceweb.stanford.edu/2004/07/iw.owl#> .
@prefix log: <http://www.w3.org/2000/10/swap/log#> .
@prefix rdf: <http://www.w3.org/1999/02/22-rdf-syntax-ns#> .
@prefix rdfs: <http://www.w3.org/2000/01/rdf-schema#> .
@prefix skolem: <http://code.google.com/p/python-dlp/wiki/SkolemTerm#> .
@prefix xml: <http://www.w3.org/XML/1998/namespace> .
@prefix xsd: <http://www.w3.org/2001/XMLSchema#> .

:ChuckNorris a :god .

:Socrates a :Mortal ;
    :drinks :whisky .
```

The output of the program tells us a few things that weren't explicitly stated in the initial knowledge base:

- Chuck Norris is a god.
- Socrates is a mortal.
- Socrates drinks whisky.

Although deriving these facts may seem obvious to most human beings, it's quite another story for a machine to have derived them—and that's what makes things exciting. Also keep in mind that the facts that are given or deduced obviously don't need to make sense in the world as we know it in order to be logically inferred from the initial information contained in the knowledge base.

 Careless assertions about Chuck Norris (even in an educational context involving a fictitious universe) could prove harmful to your computer's health, or possibly even your own health.[6]

If this simple example excites you, by all means, dig further into FuXi and the potential the semantic web holds. The example that was just provided barely scratches the surface of what it is capable of doing. There are numerous data sets available for mining, and vast technology toolchains that are a part of an entirely new realm of exciting technologies that you may not have previously encountered. The semantic web is arguably a much more advanced and complex topic than the social web, and investigating it is certainly a worthy pursuit—especially if you're excited about the possibilities that inference brings to social data. It seems pretty clear that the future of the semantic web is largely undergirded by social data and many, many evolutions of technology involving social data along the way. Whether or not the semantic web is a journey or a destination, however, is up to us.

8.5. Closing Remarks

This chapter has been an attempt to entertain you with a sort of cocktail discussion about the somewhat slippery topic of the semantic web. Volumes could be written on the history of the Web, various visions for the semantic web, and competing philosophies around all of the technologies involved; alas, this chapter has been a mere sketch intended to pique your interest and introduce you to some of the fundamentals that you can pursue as part of your ongoing professional and entrepreneurial endeavors.

If you take nothing else from this chapter, remember that microformats are a way of decorating markup with metadata to expose specific types of structured information

---

6. See *http://www.chucknorrisfacts.com*.

such as recipes, contact information, and other kinds of ubiquitous data. Microformats have vast potential to further the vision for the semantic web because they allow content publishers to take *existing* content and ensure that it conforms to a shared standard that can be understood and reasoned over by machines. Expect to see significant growth and interest in microformats in the months and years to come. Initiatives by communities of practice such as the microformats and IndieWeb communities are also notable and worth following.

While the intentional omission of semantic web discussion prior to this chapter may have created the impression of an arbitrary and rigid divide between the social and semantic webs, the divide is actually quite blurry and constantly in flux. It is likely that the combination of the undeniable proliferation of social data on the Web; initiatives such as the microformats published by parties ranging from Wikipedia to About.com, LinkedIn, Facebook's Open Graph protocol, and the open standards communities; and the creative efforts of data hackers is greatly accelerating the realization of a semantic web that may not be all that different from the one that's been hyped for the past 20 years.

The proliferation of social data has the potential to be a great catalyst for the development of a semantic web that will enable agents to make nontrivial actions on our behalf. We're not there yet, but be hopeful and heed the wise words of Epicurus, who perhaps said it best: "Don't spoil what you have by desiring what you don't have; but remember that what you now have was once among the things only hoped for."

 The source code outlined for this chapter and all other chapters is available at GitHub (*http://bit.ly/1a1kNqy*) in a convenient IPython Notebook format that you're highly encouraged to try out from the comfort of your own web browser.

8.6. Recommended Exercises

- Go hang out on the #microformats IRC (Internet Relay Chat) (*http://bit.ly/1a1phNZ*) channel and become involved in its community.

- Watch some excellent video slides (*http://bit.ly/1a1pi4G*) that present an overview on microformats by Tantek Çelik (*http://bit.ly/1a1pgcS*), a microformats community leader.

- Review the examples in the wild (*http://bit.ly/1a1oKLV*) on the microformats wiki and consider making some of your own contributions.

- Explore some websites that implement microformats and poke around in the HTML source of the pages with your browser's developer console and the built-in `document.querySelectorAll` function.

- Review and follow along with a more comprehensive FuXi tutorial (*http://bit.ly/1a1pgtA*) online.

- Review Schema.org's Getting Started Guide (*http://bit.ly/1a1piSe*)

- Review RelMeAuth (*http://bit.ly/1a1oUD4*) and attempt to implement and use web sign-in (*http://bit.ly/1a1oUDd*). You might find the Python-based GitHub project relmeauth (*http://bit.ly/1a1pkJB*) helpful as a starting point.

- Take a look at PaySwarm (*http://mzl.la/1a1pl0h*), an open initiative for web payments. (It's somewhat off topic, but an important open web initiative involving money, which is an inherently social entity.)

- Begin a survey of the semantic web (*http://bit.ly/1a1pn8o*) as part of an independent research project.

- Take a look at DBPedia (*http://bit.ly/1a1plNG*), an initiative that extracts structured data from Wikipedia for purposes of semantic reasoning. What can you do with FuXi and DBPedia data?

8.7. Online Resources

The following list of links from this chapter may be useful for review:

- *Artificial Intelligence: A Modern Approach* (*http://amzn.to/1a1pdhg*)
- Common Crawl corpus (*http://bit.ly/1a1oM6A*)
- CSS query selectors (*http://bit.ly/1a1p5hG*)
- DBPedia (*http://bit.ly/1a1plNG*)
- Firefox Operator add-on (*http://mzl.la/1a1p2Cy*)
- Forward chaining logic algorithm (*http://bit.ly/1a1pdh9*)
- FuXi (*http://bit.ly/1a1pb96*)
- FuXi tutorial (*http://bit.ly/1a1pgtA*)
- GNU Prolog (*http://bit.ly/1a1pa53*)
- Google's Structured Data Testing Tool (*http://bit.ly/1a1p5yl*)
- HTML 4.01 (*http://bit.ly/1a1oKvt*)
- IndieWeb (*http://bit.ly/1a1oWuT*)
- KML (*http://bit.ly/1a1p1Pb*)
- Microdata (*http://bit.ly/1a1oSeo*)
- microform.at (*http://bit.ly/1a1oZGX*)
- Tantek Çelik's "microformats2 & HTML5" presentation (*http://bit.ly/1a1pi4G*)

- *microformats.org*
- Notation3 (*http://bit.ly/1a1pdxO*)
- Open Graph protocol (*http://bit.ly/1a1lu3m*)
- OWL (*http://bit.ly/1a1p9Os*)
- PaySwarm (*http://mzl.la/1a1pl0h*)
- "Position Paper: A Comparison of Two Modelling Paradigms in the Semantic Web" (*http://bit.ly/1a1p9yb*)
- RDF (*http://bit.ly/1a1p6lR*)
- RDFa (*http://bit.ly/1a1oQmR*)
- RDF Schema (*http://bit.ly/1a1p8Ky*)
- RelMeAuth (*http://bit.ly/1a1oUD4*)
- Schema.org
- Semantic web (*http://bit.ly/1a1pn8o*)
- Web Data Commons (*http://bit.ly/1a1oJI1*)
- Web sign-in (*http://bit.ly/1a1oUDd*)
- XFN (*http://bit.ly/1a1oNaG*)

## PART II

Twitter Cookbook

Whereas Part I of this book featured a number of social web properties in a somewhat broadly guided tour, the remaining chapter of this book comes back full circle to where we started in Part I with Twitter. It is organized as a cookbook and features more than two dozen bite-sized recipes for mining Twitter data. Twitter's accessible APIs, inherent openness, and rampant worldwide popularity make it an ideal social website to zoom in on, and this part of the book aims to create some atomic building blocks that are highly composable to serve a wide variety of purposes.

Just like any other technical cookbook, these recipes are organized in an easy-to-navigate problem/solution format, and as you are working through them, you are sure to come up with interesting ideas that involve tweaks and modifications. Whereas Part I provided a fairly broad overview of many social web properties, Part II is designed to narrow the focus on a common set of small problems and present some patterns that you can adapt to other social web properties.

You are highly encouraged to have as much fun with these recipes as possible, and as you come up with any clever recipes of your own, consider sharing them back with the book's community by sending a pull request to its GitHub repository (*http://bit.ly/1a1kNqy*), tweeting about it (mention @SocialWebMining if you want a retweet), or posting about it on *Mining the Social Web*'s Facebook page (*http://on.fb.me/1a1kHPQ*).

Twitter Cookbook

This cookbook is a collection of recipes for mining Twitter data. Each recipe is designed to be as simple and atomic as possible in solving a particular problem so that multiple recipes can be composed into more complex recipes with minimal effort. Think of each recipe as being a building block that, while useful in its own right, is even more useful in concert with other building blocks that collectively constitute more complex units of analysis. Unlike previous chapters, which contain a lot more prose than code, this cookbook provides a relatively light discussion and lets the code do more of the talking. The thought is that you'll likely be manipulating and composing the code in various ways to achieve particular objectives.

While most recipes involve little more than issuing a parameterized API call and post-processing the response into a convenient format, some recipes are even simpler (involving little more than a couple of lines of code), and others are considerably more complex. This cookbook is designed to help you by presenting some common problems and their solutions. In some cases, it may not be common knowledge that the data you desire is really just a couple of lines of code away. The value proposition is in giving you code that you can trivially adapt to suit your own purposes.

One fundamental software dependency you'll need for all of the recipes in this chapter is the `twitter` package, which you can install with `pip` per the rather predictable **pip install twitter** command from a terminal. Other software dependencies will be noted as they are introduced in individual recipes. If you're taking advantage of the book's virtual machine (which you are highly encouraged to do), the `twitter` package and all other dependencies will be preinstalled for you.

As you know from Chapter 1, Twitter's v1.1 API requires all requests to be authenticated, so each recipe assumes that you take advantage of Section 9.1 on page 352 or Section 9.2 on page 353 to first gain an authenticated API connector to use in each of the other recipes.

Always get the latest bug-fixed source code for this chapter (and every other chapter) online at *http://bit.ly/MiningTheSocialWeb2E*. Be sure to also take advantage of this book's virtual machine experience, as described in Appendix A, to maximize your enjoyment of the sample code.

9.1. Accessing Twitter's API for Development Purposes

9.1.1. Problem

You want to mine your own account data or otherwise gain quick and easy API access for development purposes.

9.1.2. Solution

Use the twitter package and the OAuth 1.0a credentials provided in the application's settings to gain API access to your own account without any HTTP redirects.

9.1.3. Discussion

Twitter implements OAuth 1.0a (*http://bit.ly/1a1pBwg*), an authorization mechanism that's expressly designed so that users can grant third parties access to their data without having to do the unthinkable—doling out their usernames and passwords. While you can certainly take advantage of Twitter's OAuth implementation for production situations in which you'll need users to authorize your application to access their accounts, you can also use the credentials in your application's settings to gain instant access for development purposes or to mine the data in your own account.

Register an application under your Twitter account at *http://dev.twitter.com/apps* and take note of the *consumer key, consumer secret, access token,* and *access token secret,* which constitute the four credentials that any OAuth 1.0a–enabled application needs to ultimately gain account access. Figure 9-1 provides a screen capture of a Twitter application's settings. With these credentials in hand, you can use any OAuth 1.0a library to access Twitter's RESTful API (*http://bit.ly/1a1pDEq*), but we'll opt to use the twitter package, which provides a minimalist and Pythonic API wrapper around Twitter's RESTful API interface. When registering your application, you don't need to specify the callback URL since we are effectively bypassing the entire OAuth flow and simply using the credentials to immediately access the API. Example 9-1 demonstrates how to use these credentials to instantiate a connector to the API.

Example 9-1. Accessing Twitter's API for development purposes

```
import twitter

def oauth_login():
    # XXX: Go to http://twitter.com/apps/new to create an app and get values
    # for these credentials that you'll need to provide in place of these
    # empty string values that are defined as placeholders.
    # See https://dev.twitter.com/docs/auth/oauth for more information
    # on Twitter's OAuth implementation.

    CONSUMER_KEY = ''
    CONSUMER_SECRET = ''
    OAUTH_TOKEN = ''
    OAUTH_TOKEN_SECRET = ''

    auth = twitter.oauth.OAuth(OAUTH_TOKEN, OAUTH_TOKEN_SECRET,
                               CONSUMER_KEY, CONSUMER_SECRET)

    twitter_api = twitter.Twitter(auth=auth)
    return twitter_api

# Sample usage
twitter_api = oauth_login()

# Nothing to see by displaying twitter_api except that it's now a
# defined variable

print twitter_api
```

 Keep in mind that the credentials used to connect are effectively the same as the username and password combination, so guard them carefully and specify the minimal level of access required in your application's settings. Read-only access is sufficient for mining your own account data.

While convenient for accessing your own data from your own account, this shortcut provides no benefit if your goal is to write a client program for accessing someone else's data. You'll need to perform the full OAuth dance, as demonstrated in Example 9-2, for that situation.

9.2. Doing the OAuth Dance to Access Twitter's API for Production Purposes

9.2.1. Problem

You want to use OAuth so that your application can access another user's account data.

9.2.2. Solution

Implement the "OAuth dance" with the `twitter` package.

9.2.3. Discussion

The `twitter` package provides a built-in implementation of the so-called OAuth dance that works for a console application. It does so by implementing an *out of band* (oob) OAuth flow in which an application that does not run in a browser, such as a Python program, can securely gain these four credentials to access the API, and allows you to easily request access to a particular user's account data as a standard "out of the box" capability. However, if you'd like to write a web application that accesses another user's account data, you may need to lightly adapt its implementation.

Although there may not be many practical reasons to actually implement an OAuth dance from within IPython Notebook (unless perhaps you were running a hosted IPython Notebook service that was used by other people), this recipe uses Flask as an embedded web server to demonstrate this recipe using the same toolchain as the rest of the book. It could be easily adapted to work with an arbitrary web application framework of your choice since the concepts are the same.

Figure 9-1 provides a screen capture of a Twitter application's settings. In an OAuth 1.0a flow, the *consumer key* and *consumer secret* values that were introduced as part of Section 9.1 on page 352 uniquely identify your application. You provide these values to Twitter when requesting access to a user's data so that Twitter can then prompt the user with information about the nature of your request. Assuming the user approves your application, Twitter redirects back to the callback URL that you specify in your application settings and includes an *OAuth verifier* that is then exchanged for an *access token* and *access token secret*, which are used in concert with the *consumer key* and *consumer secret* to ultimately enable your application to access the account data. (For oob OAuth flows, you don't need to include a callback URL; Twitter provides the user with a PIN code as an OAuth verifier that must be copied/pasted back into the application as a manual intervention.) See Appendix B for additional details on an OAuth 1.0a flow.

Figure 9-1. Sample OAuth settings for a Twitter application

Example 9-2 illustrates how to use the consumer key and consumer secret to do the OAuth dance with the `twitter` package and gain access to a user's data. The access token and access token secret are written to disk, which streamlines future authorizations. According to Twitter's Development FAQ (*http://bit.ly/1a1pC3o*), Twitter does not currently expire access tokens, which means that you can reliably store them and use them on behalf of the user indefinitely, as long as you comply with the applicable terms of service (*http://bit.ly/1a1pEbj*).

Example 9-2. Doing the OAuth dance to access Twitter's API for production purposes

```
import json
from flask import Flask, request
import multiprocessing
from threading import Timer
from IPython.display import IFrame
from IPython.display import display
from IPython.display import Javascript as JS

import twitter
from twitter.oauth_dance import parse_oauth_tokens
```

```
from twitter.oauth import read_token_file, write_token_file

# Note: This code is exactly the flow presented in the _AppendixB notebook

OAUTH_FILE = "resources/ch09-twittercookbook/twitter_oauth"

# XXX: Go to http://twitter.com/apps/new to create an app and get values
# for these credentials that you'll need to provide in place of these
# empty string values that are defined as placeholders.
# See https://dev.twitter.com/docs/auth/oauth for more information
# on Twitter's OAuth implementation, and ensure that *oauth_callback*
# is defined in your application settings as shown next if you are
# using Flask in this IPython Notebook.

# Define a few variables that will bleed into the lexical scope of a couple of
# functions that follow
CONSUMER_KEY = ''
CONSUMER_SECRET = ''
oauth_callback = 'http://127.0.0.1:5000/oauth_helper'

# Set up a callback handler for when Twitter redirects back to us after the user
# authorizes the app

webserver = Flask("TwitterOAuth")
@webserver.route("/oauth_helper")
def oauth_helper():

    oauth_verifier = request.args.get('oauth_verifier')

    # Pick back up credentials from ipynb_oauth_dance
    oauth_token, oauth_token_secret = read_token_file(OAUTH_FILE)

    _twitter = twitter.Twitter(
        auth=twitter.OAuth(
            oauth_token, oauth_token_secret, CONSUMER_KEY, CONSUMER_SECRET),
        format='', api_version=None)

    oauth_token, oauth_token_secret = parse_oauth_tokens(
        _twitter.oauth.access_token(oauth_verifier=oauth_verifier))

    # This web server only needs to service one request, so shut it down
    shutdown_after_request = request.environ.get('werkzeug.server.shutdown')
    shutdown_after_request()

    # Write out the final credentials that can be picked up after the following
    # blocking call to webserver.run().
    write_token_file(OAUTH_FILE, oauth_token, oauth_token_secret)
    return "%s %s written to %s" % (oauth_token, oauth_token_secret, OAUTH_FILE)

# To handle Twitter's OAuth 1.0a implementation, we'll just need to implement a
# custom "oauth dance" and will closely follow the pattern defined in
# twitter.oauth_dance.
```

```
def ipynb_oauth_dance():

    _twitter = twitter.Twitter(
        auth=twitter.OAuth('', '', CONSUMER_KEY, CONSUMER_SECRET),
        format='', api_version=None)

    oauth_token, oauth_token_secret = parse_oauth_tokens(
            _twitter.oauth.request_token(oauth_callback=oauth_callback))

    # Need to write these interim values out to a file to pick up on the callback
    # from Twitter that is handled by the web server in /oauth_helper
    write_token_file(OAUTH_FILE, oauth_token, oauth_token_secret)

    oauth_url = ('http://api.twitter.com/oauth/authorize?oauth_token=' + oauth_token)

    # Tap the browser's native capabilities to access the web server through a new
    # window to get user authorization
    display(JS("window.open('%s')" % oauth_url))

# After the webserver.run() blocking call, start the OAuth Dance that will
# ultimately cause Twitter to redirect a request back to it. Once that request
# is serviced, the web server will shut down and program flow will resume
# with the OAUTH_FILE containing the necessary credentials.
Timer(1, lambda: ipynb_oauth_dance()).start()

webserver.run(host='0.0.0.0')

# The values that are read from this file are written out at
# the end of /oauth_helper
oauth_token, oauth_token_secret = read_token_file(OAUTH_FILE)

# These four credentials are what is needed to authorize the application
auth = twitter.oauth.OAuth(oauth_token, oauth_token_secret,
                           CONSUMER_KEY, CONSUMER_SECRET)

twitter_api = twitter.Twitter(auth=auth)

print twitter_api
```

You should be able to observe that the *access token* and *access token secret* that your
application retrieves are the same values as the ones in your application's settings, and
this is no coincidence. Guard these values carefully, as they are effectively the same thing
as a username and password combination.

9.3. Discovering the Trending Topics

9.3.1. Problem

You want to know what is trending on Twitter for a particular geographic area such as the United States, another country or group of countries, or possibly even the entire world.

9.3.2. Solution

Twitter's Trends API (*http://bit.ly/1a1kYSQ*) enables you to get the trending topics for geographic areas that are designated by a Where On Earth (WOE) ID (*http://yhoo.it/1a1kZ9u*), as defined and maintained by Yahoo!.

9.3.3. Discussion

A *place* is an essential concept in Twitter's development platform, and trending topics are accordingly constrained by geography to provide the best API possible for querying for trending topics (as shown in Example 9-3). Like all other APIs, it returns the trending topics as JSON data, which can be converted to standard Python objects and then manipulated with list comprehensions or similar techniques. This means it's fairly easy to explore the API responses. Try experimenting with a variety of WOE IDs to compare and contrast the trends from various geographic regions. For example, compare and contrast trends in two different countries, or compare a trend in a particular country to a trend in the world.

 You'll need to complete a short registration with Yahoo! in order to access and look up Where On Earth (WOE) IDs (*http://yhoo.it/1a1kZ9u*) as part of one of their developer products. It's painless and well worth the couple of minutes that it takes to do.

Example 9-3. Discovering the trending topics

```
import json
import twitter

def twitter_trends(twitter_api, woe_id):
    # Prefix ID with the underscore for query string parameterization.
    # Without the underscore, the twitter package appends the ID value
    # to the URL itself as a special-case keyword argument.
    return twitter_api.trends.place(_id=woe_id)

# Sample usage

twitter_api = oauth_login()
```

```
# See https://dev.twitter.com/docs/api/1.1/get/trends/place and
# http://developer.yahoo.com/geo/geoplanet/ for details on
# Yahoo! Where On Earth ID

WORLD_WOE_ID = 1
world_trends = twitter_trends(twitter_api, WORLD_WOE_ID)
print json.dumps(world_trends, indent=1)

US_WOE_ID = 23424977
us_trends = twitter_trends(twitter_api, US_WOE_ID)
print json.dumps(us_trends, indent=1)
```

9.4. Searching for Tweets

9.4.1. Problem

You want to search Twitter for tweets using specific keywords and query constraints.

9.4.2. Solution

Use the Search API to perform a custom query.

9.4.3. Discussion

Example 9-4 illustrates how to use the Search API (*http://bit.ly/1a1l398*) to perform a custom query against the entire Twitterverse. Similar to the way that search engines work, Twitter's Search API returns results in batches, and you can configure the number of results per batch to a maximum value of 200 by using the count keyword parameter. It is possible that more than 200 results (or the maximum value that you specify for count) may be available for any given query, and in the parlance of Twitter's API, you'll need to use a *cursor* to navigate to the next batch of results.

Cursors (*http://bit.ly/1a1pFMD*) are a new enhancement to Twitter's v1.1 API and provide a more robust scheme than the pagination paradigm offered by the v1.0 API, which involved specifying a page number and a results per page constraint. The essence of the cursor paradigm is that it is able to better accommodate the dynamic and real-time nature of the Twitter platform. For example, Twitter's API cursors are designed to inherently take into account the possibility that updated information may become available in real time while you are navigating a batch of search results. In other words, it could be the case that while you are navigating a batch of query results, relevant information becomes available that you would want to have included in your current results while you are navigating them, rather than needing to dispatch a new query.

Example 9-4 illustrates how to use the Search API and navigate the cursor that's included in a response to fetch more than one batch of results.

Example 9-4. Searching for tweets

```
def twitter_search(twitter_api, q, max_results=200, **kw):

    # See https://dev.twitter.com/docs/api/1.1/get/search/tweets and
    # https://dev.twitter.com/docs/using-search for details on advanced
    # search criteria that may be useful for keyword arguments

    # See https://dev.twitter.com/docs/api/1.1/get/search/tweets
    search_results = twitter_api.search.tweets(q=q, count=100, **kw)

    statuses = search_results['statuses']

    # Iterate through batches of results by following the cursor until we
    # reach the desired number of results, keeping in mind that OAuth users
    # can "only" make 180 search queries per 15-minute interval. See
    # https://dev.twitter.com/docs/rate-limiting/1.1/limits
    # for details. A reasonable number of results is ~1000, although
    # that number of results may not exist for all queries.

    # Enforce a reasonable limit
    max_results = min(1000, max_results)

    for _ in range(10): # 10*100 = 1000
        try:
            next_results = search_results['search_metadata']['next_results']
        except KeyError, e: # No more results when next_results doesn't exist
            break

        # Create a dictionary from next_results, which has the following form:
        # ?max_id=313519052523986943&q=NCAA&include_entities=1
        kwargs = dict([ kv.split('=')
                        for kv in next_results[1:].split("&") ])

        search_results = twitter_api.search.tweets(**kwargs)
        statuses += search_results['statuses']

        if len(statuses) > max_results:
            break

    return statuses

# Sample usage

twitter_api = oauth_login()

q = "CrossFit"
results = twitter_search(twitter_api, q, max_results=10)

# Show one sample search result by slicing the list...
print json.dumps(results[0], indent=1)
```

9.5. Constructing Convenient Function Calls

9.5.1. Problem

You want to bind certain parameters to function calls and pass around a reference to the bound function in order to simplify coding patterns.

9.5.2. Solution

Use Python's `functools.partial` to create fully or partially bound functions that can be elegantly passed around and invoked by other code without the need to pass additional parameters.

9.5.3. Discussion

Although not a technique that is exclusive to design patterns with the Twitter API, `functools.partial` is a pattern that you'll find incredibly convenient to use in combination with the `twitter` package and many of the patterns in this cookbook and in your other Python programming experiences. For example, you may find it cumbersome to continually pass around a reference to an authenticated Twitter API connector (`twitter_api`, as illustrated in these recipes, is usually the first argument to most functions) and want to create a function that *partially* satisfies the function arguments so that you can freely pass around a function that can be invoked with its remaining parameters.

Another example that illustrates the convenience of partially binding parameters is that you may want to bind a Twitter API connector and a WOE ID for a geographic area to the Trends API as a single function call that can be passed around and simply invoked as is. Yet another possibility is that you may find that routinely typing `json .dumps({...}, indent=1)` is rather cumbersome, so you could go ahead and partially apply the keyword argument and rename the function to something shorter like `pp` (pretty-print) to save some repetitive typing.

The possibilities are vast, and while you could opt to use Python's `def` keyword to define functions as a possibility that usually achieves the same end, you may find that it's more concise and elegant to use `functools.partial` in some situations. Example 9-5 demonstrates a few possibilities that you may find useful.

Example 9-5. Constructing convenient function calls

```
from functools import partial

pp = partial(json.dumps, indent=1)

twitter_world_trends = partial(twitter_trends, twitter_api, WORLD_WOE_ID)
```

```
print pp(twitter_world_trends())

authenticated_twitter_search = partial(twitter_search, twitter_api)
results = authenticated_twitter_search("iPhone")
print pp(results)

authenticated_iphone_twitter_search = partial(authenticated_twitter_search, "iPhone")
results = authenticated_iphone_twitter_search()
print pp(results)
```

9.6. Saving and Restoring JSON Data with Text Files

9.6.1. Problem

You want to store relatively small amounts of data that you've fetched from Twitter's API for recurring analysis or archival purposes.

9.6.2. Solution

Write the data out to a text file in a convenient and portable JSON representation.

9.6.3. Discussion

Although text files won't be appropriate for every occasion, they are a portable and convenient option to consider if you need to just dump some data out to disk to save it for experimentation or analysis. In fact, this would be considered a best practice so that you minimize the number of requests to Twitter's API and avoid the inevitable rate-limiting issues that you'll likely encounter. After all, it certainly would not be in your best interest or Twitter's best interest to repetitively hit the API and request the same data over and over again.

Example 9-6 demonstrates a fairly routine use of Python's io package to ensure that any data that you write to and read from disk is properly encoded and decoded as UTF-8 so that you can avoid the (often dreaded and not often well understood) UnicodeDeco deError exceptions that commonly occur with serialization and deserialization of text data in Python 2.x applications.

Example 9-6. Saving and restoring JSON data with text files

```
import io, json

def save_json(filename, data):
    with io.open('resources/ch09-twittercookbook/{0}.json'.format(filename),
            'w', encoding='utf-8') as f:
        f.write(unicode(json.dumps(data, ensure_ascii=False)))

def load_json(filename):
    with io.open('resources/ch09-twittercookbook/{0}.json'.format(filename),
```

```
                encoding='utf-8') as f:
        return f.read()

# Sample usage

q = 'CrossFit'

twitter_api = oauth_login()
results = twitter_search(twitter_api, q, max_results=10)

save_json(q, results)
results = load_json(q)

print json.dumps(results, indent=1)
```

9.7. Saving and Accessing JSON Data with MongoDB

9.7.1. Problem

You want to store and access nontrivial amounts of JSON data from Twitter API responses.

9.7.2. Solution

Use a document-oriented database such as MongoDB to store the data in a convenient JSON format.

9.7.3. Discussion

While a directory containing a relatively small number of properly encoded JSON files may work well for trivial amounts of data, you may be surprised at how quickly you start to amass enough data that flat files become unwieldy. Fortunately, document-oriented databases such as MongoDB are ideal for storing Twitter API responses, since they are designed to efficiently store JSON data.

MongoDB is a robust and well-documented database that works well for small or large amounts of data. It provides powerful query operators and indexing capabilities that significantly streamline the amount of analysis that you'll need to do in custom Python code.

In most cases, if you put some thought into how to index and query your data, MongoDB will be able to outperform your custom manipulations through its use of indexes and efficient BSON (*http://bit.ly/1a1pG34*) representation on disk. See Chapter 6 for a fairly extensive introduction to MongoDB in the context of storing (JSONified mailbox) data and using MongoDB's aggregation framework (*http://bit.ly/1a1pGjv*) to query it in nontrivial ways. Example 9-7 illustrates how to connect to a running MongoDB database to save and load data.

 MongoDB is easy to install and contains excellent online documentation for both installation/configuration and query/indexing operations. The virtual machine for this book takes care of installing and starting it for you if you'd like to jump right in.

Example 9-7. Saving and accessing JSON data with MongoDB

```python
import json
import pymongo # pip install pymongo

def save_to_mongo(data, mongo_db, mongo_db_coll, **mongo_conn_kw):

    # Connects to the MongoDB server running on
    # localhost:27017 by default

    client = pymongo.MongoClient(**mongo_conn_kw)

    # Get a reference to a particular database

    db = client[mongo_db]

    # Reference a particular collection in the database

    coll = db[mongo_db_coll]

    # Perform a bulk insert and  return the IDs

    return coll.insert(data)

def load_from_mongo(mongo_db, mongo_db_coll, return_cursor=False,
                    criteria=None, projection=None, **mongo_conn_kw):

    # Optionally, use criteria and projection to limit the data that is
    # returned as documented in
    # http://docs.mongodb.org/manual/reference/method/db.collection.find/

    # Consider leveraging MongoDB's aggregations framework for more
    # sophisticated queries.

    client = pymongo.MongoClient(**mongo_conn_kw)
    db = client[mongo_db]
    coll = db[mongo_db_coll]

    if criteria is None:
        criteria = {}
```

```
    if projection is None:
        cursor = coll.find(criteria)
    else:
        cursor = coll.find(criteria, projection)

    # Returning a cursor is recommended for large amounts of data

    if return_cursor:
        return cursor
    else:
        return [ item for item in cursor ]

# Sample usage

q = 'CrossFit'

twitter_api = oauth_login()
results = twitter_search(twitter_api, q, max_results=10)

save_to_mongo(results, 'search_results', q)

load_from_mongo('search_results', q)
```

9.8. Sampling the Twitter Firehose with the Streaming API

9.8.1. Problem

You want to analyze what people are tweeting about *right now* from a real-time stream of tweets as opposed to querying the Search API for what might be slightly (or very) dated information. Or, you want to begin accumulating nontrivial amounts of data about a particular topic for later analysis.

9.8.2. Solution

Use Twitter's Streaming API (*http://bit.ly/1a1l1ya*) to sample public data from the Twitter firehose.

9.8.3. Discussion

Twitter makes up to 1% of all tweets available in real time through a random sampling technique that represents the larger population of tweets and exposes these tweets through the Streaming API. Unless you want to go to a third-party provider such as GNIP (*http://bit.ly/1a1pIrB*) or DataSift (*http://bit.ly/1a1pGQE*) (which may actually be well worth the cost in many situations), this is about as good as it gets. Although you might think that 1% seems paltry, take a moment to realize that during peak loads, tweet velocity can be tens of thousands of tweets per second. For a broad enough topic, actually storing all of the tweets you sample could quickly become more of a problem than you might think. Access to up to 1% of all public tweets is significant.

Whereas the Search API is a little bit easier to use and queries for "historical" information (which in the Twitterverse could mean data that is minutes or hours old, given how fast trends emerge and dissipate), the Streaming API provides a way to sample from *worldwide information* in as close to real time as you'll ever be able to get. The `twit ter` package exposes the Streaming API in an easy-to-use manner in which you can filter the firehose based upon keyword constraints, which is an intuitive and convenient way to access this information. As opposed to constructing a `twitter.Twitter` connector, you construct a `twitter.TwitterStream` connector, which takes a keyword argument that's the same `twitter.oauth.OAuth` type as previously introduced in Section 9.1 on page 352 and Section 9.2 on page 353. The sample code in Example 9-8 demonstrates how to get started with Twitter's Streaming API.

Example 9-8. Sampling the Twitter firehose with the Streaming API

```
# Finding topics of interest by using the filtering capablities it offers.

import twitter

# Query terms

q = 'CrossFit' # Comma-separated list of terms

print >> sys.stderr, 'Filtering the public timeline for track="%s"' % (q,)

# Returns an instance of twitter.Twitter
twitter_api = oauth_login()

# Reference the self.auth parameter
twitter_stream = twitter.TwitterStream(auth=twitter_api.auth)

# See https://dev.twitter.com/docs/streaming-apis
stream = twitter_stream.statuses.filter(track=q)

# For illustrative purposes, when all else fails, search for Justin Bieber
# and something is sure to turn up (at least, on Twitter)

for tweet in stream:
    print tweet['text']
    # Save to a database in a particular collection
```

9.9. Collecting Time-Series Data

9.9.1. Problem

You want to periodically query Twitter's API for specific results or trending topics and store the data for time-series analysis.

9.9.2. Solution

Use Python's built-in `time.sleep` function inside of an infinite loop to issue a query and store the results to a database such as MongoDB if the use of the Streaming API as illustrated in Section 9.8 on page 365 won't work.

9.9.3. Discussion

Although it's easy to get caught up in pointwise queries on particular keywords at a particular instant in time, the ability to sample data that's collected over time and detect trends and patterns gives us access to a radically powerful form of analysis that is commonly overlooked. Every time you look back and say, "I wish I'd known…" could have been a potential opportunity if you'd had the foresight to preemptively collect data that might have been useful for extrapolation or making predictions about the future (where applicable).

Time-series analysis of Twitter data can be truly fascinating given the ebbs and flows of topics and updates that can occur. Although it may be useful for many situations to sample from the firehose and store the results to a document-oriented database like MongoDB, it may be easier or more appropriate in some situations to periodically issue queries and record the results into discrete time intervals. For example, you might query the trending topics for a variety of geographic regions throughout a 24-hour period and measure the rate at which various trends change, compare rates of change across geographies, find the longest- and shortest-lived trends, and more.

Another compelling possibility that is being actively explored is correlations between sentiment as expressed on Twitter and stock markets. It's easy enough to zoom in on particular keywords, hashtags, or trending topics and later correlate the data against actual stock market changes; this could be an early step in building a bot to make predictions about markets and commodities.

Example 9-9 is essentially a composition of Section 9.1 on page 352, Example 9-3, and Example 9-7, and it demonstrates how you can use recipes as primitive building blocks to create more complex scripts with a little bit of creativity and copy/pasting.

Example 9-9. Collecting time-series data

```
import sys
import datetime
```

```
import time
import twitter

def get_time_series_data(api_func, mongo_db_name, mongo_db_coll,
                        secs_per_interval=60, max_intervals=15, **mongo_conn_kw):

    # Default settings of 15 intervals and 1 API call per interval ensure that
    # you will not exceed the Twitter rate limit.

    interval = 0

    while True:

        # A timestamp of the form "2013-06-14 12:52:07"
        now = str(datetime.datetime.now()).split(".")[0]

        ids = save_to_mongo(api_func(), mongo_db_name, mongo_db_coll + "-" + now)

        print >> sys.stderr, "Write {0} trends".format(len(ids))
        print >> sys.stderr, "Zzz..."
        print >> sys.stderr.flush()

        time.sleep(secs_per_interval) # seconds
        interval += 1

        if interval >= 15:
            break

# Sample usage

get_time_series_data(twitter_world_trends, 'time-series', 'twitter_world_trends')
```

9.10. Extracting Tweet Entities

9.10.1. Problem

You want to extract entities such as *@username* mentions, #hashtags, and URLs from tweets for analysis.

9.10.2. Solution

Extract the tweet entities from the `entities` field of tweets.

9.10.3. Discussion

Twitter's API now provides tweet entities (*http://bit.ly/1a1pIYA*) as a standard field for most of its API responses, where applicable. The `entities` field, illustrated in Example 9-10, includes user mentions, hashtags, references to URLs, media objects (such as images and videos), and financial *symbols* such as stock tickers. At the current time, not all fields may apply for all situations. For example, the media field will appear and be populated in a tweet only if a user embeds the media using a Twitter client that specifically uses a particular API for embedding the content; simply copying/pasting a link to a YouTube video won't necessarily populate this field.

See the Tweet Entities API documentation (*http://bit.ly/1a1pIYA*) for more details, including information on some of the additional fields that are available for each type of entity. For example, in the case of a URL, Twitter offers several variations, including the shortened and expanded forms as well as a value that may be more appropriate for displaying in a user interface for certain situations.

Example 9-10. Extracting tweet entities

```
def extract_tweet_entities(statuses):

    # See https://dev.twitter.com/docs/tweet-entities for more details on tweet
    # entities

    if len(statuses) == 0:
        return [], [], [], [], []

    screen_names = [ user_mention['screen_name']
                        for status in statuses
                            for user_mention in status['entities']['user_mentions'] ]

    hashtags = [ hashtag['text']
                    for status in statuses
                        for hashtag in status['entities']['hashtags'] ]

    urls = [ url['expanded_url']
                for status in statuses
                    for url in status['entities']['urls'] ]

    symbols = [ symbol['text']
                  for status in statuses
                      for symbol in status['entities']['symbols'] ]

    # In some circumstances (such as search results), the media entity
    # may not appear
    if status['entities'].has_key('media'):
        media = [ media['url']
                    for status in statuses
                        for media in status['entities']['media'] ]
    else:
        media = []

    return screen_names, hashtags, urls, media, symbols

# Sample usage

q = 'CrossFit'
```

```
statuses = twitter_search(twitter_api, q)

screen_names, hashtags, urls, media, symbols = extract_tweet_entities(statuses)

# Explore the first five items for each...

print json.dumps(screen_names[0:5], indent=1)
print json.dumps(hashtags[0:5], indent=1)
print json.dumps(urls[0:5], indent=1)
print json.dumps(media[0:5], indent=1)
print json.dumps(symbols[0:5], indent=1)
```

9.11. Finding the Most Popular Tweets in a Collection of Tweets

9.11.1. Problem

You want to determine which tweets are the most popular among a collection of search results or any other batch of tweets, such as a user timeline.

9.11.2. Solution

Analyze the `retweet_count` field of a tweet to determine whether or not a tweet was retweeted and, if so, how many times.

9.11.3. Discussion

Analyzing the `retweet_count` field of a tweet, as shown in Example 9-11, is perhaps the most straightforward measure of a tweet's popularity because it stands to reason that popular tweets will be shared with others. Depending on your particular interpretation of "popular," however, another possible value that you could incorporate into a formula for determining a tweet's popularity is its `favorite_count`, which is the number of times a user has bookmarked a tweet.

For example, you might weight the `retweet_count` at 1.0 and the `favorite_count` at 0.1 to add a marginal amount of weight to tweets that have been both retweeted and favorited if you wanted to use `favorite_count` as a tiebreaker. The particular choice of values in a formula is entirely up to you and will depend on how important you think each of these fields is in the overall context of the problem that you are trying to solve. Other possibilities, such as incorporating an exponential decay (*http://bit.ly/ 1a1pHEe*) that accounts for time and weights recent tweets more heavily than less recent tweets, may prove useful in certain analyses.

See also Section 9.14 on page 374 and Section 9.15 on page 376 for some additional discussion that may be helpful in navigating the space of analyzing and applying attribution to retweets, which can be slightly more confusing than it initially seems.

Example 9-11. Finding the most popular tweets in a collection of tweets

```
import twitter

def find_popular_tweets(twitter_api, statuses, retweet_threshold=3):

    # You could also consider using the favorite_count parameter as part of
    # this  heuristic, possibly using it to provide an additional boost to
    # popular tweets in a ranked formulation

    return [ status
                for status in statuses
                    if status['retweet_count'] > retweet_threshold ]

# Sample usage

q = "CrossFit"

twitter_api = oauth_login()
search_results = twitter_search(twitter_api, q, max_results=200)

popular_tweets = find_popular_tweets(twitter_api, search_results)

for tweet in popular_tweets:
    print tweet['text'], tweet['retweet_count']
```

 The `retweeted` attribute in a tweet is *not* a shortcut for telling you whether or not a tweet has been retweeted. It is a so-called "perspectival" attribute that tells you whether or not the authenticated user (which would be you in the case that you are analyzing your own data) has retweeted a status, which is convenient for powering markers in user interfaces. It is called a perspectival attribute because it provides perspective from the standpoint of the authenticating user.

9.12. Finding the Most Popular Tweet Entities in a Collection of Tweets

9.12.1. Problem

You'd like to determine if there are any popular tweet entities, such as *@username* mentions, #hashtags, or URLs, that might provide insight into the nature of a collection of tweets.

9.12.2. Solution

Extract the tweet entities with a list comprehension, count them, and filter out any tweet entity that doesn't exceed a minimal threshold.

9.12.3. Discussion

Twitter's API provides access to tweet entities directly in the metadata values of a tweet through the `entities` field, as demonstrated in Section 9.10 on page 368. After extracting the entities, you can compute the frequencies of each and easily extract the most common entities with a `collections.Counter` (shown in Example 9-12), which is a staple in Python's standard library and a considerable convenience in any frequency analysis experiment with Python. With a ranked collection of tweet entities at your fingertips, all that's left is to apply filtering or other threshold criteria to the collection of tweets in order to zero in on particular tweet entities of interest.

Example 9-12. Finding the most popular tweet entities in a collection of tweets

```
import twitter
from collections import Counter

def get_common_tweet_entities(statuses, entity_threshold=3):

    # Create a flat list of all tweet entities
    tweet_entities = [  e
                        for status in statuses
                            for entity_type in extract_tweet_entities([status])
                                for e in entity_type
                     ]

    c = Counter(tweet_entities).most_common()

    # Compute frequencies
    return [ (k,v)
             for (k,v) in c
                 if v >= entity_threshold
           ]

# Sample usage
```

```
q = 'CrossFit'

twitter_api = oauth_login()
search_results = twitter_search(twitter_api, q, max_results=100)
common_entities = get_common_tweet_entities(search_results)

print "Most common tweet entities"
print common_entities
```

9.13. Tabulating Frequency Analysis

9.13.1. Problem

You'd like to tabulate the results of frequency analysis experiments in order to easily skim the results or otherwise display them in a format that's convenient for human consumption.

9.13.2. Solution

Use the prettytable package to easily create an object that can be loaded with rows of information and displayed as a table with fixed-width columns.

9.13.3. Discussion

The prettytable package is very easy to use and incredibly helpful in constructing an easily readable, text-based output that can be copied and pasted into any report or text file (see Example 9-13). Just use **pip install prettytable** to install the package per the norms for Python package installation. A prettytable.PrettyTable is especially handy when used in tandem with a collections.Counter or other data structure that distills to a list of tuples that can be ranked (sorted) for analysis purposes.

 If you are interested in storing data for consumption in a spreadsheet, you may want to consult the documentation on the csv package (*http://bit.ly/1a1pHUH*) that's part of Python's standard library. However, be aware that there are some known issues (as documented) regarding its support for Unicode.

Example 9-13. Tabulating frequency analysis

```
from prettytable import PrettyTable

# Get some frequency data

twitter_api = oauth_login()
```

```
search_results = twitter_search(twitter_api, q, max_results=100)
common_entities = get_common_tweet_entities(search_results)

# Use PrettyTable to create a nice tabular display

pt = PrettyTable(field_names=['Entity', 'Count'])
[ pt.add_row(kv) for kv in common_entities ]
pt.align['Entity'], pt.align['Count'] = 'l', 'r' # Set column alignment
print pt
```

9.14. Finding Users Who Have Retweeted a Status

9.14.1. Problem

You'd like to discover all of the users who have ever retweeted a particular status.

9.14.2. Solution

Use the `GET retweeters/ids` API endpoint to determine which users have retweeted the status.

9.14.3. Discussion

Although the `GET retweeters/ids` API (*http://bit.ly/1a1pJvI*) returns the IDs of any users who have retweeted a status, there are a couple of subtle caveats that you should know about. In particular, keep in mind that this API reports only users who have retweeted by using Twitter's *native retweet API*, as opposed to users who have copy/pasted a tweet and prepended it with "RT," appended attribution with "(via @exampleUser)," or used another common convention.

Most Twitter applications (including the *twitter.com* user interface) use the native retweet API, but some users may still elect to share a status by "working around" the native API for the purposes of attaching additional commentary to a tweet or inserting themselves into a conversation that they'd otherwise be broadcasting only as an intermediary. For example, a user may suffix "< AWESOME!" to a tweet to display like-mindedness about it, and although the user may think of this as a retweet, he is actually *quoting* the tweet as far as Twitter's API is concerned. At least part of the reason for the confusion between quoting a tweet and retweeting a tweet is that Twitter has not always offered a native retweet API. In fact, the notion of retweeting is a phenomenon that evolved organically and that Twitter eventually responded to by providing first-class API support back in late 2010.

An illustration may help to drive home this subtle technical detail: suppose that @fperez_org posts a status and then @SocialWebMining retweets it. At this point in time, the `retweet_count` of the status posted by @fperez_org would be equal to 1, and

@SocialWebMining would have a tweet in its user timeline that indicates a retweet of @fperez_org's status.

Now let's suppose that @jyeee notices @fperez_org's status by examining @SocialWebMining's user timeline through *twitter.com* or an application like TweetDeck (*http://bit.ly/1a1pIbh*) and clicks the retweet button. At this point in time, @fperez_org's status would have a `retweet_count` equal to 2 and @jyeee would have a tweet in his user timeline (just like @SocialWebMining's last status) indicating a retweet of @fperez_org.

Here's the important point to understand: *from the standpoint of any user browsing @jyeee's timeline, @SocialWebMining's intermediary link between @fperez_org and @jyeee is effectively lost.* In other words, @fperez_org will receive the attribution for the original tweet, regardless of what kind of chain reaction gets set off involving multiple layers of intermediaries for a popular status.

With the ID values of any user who has retweeted the tweet in hand, it's easy enough to get profile details using the GET users/lookup API. See Section 9.17 on page 380 for more details.

Given that Example 9-14 may not fully satisfy your needs, be sure to also carefully consider Section 9.15 on page 376 as an additional step that you can take to discover broadcasters of a status. It provides an example that uses a regular expression to analyze the 140 characters of a tweet's content to extract the attribution information for a *quoted* tweet if you are processing a historical archive of tweets or otherwise want to double-check the content for attribution information.

Example 9-14. Finding users who have retweeted a status

```
import twitter

twitter_api = oauth_login()

print """User IDs for retweeters of a tweet by @fperez_org
that was retweeted by @SocialWebMining and that @jyeee then retweeted
from @SocialWebMining's timeline\n"""
print twitter_api.statuses.retweeters.ids(_id=334188056905129984)['ids']
print json.dumps(twitter_api.statuses.show(_id=334188056905129984), indent=1)
print

print "@SocialWeb's retweet of @fperez_org's tweet\n"
print twitter_api.statuses.retweeters.ids(_id=345723917798866944)['ids']
print json.dumps(twitter_api.statuses.show(_id=345723917798866944), indent=1)
print

print "@jyeee's retweet of @fperez_org's tweet\n"
print twitter_api.statuses.retweeters.ids(_id=338835939172417537)['ids']
print json.dumps(twitter_api.statuses.show(_id=338835939172417537), indent=1)
```

Some Twitter users intentionally quote tweets as opposed to using the retweet API in order to inject themselves into conversations and potentially be retweeted themselves, and it is still quite common to see the *RT* and *via* functionality widely used. In fact, popular applications such as TweetDeck include functionality for distinguishing between "Edit and RT" and a native "Retweet," as illustrated in Figure 9-2.

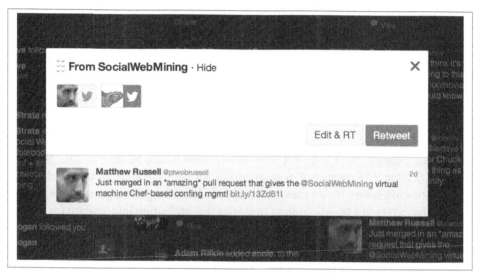

Figure 9-2. Popular applications such as Twitter's own TweetDeck provide "Edit and RT" functionality to "quote" a tweet as well as the newer and more native functionality for "Retweet"

9.15. Extracting a Retweet's Attribution

9.15.1. Problem

You'd like to determine the original attribution of a tweet.

9.15.2. Solution

Analyze the 140 characters of the tweet with regular expression heuristics for the presence of conventions such as "RT @SocialWebMining" or "(via @SocialWebMining)."

9.15.3. Discussion

Examining the results of Twitter's native retweet API as described in Section 9.14 on page 374 can provide the original attribution of a tweet in some, but certainly not all, circumstances. As noted in that recipe, it is sometimes the case that users will inject themselves into conversations for various reasons, so it may be necessary to analyze certain tweets in order to discover the original attribution. Example 9-15 demonstrates how to use regular expressions in Python to detect a couple of commonly used conventions that were adopted prior to the release of Twitter's native retweet API and that are still in common use today.

Example 9-15. Extracting a retweet's attribution

```
import re

def get_rt_attributions(tweet):

    # Regex adapted from Stack Overflow (http://bit.ly/1821y0J)

    rt_patterns = re.compile(r"(RT|via)((?:\b\W*@\w+)+)", re.IGNORECASE)
    rt_attributions = []

    # Inspect the tweet to see if it was produced with /statuses/retweet/:id.
    # See https://dev.twitter.com/docs/api/1.1/get/statuses/retweets/%3Aid.

    if tweet.has_key('retweeted_status'):
        attribution = tweet['retweeted_status']['user']['screen_name'].lower()
        rt_attributions.append(attribution)

    # Also, inspect the tweet for the presence of "legacy" retweet patterns
    # such as "RT" and "via", which are still widely used for various reasons
    # and potentially very useful. See https://dev.twitter.com/discussions/2847
    # and https://dev.twitter.com/discussions/1748 for some details on how/why.

    try:
        rt_attributions += [
                        mention.strip()
                        for mention in rt_patterns.findall(tweet['text'])[0][1].split()
                    ]
    except IndexError, e:
        pass

    # Filter out any duplicates

    return list(set([rta.strip("@").lower() for rta in rt_attributions]))

# Sample usage
twitter_api = oauth_login()

tweet = twitter_api.statuses.show(_id=214746575765913602)
print get_rt_attributions(tweet)
```

```
print
tweet = twitter_api.statuses.show(_id=345723917798866944)
print get_rt_attributions(tweet)
```

9.16. Making Robust Twitter Requests

9.16.1. Problem

In the midst of collecting data for analysis, you encounter unexpected HTTP errors that range from exceeding your rate limits (429 error) to the infamous "fail whale" (503 error) that need to be handled on a case-by-case basis.

9.16.2. Solution

Write a function that serves as a general-purpose API wrapper and provides abstracted logic for handling various HTTP error codes in meaningful ways.

9.16.3. Discussion

Although Twitter's rate limits are arguably adequate for most applications, they are generally inadequate for data mining exercises, so it's common that you'll need to manage the number of requests that you make in a given time period and also account for other types of HTTP failures, such as the infamous "fail whale" or other unexpected network glitches. One approach, shown in Example 9-16, is to write a wrapper function that abstracts away this messy logic and allows you to simply write your script as though rate limits and HTTP errors do not exist for the most part.

 See Section 9.5 on page 361 for inspiration on how you could use the standard library's functools.partial function to simplify the use of this wrapper function for some situations. Also be sure to review the complete listing of Twitter's HTTP error codes (*http://bit.ly/ 1a1pL6O*). Section 9.19 on page 382 provides a concrete implementation that illustrates how to use a function called make twitter_re quest that should simplify some of the HTTP errors you may experience in harvesting Twitter data.

Example 9-16. Making robust Twitter requests

```
import sys
import time
from urllib2 import URLError
from httplib import BadStatusLine
import json
import twitter
```

```
def make_twitter_request(twitter_api_func, max_errors=10, *args, **kw):

    # A nested helper function that handles common HTTPErrors. Return an updated
    # value for wait_period if the problem is a 500 level error. Block until the
    # rate limit is reset if it's a rate limiting issue (429 error). Returns None
    # for 401 and 404 errors, which requires special handling by the caller.
    def handle_twitter_http_error(e, wait_period=2, sleep_when_rate_limited=True):

        if wait_period > 3600: # Seconds
            print >> sys.stderr, 'Too many retries. Quitting.'
            raise e

        # See https://dev.twitter.com/docs/error-codes-responses for common codes

        if e.e.code == 401:
            print >> sys.stderr, 'Encountered 401 Error (Not Authorized)'
            return None
        elif e.e.code == 404:
            print >> sys.stderr, 'Encountered 404 Error (Not Found)'
            return None
        elif e.e.code == 429:
            print >> sys.stderr, 'Encountered 429 Error (Rate Limit Exceeded)'
            if sleep_when_rate_limited:
                print >> sys.stderr, "Retrying in 15 minutes...ZzZ..."
                sys.stderr.flush()
                time.sleep(60*15 + 5)
                print >> sys.stderr, '...ZzZ...Awake now and trying again.'
                return 2
            else:
                raise e # Caller must handle the rate limiting issue
        elif e.e.code in (500, 502, 503, 504):
            print >> sys.stderr, 'Encountered %i Error. Retrying in %i seconds' % \
                (e.e.code, wait_period)
            time.sleep(wait_period)
            wait_period *= 1.5
            return wait_period
        else:
            raise e

    # End of nested helper function

    wait_period = 2
    error_count = 0

    while True:
        try:
            return twitter_api_func(*args, **kw)
        except twitter.api.TwitterHTTPError, e:
            error_count = 0
            wait_period = handle_twitter_http_error(e, wait_period)
            if wait_period is None:
```

```
            return
    except URLError, e:
        error_count += 1
        print >> sys.stderr, "URLError encountered. Continuing."
        if error_count > max_errors:
            print >> sys.stderr, "Too many consecutive errors...bailing out."
            raise
    except BadStatusLine, e:
        error_count += 1
        print >> sys.stderr, "BadStatusLine encountered. Continuing."
        if error_count > max_errors:
            print >> sys.stderr, "Too many consecutive errors...bailing out."
            raise

# Sample usage

twitter_api = oauth_login()

# See https://dev.twitter.com/docs/api/1.1/get/users/lookup for
# twitter_api.users.lookup

response = make_twitter_request(twitter_api.users.lookup,
                                screen_name="SocialWebMining")

print json.dumps(response, indent=1)
```

9.17. Resolving User Profile Information

9.17.1. Problem

You'd like to look up profile information for one or more user IDs or screen names.

9.17.2. Solution

Use the GET users/lookup API to exchange as many as 100 IDs or usernames at a time for complete user profiles.

9.17.3. Discussion

Many APIs, such as GET friends/ids and GET followers/ids, return opaque ID values that need to be resolved to usernames or other profile information for meaningful analysis. Twitter provides a GET users/lookup API that can be used to resolve as many as 100 IDs or usernames at a time, and a simple pattern can be employed to iterate over larger batches. Although it adds a little bit of complexity to the logic, a single function can be constructed that accepts keyword parameters for your choice of either usernames or IDs that are resolved to user profiles. Example 9-17 illustrates such a function that can be adapted for a large variety of purposes, providing ancillary support for situations in which you'll need to resolve user IDs.

Example 9-17. Resolving user profile information

```
def get_user_profile(twitter_api, screen_names=None, user_ids=None):

    # Must have either screen_name or user_id (logical xor)
    assert (screen_names != None) != (user_ids != None), \
    "Must have screen_names or user_ids, but not both"

    items_to_info = {}

    items = screen_names or user_ids

    while len(items) > 0:

        # Process 100 items at a time per the API specifications for /users/lookup.
        # See https://dev.twitter.com/docs/api/1.1/get/users/lookup for details.

        items_str = ','.join([str(item) for item in items[:100]])
        items = items[100:]

        if screen_names:
            response = make_twitter_request(twitter_api.users.lookup,
                                            screen_name=items_str)
        else: # user_ids
            response = make_twitter_request(twitter_api.users.lookup,
                                            user_id=items_str)

        for user_info in response:
            if screen_names:
                items_to_info[user_info['screen_name']] = user_info
            else: # user_ids
                items_to_info[user_info['id']] = user_info

    return items_to_info

# Sample usage

twitter_api = oauth_login()

print get_user_profile(twitter_api, screen_names=["SocialWebMining", "ptwobrussell"])
#print get_user_profile(twitter_api, user_ids=[132373965])
```

9.18. Extracting Tweet Entities from Arbitrary Text

9.18.1. Problem

You'd like to analyze arbitrary text and extract tweet entities such as *@username* mentions, #hashtags, and URLs that may appear within it.

9.18.2. Solution

Use a third-party package like `twitter_text` to extract tweet entities from arbitrary text such as historical tweet archives that may not contain tweet entities as currently provided by the v1.1 API.

9.18.3. Discussion

Twitter has not always extracted tweet entities but you can easily derive them yourself with the help of a third-party package called `twitter_text`, as shown in Example 9-18. You can install `twitter-text` with `pip` using the command **pip install twitter-text-py**.

Example 9-18. Extracting tweet entities from arbitrary text

```
import twitter_text

# Sample usage

txt = "RT @SocialWebMining Mining 1M+ Tweets About #Syria http://wp.me/p3QiJd-1I"

ex = twitter_text.Extractor(txt)

print "Screen Names:", ex.extract_mentioned_screen_names_with_indices()
print "URLs:", ex.extract_urls_with_indices()
print "Hashtags:", ex.extract_hashtags_with_indices()
```

9.19. Getting All Friends or Followers for a User

9.19.1. Problem

You'd like to harvest all of the friends or followers for a (potentially very popular) Twitter user.

9.19.2. Solution

Use the `make_twitter_request` function introduced in Section 9.16 on page 378 to simplify the process of harvesting IDs by accounting for situations in which the number of followers may exceed what can be fetched within the prescribed rate limits.

9.19.3. Discussion

The GET followers/ids and GET friends/ids provide an API that can be navigated to retrieve all of the follower and friend IDs for a particular user, but the logic involved in retrieving all of the IDs can be nontrivial since each API request returns at most 5,000 IDs at a time. Although most users won't have anywhere near 5,000 friends or followers, some celebrity users, who are often interesting to analyze, will have hundreds of thousands or even millions of followers. Harvesting all of these IDs can be challenging because of the need to walk the cursor for each batch of results and also account for possible HTTP errors along the way. Fortunately, it's not too difficult to adapt `make_twit ter_request` and previously introduced logic for walking the cursor of results to systematically fetch all of these ids.

Techniques similar to those introduced in Example 9-19 could be incorporated into the template supplied in Section 9.17 on page 380 to create a robust function that provides a secondary step, such as resolving a subset (or all) of the IDs for usernames. It is advisable to store the results into a document-oriented database such as MongoDB (as illustrated in Section 9.7.1 on page 363) after each result so that no information is ever lost in the event of an unexpected glitch during a large harvesting operation.

 You may be better off paying a third party such as DataSift (*http://bit.ly/ 1a1pKje*) for faster access to certain kinds of data, such as the complete profiles for all of a very popular user's (say, @ladygaga) followers. Before you attempt to collect such a vast amount of data, at least do the arithmetic and determine how long it will take, consider the possible (unexpected) errors that may occur along the way for very long-running processes, and consider whether it would be better to acquire the data from another source. What it may cost you in money, it may save you in time.

Example 9-19. Getting all friends or followers for a user

```
from functools import partial
from sys import maxint

def get_friends_followers_ids(twitter_api, screen_name=None, user_id=None,
                              friends_limit=maxint, followers_limit=maxint):

    # Must have either screen_name or user_id (logical xor)
    assert (screen_name != None) != (user_id != None), \
    "Must have screen_name or user_id, but not both"

    # See https://dev.twitter.com/docs/api/1.1/get/friends/ids and
    # https://dev.twitter.com/docs/api/1.1/get/followers/ids for details
    # on API parameters

    get_friends_ids = partial(make_twitter_request, twitter_api.friends.ids,
                              count=5000)
    get_followers_ids = partial(make_twitter_request, twitter_api.followers.ids,
                                count=5000)

    friends_ids, followers_ids = [], []

    for twitter_api_func, limit, ids, label in [
```

```
                [get_friends_ids, friends_limit, friends_ids, "friends"],
                [get_followers_ids, followers_limit, followers_ids, "followers"]
            ]:

        if limit == 0: continue

        cursor = -1
        while cursor != 0:

            # Use make_twitter_request via the partially bound callable...
            if screen_name:
                response = twitter_api_func(screen_name=screen_name, cursor=cursor)
            else: # user_id
                response = twitter_api_func(user_id=user_id, cursor=cursor)

            if response is not None:
                ids += response['ids']
                cursor = response['next_cursor']

            print >> sys.stderr, 'Fetched {0} total {1} ids for {2}'.format(len(ids),
                                            label, (user_id or screen_name))

            # XXX: You may want to store data during each iteration to provide an
            # an additional layer of protection from exceptional circumstances

            if len(ids) >= limit or response is None:
                break

    # Do something useful with the IDs, like store them to disk...
    return friends_ids[:friends_limit], followers_ids[:followers_limit]

# Sample usage

twitter_api = oauth_login()

friends_ids, followers_ids = get_friends_followers_ids(twitter_api,
                                        screen_name="SocialWebMining",
                                        friends_limit=10,
                                        followers_limit=10)

print friends_ids
print followers_ids
```

9.20. Analyzing a User's Friends and Followers

9.20.1. Problem

You'd like to conduct a basic analysis that compares a user's friends and followers.

9.20.2. Solution

Use setwise operations such as *intersection* and *difference* to analyze the user's friends and followers.

9.20.3. Discussion

After harvesting all of a user's friends and followers, you can conduct some primitive analyses using only the ID values themselves with the help of setwise operations such as *intersection* and *difference*, as shown in Example 9-20.

Given two sets, the intersection of the sets returns the items that they have in common, whereas the difference between the sets "subtracts" the items in one set from the other, leaving behind the difference. Recall that intersection is a commutative operation, while difference is *not* commutative.[1]

In the context of analyzing friends and followers, the intersection of two sets can be interpreted as "mutual friends" or people you are following who are also following you back, while the difference of two sets can be interpreted as followers who you aren't following back or people you are following who aren't following you back, depending on the order of the operands.

Given a complete list of friend and follower IDs, computing these setwise operations is a natural starting point and can be the springboard for subsequent analysis. For example, it probably isn't necessary to use the GET users/lookup API to fetch profiles for millions of followers for a user as an immediate point of analysis.

You might instead opt to calculate the results of a setwise operation such as mutual friends (for which there are likely much stronger affinities) and hone in on the profiles of these user IDs before spidering out further.

Example 9-20. Analyzing a user's friends and followers

```
def setwise_friends_followers_analysis(screen_name, friends_ids, followers_ids):

    friends_ids, followers_ids = set(friends_ids), set(followers_ids)

    print '{0} is following {1}'.format(screen_name, len(friends_ids))

    print '{0} is being followed by {1}'.format(screen_name, len(followers_ids))

    print '{0} of {1} are not following {2} back'.format(
            len(friends_ids.difference(followers_ids)),
            len(friends_ids), screen_name)
```

---

1. A commutative operation is one in which the order of the operands does not matter—the operands can commute—as is the case with addition or multiplication.

```
print '{0} of {1} are not being followed back by {2}'.format(
        len(followers_ids.difference(friends_ids)),
        len(followers_ids), screen_name)

print '{0} has {1} mutual friends'.format(
        screen_name, len(friends_ids.intersection(followers_ids)))

# Sample usage

screen_name = "ptwobrussell"

twitter_api = oauth_login()

friends_ids, followers_ids = get_friends_followers_ids(twitter_api,
                                                screen_name=screen_name)
setwise_friends_followers_analysis(screen_name, friends_ids, followers_ids)
```

9.21. Harvesting a User's Tweets

9.21.1. Problem

You'd like to harvest all of a user's most recent tweets for analysis.

9.21.2. Solution

Use the GET statuses/user_timeline API endpoint to retrieve as many as 3,200 of the most recent tweets from a user, preferably with the added help of a robust API wrapper such as make_twitter_request (as introduced in Section 9.16 on page 378) since this series of requests may exceed rate limits or encounter HTTP errors along the way.

9.21.3. Discussion

Timelines are a fundamental concept in the Twitter developer ecosystem, and Twitter provides a convenient API endpoint for the purpose of harvesting tweets by user through the concept of a "user timeline." Harvesting a user's tweets, as demonstrated in Example 9-21, is a meaningful starting point for analysis since a tweet is the most fundamental primitive in the ecosystem. A large collection of tweets by a particular user provides an incredible amount of insight into what the person talks (and thus cares) about. With an archive of several hundred tweets for a particular user, you can conduct dozens of experiments, often with little additional API access. Storing the tweets in a particular collection of a document-oriented database such as MongoDB is a natural way to store and access the data during experimentation. For longer-term Twitter users, performing a time series analysis of how interests or sentiments have changed over time might be a worthwhile exercise.

Example 9-21. Harvesting a user's tweets

```python
def harvest_user_timeline(twitter_api, screen_name=None, user_id=None, max_results=1000):

    assert (screen_name != None) != (user_id != None), \
    "Must have screen_name or user_id, but not both"

    kw = {  # Keyword args for the Twitter API call
        'count': 200,
        'trim_user': 'true',
        'include_rts' : 'true',
        'since_id' : 1
        }

    if screen_name:
        kw['screen_name'] = screen_name
    else:
        kw['user_id'] = user_id

    max_pages = 16
    results = []

    tweets = make_twitter_request(twitter_api.statuses.user_timeline, **kw)

    if tweets is None: # 401 (Not Authorized) - Need to bail out on loop entry
        tweets = []

    results += tweets

    print >> sys.stderr, 'Fetched %i tweets' % len(tweets)

    page_num = 1

    # Many Twitter accounts have fewer than 200 tweets so you don't want to enter
    # the loop and waste a precious request if max_results = 200.

    # Note: Analogous optimizations could be applied inside the loop to try and
    # save requests. e.g. Don't make a third request if you have 287 tweets out of
    # a possible 400 tweets after your second request. Twitter does do some
    # post-filtering on censored and deleted tweets out of batches of 'count', though,
    # so you can't strictly check for the number of results being 200. You might get
    # back 198, for example, and still have many more tweets to go. If you have the
    # total number of tweets for an account (by GET /users/lookup/), then you could
    # simply use this value as a guide.

    if max_results == kw['count']:
        page_num = max_pages # Prevent loop entry

    while page_num < max_pages and len(tweets) > 0 and len(results) < max_results:

        # Necessary for traversing the timeline in Twitter's v1.1 API:
        # get the next query's max-id parameter to pass in.
        # See https://dev.twitter.com/docs/working-with-timelines.
```

```
        kw['max_id'] = min([ tweet['id'] for tweet in tweets]) - 1

        tweets = make_twitter_request(twitter_api.statuses.user_timeline, **kw)
        results += tweets

        print >> sys.stderr, 'Fetched %i tweets' % (len(tweets),)

        page_num += 1

    print >> sys.stderr, 'Done fetching tweets'

    return results[:max_results]

# Sample usage

twitter_api = oauth_login()
tweets = harvest_user_timeline(twitter_api, screen_name="SocialWebMining", \
                                max_results=200)

# Save to MongoDB with save_to_mongo or a local file with save_json...
```

9.22. Crawling a Friendship Graph

9.22.1. Problem

You'd like to harvest the IDs of a user's followers, followers of those followers, followers of followers of those followers, and so on, as part of a network analysis—essentially crawling a friendship graph of the "following" relationships on Twitter.

9.22.2. Solution

Use a breadth-first search to systematically harvest friendship information that can rather easily be interpreted as a graph for network analysis.

9.22.3. Discussion

A breadth-first search is a common technique for exploring a graph and is one of the standard ways that you would start at a point and build up multiple layers of context defined by relationships. Given a starting point and a depth, a breadth-first traversal systematically explores the space such that it is guaranteed to eventually return all nodes in the graph up to the said depth, and the search explores the space such that each depth completes before the next depth is begun (see Example 9-22).

Keep in mind that it is quite possible that in exploring Twitter friendship graphs, you may encounter *supernodes*—nodes with very high degrees of outgoing edges—which can very easily consume computing resources and API requests that count toward your rate limit. It is advisable that you provide a meaningful cap on the maximum number of followers you'd like to fetch for each user in the graph, at least during preliminary analysis, so that you know what you're up against and can determine whether the supernodes are worth the time and trouble for solving your particular problem. Exploring an unknown graph is a complex (and exciting) problem to work on, and various other tools, such as sampling techniques, could be intelligently incorporated to further enhance the efficacy of the search.

Example 9-22. Crawling a friendship graph

```python
def crawl_followers(twitter_api, screen_name, limit=1000000, depth=2):

    # Resolve the ID for screen_name and start working with IDs for consistency
    # in storage

    seed_id = str(twitter_api.users.show(screen_name=screen_name)['id'])

    _, next_queue = get_friends_followers_ids(twitter_api, user_id=seed_id,
                                              friends_limit=0, followers_limit=limit)

    # Store a seed_id => _follower_ids mapping in MongoDB

    save_to_mongo({'followers' : [ _id for _id in next_queue ]}, 'followers_crawl',
                  '{0}-follower_ids'.format(seed_id))

    d = 1
    while d < depth:
        d += 1
        (queue, next_queue) = (next_queue, [])
        for fid in queue:
            follower_ids = get_friends_followers_ids(twitter_api, user_id=fid,
                                                     friends_limit=0,
                                                     followers_limit=limit)

            # Store a fid => follower_ids mapping in MongoDB
            save_to_mongo({'followers' : [ _id for _id in next_queue ]},
                          'followers_crawl', '{0}-follower_ids'.format(fid))

            next_queue += follower_ids

# Sample usage

screen_name = "timoreilly"

twitter_api = oauth_login()

crawl_followers(twitter_api, screen_name, depth=1, limit=10)
```

9.23. Analyzing Tweet Content

9.23.1. Problem

Given a collection of tweets, you'd like to do some cursory analysis of the 140 characters of content in each to get a better idea of the nature of discussion and ideas being conveyed in the tweets themselves.

9.23.2. Solution

Use simple statistics, such as lexical diversity and average number of words per tweet, to gain elementary insight into what is being talked about as a first step in sizing up the nature of the language being used.

9.23.3. Discussion

In addition to analyzing the content for tweet entities and conducting simple frequency analysis of commonly occurring words, you can also examine the *lexical diversity* of the tweets and calculate other simple statistics, such as the average number of words per tweet, to better size up the data (see Example 9-23). Lexical diversity is a simple statistic that is defined as the number of unique words divided by the number of total words in a corpus; by definition, a lexical diversity of 1.0 would mean that all words in a corpus were unique, while a lexical diversity that approaches 0.0 implies more duplicate words.

Depending on the context, lexical diversity can be interpreted slightly differently. For example, in contexts such as literature, comparing the lexical diversity of two authors might be used to measure the richness or expressiveness of their language relative to each other. Although not usually the end goal in and of itself, examining lexical diversity often provides valuable preliminary insight (usually in conjunction with frequency analysis) that can be used to better inform possible follow-up steps.

In the Twittersphere, lexical diversity might be interpreted in a similar fashion if comparing two Twitter users, but it might also suggest a lot about the relative diversity of overall content being discussed, as might be the case with someone who talks only about technology versus someone who talks about a much wider range of topics. In a context such as a collection of tweets by multiple authors about the same topic (as would be the case in examining a collection of tweets returned by the Search API or the Streaming API), a much lower than expected lexical diversity *might* also imply that there is a lot of "group think" going on. Another possibility is a lot of retweeting, in which the same information is more or less being regurgitated. As with any other analysis, no statistic should be interpreted devoid of supporting context.

Example 9-23. Analyzing tweet content

```
def analyze_tweet_content(statuses):

    if len(statuses) == 0:
        print "No statuses to analyze"
        return

    # A nested helper function for computing lexical diversity
    def lexical_diversity(tokens):
        return 1.0*len(set(tokens))/len(tokens)

    # A nested helper function for computing the average number of words per tweet
    def average_words(statuses):
        total_words = sum([ len(s.split()) for s in statuses ])
        return 1.0*total_words/len(statuses)

    status_texts = [ status['text'] for status in statuses ]
    screen_names, hashtags, urls, media, _ = extract_tweet_entities(statuses)

    # Compute a collection of all words from all tweets
    words = [ w
            for t in status_texts
                for w in t.split() ]

    print "Lexical diversity (words):", lexical_diversity(words)
    print "Lexical diversity (screen names):", lexical_diversity(screen_names)
    print "Lexical diversity (hashtags):", lexical_diversity(hashtags)
    print "Averge words per tweet:", average_words(status_texts)


# Sample usage

q = 'CrossFit'
twitter_api = oauth_login()
search_results = twitter_search(twitter_api, q)

analyze_tweet_content(search_results)
```

9.24. Summarizing Link Targets

9.24.1. Problem

You'd like to have a cursory understanding of what is being talked about in a link target, such as a URL that is extracted as a tweet entity, to gain insight into the nature of a tweet or the interests of a Twitter user.

9.24.2. Solution

Summarize the content in the URL to just a few sentences that can easily be skimmed (or more tersely analyzed in some other way) as opposed to reading the entire web page.

9.24.3. Discussion

Your imagination is the only limitation when it comes to trying to understand the human language data in web pages. Example 9-24 is an attempt to provide a template for processing and distilling that content into a terse form that could be quickly skimmed or analyzed by alternative techniques. In short, it demonstrates how to fetch a web page, isolate the meaningful content in the web page (as opposed to the prolific amounts of boilerplate text in the headers, footers, sidebars, etc.), remove the HTML markup that may be remaining in that content, and use a simple summarization technique to isolate the most important sentences in the content.

The summarization technique basically rests on the premise that the most important sentences are a good summary of the content if presented in chronological order, and that you can discover the most important sentences by identifying frequently occurring words that interact with one another in close proximity. Although a bit crude, this form of summarization works surprisingly well on reasonably well-written Web content.

Example 9-24. Summarizing link targets

```
import sys
import json
import nltk
import numpy
import urllib2
from boilerpipe.extract import Extractor

def summarize(url, n=100, cluster_threshold=5, top_sentences=5):

    # Adapted from "The Automatic Creation of Literature Abstracts" by H.P. Luhn
    #
    # Parameters:
    # * n   - Number of words to consider
    # * cluster_threshold - Distance between words to consider
    # * top_sentences - Number of sentences to return for a "top n" summary

    # Begin - nested helper function
    def score_sentences(sentences, important_words):
        scores = []
        sentence_idx = -1

        for s in [nltk.tokenize.word_tokenize(s) for s in sentences]:

            sentence_idx += 1
            word_idx = []
```

```python
        # For each word in the word list...
        for w in important_words:
            try:
                # Compute an index for important words in each sentence

                word_idx.append(s.index(w))
            except ValueError, e: # w not in this particular sentence
                pass

    word_idx.sort()

    # It is possible that some sentences may not contain any important words
    if len(word_idx)== 0: continue

    # Using the word index, compute clusters with a max distance threshold
    # for any two consecutive words

    clusters = []
    cluster = [word_idx[0]]
    i = 1
    while i < len(word_idx):
        if word_idx[i] - word_idx[i - 1] < cluster_threshold:
            cluster.append(word_idx[i])
        else:
            clusters.append(cluster[:])
            cluster = [word_idx[i]]
        i += 1
    clusters.append(cluster)

    # Score each cluster. The max score for any given cluster is the score
    # for the sentence.

    max_cluster_score = 0
    for c in clusters:
        significant_words_in_cluster = len(c)
        total_words_in_cluster = c[-1] - c[0] + 1
        score = 1.0 * significant_words_in_cluster \
            * significant_words_in_cluster / total_words_in_cluster

        if score > max_cluster_score:
            max_cluster_score = score

    scores.append((sentence_idx, score))

    return scores

# End - nested helper function

extractor = Extractor(extractor='ArticleExtractor', url=url)

# It's entirely possible that this "clean page" will be a big mess. YMMV.
```

```python
# The good news is that the summarize algorithm inherently accounts for handling
# a lot of this noise.

txt = extractor.getText()

sentences = [s for s in nltk.tokenize.sent_tokenize(txt)]
normalized_sentences = [s.lower() for s in sentences]

words = [w.lower() for sentence in normalized_sentences for w in
         nltk.tokenize.word_tokenize(sentence)]

fdist = nltk.FreqDist(words)

top_n_words = [w[0] for w in fdist.items()
        if w[0] not in nltk.corpus.stopwords.words('english')][:n]

scored_sentences = score_sentences(normalized_sentences, top_n_words)

# Summarization Approach 1:
# Filter out nonsignificant sentences by using the average score plus a
# fraction of the std dev as a filter

avg = numpy.mean([s[1] for s in scored_sentences])
std = numpy.std([s[1] for s in scored_sentences])
mean_scored = [(sent_idx, score) for (sent_idx, score) in scored_sentences
                if score > avg + 0.5 * std]

# Summarization Approach 2:
# Another approach would be to return only the top N ranked sentences

top_n_scored = sorted(scored_sentences, key=lambda s: s[1])[-top_sentences:]
top_n_scored = sorted(top_n_scored, key=lambda s: s[0])

# Decorate the post object with summaries

return dict(top_n_summary=[sentences[idx] for (idx, score) in top_n_scored],
        mean_scored_summary=[sentences[idx] for (idx, score) in mean_scored])

# Sample usage

sample_url = 'http://radar.oreilly.com/2013/06/phishing-in-facebooks-pond.html'
summary = summarize(sample_url)

print "----------------------------------------------"
print "              'Top N Summary'"
print "----------------------------------------------"
print " ".join(summary['top_n_summary'])
print
print
print "----------------------------------------------"
print "              'Mean Scored' Summary"
```

```
print "-------------------------------------------------"
print " ".join(summary['mean_scored_summary'])
```

9.25. Analyzing a User's Favorite Tweets

9.25.1. Problem

You'd like to learn more about what a person cares about by examining the tweets that a person has marked as favorites.

9.25.2. Solution

Use the GET favorites/list API endpoint to fetch a user's favorite tweets and then apply techniques to detect, extract, and count tweet entities to characterize the content.

9.25.3. Discussion

Not all Twitter users take advantage of the bookmarking feature to identify favorites, so you can't consider it a completely dependable technique for zeroing in on content and topics of interest; however, if you are fortunate enough to encounter a Twitter user who tends to bookmark favorites as a habit, you'll often find a treasure trove of curated content. Although Example 9-25 shows an analysis that builds upon previous recipes to construct a table of tweet entities, you could apply more advanced techniques to the tweets themselves. A couple of ideas might include separating the content into different topics, analyzing how a person's favorites have changed or evolved over time, or plotting out the regularity of when and how often a person marks tweets as favorites.

Keep in mind that in addition to favorites, any tweets that a user has retweeted are also promising candidates for analysis, and even analyzing patterns of behavior such as whether or not a user tends to retweet (and how often), bookmark (and how often), or both is an enlightening survey in its own right.

Example 9-25. Analyzing a user's favorite tweets

```
def analyze_favorites(twitter_api, screen_name, entity_threshold=2):

    # Could fetch more than 200 by walking the cursor as shown in other
    # recipes, but 200 is a good sample to work with.
    favs = twitter_api.favorites.list(screen_name=screen_name, count=200)
    print "Number of favorites:", len(favs)

    # Figure out what some of the common entities are, if any, in the content

    common_entities = get_common_tweet_entities(favs,
                                        entity_threshold=entity_threshold)

    # Use PrettyTable to create a nice tabular display
```

```
pt = PrettyTable(field_names=['Entity', 'Count'])
[ pt.add_row(kv) for kv in common_entities ]
pt.align['Entity'], pt.align['Count'] = 'l', 'r' # Set column alignment

print
print "Common entities in favorites..."
print pt


# Print out some other stats
print
print "Some statistics about the content of the favorites..."
print
analyze_tweet_content(favs)

# Could also start analyzing link content or summarized link content, and more.

# Sample usage

twitter_api = oauth_login()
analyze_favorites(twitter_api, "ptwobrussell")
```

Check out *http://favstar.fm* for an example of a popular website that aims to help you find "the best tweets" by tracking and analyzing what is being favorited and retweeted on Twitter.

9.26. Closing Remarks

Although this cookbook is really just a modest collection when compared to the hundreds or even thousands of possible recipes for manipulating and mining Twitter data, hopefully it has provided you with a good springboard and a sampling of ideas that you'll be able to draw upon and adapt in many profitable ways. The possibilities for what you can do with Twitter data (and most other social data) are broad, powerful, and (perhaps most importantly) fun!

Pull requests for additional recipes (as well as enhancements to these recipes) are welcome and highly encouraged, and will be liberally accepted. Please fork this book's source code from its GitHub repository (*http://bit.ly/1a1kNqy*), commit a recipe to this chapter's IPython Notebook, and submit a pull request! The hope is that this collection of recipes will grow in scope, provide a valuable starting point for social data hackers, and accumulate a vibrant community of contributors around it.

9.27. Recommended Exercises

- Review the Twitter Platform API (*http://bit.ly/1a1kSKQ*) in depth. Are there APIs that you are surprised to find (or not find) there?

- Analyze all of the tweets that you have ever retweeted. Are you at all surprised about what you have retweeted or how your interests have evolved over time?

- Juxtapose the tweets that you author versus the ones that you retweet. Are they generally about the same topics?

- Write a recipe that loads friendship graph data from MongoDB into a true graphical representation with NetworkX and employ one of NetworkX's built-in algorithms, such as centrality measurement or clique analysis, to mine the graph. Chapter 7 provides an overview of NetworkX that you may find helpful to review before completing this exercise.

- Write a recipe that adapts visualizations from previous chapters for the purpose of visualizing Twitter data. For example, repurpose a graph visualization to display a friendship graph, adapt a plot or histogram in IPython Notebook to visualize tweeting patterns or trends for a particular user, or populate a tag cloud (such as Word Cloud Layout (*http://bit.ly/1a1n5pO*)) with content from tweets.

- Write a recipe to identify followers that you are not following back but perhaps should follow back based upon the content of their tweets. A few similarity measurements that may make suitable starting points were introduced in Section 3.3.3 on page 112.

- Write a recipe to compute the similarity of two users based upon the content that they tweet about.

- Review Twitter's Lists API, in particular the /lists/list (*http://bit.ly/1a1pMrv*) and /lists/memberships (*http://bit.ly/1a1pOj5*) API endpoints, which tell you the lists a user subscribes to and the lists that a member has been added to by other users, respectively. What can you learn about users from the lists they subscribe to and/or have been added to by other users?

- Try to apply techniques for processing human language to tweets. Carnegie Mellon has a Twitter NLP and Part-of-Speech Tagging (*http://bit.ly/1a1n84Y*) project that provides a good starting point.

- If you follow many Twitter accounts, it is virtually impossible to keep up with all of the activity. Write an algorithm that ranks the tweets that appear in your home timeline by importance rather than chronology. Are you able to effectively filter out noise and gain more signal? Can you compute a meaningful digest of the top tweets for the day based on your own personal interests?

- Begin amassing a collection of recipes for other social websites like Facebook, LinkedIn, or Google+.

9.28. Online Resources

The following list of links from this chapter may be useful for review:

- BSON (*http://bit.ly/1a1pG34*)
- d3-cloud GitHub repository (*http://bit.ly/1a1n5pO*)
- Exponential decay (*http://bit.ly/1a1pHEe*)
- MongoDB data aggregation framework (*http://bit.ly/1a1pGjv*)
- OAuth 1.0a (*http://bit.ly/1a1pBwg*)
- Twitter API HTTP error codes (*http://bit.ly/1a1pL6O*)
- Twitter Developer API (*http://bit.ly/1a1kSKQ*)
- Twitter Development FAQ (*http://bit.ly/1a1pC3o*)
- Twitter NLP and Part-of-Speech Tagging (*http://bit.ly/1a1n84Y*)
- Twitter Streaming API (*http://bit.ly/1a1l1ya*)
- Yahoo! Where On Earth (WOE) ID (*http://yhoo.it/1a1kZ9u*)

## PART III

Appendixes

The appendixes of this book present some crosscutting material that undergirds much of the content that precedes it:

- Appendix A presents a brief overview of the technology that powers the virtual machine experience that accompanies this book, as well as a brief discussion on the scope and purpose of the virtual machine.

- Appendix B provides a short discussion of Open Authorization (OAuth), the industry protocol that undergirds accessing social data from just about any notable social website with an API.

- Appendix C is a very short primer on some common Python idioms that you'll encounter in the source code for this book; it highlights some subtleties about IPython Notebook that you may benefit from knowing about.

Information About This Book's Virtual Machine Experience

Just as each chapter in this book has a corresponding IPython Notebook, each appendix also has a corresponding IPython Notebook. All notebooks, regardless of purpose, are maintained in the book's GitHub source code repository (*http://bit.ly/1a1kNqy*). The particular appendix that you are reading here "in print" serves as a special cross-reference to the IPython Notebook that provides step-by-step instructions for how to install and configure the book's virtual machine.

You are strongly encouraged to install the virtual machine as a development environment instead of using your existing Python installation, because there are some non-trivial configuration management issues involved in installing IPython Notebook and all of its dependencies for scientific computing. The various other third-party Python packages that are used throughout the book and the need to support users across multiple platforms only exacerbate the complexity that can be involved in getting a basic development environment up and running. Therefore, this book comes with a virtual machine that provides all readers and consumers of the source code with the least amount of friction possible to interactively follow along with the examples. *Even if you are an expert in working with Python developer tools, you will still likely save some time by taking advantage of the book's virtual machine experience on your first pass through the text.* Give it a try. You'll be glad that you did.

 The corresponding read-only IPython Notebook, Appendix A: Virtual Machine Experience (*http://bit.ly/1a1pSiI*), is maintained with the book's GitHub source code repository (*http://bit.ly/1a1kNqy*) and contains step-by-step instructions for getting started.

OAuth Primer

Just as each chapter in this book has a corresponding IPython Notebook, each appendix also has a corresponding IPython Notebook. All notebooks, regardless of purpose, are maintained in the book's GitHub source code repository (*http://bit.ly/1a1kNqy*). The particular appendix that you are reading here "in print" serves as a special cross-reference to the IPython Notebook that provides example code demonstrating interactive OAuth flows that involve explicit user authorization, which is needed if you implement a user-facing application.

The remainder of this appendix provides a terse discussion of OAuth as a basic orientation. The sample code for OAuth flows for popular websites such as Twitter, Facebook, and LinkedIn is in the corresponding IPython Notebook that is available with this book's source code.

Like the other appendixes, this appendix has a corresponding IPython Notebook entitled Appendix B: OAuth Primer (*http://bit.ly/1a1pW1V*) that you can view online.

Overview

OAuth stands for "open authorization" and provides a means for users to *authorize* an application to access their account data through an API without the users needing to hand over sensitive credentials such as a username and password combination. Although OAuth is presented here in the context of the social web, keep in mind that it's a specification that has wide applicability in any context in which users would like to authorize an application to take certain actions on their behalf. In general, users can control the level of access for a third-party application (subject to the degree of API granularity that the provider implements) and revoke it at any time. For example, consider the case of Facebook, in which extremely fine-grained permissions are implemented and enable users to allow third-party applications to access very specific pieces of sensitive account information.

Given the nearly ubiquitous popularity of platforms such as Twitter, Facebook, LinkedIn, and Google+, and the vast utility of third-party applications that are developed on these social web platforms, it's no surprise that they've adopted OAuth as a common means of opening up their platforms. However, like any other specification or protocol, OAuth implementations across social web properties currently vary with regard to the version of the specification that's implemented, and there are sometimes a few idiosyncrasies that come up in particular implementations. The remainder of this section provides a brief overview of OAuth 1.0a, as defined by RFC 5849 (*http://bit.ly/1a1pWio*), and OAuth 2.0, as defined by RFC 6749 (*http://bit.ly/1a1pWiz*), that you'll encounter as you mine the social web and engage in other programming endeavors involving platform APIs.

OAuth 1.0A

OAuth 1.0[1] defines a protocol that enables a web *client* to access a *resource owner's protected resource* on a *server* and is described in great detail in the OAuth 1.0 Guide (*http://bit.ly/1a1pYHe*). As you already know, the reason for its existence is to avoid the problem of users (resource owners) sharing passwords with web applications, and although it is fairly narrowly defined in its scope, it does do very well the one thing it claims to do. As it turns out, one of the primary developer complaints about OAuth 1.0 that initially hindered adoption was that it was very tedious to implement because of the various encryption details involved (such as HMAC signature generation (*http://bit.ly/1a1pZe1*)), given that OAuth 1.0 does not assume that credentials are exchanged over a secure SSL connection using an HTTPS protocol. In other words, OAuth 1.0 uses cryptography as part of its flow to guarantee security during transmissions over the wire.

Although we'll be fairly informal in this discussion, you might care to know that in OAuth parlance, the application that is requesting access is often known as the *client* (sometimes called the *consumer*), the social website or service that houses the *protected resources* is the *server* (sometimes called the *service provider*), and the user who is granting access is the *resource owner*. Since there are three parties involved in the process, the series of redirects among them is often referred to as a *three-legged flow*, or more colloquially, the "OAuth dance." Although the implementation and security details are a bit messy, there are essentially just a few fundamental steps involved in the OAuth dance that ultimately enable a client application to access protected resources on the resource owner's behalf from the service provider:

---

1. Throughout this discussion, use of the term "OAuth 1.0" is technically intended to mean "OAuth 1.0a," given that OAuth 1.0 revision A obsoleted OAuth 1.0 and is the widely implemented standard.

1. The client obtains an unauthorized request token from the service provider.

2. The resource owner authorizes the request token.

3. The client exchanges the request token for an access token.

4. The client uses the access token to access protected resources on behalf of the re-source owner.

In terms of particular credentials, a client starts with a *consumer key* and *consumer secret* and by the end of the OAuth dance winds up with an *access token* and *access token secret* that can be used to access protected resources. All things considered, OAuth 1.0 sets out to enable client applications to securely obtain authorization from resource owners to access account resources from service providers, and despite some arguably tedious implementation details, it provides a broadly accepted protocol that makes good on this intention. It is likely that OAuth 1.0 will be around for a while.

 "Introduction to OAuth (in Plain English)" (*http://bit.ly/1a1pXD7*) illustrates how an end user (as a resource owner) could authorize a link-shortening service such as bit.ly (as a client) to automatically post links to Twitter (as a service provider). It is worth reviewing and drives home the abstract concepts presented in this section.

OAuth 2.0

Whereas OAuth 1.0 enables a useful, albeit somewhat narrow, authorization flow for web applications, OAuth 2.0 was originally intended to significantly simplify imple-mentation details for web application developers by relying completely on SSL for se-curity aspects, and to satisfy a much broader array of use cases. Such use cases ranged from support for mobile devices to the needs of the enterprise, and even somewhat futuristically considered the needs of the "Internet of Things," such as devices that might appear in your home.

Facebook was an early adopter, with migration plans dating back to early drafts of OAuth 2.0 in 2011 (*http://bit.ly/1a1pYa9*) and a platform that quickly relied exclusively on a portion of the OAuth 2.0 specification, while LinkedIn waited to implement support for OAuth 2.0 until early 2013 (*http://linkd.in/1a1q1mk*). Although Twitter's standard user-based authentication is still based squarely on OAuth 1.0a, it implemented application-based authentication (*http://bit.ly/1a1q0Ph*) in early 2013 that's modeled on the Client Credentials Grant (*http://bit.ly/1a1q3KT*) flow of the OAuth 2.0 spec. Finally, Google currently implements OAuth 2.0 for services such as Google+ (*http://bit.ly/1a1q29X*), and has deprecated support for OAuth 1.0 (*http://bit.ly/1a1q4i3*) as of April 2012. As you can see, the reaction was somewhat mixed in that not every social website immediately scrambled to implement OAuth 2.0 as soon as it was announced.

Still, it's a bit unclear whether or not OAuth 2.0 as originally envisioned will ever become the new industry standard. One popular blog post, entitled "OAuth 2.0 and the Road to Hell" (*http://bit.ly/1a1q4yr*) (and its corresponding Hacker News discussion (*http://bit.ly/1a1q2Xg*)) is worth reviewing and summarizes a lot of the issues. The post was written by Eran Hammer, who resigned his role as lead author and editor of the OAuth 2.0 specification as of mid-2012 after working on it for several years. It appears as though "design by committee" around large open-ended enterprise problems suffocated some of the enthusiasm and progress of the working group, and although the specification was published in late 2012, it is unclear as to whether it provides an actual specification or a blueprint for one. Fortunately, over the previous years, lots of terrific OAuth frameworks have emerged to allay most of the OAuth 1.0 development pains associated with accessing APIs, and developers have continued innovating despite the initial stumbling blocks with OAuth 1.0. As a case in point, in working with Python packages in earlier chapters of this book, you haven't had to know or care about any of the complex details involved with OAuth 1.0a implementations; you've just had to understand the gist of how it works. What does seem clear despite some of the analysis paralysis and "good intentions" associated with OAuth 2.0, however, is that several of its flows seem well-defined enough that large social web providers are moving forward with them.

As you now know, unlike OAuth 1.0 implementations, which consist of a fairly rigid set of steps, OAuth 2.0 implementations can vary somewhat depending on the particular use case. A typical OAuth 2.0 flow, however, does take advantage of SSL and essentially just consists of a few redirects that, at a high enough level, don't look all that different from the previously mentioned set of steps involving an OAuth 1.0 flow. For example, Twitter's recent application-only authentication (*http://bit.ly/1a1q0Ph*) involves little more than an application exchanging its *consumer key* and *consumer secret* for an access token over a secure SSL connection. Again, implementations will vary based on the particular use case, and although it's not exactly light reading, Section 4 of the OAuth 2.0 spec (*http://bit.ly/1a1q3uv*) is fairly digestible content if you're interested in some of the details. If you choose to review it, just keep in mind that some of the terminology differs between OAuth 1.0 and OAuth 2.0, so it may be easier to focus on understanding one specification at a time as opposed to learning them both simultaneously.

 Chapter 9 of Jonathan LeBlanc's *Programming Social Applications* (O'Reilly) provides a nice discussion of OAuth 1.0 and OAuth 2.0 in the context of building social web applications.

The idiosyncrasies of OAuth and the underlying implementations of OAuth 1.0 and OAuth 2.0 are generally not going to be all that important to you as a social web miner. This discussion was tailored to provide some surrounding context so that you have a basic understanding of the key concepts involved and to provide some starting points for further study and research should you like to do so. As you may have already gathered, the devil really is in the details. Fortunately, nice third-party libraries largely obsolete the need to know much about those details on a day-to-day basis, although they can sometimes come in handy. The online code for this appendix features both OAuth 1.0 and OAuth 2.0 flows, and you can dig into as much detail with them as you'd like.

Python and IPython Notebook Tips & Tricks

Just as each chapter in this book has a corresponding IPython Notebook, each appendix also has a corresponding IPython Notebook. Like Appendix A, this "in print" appendix serves as a special cross-reference to an IPython Notebook that's maintained in the book's GitHub source code repository (*http://bit.ly/1a1kNqy*) and includes a collection of Python idioms as well as some helpful tips for using IPython Notebook.

 The corresponding IPython Notebook for this appendix, Appendix C: Python and IPython Notebook Tips & Tricks (*http://bit.ly/1a1q6GI*), contains additional examples of common Python idioms that you may find of particular relevance as you work through this book. It also contains some helpful tips about working with IPython Notebook that may save you some time.

Even though it's not that uncommon to hear Python referred to as "executable pseudocode," a brief review of Python as a general-purpose programming language may be worthwhile for readers new to Python. Please consider following along with Sections 1 through 8 of the Python Tutorial (*http://bit.ly/1a1q6Xe*) as a means of basic familiarization if you feel that you could benefit from a general-purpose introduction to Python as a programming language. It's a worthwhile investment and will maximize your enjoyment of this book.

Index

We'd like to hear your suggestions for improving our indexes. Send email to index@oreilly.com.

ontologies, 340
operator.itemgetter Python function, 73
OWL language, 291, 342

P

parsing
    email messages with IMAP, 271–273
    feeds, 184–185, 196–200
part-of-speech (POS) tagging, 194, 212
Patel-Schneider, Peter, 342
patterns
    in retweets, 34–37, 374–376
    in sender/recipient communications, 250–255
    visualizing in Gmail, 273–274
PaySwarm, 347
Pearson's chi-square test, 176
Penn Treebank Project, 194, 209
people (Google+), 137, 140–142
People API (Google+), 140
personal API access token (OAuth), 282
pip instal command
    google-api-python-client Python package, 140
pip install command
    beautifulsoup Python package, 144
    cluster Python package, 120
    envoy Python package, 241
    facebook-sdk Python package, 59
    feedparser Python package, 184
    geopy Python package, 107
    networkx Python package, 81, 288
    nltk Python package, 112
    numpy Python package, 201
    oauth2 Python package, 270
    prettytable Python package, 72, 94, 373
    PyGithub Python package, 283
    pymongo Python package, 242, 244
    python-boilerpipe package, 183
    python-linkedin Python package, 92
    python_dateutil Python package, 235
    requests Python package, 53, 283
    twitter Python package, 12, 351
    twitter-text-py Python package, 382
places (Twitter), 9, 358
PMI (Pointwise Mutual Information), 176
Pointwise Mutual Information (PMI), 176
POS (part-of-speech) tagging, 194, 212
prettytable Python package, 72, 94, 267, 373

privacy controls
    Facebook and, 45, 47, 71
    LinkedIn and, 91
projects (GitHub), 281
Prolog programming language, 341
property graphs, modeling data with, 288–291
public firehose (tweets), 11
public streams API, 11
pull requests (Git), 279
PunktSentenceTokenizer Python class, 199
PunktWordTokenizer Python class, 200
PuTTY (Windows SSH client), 243
pydoc Python package, 12, 140, 199, 287
PyGithub Python package, 283, 286–287, 308
PyLab, 37, 76
pymongo Python package, 242, 244–246, 260
python-boilerpipe Python package, 183
python-oauth2 Python package, 270
PYTHONPATH environment variable, 12

Q

quality of analytics for human language data, 219–222
queries
    advanced, 255–259
    by date/time range, 248–250
    Facebook Social Graph API, 60–63
    GitHub API, 286
    Google+ API, 140–147
    human language data, 155–178
    LinkedIn data, 89, 93
    nodes as pivots for, 311–315
    TF-IDF support, 148–166
    Twitter API, 16–26
quopri Python package, 239
quoting tweets, 34

R

rate limits
    Facebook Social Graph API, 60
    GitHub API, 284, 300
    LinkedIn API, 93
    Twitter API, 17
raw frequency, 175
RDF (Resource Description Framework), 340–345
RDF Schema language, 291, 342

Subversion version control system, 279
supernodes, 307, 388
supervised learning, 183, 221
syllogisms, 342

T

tag clouds, 213, 397
taxonomies, 9
term frequency (TF), 148–149
Term Frequency–Inverse Document Frequency
    (see TF-IDF)
text field (tweets), 26
TF (term frequency), 148–149
TF-IDF (Term Frequency–Inverse Document
    Frequency)
    about, 136, 147
    applying to human language, 158–160
    finding similar documents, 160–167
    inverse document frequency, 150
    querying human language data with, 155–
        178
    running on sample data, 151–155
    term frequency, 148–149
thread pool, 190, 300
time-series trends, 264–268, 367
time.sleep Python function, 367
timelines (Twitter), 9–11, 386
timestamps, 227
Titan big graph database, 291
tokenization, 157, 193, 197–200
Travelling Salesman probems, 130
TreebankWordTokenizer Python class, 199
trends (Twitter), 16–19, 358
TrigramAssociationMeasures Python class, 114
trigrams, 114
true error, 219
true negatives, 220
true positives, 220
Turing Test, 190
tweet entities
    analyzing, 26–28, 30–32
    composition of, 9
    extracting, 28, 368, 372, 381
    finding most popular, 372
    searching for, 10, 20–26
TweetDeck, 10
tweets
    about, 9–11
    analyzing, 26–28, 30–32, 390

composition of, 9
finding most popular, 370
harvesting, 386
lexical diversity of, 32–34, 390
quoting, 34
retweeting, 34–37, 39, 374–376
searching for, 10, 20–26, 359, 370
timelines and, 9–11, 386
Twitter
    about, 6–8
    fundamental terminology, 9–11
    interest graphs and, 36, 292
    recommended exercises, 397
Twitter accounts
    creating, 11
    governance of, 8
    logging into, 10
    recommended exercises, 43, 397
    resolving user profile information, 380
Twitter API
    accessing for development purposes, 352–
        353
    collecting time-series data, 367
    convenient function calls, 361
    creating connections, 12–15
    fundamental terminology, 9–11
    making robust requests, 378–380
    online resources, 44, 398
    rate limits, 17
    recommended exercises, 43, 397
    sampling public data, 365
    saving and restoring JSON data with text
        files, 362–364
    searching for tweets, 20–26, 359, 370
    trending topics, 16–19, 358
Twitter platform objects
    about, 9–11
    analyzing tweets, 26–42
    searching for tweets, 20–26, 359, 370
Twitter Python class, 17
twitter Python package, 12, 351
twitter_text Python package, 382
Twurl tool (Twitter API), 11

U

UnicodeDecodeError (Python), 237, 362
Unix mailboxes
    about, 227–232
    converting mail corpus to, 235–236

About the Author

Matthew Russell (*@ptwobrussell*) is Chief Technology Officer at Digital Reasoning (*http://www.digitalreasoning.com/*), Principal at Zaffra, and author of several books on technology, including *Mining the Social Web* (O'Reilly, 2013), now in its second edition. He is passionate about open source software development, data mining, and creating technology to amplify human intelligence. Matthew studied computer science and jumped out of airplanes at the United States Air Force Academy. When not solving hard problems, he enjoys practicing Bikram Hot Yoga, CrossFitting, and participating in triathlons.

Colophon

The animal on the cover of *Mining the Social Web* is a groundhog (*Marmota monax*), also known as a woodchuck (a name derived from the Algonquin name *wuchak*). Groundhogs are famously associated with the US/Canadian holiday Groundhog Day, held every February 2nd. Folklore holds that if the groundhog emerges from its burrow that day and sees its shadow, winter will continue for six more weeks. Proponents say that the rodents forecast accurately 75 to 90 percent of the time. Many cities host famous groundhog weather prognosticators, including Punxsutawney Phil (of Punxsutawney, Pennsylvania, and the 1993 Bill Murray film *Groundhog Day*).

This legend perhaps originates from the fact that the groundhog is one of the few species that enters true hibernation during the winter. Primarily herbivorous, groundhogs will fatten up in the summer on vegetation, berries, nuts, insects, and the crops in human gardens, causing many people to consider them pests. They then dig a winter burrow, and remain there from October to March (although they may emerge earlier in temperate areas, or, presumably, if they will be the center of attention on their eponymous holiday).

The groundhog is the largest member of the squirrel family, around 16–26 inches long and weighing 4–9 pounds. It is equipped with curved, thick claws ideal for digging, and two coats of fur: a dense grey undercoat and a lighter-colored topcoat of longer hairs, which provides protection against the elements.

Groundhogs range throughout most of Canada and northern regions of the United States, in places where open space and woodlands meet. They are capable of climbing trees and swimming but are usually found on the ground, not far from the burrows they dig for sleeping, rearing their young, and seeking protection from predators. These burrows typically have two to five entrances, and up to 46 feet of tunnels.

The cover image is from Wood's *Animate Creatures*, Volume 1. The cover font is Adobe ITC Garamond. The text font is Adobe Minion Pro; the heading font is Adobe Myriad Condensed; and the code font is Dalton Maag's Ubuntu Mono.

Get even more for your money.

Join the O'Reilly Community, and register the O'Reilly books you own. It's free, and you'll get:

- $4.99 ebook upgrade offer
- 40% upgrade offer on O'Reilly print books
- Membership discounts on books and events
- Free lifetime updates to ebooks and videos
- Multiple ebook formats, DRM FREE
- Participation in the O'Reilly community
- Newsletters
- Account management
- 100% Satisfaction Guarantee

Signing up is easy:

1. Go to: oreilly.com/go/register
2. Create an O'Reilly login.
3. Provide your address.
4. Register your books.

Note: English-language books only

To order books online:

oreilly.com/store

For questions about products or an order:

orders@oreilly.com

To sign up to get topic-specific email announcements and/or news about upcoming books, conferences, special offers, and new technologies:

elists@oreilly.com

For technical questions about book content:

booktech@oreilly.com

To submit new book proposals to our editors:

proposals@oreilly.com

O'Reilly books are available in multiple DRM-free ebook formats. For more information:

oreilly.com/ebooks

O'REILLY®

Spreading the knowledge of innovators

oreilly.com

CPSIA information can be obtained at www.ICGtesting.com
Printed in the USA
BVOW10s1411151113

336403BV00005B/21/P